Garden and Landscape History

TRANSHUMANCE AND THE MAKING OF IRELAND'S UPLANDS (1550–1900)

Garden and Landscape History

ISSN 1758-518X

General Editor
Tom Williamson

This exciting series offers a forum for the study of all aspects of the subject. It takes a deliberately inclusive approach, aiming to cover both the 'designed' landscape and the working, 'vernacular' countryside; topics embrace, but are not limited to, the history of gardens and related subjects, biographies of major designers, in-depth studies of key sites, and regional surveys.

Proposals or enquiries may be sent directly to the editor or the publisher at the addresses given below; all submissions will receive prompt and informed consideration.

Professor Tom Williamson, School of History, University of East Anglia, Norwich, Norfolk NR4 7TJ, UK.

Boydell & Brewer, PO Box 9, Woodbridge, Suffolk, England, UK IP12 3DF, UK.

Previously published volumes in the series are listed at the back of this book

TRANSHUMANCE AND THE MAKING OF IRELAND'S UPLANDS (1550–1900)

EUGENE COSTELLO

THE BOYDELL PRESS

First published 2020
The Boydell Press, Woodbridge
Paperback edition 2024

ISBN 978-1-78327-531-1 hardback
ISBN 978-1-83765-147-4 paperback

The Boydell Press is an imprint of Boydell & Brewer Ltd
PO Box 9, Woodbridge, Suffolk IP12 3DF, UK
and of Boydell & Brewer Inc.
668 Mt Hope Avenue, Rochester, NY 14620–2731, USA
website: www.boydellandbrewer.com

A CIP catalogue record for this book is available
from the British Library

The publisher has no responsibility for the continued existence or accuracy of URLs
for external or third-party internet websites referred to in this book, and does
not guarantee that any content on such websites is, or will remain, accurate or
appropriate

CONTENTS

ILLUSTRATIONS

The author and publisher are grateful to all the institutions and individuals listed
in the figure captions for permission to reproduce the materials in which they hold
copyright. Every effort has been made to trace the copyright holders; apologies are
offered for any omission, and the publisher will be pleased to add any necessary
acknowledgement in subsequent editions.

PREFACE AND ACKNOWLEDGEMENTS

This book is a product of my curiosity about farming practices and peoples – in the past, present and future. Growing up on an organic suckler cow farm in south County Limerick, Ireland, I have long been aware of the importance of food production and how it happens on a daily basis. Over the years, I have also grown to know the land and what it supports in terms of vegetation – the life blood of all animal husbandry. With some observation, it becomes clear that farming landscapes in Ireland and other parts of the world are the product of human action over generations, some buildings being constructed in living memory, subtle earthen features melting gradually back into the ground, others lying under the surface, others gone forever. It was these observations on the physical legacy of farming practices in the landscape that got me interested in archaeology. At least where I grew up, you simply could not understand how past humans interacted with and inhabited the landscape without going out and actually looking at it. And, with my experience of livestock, it was only natural that the study of pastoralism would attract me most.

Of course, in Ireland and much of Europe today, livestock rearing is a fairly sedentary practice. Farmers do not move with their animals as some pastoralists in Central Asia, the Near East and Sub-Saharan Africa do to this day. Typically, they stay put on a farm that has fixed boundaries, with cattle either moving between narrow fenced strips on a rotational basis or grazed on larger blocks of land containing several ditched or hedged fields. Depending on the number of cattle, another few fields would be closed off as meadows and cut as hay or, more commonly, silage during summer and early autumn (twice or even three times in a year of good growth). Once baled, this grass acts as winter fodder for the cattle after they are brought into sheds for the wettest and coldest months of the year. This is the 'system' of pastoralism that I grew up in and took for granted.

So, for that reason, it came as a great surprise in my undergraduate days at University College Cork to discover that Irish farming might once have involved more mobility. The phenomenon of 'booleying', or seasonal grazing of cows in upland pastures, captured my attention; and even more so when I realised that this practice also involved the movement of people to upland booley huts, where they would have taken shelter while tending to the livestock. But all of this was mentioned only in passing by textbooks and lecturers, and brushed over as inconsequential and uncertain. It was as if most archaeologists and historians were nonplussed by the practice, and found it difficult to relate to. For archaeologists, the booley huts were perhaps too small and high up in the hills to be worth the effort. For historians, the practice hardly registered at all, as there were so few detailed written records relating to pastoralism before the 1840s. Whatever the reasons, it seemed a monstrous oversight to me. Ireland's great characteristics in the imagination of people worldwide are its green fields and grassy countryside, and the rearing of cattle for beef and dairy production is a vital sector of the national economy today. Indeed, it is quite accurate to say that cattle and cows in particular have long had an important role in Irish society and landscape. So to shy away from a potentially very significant aspect of this history means that the story of Ireland as a whole suffers.

However, the practice of transhumance was not completely 'virgin' ground as a subject of enquiry. Every scholar builds on previous knowledge to some extent, and if they are lucky they find something inspiring. For me, it was my encounter with an article published in 1945 in the *Journal of the Royal Society of Antiquaries of Ireland*. The folklife expert Caoimhín Ó Danachair (Kevin Danaher), from Athea in my own county, had published a short piece entitled 'Traces of the *Buaile* in the Galtee Mountains' on booleying, which was practised in Kilbeheny, in the south-east of County Limerick, up to approximately 1875. He provided a fascinating local account of what this system of farming involved and how young people looked after and milked cows on the mountain over the summer, basing themselves in booley houses. It seemed so recent and immediate – it was no longer a distant early modern or medieval curiosity but something that farmers not very far away were actively making use of. I knew then that I had to find out more, and soon I was up in the Galtee Mountains myself, tracking down the remains of booley houses during initial fieldwork in late 2010 and early 2011. I had productive initial discussions on the historiography of Irish booleying with Dr Colin Rynne at University College Cork and on relevant methods in landscape research with Dr Bob Johnston at the University of Sheffield.

My plan for a book on the practice of transhumance received a major boost in 2012 after I received funding from both the Irish Research Council and the Hardiman Scholars scheme at National University of Ireland, Galway. Here, in the School of Geography and Archaeology, Dr Kieran O'Conor provided advice and encouragement from start to finish, while Professor Elizabeth FitzPatrick was keen to encourage my project and give constructive criticism when needed. I would also like to thank Dr Michelle Comber for commenting on an earlier draft of my work. Joe Fenwick was vital to the fieldwork aspects of my research, training me in the use of various sorts of equipment and making sure it was available to me. Meanwhile, Dr Ronan Hennessy, Senior Technical Officer in the Ryan Institute, provided me with important topographic data for use in Geographic Information Systems (GIS).

In my office, Dr Richard Clutterbuck was a friend and colleague who always had an answer to my queries about GIS and was there to discuss post-medieval archaeology with me in detail. In the office next door, Lynda McCormack and

Dr Yolande O'Brien took valuable time out of their schedules on more than one occasion to help me with fieldwork in Connemara and Donegal. Dr Paul Naessens was very good to me, taking out his UAV to survey one of my more difficult sites in Connemara. I also had good discussions with Dr Theresa McDonald on our shared interest in booleying.

There are others, too. Michael Gibbons and Con Moriarty kindly showed me around parts of Connemara and the McGillycuddy's Reeks, generously imparting to me the kind of knowledge that comes only after many years of walking the landscape. In the Galtee Mountains, Michael Lewis, John Cunningham, Patsy King, Michael Kearney and Mike Henebry gave local words of advice. Seosamh Ó Cuaig, Máirtín Ó Catháin, Beartla King, Josie Moylan and Kieran Moylan provided especially valuable information on how booleying and farming once operated in the south Connemara area. Beanachtaí leo go léir! Séamus McGinley, a native of Carrick, did his level best to point the way in Gleann Cholm Cille in Donegal. Closer to home, the skilful Kieran O'Regan showed great accuracy on the total station during Galtee Mountains fieldwork. My sisters Niamh and Deirdre and father Mícheál also braved the tiring slopes of the Galtees on different days to help me out. As much as I enjoy solo fieldwork, there is nothing like a bit of company out there. My mother Mairéad, too, was always ready to encourage and reassure.

Outside archaeology, the eminent palaeobotanist Professor Michael O'Connell showed great enthusiasm about my subject and sent me helpful papers. In the Department of Irish (Roinn na Gaeilge) I received valuable guidance on folklore and place-names from Dr Lillis Ó Laoire and Dr Nollaig Ó Muraíle respectively. Dr Christy Cunniffe and his infectious enthusiasm for field survey made sure that I was introduced to the secrets of the Slieve Aughty landscape, which he continues to uncover. Further afield, Dr Mark Gardiner of the University of Lincoln (then at Queen's University Belfast) and Professor Eva Svensson at Karlstad University introduced me to a raft of like-minded researchers on the international stage. Indeed, Mark's analysis of an earlier version of my book proved vital.

Subsequently, as a National Endowment for the Humanities Fellow at the University of Notre Dame, I was given the space and time to further develop and finalise the book. For this I must thank Professor Ian Kuijt and Professor Meredith Chesson in the Department of Anthropology, Professor Diarmuid Ó Giolláin in the Department of Irish Language and Literature and above all Professor Chris Fox, then Director of the Keough-Naughton Institute for Irish Studies. He brought two renowned external readers to Notre Dame in April 2017 to offer me advice on the book – namely Professor Mary Beaudry of Boston University and Professor Stephen Rippon of the University of Exeter. Their very thorough reviews were instrumental to my improvement of the book manuscript after I returned to Ireland and in my current position as Postdoctoral Fellow at Stockholm University. On that note, I give my sincerest thanks to Professor Kerstin Lidén, Head of the Department of Archaeology and Classical Studies, and to the Environmental Research in Human Sciences initiative at Stockholm University, for providing the funding to publish the book.

Finally, I am very grateful to Professor Tom Williamson of the University of East Anglia for including this book in his exciting book series, *Garden and Landscape History*, to the peer-reviewers who read my book proposal and manuscript, and especially to Boydell and Brewer's commissioning editor Caroline Palmer, whose patience and clarity ensured my timely completion of the book. Assistant production editor Emily Champion has also provided clear guidance and help in the final stages.

And so I leave you to read. Any mistakes are my own.

Dr Eugene Costello
Department of Archaeology and Classical Studies
Stockholm University, Sweden
5 November 2019

NOTE ON CHRONOLOGY

The following are the main chronological divisions used in the book:

Early medieval period: *c.* AD 500–1100
Later medieval period: *c.* AD 1100–1550
   High medieval: *c.* AD 900–1350
   Late medieval: *c.* AD 1350–1550
Post-medieval period: *c.* AD 1550–1950
Early modern: *c.* AD 1550–1700

INTRODUCTION

BACKGROUND AND JUSTIFICATION

Transhumance is a form of seasonal pastoralism that has been practised around the world for many thousands of years. In basic terms, it is the seasonal movement of people and livestock from one environmental context to another, with the home settlement and main zone of crop production usually found in fertile lowlands or valleys and the summer pastures, such as heaths, wetlands, forests, hills and mountains, located over a wider area in a marginal zone of production. The people who move with the livestock occupy small dwellings in these marginal zones until they all return home for the winter half of the year or longer. As with all definitions of farming systems, however, this statement fails to acknowledge a lot of diversity. Every farming practice is a social practice, influenced by the needs and capabilities of different people and their interactions with one another. Every farming practice is also shaped by the environment, no two farmers having to deal with exactly the same soil fertility, topography or climate. Transhumance is an especially complex farming and social phenomenon in which people exploit, via movement, the seasonality of *different* environments. If communities are organised to cope with the absence of many of their members and most of their livestock for up to half the year, it becomes possible for them to spare more land for tillage crops and winter fodder, the latter, in turn, allowing them to maximise the size of herd that can be sustained through the winter.

Transhumance was practised in many parts of Ireland up to the nineteenth century and as late as the early twentieth century in the western regions of Connemara and Achill Island. Thus, the question of seasonal pastoral movement and settlement in Ireland is one for students of the past. In the Anglophone scholarship Irish transhumance is often known as 'booleying', a term derived from the practice of removing with dairy cattle to summer 'booley' settlements in rough hill pastures. However convenient the term may be for an Irish context, its application across the island masks a great deal of regional and local nuance over time. For one thing, 'booley' stems from the Irish-language word *buaile*, which has more than one meaning. While its main interpretation in modern Irish would be a 'milking place in summer pasturage', this is not always the case: 'fold', 'small grazing field' and 'dung-yard' are alternative translations (Ó Dónaill 1977). In Old and Middle Irish, depending on the context, it could be used to indicate an 'enclosure', 'cow-house', 'cattle-pen', or 'cattlefold at times of summer pasturage' (eDIL, 7236). Moreover, the names given to seasonal pastoral sites varied according to the locality – *bráca*, *bothóg* and *áirí* are just some of the words associated with transhumant settlements in place-names and oral history. And, in terms of the motivating factors and patterns in the practice of seasonal movement and grazing, there were significant differences over time and space even within Ireland. One assumption about 'booleying' that is likely to hold up, however, is the special role of cattle, and dairy cows in particular. While this work points out evidence for the presence of sheep and goats on upland pastures, readers will note that in post-medieval Ireland the story of transhumance *sensu stricto* is primarily bovine.

As the first major work to examine seasonal movement and settlement in multiple areas of Ireland from a cross-disciplinary perspective, this book will uncover the commonalities and differences that characterise post-medieval transhumance on the island. Previous studies either have been undertaken from the point of view of folklife and/or geography or, if archaeological, have focused on only one part of Ireland. This has left scholars with little idea as to whether Irish transhumance was homogeneous as a practice or if it contained important regional differences. In archaeology, there has been no understanding of the material culture of transhumance at a national level. A multi-disciplinary discussion that incorporates field archaeology, historical documentation and oral tradition will begin to fill this obvious gap in knowledge about the evolution of the Irish landscape, and of upland pastoral landscapes in particular.

AIMS AND RESEARCH QUESTIONS

On one level, then, this book provides a fundamental study of transhumance in Irish society and settlement from *circa* AD 1550 to 1920, which will be of interest to scholars of transhumance in other countries in north-west Europe, such as Britain, France, Iceland, Norway and Sweden. Yet on another, deeper, level it counters the view that pre-Improvement farming practices, particularly in upland areas, were not as sophisticated as modern scientific agriculture. It explores how agro-pastoral communities in a supposedly peripheral part of Europe used complex systems of mobility to exploit seasonal variation in the physical environment, and it asks how they interacted with hill and mountain landscapes as seasonal zones of work and habitation. The juxtaposition of permanent and seasonal settlement patterns over time will also allow me to address the agency of subaltern rural dwellers in historically attested social and economic trends such as population growth, settlement expansion and integration with global food markets – that is, some of the hallmarks of modernity. In pursuit of these aims, I have the following more specific research goals:

- **To ascertain how seasonal movement and settlement manifested itself in the landscape.**

   What is the archaeological evidence for structures inhabited in summertime by transhumant herders in Ireland's hills and mountains, in view of the evidence for upland shielings in parts of Britain and summer farms in the Scandinavian countries?

To what extent were the location, form and distribution of these structures influenced by time and the landscape? What spatial and social relationships did summer settlements have with permanent settlements? How can these seasonal sites be distinguished from permanent ones in terms of architecture and location?

- **To understand how transhumant systems operated in Ireland before the Cromwellian conquest and settlement.**

  Was transhumance practised in the medieval period and how widespread was the practice in the sixteenth and early seventeenth centuries? What livestock were moved on a seasonal basis and how far? What contemporary environmental and social factors required the seasonal removal of livestock? Did whole families and communities relocate with them? What role did Gaelic and Hiberno-Norman lords play in transhumance? What difficulties do archaeologists face when trying to identify seasonal settlements from this period?

- **To show how non-elite rural communities used transhumance to adapt to wider socio-economic trends from the mid-seventeenth century onwards.**

  How did the emergence of landed estates influence the organisation of transhumance and elite participation in the practice? What effect did landlord improvements have on upland commons and settlement patterns associated with transhumance, and how does the agency of peasant farmers in Ireland compare with that in Highland Scotland? How did tenants cope with and contribute to population expansion onto common pastures through their use of seasonal sites? What role did seasonal removal to upland pastures have in the cultural formation of rural landscapes of Ireland and north-west Europe, particularly in the domestication of 'wild' upland spaces and the development of gender roles?

- **To explain the eventual decline of transhumance in Ireland.**

  In what ways did the growth of a global capitalist economy with access to its markets impact on transhumance, both positively and negatively? How did new forms of upland animal husbandry reduce the need for the seasonal movement of people and what changes in rural society during the late nineteenth century disrupted the practice? Why did people continue practising transhumance longer in certain upland areas? How does the timing of its decline in Ireland compare with the situation in similar regions in Britain, particularly Scotland?

STRUCTURE OF BOOK AND STUDY AREAS

Situating the study

Given the worldwide distribution of pastoralism, and the well-known presence of transhumant pastoralism in many parts of Europe, it is essential that this book is placed in a broader context. This is what Chapter 1 sets out to do. It introduces the key conceptual issues involved in studies of seasonally mobile pastoral societies on an international stage, distinguishing transhumance from related forms of pastoralism. It then goes on to outline previous work on the subject in north-west Europe and particularly in Ireland's nearest neighbour, Britain. The most attention is given to Scotland, as it shares many environmental and cultural–historical traits with Ireland. I outline the archaeological evidence for seasonal settlement and discuss probable factors in the decline of transhumance in different parts of the country.

Chapter 2 then moves the focus to Ireland, discussing the historical basis for viewing seasonal pastoralism as an important aspect of society from the early medieval period onwards and identifying those areas where the practice of transhumance can be attested in the early modern period. It also discusses how pastoral mobility has been perceived since the late sixteenth century, first of all by English writers in the era of Tudor and Cromwellian conquests and secondly by scholars of various disciplines in the twentieth and twenty-first centuries. In particular, it outlines previous archaeological fieldwork in upland areas around Ireland and critically assesses the evidence for seasonal 'booley' sites associated with livestock herding. It then examines previous research on the transhumant systems in which such sites were used. Important first steps were taken in historical geography and folklife studies many decades ago, but by portraying it as a 'traditional' practice that belonged in the past they partly held back deeper investigations of transhumance and landscape change in the uplands.

Choice of study areas

Since a detailed interdisciplinary study of every hill and mountain range in Ireland would probably delay progress on the subject of transhumance for another decade or two, it was decided to focus on three study areas. These were chosen based on a number of factors: the level of previous research locally, the availability of suitable documentary sources, the survival of archaeological evidence for seasonal settlement and the overall complementarity of the study areas in a synthetic discussion on transhumance. For example, the civil parish of Achill, County Mayo, was not very suitable, given the in-depth research already undertaken on summer booley settlements there by Theresa McDonald (2014). At the same time, although virtually unexplored and presenting good archaeological potential (evident from Digital Globe and Google satellite imagery and my own preliminary fieldwork), the Wicklow Mountains, Comeragh Mountains and the MacGillycuddy's Reeks were all poor in terms of folk memory of transhumance. Other uplands, such as the Ballyhoura Hills and west Limerick hills, have been largely covered with swathes of commercial forestry since the 1980s, dashing any hope of informative fieldwork immediately.

Ultimately, the three chosen study areas – the Carna peninsula in Connemara, County Galway; the parish of Gleann Cholm Cille in south-west County Donegal; and the Galtee Mountains in Counties Limerick and Tipperary – contained what were seen as a good mixture of all factors (Figure 0.1). All have solid ethnographic evidence for the existence of some form of transhumance up to at least the mid-nineteenth century, all have potential archaeological evidence for seasonal settlement and none has been studied in an in-depth manner before from the point of view of transhumance. Furthermore, there are differences between them in terms of topography, quality of soil and recent socio-economic history that introduces a timely regional aspect to research on Irish transhumance. For instance, the Galtee Mountains reach over 900m in altitude, which in Ireland gives rise to a sub-Alpine environment where vegetation and temperature change perceptibly. By contrast, the Carna peninsula is much lower. Nearly all of the rough pasture that cattle grazed on is found below 100m a.s.l., and only the rocky ridge of Cnoc Mordáin running down its eastern side exceeds 150m. The third study area, Gleann Cholm Cille, offers elements of both these environments insofar as it contains low-lying valleys but also hills and plateaus that lie between 100m

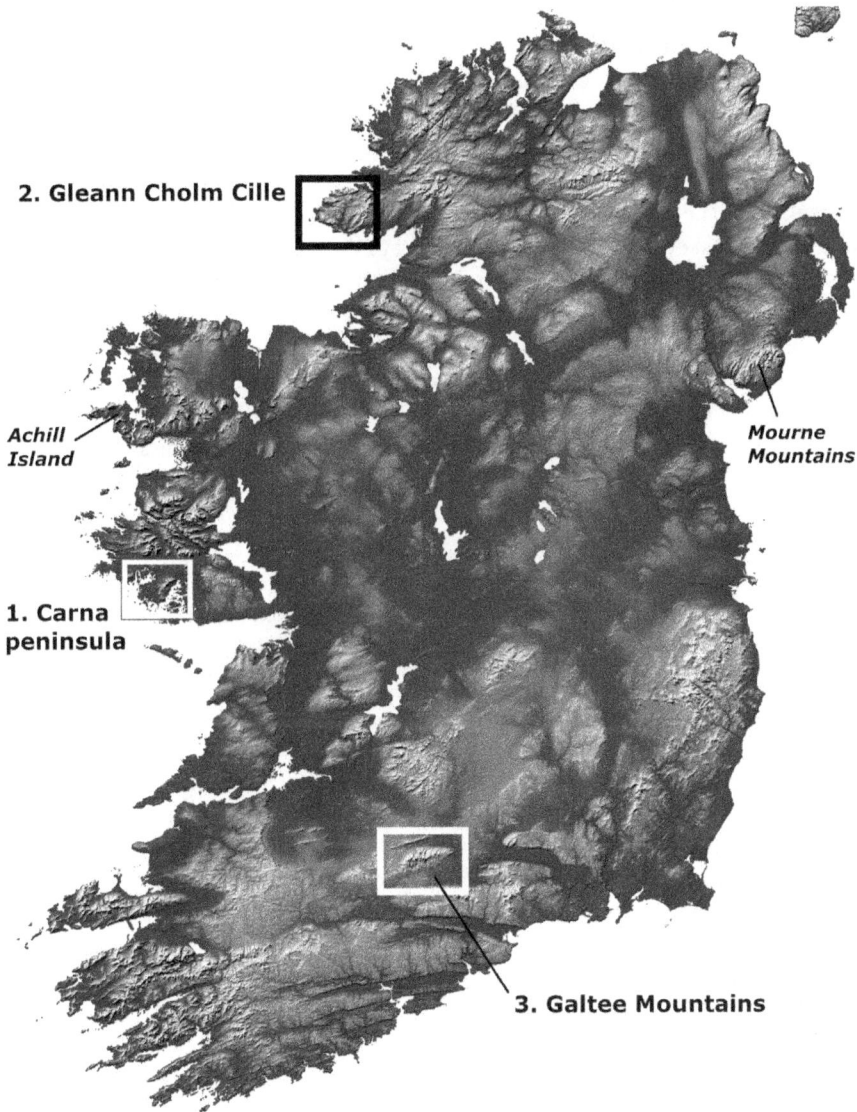

Figure 0.1 Study areas 1–3, and two other areas with significant previous archaeological fieldwork.

and 400m a.s.l. As such, the book deliberately reflects the wide variety of 'upland' found in the Irish landscape. In addition, there is much more agriculturally productive land around the Galtees than in the two western study areas, where fertile soils (i.e. highly productive grasslands and arable) are by and large limited to small pockets by the coast in Carna and along narrow valleys in Gleann Cholm Cille. The settlement and land-use history of each study area is influenced by all of these topographic and geomorphological differences, with consequences for the kind of transhumance that was practised regionally.

Addressing the question of transhumance in Ireland, 1550–1900

Each of these study areas is given its own chapter. While they each seek to understand how transhumance operated and changed over time in that area using a range of sources, they also deliver their own message on the practice and its role in the history of Ireland's uplands. Thus, Chapter 3 reconstructs the practice of transhumance in the Carna peninsula from the late sixteenth century onwards but, because of rich archaeological and oral historical evidence in that area relating to the life of transhumant cow herders, it focuses much of its discussion on the organisation and negotiation of space in summer pastures. Likewise, Chapter 4 pieces together the role of transhumance in Gleann Cholm Cille but, thanks to unusually rich documentary evidence, it is able to go into more detail on the evolution of the links between home farms and hill pastures and their exploitation by tenant farmers during population growth in the late eighteenth and early nineteenth centuries. Finally, Chapter 5 uses seasonal movement and settlement in the Galtee Mountains to understand the importance of uplands in facilitating peasant responses to two key aspects of the modern world – the reorganisation of rural landscapes by elites and the globalisation of food markets.

Chapter 6 then draws the lessons from each case study together in an extended comparative discussion that addresses a number of issues in detail. First, at a macro-level, I tackle the question of how changes in the ethno-religious composition and outlook of elite early modern society in Ireland affected the practice of transhumance and the wider social structures in which it took place. I also model the different forms of settlement expansion associated with rural population growth after the seventeenth century in order to understand how transhumant patterns were impacted and altered in the landscape, placing particular emphasis on the agency of tenant farmers in different part of the country.

With that as a basis, I examine the archaeology of summer settlement across my three study areas and other uplands where field survey and/or excavation has taken place. I start with the morphology of the booley dwellings themselves, weighing up the various factors that determined their size and design and considering the role of chronology especially. I then compare the different patterns of seasonal settlement in uplands with patterns of permanent settlement on lower ground or by the coast. I highlight the clear regionality in settlement patterns and what this tells us about social organisation in different parts of the country. Finally, I address the question of how many people in a community actually moved with cattle to summer pastures, from early modern times to the early twentieth century. Based on this, I discuss the socio-cultural role of transhumant movements, both for the people involved and for the uplands as a marginal or liminal space.

The last third of the chapter considers what developments in the growing capitalist world system meant for the practice of transhumance at a local level across Ireland. It discusses the various trajectories of specialisation that pastoralism followed in the country – beef versus dairy, for example – and highlights the differing outcomes for transhumance as a result. It highlights how upland pastures allowed supposedly 'marginal' rural communities to adapt to and interact with new markets on the international stage. The chapter is rounded off with a detailed breakdown of the factors that contributed to the final decline of seasonal human and livestock movements during the late nineteenth and early twentieth centuries. It pinpoints how changes in herd composition, the proprietorship of uplands and the phenomenon of emigration contributed to the cessation of an (at least) millennium-long tradition of booley settlement in Ireland's hills and mountains. The conclusion then summarises the most important messages in the book and outlines how future work on pastoralism in the historic north-west of Europe might proceed.

Transhumance and the future

As we enter an uncertain chapter in the Earth's history, the Anthropocene, this book serves as an important reminder that farming practices in Ireland and elsewhere have the potential to change. The relatively sedentary and intensive nature of cattle farming in much of north-west Europe over the last 100 years is not necessarily reflective of livestock husbandry in preceding centuries, when mobility, at least on a seasonal basis, was far more common. This is especially striking in Ireland. The rearing of cows is a cornerstone of Ireland's cultural heritage and even its economy, yet among the public the story of mobile pastoralism in the not-so-distant past is virtually unknown. The same goes for the uplands that served as summer pastures, now largely overlooked and given over to low-input sheep grazing and commercial forestry.

Rural landscape and society has changed greatly since the sixteenth century and, indeed, this is part of the reason why transhumance declined in Ireland and neighbouring countries in this corner of Europe. Reviving seasonal movements and the practice of summer settlement in upland pastures is clearly not a realistic prospect in the near future, therefore. However, a history of transhumance still provides useful lessons as we face a period of global adversity. For one thing, it helps us to understand the long-term origins of problems in pasture management, which can often lead to over-grazing and vegetation change. At a socio-economic level, it provides a crucial insight into the adaptive capacity of rural communities over multiple generations, as they reacted to shocks such as conquest, elite change and famine, as well as to wider economic opportunities. The fate of transhumance in Ireland from 1550 to 1900 is therefore a microcosm of the fundamental and potentially planet-altering revolution in agricultural life that we are living with today.

CHAPTER 1

SEASONAL MOVEMENT AND SETTLEMENT IN A WORLD OF PASTORALISM

MOBILE PASTORALISM AND ARCHAEOLOGY

Mobility in past societies can be approached in many different ways. The word itself may refer to the physical movement or migration of groups of people, the vertical or horizontal movement of individuals within society, the trade and exchange of their objects or the diffusion of different technologies and ways of seeing the world between regions (e.g. Beaudry et al. 2013). Where the archaeology of farming societies[1] is concerned, regular movement across the landscape by humans and their domesticated animals has gained increasing amounts of attention in recent decades. Pastoral movements tend to be more structured and repetitive than other forms of physical human mobility (e.g. refuge, colonisation, invasion) because the herding of livestock always revolves around the availability of pasture. This introduces certain limitations on how far pastoralists may travel and when. For socio-political reasons they may not have access to certain tracts of grassland, while climate and topography may render other areas undesirable. Having said that, seasonal variations in climate and vegetation are often what encourage pastoralists to move out of one region for part of the year, in order to take advantage of better pasture in one or more areas elsewhere. Indeed, for husbandmen and women in some parts of the world these variations can be so extreme as to make movement an absolute necessity. For example, it was and is common for people and their livestock to follow rainfall in the Central Andes (Browman 1997, 24–26), the Libyan Desert (Roe 2008, 494) and the arid Egypt/ Sudan border area (Wendrich 2008, 534).

Ethnographers, anthropologists and geographers have carried out many studies of mobile pastoralists in present-day contexts, as living societies worth studying in their own right (Barth 1961; Johnson 1969; Ingold 1980; Galaty and Johnson 1990; Chang and Koster 1994; Khazanov 1994; Salzmann 2004). It is naturally more difficult to gather information on past mobility by pastoralists not simply because direct observations are now impossible but also owing to the difficulty of tracing regular movement across

---

[1] In this book, the term 'farming' refers not only to arable farming or the cultivation of domesticated plants but also to the rearing of livestock. However, 'agriculture' is used to refer specifically to plant cultivation, and 'pastoralism' to the management and breeding of livestock.

past landscapes. With some justification, Vere Gordon Childe has been lambasted for pronouncing over eighty years ago that 'pastoralists are not likely to leave many vestiges by which the archaeologist could recognize their presence' (Childe 1936, 81; see Cribb 1991, 65). His claim that they do not tend to use pots and live in tents rather than built structures is false, as amply demonstrated by landscape archaeologists since the 1980s. Past nomadic and semi-nomadic peoples did use and even make pottery and frequently constructed fixed buildings in the pastures they visited (Bar-Yosef and Khazanov 1991; Cribb 1991; Barnard and Wendrich 2008). Furthermore, since many pastoral groups in recent times are known to have cultivated grain crops in order to manage risk, such as the Bamadi and Qashqaaii tribes of western Iran (Alizadeh 2008, 89–90), archaeologists might also expect to find the remains of grain stores, drying kilns and perhaps charred grains at or near their winter quarters.

Archaeological methods have certainly not come far enough to make pastoralism *easy* to track, however, and they will never alter the nature of deposition in contexts associated with pastoral peoples. The buildings that herders erected for their own shelter, while not necessarily tent-like, were very often less substantial than structures occupied on a year-round basis. In County Down in Ireland, for example, mid-eighteenth-century cattle-owners would travel to common pasture in the Mourne Mountains, bringing 'with them their Wives, Children, and little wretched Furniture, erect Huts, and there live for two Months, and sometimes more' (Smith and Harris 1744, 125). Moreover, the preservation of these structures and any material culture associated with their occupation can be quite poor in some environments used on a seasonal basis. Semi-arid environments of the Near East and other sub-tropical climates may help to preserve organic materials, but this is not the case in many of the wetter, acidic soils of northern Europe's upland and heathland pastures.

There are, thankfully, other sources of information on which archaeologists may draw to elucidate daily life and economy among mobile pastoralists. Perhaps the greatest source of non-archaeological information used to date has come from ethnographic observations of modern pastoralists. Their practices cannot be assumed to represent fossilisations of earlier herding practices, but they do offer a rich source of analogy. As Wendrich and Barnard (2008, 14) point out, 'ethnographies and ethno-archaeological studies provide an inventory of known occurrences: a palette of different types of organization, forms of habitation and human reactions to and interactions with a wide range of physical, social and spiritual circumstances.' Either by making their own observations or by using existing 'inventories', many archaeologists have been able to offer new explanations of the material remains of pastoralism, or the lack thereof, by reference to modern societies (e.g. Lewthwaite 1984; Gamble and Boismier 1991; Chang and Tourtellotte 1993; Alizadeh 2008; Carrer 2013). The emphasis in these ethnoarchaeological studies has largely been on the more distant past, however, such as the Classical Mediterranean or the ancient Near East (but see, for medieval Spain, Moreno-Garcia 2001). There is no reason why more recent time periods should not interest archaeologists. Not only is modern ethnographic information potentially more applicable to medieval and especially post-medieval times (in a European context), historical records and maps also encourage one to ask more penetrating questions of the landscape (e.g. Rippon 2012). Historical archaeologists can even be said to 'revel in the availability of non-excavation-based sources of information ... [and the] appropriation of information from all useful sources' (Orser 2006a, 13). Numerous scholars now agree that texts, oral history and material culture are equally valid as sources of information on the past (Comaroff and Comaroff 1992; Hall 2000; Hicks and Beaudry 2006; Wilkie 2006). The present writer is in broad agreement with these sentiments. So long as archaeologists are aware of the limitations of a source material, their 'historical archaeologies' will be all the stronger for having a diverse evidence base.

The greater resolution that can be obtained in historical times means that they offer archaeologists a special laboratory for categorising mobility and for characterising the drivers and consequences of change within different groups of pastoralists. Of course, the various contexts (political, social, economic and ecological) in which historical pastoralists operated will not be the same for prehistoric people: sustained major population growth and a greater emphasis on surpluses are two notable developments in Europe after the medieval period, for example. Drawing firmer conclusions about historical pastoralists will therefore not uncover anything new about the conditions facing earlier farmers. However, it will facilitate more accurate modelling of human agency and mobility in pastoral societies, which might be applied and tested in different contexts.

TRANSHUMANCE: SEASONAL MOBILITY WITH ROOTS

The present study starts this process by focusing on the form of mobile pastoralism known as transhumance, asking questions about its changing nature in post-medieval Ireland. The *Oxford English Dictionary* defines transhumance as 'the action or practice of moving livestock from one grazing ground to another in a seasonal cycle, typically to lowlands in winter and highlands in summer'. While adequate as a general statement, this insufficiently distinguishes the human participants in transhumance from other kinds of pastoralist – that is, anyone 'whose livelihood comes from tending grazing animals' (Gefu and Gilles 1990, 35). The world of pastoralism is hugely diverse, over space as well as time, and seasonality may also play a role in nomadic pastoralism. Yet nomadic pastoralists lead a very different life to people who depend on transhumance. Cribb (1991, 19) attempted to resolve the confusion by arguing that the term 'transhumance' should be 'confined to a form of livestock management making use of seasonal variations in the availability of pasture'. He maintains that 'transhumance' refers simply to the movement of livestock and that 'nomadism', 'semi-nomadism' and 'sedentism' denote *how* mobile humans would be in a transhumant system. But since pastoralism's core characteristic is human–animal interdependency, describing the organisation of humans and animals separately is unhelpful. The terminology of mobile pastoralism needs to take humans and animals into account at the same time, otherwise we risk losing sight of the economic motivations for rearing livestock and the reliance of domesticated livestock on human protection and management.

Of course, strict definitions are impossible to make, and are undesirable given the overlapping characteristics of different forms of pastoralism. Nonetheless, it is fairly easy to distinguish transhumance from nomadic pastoralism, which, in its purest form, does not require a fixed base and is characterised by a complete lack of agriculture or arable farming; in modern times this is recorded only in North Eurasia, High Inner Asia, the Eurasian steppes, Arabia and the Sahara (Khazanov 1994, 19). Transhumance, by contrast, always involves a degree of sedentism whereby a family or community maintains a fixed base where crops (including winter fodder) are grown. The removal of livestock from this core area (usually over the summer) enables these people to exploit seasonally productive pastures in another ecological zone, at the same time freeing up ground around the main settlement for the community's crops and giving pastures time to recover, especially if conditions are hot in the lowlands over the summer. As such, people who rely on transhumance can be said to have a fixed base and are involved in *agro-pastoralism*, as opposed to animal husbandry alone. It is also important to emphasise the role of seasonal *human* settlement in transhumance. The necessity for this can vary widely depending on the amount of labour needed on the summer pastures, for herding, dairying and perhaps small-scale cultivation, and at home, for protecting and harvesting crops, fishing, industrial activity and/or warfare. The distance to the summer pastures and the availability of knowledge about those landscapes are important considerations for livestock owners as well. In general, however, if livestock are being moved so far that they enter a different ecological or climatic zone then at least some human presence is necessary at those seasonal pastures. Across medieval and modern Europe, this might involve the relocation of entire families, a few family members or professional herdsmen (Costello and Svensson 2018a).

Some scholars have a particular type of seasonal movement in mind when they employ the term 'transhumance'. To some extent, uncertainty about the word is due to the fact that it was borrowed into English from Romance languages and its usage in English is now broader than in French, (Castilian) Spanish, Italian, Romanian, and so on (respectively, *transhumance, transhumancia, transhumanza, transhumanța*). In parts of Europe where these languages are spoken the idea of transhumance is most strongly associated with long-distance movements of wool-producing sheep that emerged in the sixteenth century; other terms, such as *monticazione* (northern Italy) and *transterminancia* (Spain), are used to single out seasonal mobility on a local scale (Braudel 1972, 85–87; Rendu 2006; Brigand *et al.* 2018; Burri *et al.* 2018; López-Sáez *et al.* 2018; Stagno 2018). Referring to German-speaking parts of the Alps and further north, Luick (2004, 2–3) also prefers to associate 'transhumance' with large-scale sheep movements, relegating the shorter, family-based system of *alpwirtschaft* to the status of pseudo-transhumance. For all its current popularity, however, Rendu (2006, 9) notes that the term *transhumance* is not attested in the French language until 1791, when the citizens of Bouches-du-Rhône, and especially the town and territory of Arles, sought protection from the National Assembly for their *troupeaux transhumants*. Just under thirty years later, *Le Robert de la langue française* defines transhumance rather broadly as the 'the periodic migration of lowland livestock, which change (move) pasture in summer and settle in the mountains' (own translation; Rendu 2006, 9). Considering the relatively recent spread of the word, it may be unwise for scholars of seasonal pastoralism to become too settled in their own definitions.

Recent archaeological work across Europe has shown that scholars of seasonal human–livestock mobility (between fixed areas of the landscape) actually have a lot in common in spite of the variable distances, scales and motivations for movement. For this reason, 'transhumance' undoubtedly serves as a convenient umbrella term (Collis *et al.* 2016; Costello and Svensson, 2018a). Rather than see it as a strictly defined practice, it might be thought of as a 'boundary object' – that is, an object that is

> plastic enough to adapt to local needs and the constraints of the several parties employing [it], yet robust enough to maintain a common identity across sites … [Boundary objects] have different meanings in different social worlds but their structure is common enough to more than one world to make them recognizable, a means of translation. The creation and management of boundary objects is a key process in developing and maintaining coherence across intersecting social worlds. (Star and Griesemer 1989, 393, cited by Costello and Svensson 2018b, 3).

Thus, Costello and Svensson (2018b) argue that transhumant mobility is an 'elastic strategy' that people with individual and collective agency use to navigate through a range of factors, among them socio-political structure, economic opportunity and environmental limitation.

HISTORICAL TRANSHUMANCE IN NORTH-WEST EUROPE: ISSUES AND OPPORTUNITIES

Over the last millennium or so transhumant practices in north-western Europe (Ireland and Britain specifically) have exhibited some distinctive characteristics. For a start, most seasonal movements of people and livestock appear to have taken place over significantly shorter distances than on the Continent. In some cases 30–50km might be covered before summer pastures were reached, but the majority of journeys, at least in post-medieval times, were only 2–12km in distance (see pages 33–37). This is clearly not of the same magnitude as the 'Great Transhumance', various incarnations of which flourished economically in southern France, Iberia, Italy and the Balkans during the period 1500–1900 (Klein 1920; Braudel 1972, 85–102; Lebaudy 2006; Dunăre 1984). On current evidence, systems of seasonal mobility in Ireland and Britain are more akin to localised movements of dairy animals attested in mountain valleys of the Pyrenees, Alps and other upland regions of Continental Europe, which often took place in competition with long-distance transhumance (Lévêque 2013; Lozny 2013b; Andres 2016; Daugstad and Schippers 2016; González-Álvarez *et al.* 2016). That said, even where small-scale movements occurred on the Continent, summer pastures were usually located at significantly higher altitudes (1200–2500m) than in Ireland and Britain, and movements could involve the use of intermediate grazing grounds.

Somewhat closer parallels are available in Scandinavian countries. Recent studies in western and central Sweden, Norway and Iceland have shown that agro-pastoral communities made use of summer sites from at least later medieval times (Emanuelsson *et al.* 2003; Larsson 2012; Daugstad and Schippers 2016; Kupiec *et al.* 2016; Kupiec and Milek 2018; Pettersson 2018). Known respectively in the three countries as *fäbod* or *säter*, *seter* and *sel*, these sites were typically located in mountainous or Boreal forest outlands and were particularly associated with women, who looked after and milked cows for the duration of their stay; hay would also be made at these sites to bolster supplies of winter fodder. Although in the late eighteenth century some farms in central southern Norway used *seter* sites 100–120km away (Pedersen 1974), distances were for the most part comparable to those travelled in Ireland and Britain. Furthermore, ethno-historical information described below and in subsequent chapters shows that later systems in western Ireland and Scotland also tended to devolve significant responsibility on young women (see also Costello 2017; 2018).

Yet important differences still emerge in a comparison of Irish and British transhumance and the Scandinavian practices. In terms of landscape there is a far clearer divide between infield and outland (*utmark*) in Nordic countries than in Britain or Ireland. With a longer growing season and relatively small tracts of uncultivated land compared with Scandinavia and Iceland, the overall extent of summer commons has expanded and receded more noticeably in the long term in Ireland and Britain. Colonisation and improvement of marginal land could and did occur in Scandinavian countries (e.g. Lindholm *et al.* 2013, 30) but large blocks of upland, forest and heath have remained essentially intact. Some of the ambiguity surrounding summer pastures in Irish and British landscapes may be attributed to the fact that seasonal movements of people and livestock came to an end sooner than in Scandinavia, where, as on the Continent, though to a lesser degree, some summer sites are still being used by farmers. Indeed, in England, the use of summer shielings died out as early as *c.*1600 (see below). From a methodological point of view the loss of oral history about transhumance and the subsequent emergence of new forms of land-use (mining/quarrying, permanent settlement, forestry, and so on) can make it difficult to identify seasonal mobility and settlement. Moreover, one is obliged to ask why there was an earlier decline in Ireland and Britain. The rest of this chapter outlines the archaeological and historical evidence for transhumance in medieval and post-medieval England, Wales and Scotland, and particularly examines the trend of decline in Scotland – Ireland's closest neighbour geographically and culturally. This will highlight potential points of comparison with the less well-known Irish material and demonstrate the importance of a cross-disciplinary approach to the topic of seasonal movement and settlement.

ENGLAND

The English landscape is more diverse than that of either of its two neighbours on the island of Britain. The north contains large areas of peat-covered upland, such as the Cumbrian Mountains and the long broad mountainous spine of the Pennines, with slightly lower and less extensive uplands found in Devon. Much of the rest of England, however, is characterised by low rolling countryside interrupted occasionally by ridges, plateaus and – before post-medieval drainage – wetlands. As such, transhumant practices in England, where and if they were necessary, should not be expected to replicate the vertical nature of movements that seem to have predominated elsewhere in Britain. While upland shielings were widely used in the Lake District and the Border Country up to the early seventeenth century (Ramm *et al.* 1970, 9–43; Whyte 1985; Winchester 2000, 78–102), and upland moors were utilised in summertime in medieval Devon and Cornwall (Fox 2012; Herring 2012), there are also indications of seasonal movements of livestock in parts of the country where mountainous terrain was absent. In pre-Norman Warwickshire, for example, several manors in the Avon valley were connected to detached pieces of territory in the Arden woodlands, a pattern that almost certainly points to the possession of seasonal grazing rights in the woods (Ford 1976). Similar arrangements were in place in the forested Weald of Kent (Hooke 2012, 33–34). In addition, it is now clear that across much of eastern and southern England low hills and plateaus that hardly exceeded 150m a.s.l. – often known as 'wolds' because of their wooded state earlier in the Anglo-Saxon period – played an important role in transhumance up to the late first millennium AD (Everitt 1977; Gardiner 2018, 110–11). Place-name evidence suggests that goats formed a significant presence in these early medieval movements, along with cattle and sheep, though it is clear that their importance in later medieval and post-medieval times was increasingly limited to the rocky uplands of south-western and northern England (Dyer 2004). The scarcity of goats in the transhumant flocks and herds of post-medieval Ireland is also noticeable, where cattle and dairy cows in particular dominate the narrative.[2]

While it has proved difficult to identify archaeological traces of people travelling and staying with livestock in the woodlands and wolds of Anglo-Saxon England, it is highly likely that some on-site herding facilities were necessary given the pastures' separation from parent settlements. Citing examples in the Yorkshire Wolds and Sussex Downs, Gardiner (2011b, 211–13; 2018, 110–11) argues that the excavation of isolated 'sunken dwellings' has provided a possible glimpse of transhumant herders' huts in Anglo-Saxon England. In the late first millennium AD, however, there was a trend towards the colonisation of seasonally grazed woodlands and wolds, and the new landscape of villages, farmsteads and fields is likely to have obscured a lot of older archaeology associated with herding. One of the best examples of this transition comes from Wharram Percy in the Yorkshire Wolds, where the excavation of small sunken dwellings suggests at least one phase of seasonal occupation before permanent settlement accompanied by cereal cultivation was established in the tenth century (lasting until shortly after 1500; Wrathmell 2012, 95; Everson and Stocker 2012, 204). The replacement of seasonal sites by year-round agrarian settlements

---

[2]   In Ireland, as subsequent chapters will show, the evidence for goats survives mainly in the form of place-names, and these are difficult to date. The only landscape in Ireland where there is clear historical evidence for the importance of goats up to the nineteenth century is the MacGillycuddy's Reeks in County Kerry, a range that contains the rockiest and steepest mountain slopes anywhere in the country (Weld 1807, 164).

continued in the more elevated parts of England in the second millennium AD, most notably at Hound Tor in Dartmoor, where sunken dwellings were found to underlie a thirteenth-/fourteenth-century hamlet (Beresford 1979, 110–12), and in the Pennines and Lake District, where *skáli* place-names strongly suggest seasonal origins for many upland farmsteads (Whyte 1985; Winchester 2000, Chapter 7). The phenomenon of permanent settlement succeeding seasonal occupation is evident in parts of Wales and Scotland too (see below), and formed an important driver of change in transhumant systems of post-medieval Ireland. However, the timing of colonisation could vary considerably and it is a mistake to assume that transitions to permanent settlement were irreversible. Indeed, the well-attested abandonment of villages in England during the late medieval period may have provided a (brief) opportunity for the revival of transhumance in some wold landscapes. In the fourteenth and fifteenth centuries, for example, the ewe flocks of manor lords and possibly their peasants were kept on summer pastures in the north Cotswolds, and some of the sheepcotes involved were set up on land that had been cultivated and settled on a year-round basis until *c.*1350 (Dyer 1996). Uplands must therefore be viewed as dynamic places where the role of transhumance could fluctuate in importance over time as social, economical and environmental conditions dictated.

Another central but unresolved issue in medieval English pastoralism is the extent to which animal husbandry on summer pastures was carried out by people who hailed from the parent settlements or by hired herdsmen living beside or on the summer pastures. Post-medieval transhumant movements in Scotland, Ireland and perhaps Wales can be said with a degree of certainty to have involved families or at least a few of their members because these practices were observed and recorded by others, but for most of England – where transhumance did not survive as long – medieval records tend to be a little opaque. As a result, most scholars have not been able to tackle the subject in any depth. Although the nearest villages were only 1.5 to 2.5km away, historical evidence for sheep milking leads Dyer (1996) to suggest that many sheepcotes accommodated shepherds and possibly dairymaids. The retrieval of ceramics from excavations of small buildings at sheepcotes on Bredon Hill and Chalk Hill (Dyer 1996, 28–31) certainly adds weight to the idea of an overnight human presence, but as yet there has been no detailed investigation of who, or how many people, might have been living there. Recent work that does shine a light on the issue is a study of Dartmoor by the late historical geographer Harold Fox, arguably the most comprehensive undertaken to date on British transhumance. Here there is clear documentary evidence from the later medieval period for professional herdsmen and moor-edge farmers (acting as middlemen) looking after cattle that were brought from farms up to 20–35km away – what Fox calls 'impersonal' transhumance (Fox 2012, 49, 61–69); in the Anglo-Saxon period, however, he argues that 'personal' transhumance had taken place between the lowlands and seasonal settlements on detachments of manors found on or beside the outer moor, land that was eventually colonised fully by would-be middlemen (Fox 2012, 108–11, 158–66). Significantly, the labour-intensive task of dairying would appear to have taken place on Dartmoor in this earlier phase (Fox 2012, 148–54). While these ideas have yet to be tested rigorously through an examination of the archaeology, they do raise the question of whether similar transitions could have occurred elsewhere in England and, on the other side of the coin, whether 'impersonal' systems ever formed an important aspect of seasonal pastoralism in the rest of Britain and in Ireland.

WALES

Transhumance to upland grazing grounds looms large in the later medieval and early post-medieval written sources of Wales, with the practice known as *hafod a hendre* – literally 'summer and winter dwellings'. Tradition places the upward movement of people and their livestock to the *hafod* on May Day, with the return to the *hendre* occurring on All Saints' Day (Davies 1984–85, 76–77), a schedule that agrees with movements recorded in nineteenth-century Donegal, in Ireland (Morris *et al.* 1939, 289; Ó hEochaidh 1943, 141, 143), as well as in eighteenth-century Aberdeenshire (Smith 1986, 451). However, there was probably some deviation from these very specific dates in years of unusually early or late growth and according to the soil quality at various summer grazing grounds across Wales.

Elwyn Davies has shed more light on the history of transhumance in Welsh farming than any other scholar to date, having trawled through historical records, maps and place-names for the whole country (Davies 1973; 1977; 1979; 1980; 1984–85). His work has shown that *hafod/hafoty* names are to be found throughout most of upland Wales, with the greatest densities in the north (Davies 1984–85, 89, fig. 6), and that they are mentioned quite regularly in documents from the late fifteenth to the nineteenth century (Davies 1980, Appendices A and B). Interestingly, however, many instances of *hafod* place-names mark the locations of permanent farmsteads rather than summer dwellings (that is, either now or at the time of their recording). Davies explains this discrepancy in the context of colonisation, which in Wales seems to have started at many of the lower seasonal sites from the sixteenth century as a result of land pressure in lower areas and the replacement of partible inheritance with primogeniture – a shift that may have left many disenfranchised sons with no option but to settle on *hafod* sites (Davies 1984–85, 84–86). That the *hafod* name clung to these newly established farmsteads is a potential aid in reconstructing the former extent of seasonally used grazing grounds in Wales. Equally, it is a reminder that in Ireland the occurrence of *buaile* and *áirí* place-names in what are now – or were recently – permanently settled contexts should not come as a surprise.

More recent research has shown that, in the later medieval period, transhumance played an important role at a high level in Welsh society. The princes of Gwynedd, for example, are recorded as having the use of *hafodydd* on royal *friddoedd*, or 'uncultivated lands', in central Snowdonia, while many late twelfth- and early thirteenth-century stone castles built by them and others in this region are located in valley floors giving access to the mountain pasture – presumably with the intention of controlling access to that resource (Longley 2006, 77–79). To what extent client farmers of the nobility took part in this transhumance is difficult to gauge, but it would be surprising if they were excluded totally. After the conquest of Gwynedd in 1283 control of the territory's *hafodydd* seems to have become devolved to individuals who, initially at least, were of

Anglo-Norman stock (Longley 2006, 79). This marks the beginning of a move towards private ownership at the expense of ideas of common ownership that were integral to the native Welsh 'commote', and ultimately probably made it easier for individuals to enclose and settle on sections of summer pasture.

Notwithstanding these changes in Welsh society, transhumance continued to be practised by certain farmers with access to mountain pasture well into the post-medieval period, though the last instances of its existence are confined to Snowdonia. Pennant, in 1773, describes the upward movement of whole families with cattle, sheep and goats to 'havodtys or summer-dairy-houses' in Llanberis – a custom not unlike the driving of dairy cows to summer shielings observed subsequently by him in the Scottish islands (Pennant 1810, 334–35). Twenty years later, however, this practice had apparently ceased in Llanberis (Kay 1794, 17). The latest attested use of a summer dwelling for transhumance anywhere in Wales comes from Cwm Llydaw (also in Snowdonia), which, as late as 1862, was linked with settlements over 2km away in the Glaslyn valley (Roberts 1968, 7): other late references to transhumance hail from North Wales also (Davies 1984–85, 84, 88). Just as in Ireland and Scotland, then, there is clear evidence for the practice of transhumance in certain upland districts of Wales up to the nineteenth century. In Wales, however, there is not the same level of cultural richness around transhumance in the form of folklore and first-hand observations: had people remained at the *hafodydd* for two or three decades longer, it is possible that more specific details on the inner workings of recent Welsh transhumance might have survived to be recorded.

With regard to the post-medieval history of transhumance in Wales, the term *lluest* is of interest. Like *hafod*, it is used to denote upland sites associated with pastoralism, though it is not exactly clear how it differs from the former. In the literature there is a sense that *lluestau* are later because they are not recorded in the main until the tithe surveys of the early nineteenth century (Davies 1984–85, 87). It is also assumed that they functioned as small shepherding stations – as distinct from summer settlements like the *hafodydd*, to which larger numbers of people (i.e., families, communities or several members thereof) would have moved with dairy cattle (Davies 1980, 25; Roberts 2006, 180; Leighton 2012, 103). The association of *lluestau* with eighteenth- and nineteenth-century shepherding is hardly concrete enough to make these assumptions, however. One of the only references to their use by shepherds comes from Thomas Jones' 1688 explanation of the word in his dictionary as 'A shepherd's Cottage, also a Tent' (quoted in Sambrook 2006, 100), while the field evidence for them is difficult to distinguish from that of *hafod* structures where the former are not specifically marked on maps (Silvester 2006, 33). Also strange is the fact that *lluest* only occurs commonly in place-names in central Wales, and is entirely absent north of Harlech (Davies 1984–85, 91. fig. 7). Thus, while there may be merit in Davies' suggestion that *lluestau* were established at higher altitudes as *hafodydd* were taken over as permanent farms (Davies 1984–85, 87), one wonders whether this model is applicable outside Wales' central uplands. It is possible that too much significance has been placed on what may amount to no more than a difference in terminology. In any case, if people travelled seasonally with livestock to *lluestau* just as they did to *hafodydd*, albeit in lesser numbers, then they were still clearly practising a form of transhumance.

Archaeological evidence

Comprehensive fieldwork is beginning to build up a picture of the distribution of seasonally occupied *hafodydd* and *lluestau*. The two most commonly encountered forms of deserted settlement over 200m a.s.l. in Wales today are roughly rectangular or sub-rectangular 'long huts' constructed of earth and/or stones, and earthwork 'platforms', many of which display the remains of possible long huts (Roberts 2006, 174, fig. 9.1; 175, 9.2). Where these structures are found in remote locations on unenclosed mountains they tend to be seen as the likely remains of summer habitations used as part of transhumance (Silvester 2006, 34). However, these classifications need to be treated with some caution, as they are intended only as general indications of form – of the 330 long huts identified in central and north-east Wales, for example, internal length varies from 4m to 7m in 43 per cent of cases, with the rest either longer or shorter (Silvester 2006, 34). Rectangular and sub-rectangular stone huts built on platforms predominate in the Black Mountain area of the western Brecon Beacons, although here many of the huts are multi-celled and occasionally have pens and outbuildings attached – that is, of course, to say nothing of the wide range of sizes that all of the encountered sites encompass (Ward 1997, 99–100, figs 8.3–8.4). A similar picture emerges from the upper Taf Fechan valley, further east along the Beacons, albeit with the additional presence of oval-shaped structures (Miller 1967b, 107–10).

In short, the material evidence for seasonal settlement in Wales is complex. Not only is the significance of the various shapes and sizes of structure found in the Welsh uplands uncertain, it is still early days in terms of understanding their chronology. In general, owing to the historical evidence, long huts are assumed to date to the later medieval or early modern periods. However, a recent excavation at Carn Goedog in the Preseli hills of south-west Wales has placed an eleventh- to twelfth-century occupation date on a sub-rectangular hut measuring 4.5m × 2.2m internally (Schlee *et al.* 2018; Comeau 2019, 143–44), while the excavation of a slightly larger rectangular hut at Ynys Ettws in north-west Wales gave a (primary) occupation date in the twelfth to fourteenth centuries (Smith and Thompson 2006, 114–17). Lying at the relatively low altitudes of 250m and 270m respectively, the Ynys Ettws and Carn Goedog structures possibly offer a glimpse of *hafod* settlement in the high medieval period, surviving when similar hillsides elsewhere in Wales were, as Elwyn Davies documents, settled on a year-round basis.

Determining whether a particular site is seasonal or not is rarely clear cut, however. Ward has drawn attention to some inconsistencies in attempts to characterise excavated upland settlements across Wales, whereby sites with scant finds have been considered permanent while others with comparatively rich assemblages are deemed seasonal just because they are located at higher altitudes and/or are associated with a *hafod* place-name (Ward 1997, 105–06). For example, the 'centre house' excavated on Gelligaer East in the south of Wales was believed to represent a year-round homestead because of its large size (20m × 7.5m, internally) and the presence of pottery from the thirteenth to fourteenth centuries (Fox 1939). However, it is located at almost 400m a.s.l. and there are no surface traces of contemporary fields or cultivation ridges in the vicinity, leading some to doubt as to its permanence (Locock 2006, 55).

Furthermore, palaeoecological sampling at Ynys Ettws has thrown up evidence for cereal-type pollen during the later medieval period (Caseldine 2006, fig.7.3), which suggests either that the site was occupied on a year-round basis on a few occasions or that people used it for long enough each year to justify cultivating a small amount of cereals. In view of these uncertainties, Ward (1997, 107–08) proposes a scenario whereby evidence of upland settlement should be viewed in a fluid way, with ruined structures representing past communities' attempts to manage environmental risk on an exceptional as well as a seasonal basis, or even, in some cases, as short-lived attempts at outright colonisation. This may be a slightly pessimistic view of what can be achieved, but it is a reminder of the importance of maintaining an open mind when investigating what may be the physical remains of seasonal settlement.

SCOTLAND

Shieling systems in southern Scotland

Southern Scotland, and the Border region in particular, bears many similarities to adjoining parts of northern England, at least in terms of environmental and population history during the second millennium AD. Here, too, transhumance had all but disappeared by the seventeenth century. Two of the last references to the use of summer shielings come from near the English border – Kershopefoot on the West March in 1583 and the Middle March in 1584 (Bain 1894, nos 182, 2214, 217). Prior to the sixteenth century, transhumant activity appears to have been more common. Numerous grants of land in twelfth-century Lowland charters are termed *scalinga*, which is thought to be a latinised version of 'shieling grounds' (Whitaker 1959, 169). Furthermore, place-names containing *schele* and occasionally *skāli* elements – both possibly related to summer settlement – have been found across most of southern Scotland (Winchester 2012, fig. 9.2). As a result of historical research and archaeological field survey in Liddesdale, near the English border, Dixon (2009, 39) has suggested that the cessation of shieling use during the seventeenth century was associated with the expansion of permanent settlement beyond the deer dykes (boundaries that marked off the unenclosed mountain pasture) (Dixon 2009, 39). In addition, he points out that the local landlord placed a great deal more emphasis on sheep farming from the early seventeenth century (Dixon 2009, 44), a shift that would have negated the need for summer upland settlement because of the reduced attention mutton and wool-producing sheep required compared with dairy cattle.

Shieling systems in Highland Scotland

North of the Forth–Clyde isthmus transhumance was practised well into the post-medieval period and as a result attracted a significant accumulation of documentary evidence, as well as more intensive archaeological research today. In a preliminary but nonetheless fairly extensive survey of documentary and ethnohistorical sources, Whitaker has shown that there were numerous instances of in-use shieling sites in (mainland) Highland Scotland between 1501 and 1800. These are mainly concentrated in the Central and East Highland zone, with a noticeable fall-off near the low-lying eastern coast and the most northerly parts of the Highlands (Whitaker 1959, figs 1–3). Removal to summer shielings was a typical element of runrig farming (see Whittington 1970 and Hodd 1974), in which small clustered settlements had to depend on narrow stretches of cultivable land in the valleys that divide up the great mass of the Highlands. The distances separating these valley and lakeside townships from their shielings in adjacent mountains were usually no more than 3–7km (MacSween 1959, fig. 1, 81; Miller 1967a, 202; Love 1981, 43; Bil 1990, fig. 6); however, it cannot be ruled out that some, perhaps wealthier, farmers in the east of northern Scotland once maintained long-distance connections with summer pastures in the Highland zone. For instance, there is evidence from Aberdeenshire that lowland farmers in Monymusk had rights to shieling grounds some 48km away in the Cabrach up to the mid-eighteenth century (RCAHMS 2007, 205).

After 1800 there are far fewer references to shielings being used, and only one after 1901, indicating that the system had broken down in most areas of mainland Scotland by the nineteenth century (Whitaker 1959, figs 4, 5). Of course, because Whitaker consults only the written material, his distribution maps can be seen as only rough estimations of the contraction of transhumance; it is possible, for example, that the apparent lack of shielings in the far north may have resulted from a disinterest on the part of contemporary authorities in documenting customary farming practices in that area. Other scholars dealing solely with documentary evidence have also gravitated towards the Central Highlands. Gaffney (1967) has revealed several useful maps and other records of eighteenth-century shielings for the Drumochter area, while Albert Bil (1989; 1990) has delved in great detail into shieling systems that were in operation throughout Perthshire from 1600 to 1840. Using nineteenth-century Ordnance Survey maps, place-names, historical accounts and earlier legal and estate records, Bil has shown that distances between home farms and their shielings (known in Scots Gaelic as *àirighean* or *àiridhean*) could vary substantially according to locality and that, while women carried out dairying tasks at shieling huts, their menfolk would be in charge of herding the cows in the wider landscape (Bil 1990, 199–205).

Archaeological research has taken advantage of the relatively plentiful supporting evidence available in the Central Highlands; initially Miller (1967a, 204) was able to identify examples of shieling huts that were marked on an estate map of North Lochtayside in 1769 and, more recently, the Ben Lawers Historic Landscape project undertook in-depth field survey, excavation and palaeoenvironmental proxy studies of the area (Atkinson 2016). The results of this study, and of wider reconnaissance surveys by the Royal Commission on the Ancient and Historical Monuments of Scotland (CANMORE), mean that we now have a fairly decent overall impression of the architecture of former shieling huts as well as of their size and distribution. Summarising the results of fieldwork, Dixon (2018) has pointed out that most summer dwellings are sub-rectangular, with a mean internal space of 3.98m (±1.65m) by 2m (±0.7m). Roughly half were built of sods and half of stone, though this could vary depending on the raw materials that were available in a given space and time. Shieling huts are generally found in loose groups, with 20–30m between each building.

Dixon (2009, 38, 44) suggests a development from sod-building to stone-building as a result of improvement-driven estate policies in the post-medieval period, but there is not enough absolute dating evidence to confirm this. Excavation of ten probable summer dwellings in Lochtayside revealed that occupation took place mainly over the period 1450–1775, and radiocarbon date-ranges overlapped for sod- and stone-built huts (that said, larger sod-walled structures just above Kiltyrie township that were deemed to represent a short-lived phase of year-round settlement produced high medieval dates – earlier than any of the others; Atkinson 2016, 92–94). The possibility of chronological development from mostly or entirely sod-built structures with curving walls to more rectangular stone structures has emerged in debates about seasonal settlement in Ireland too. As discussed later, the answer cannot always be reduced to a simple 'earlier' or 'later' choice – raw materials, topography and human agency are also important factors in the morphology of seasonal settlements.

Nevertheless, the overall date range for shieling hut construction and occupation in Lochtayside does match up reasonably well with recent palynological studies in the Scottish Highlands, which show a gradual intensification of upland grazing in late medieval times (Davies 2016). The excavation results also agree with later historical records that document the abandonment of shieling huts by tenant families and their cows in the late eighteenth and early nineteenth centuries (Bil 1990).

Factors in the decline of Highland shieling practices

The decay of seasonal mobility across northern Scotland varied according to the nature of the local economy, the policies of landlords and their tenants' means of subsistence. Some general trends can be discerned, however.

Upland colonisation

There is evidence from some areas that permanent farming settlements began to encroach upon summer grazing grounds at higher altitudes in the late eighteenth century. For the Braemar area Smith (1986, 451) has put forward a model in which some of the lower shieling sites began to attract cultivation before being colonised fully in the decades c.1800, when population pressure reached a high point (although it seems that shielings at still greater altitudes did continue to be used seasonally for a short time). Similarly, in Corgarff, to the north, shieling sites started to be cultivated in the late eighteenth century as they made the transition from seasonal sites to permanent crofts; indeed, it was even a stipulation of leases from the landlord there – the duke of Gordon – that shielings be improved by tenants (Gaffney 1959, 32–34). This pattern of upland colonisation would have curtailed the seasonal use of mountain grazing by severing the link between older permanent settlements and their shielings.

Other factors too were at work in altering the Highland economy in the late eighteenth and early nineteenth centuries, and these ultimately proved to be of even greater detriment to the shieling system. At the same time as nascent settlement expansion, there was a growing desire by Highland landlords to establish hunting and shooting grounds on their estates and also to replace dairy cattle with less labour-intensive forms of pastoralism. These policy shifts ultimately prevented population pressure from reaching anything near the proportions seen in Ireland, where, it is worth adding, unoccupied marginal land was less extensive. Exactly when and in what order these new policies were brought in varies, rather unsurprisingly, from one estate to another – and this as a research theme is worthy of further scrutiny on a nationwide scale. Nevertheless, there is no doubting that, sooner or later, they overrode the process of shieling colonisation and themselves played decisive roles in bringing an end to transhumance.

Hunting

As Dixon (2009) has highlighted, many areas of the Highlands were reserved from later medieval times for deer hunting by the nobility. These deer parks or 'forests' co-existed with shieling systems for several centuries in areas such as the Mar in the Upper Dee valley and nearby on the Don in Corgarff, both of which had hunting reserves from the fourteenth century onwards (Dixon 2009, 39). Settlement – seasonal or otherwise – was not permitted on the reserves, but it seems that they were sometimes encroached upon illegally by the cattle of those who used nearby shielings, as was the case in the Forests of Drumochter (Gaffney 1967, 91). However, in the eighteenth and nineteenth centuries Highland landlords came increasingly to expand their deer forests at the expense of both permanent settlements and summer grazing grounds. In the Lui valley, a tributary of the Dee, settlements dating back to the seventeenth century were removed for good in 1776 by the earl of Fife (Dixon 2009, 44), a move that obviously brought an end to the use of shieling huts associated with them. The enlargement of hunting grounds gained pace in the nineteenth century, with the Braemar and Crathie parish a few kilometres further down the Dee valley being depopulated in 1811, apparently for the same reasons (though this was debated by a representative of the earl; Smith 1986, 452). The same pattern was eventually repeated to the north in Glenavon, Banffshire, where grazings were sacrificed in 1841 (Gaffney 1959, 34). While it may appear counter-intuitive for landlords to clear rent-paying tenants off their land, the reality is that these holdings and grazing grounds yielded a greater return when hired out for deer hunting and grouse shooting. As the *Inverness Courier* reported in 1835, 'at the present moment, we believe, many Highland proprietors derive a greater revenue from their moors alone, for grouse shooting, than their whole rental amounted to sixty years since' (quoted in Devine 1994, 78).

Sheep farming and the Clearances

The commercial motivations evident in the expansion of deer forests also manifest themselves in developments in post-medieval Highland farming. Their origins can first be seen in the growth in the trade of 'black' cattle raised solely for beef production. After the union of the Scottish and English crowns in 1603 demand for meat surged in England, especially amongst London's growing population – a demand that landlords north of the Border happily met by sending dry cattle to be fattened on the uplands before eventually droving them south to the markets (MacSween 1959, 81; Riley 1978, 200; Fenton 1987, 27). As these animals required less attention than dairy cows, there was probably little or no increase in the use of shieling sites; indeed, if anything, the growth of this form of pastoralism may have placed shieling systems under some pressure as landlord herds competed for grazing with the smaller dairy herds of their tenants.

This early phase of commercialisation did not by any means strike a fatal blow to transhumance in the Highlands, but it did foreshadow a more complete change that was to come. As landlords continued to seek out more profitable uses for mountainous terrain on their estates, Blackface sheep were introduced in large numbers from the Lowlands during the later eighteenth and nineteenth centuries (Bil 1990, 308; Whyte and Whyte 1991, 167–69; Bangor-Jones 2002, 181). Sheep were certainly not unknown in the north of Scotland before this; in pre-Norse and Norse excavated horizons at Buckquoy in Orkney, for example, sheep account for roughly 30 per cent of animal bone (Ritchie 1977, 202, table 1). Much later, in a case study of early seventeenth- and eighteenth-century Glenorchy in Argyll, Dodgshon has demonstrated that sheep were just as numerous as cattle (Dodgshon 1998, 175, 180, figs 7.5, 7.9), while in Perthshire sheep were also regularly listed among the movable properties of deceased people from the sixteenth to eighteenth centuries (Bil 1990, 306). Indeed, these 'Whitefaced' sheep are said to have grazed alongside cows at upland shielings and were often kept for their milk as well as their wool (Bil 1990, 161, 307). On the whole, however, it seems that, before the late eighteenth century, these herds of sheep formed just one element of a mixed farming economy. In other words, as Gray has put it, 'there were many sheep but no sheep farms' (Gray 1957, 38). What marks subsequent sheep farming out as different is its scale and the fact that its introduction came at the expense of the mixed subsistence farming of which the shieling system had been part and parcel. In Perthshire several upland parishes had been converted to sheep farms by the 1770s, with the process accelerating greatly after 1790 – one of the later examples of this process being the parish of Fortingall, where the sheep population rocketed from 27,286 in 1790 to 62,000 in 1838 (Bil 1990, 320–21). In the Northern Highlands of Sutherland, after an initial period of experimentation by landlords, sheep farms also came to dominate the pastoral landscape in the last quarter of the eighteenth century (Bangor-Jones 2002, 200).

The socio-economic situation that encouraged specialisation in sheep farming is a complex one, but a number of factors stand out. First, while prices for cattle rose in the late eighteenth century, prices for Blackface sheep and their wool rose quicker, and this naturally led to them being favoured over the former – as well as over the 'Whitefaced' native breed, which produced little wool (Richards 2000, 71–72). Secondly, in the aftermath of the Battle of Culloden in 1746 – which ended the '45 Rebellion – the Highland nobility sought to bring their style of estate management into line with changes that had already taken hold of the south of Scotland – changes that involved a greater emphasis on a market economy and cash payment of rent (Dodgshon 1998, 233–39). This placed a strain on the subsistence lifestyle of Highland tenants, who were used to the old clan-based system of payment in kind, and ultimately, as Dodgshon has argued convincingly, drove a wedge between them and their increasingly detached lords (Dodgshon 1998, 243). Frustrations were created for both parties by this new relationship, not least because smallholders struggled to procure the necessary cash (Dodgshon 1998, 235). In the end, however, the nobility were in a stronger position to change the situation and in their search for steadier forms of income the idea gradually took root that having fewer tenants and more sheep might streamline the running of their estates.

Widespread clearances of townships followed from the end of the eighteenth century and gathered pace in the first two decades of the next. As explained above, depopulation had already been witnessed to an extent with the first expansion of the deer forests, but now it proceeded more vigorously. Writing in 1791, Robert Newte claimed that between a half and two-thirds of upland Perthshire's population melted away to the coast and farther still to North America as sheep farming engulfed the uplands (Newte 1791, 236). Elsewhere, the clearance of upland tenants seems to have involved somewhat more force on the part of landlords, as attested by upheavals in Strathnaver and Kildonan, Sutherland, in the years 1818–19 (Richards 2000, chapter 10). Whatever the method, however, the outcome was eventually the same: the focus on sheep, which required less attention than dairy cattle and certainly less than arable crops, meant that a large labour force was no longer required. Landlords could make do with employing a few shepherds to attend their cash-generating flocks (Bil 1990, 362–63). Although sheep farming was itself to lose favour in the late nineteenth century as hunting and shooting game became ever more lucrative (Orr 1982, 91–92), the great damage inflicted upon rural Highland populations up to that point ensured that the shieling system, which depended on people as well as livestock, had well and truly disappeared.

Shieling practices on Scotland's islands

The islands off Scotland's west coast are worth considering separately because there small-scale transhumance continued well into the nineteenth and twentieth centuries, ensuring greater numbers of historical references and surviving oral traditions. On the Isle of Skye shielings are mentioned as early as the sixteenth century and on South Uist and Benbecula from the seventeenth century (Whitaker 1959, fig. 1). As more people visited and wrote about the islands, shieling customs on Lewis and the rest of the Hebrides start to be attested more frequently in the late eighteenth century (Whitaker 1959, figs 3–5). Among these references is the well-known account of Thomas Pennant in 1772 – the first in detail anywhere in Scotland. Arriving on Jura, he recorded his observations of 'sheelins [shielings], the temporary habitations of some peasants who tend the herds of milch cows', and depicts the structures as tepee- and beehive-shaped huts consisting of a light timber framework and sod walls (Pennant 1776, 205, 246). Pennant's depiction offers a rare glimpse of the appearance of shieling huts while they were still in use and suggests two methods of roofing structures with circular or oval ground plans. Superstructures are an important indicator of building style and potentially chronology but they rarely survive intact at seasonal sites. In the absence of more widespread excavation, archaeological interpretation of ground plans must therefore be supplemented with pictorial evidence and folk memories in order to form reasonable hypotheses about the appearance of different transhumant dwellings.

On Skye – the most populated of the Hebrides for much of the post-medieval period – shielings may have been used as late as the 1850s in East Trotternish, according to local tradition (MacSween 1959, 76). However, the dairy-based transhumant lifestyle may have faced competition from an earlier period; in Skye the rearing of black cattle for the beef trade featured prominently on rough grazing from the sixteenth century, with the Kingsburgh MacDonalds beginning the first southward droves in 1502 (Haldane 1952, 20). Much later again, clearances for sheep farming towards the end of the eighteenth century and the reorganisation of the island's runrig system in 1811 (MacSween 1959, 82) are likely to have broken up the shieling system in much the same fashion that similar pressures had done, or were still doing, in the Highlands. South of Skye, the links between Rum's twelve permanent settlements and their inland shielings was severed in 1826–28 when the island was entirely cleared to make way for the establishment of an 8,000-strong sheep flock tended to by a few shepherds who were strangers to the island (Love 1981, 39). Love (1981) and Miller (1967a) have reported close to 300 structures in the island's interior, many of which were probably associated with summer settlement and dairying before 1826.

In the Western Isles or Outer Hebrides transhumance continued to be practised into the twentieth century and this, thankfully, received the attention of curious visitors (see Whitaker 1959, 172, fig. 5). One account describes how, 'having finished their tillage, the people go early in June to the hill-grazing with their flocks', sheep going first, cattle next and horses last (Skene 1880, 385). Here, evidently, a mixed farming economy was still operating in the late nineteenth century, several decades after that had given way to specialised sheep farming and hunting throughout most of Highland Scotland. Early antiquarian work also provides an insight into the materiality of seasonal settlement in post-medieval transhumance. Visiting Uig on the Isle of Lewis in the 1850s, Thomas (1857, 143–44, Plates X–XVIII) describes a series of *bothan* or beehive-shaped huts constructed partly or mostly of stone (and cased in peat) that had been falling out of use as summer dwellings in the preceding decades; indeed, one remarkable site thought to have been abandoned in 1823 consisted of twelve conjoined beehive huts. He draws a distinction between these and the rectangular, timber-roofed summer dwellings known as *àiridhean* that were common across Lewis (Thomas 1857, 135, 138). Modern archaeological survey confirms the presence of corbelled and sometimes multi-celled beehive huts on Uig and Harris (Dixon 2018, 63).

When these *bothan* were constructed remains uncertain, however. According to Thomas, there was almost no local memory of how old they were or who had built them. One potential indicator of chronology, if assessed in a wider context, is their form of construction. While Dixon may well be correct that beehive stone corbelling is unique to shieling huts on Uig and Harris, owing to the plentiful supply of suitable stone and a lack of timber (Dixon 2018, 63), their undifferentiated form does have parallels. In terms of shape, if not raw materials, the *bothan* are similar to the beehive huts depicted by Pennant several decades previously on Jura, and also those found in various parts of Ireland *c.*1600, according to illustrations in the *Pacata Hibernia* (see Andrews 2001). The construction of circular and oval dwellings – sometimes with beehive-like superstructures – had remained common at a non-elite level in later medieval Ireland, but from the seventeenth century it seems that rectangular house forms became increasingly dominant throughout society (e.g. Aalen 1997; O'Conor 2002; Orser 2010; Gardiner 2012b). One emerging hypothesis is therefore that the beehive huts found on Uig and Harris belong to an older tradition of construction that overlapped in terms of occupation with timber-roofed rectangular forms. This remains to be tested, but recently unearthed photographic evidence from the 1940s does demonstrate that it was the larger rectangular shielings that continued in use longest (Kupiec 2016, figs 3.3, 3.10). Indeed, in what must have been an attempt to imitate the permanent 'blackhouses' at home, their interiors were even wallpapered.

The social role of shielings for tenant communities in the Outer Hebrides is another issue of direct relevance to the Irish debate on transhumance. Skene (1880, 386–87) outlines the annual festivities that marked the movement to the summer pastures in Lewis: the 'removing' feast, or *Feisd na h-imrig*. Prayers would be sung and cheese shared out between the participants, before the younger women and girls were left to take care of the livestock. Clearly, the practice of transhumance had a role not only in making sensible use of land but also as a force for social cohesion. Thomas (1857, 130–32), furthermore, records a story of a human-like but evil *each-uisge* (water-horse) coming to visit a dairymaid in her shieling, the girl immediately fleeing back to her home. The potential for mystery and otherworldliness at seasonal sites is echoed in oral traditions about booleying in Ireland, with one story from Connemara, for example, telling of an old woman who shape-shifted into a hare in order to steal milk from a cow (Mac Giollarnáth 1934, 105). Other unusual aspects of life at summer pastures in Ireland – both real and imagined – will be highlighted in each case study, before the socio-cultural role of transhumance is discussed in Chapter 6.

Without doubt, the continued usage of shielings in the Outer Hebrides until well into the twentieth century helps to explain the survival of oral traditions about the practice. Curwen speaks of shieling sites that were still occupied shortly before the outbreak of World War II, and from which 'no visitor is allowed to go away without at least a large glass of creamy milk' (Curwen 1938, 270). A few years later the remaining shielings of Lewis were abandoned by the last transhumant dairymaids, although some structures continued to be used as summer holiday homes or shelters for peat-cutters (Miller 1967a, 215). It seems likely that one of the final triggers for the abandonment of shielings as transhumant sites was the increased need for women at home farms during the 1940s, many of the young men having departed for war.

Nevertheless, the apparent local 'survival' of shieling practices requires explanation. Fenton argues that clearances for sheep farms could not proceed on Lewis as they had done on Skye and the mainland because the Seaforth landlords, and subsequently Sir James Mathieson, were less ruthless in their estate management (Fenton 1987, 35). He also makes the case that, in the second half of the eighteenth century, extreme population growth on what little tillable land Lewis contained rendered the continued summer use of shielings vital for the survival of small farmers (Fenton 1987, 35). While this theory seems plausible, it does present a paradox whereby, as seen above, seasonal movement to shieling sites in parts of the Highlands were hampered rather than encouraged by population growth (due to the colonisation of shielings).

Ultimately, in explaining the apparently contradictory consequences of post-medieval population expansion for transhumance, it is likely that a number of issues need further consideration, including: the nature and quality of upland/moorland grazing available to different communities; how they adapted at an organisational level to having more people around; and the difficulty of negotiating the landscape as a herder after encroachment on grazing grounds had begun. Increasing population is an even more significant theme in post-medieval Ireland, and teasing out its effects on transhumance in different regions is a central issue for this book.

Conclusions

Pastoralism, or the rearing and herding of livestock, is a vast and diverse area of study in anthropology with potentially significant implications for our understanding of the evolution of human societies and the landscapes they depend on. Having been dismissed as a fleeting phenomenon that has little archaeological visibility, decades of interdisciplinary research have now made clear that pastoral groups around the world are indeed traceable. The regularity of transhumant pastoralism, particularly, facilitates identification. While the term speaks to a highly varied set of practices, at their core they all typically involve a primary settlement, at which crops are typically grown in summer and from which herders remove with livestock on a seasonal basis to another environmental context.

In mainland Europe, and indeed Scandinavia, significant progress has been made in understanding the nature of transhumant practices over time and the role they played in the development of Alpine and Mediterranean cultural landscapes, either because seasonal movements to upland pastures still take place or because the idea of that lifestyle remains alive somehow in the public consciousness. However, in Britain and Ireland the cessation of transhumance over the course of recent centuries means that living memories of seasonal movement have disappeared and historic farming practices are studied mainly through the lens of sedentism. This is most obvious in England, where research has been piecemeal and relatively light on archaeological investigation. Historical records and place-names suggest that the seasonal grazing of livestock was common in many woodland and wold regions prior to the late Anglo-Saxon period, although physical evidence of human relocation is limited to a small number of sunken dwellings found through excavation. On current evidence it seems that the general trend in high medieval times was towards the colonisation of these lower pastures, leaving the mountainous north of England as the only region with historical and archaeological evidence for seasonal movements of people with livestock in the late medieval and early modern periods. Conversely, we have so little detailed information about the operation of *early* medieval animal husbandry in the northern Pennines and Lake District that it cannot be assumed that later shieling systems in these areas represent a continuing tradition of transhumance.

Similarly, for Wales and Scotland it is unclear how and indeed if transhumance operated in the first millennium AD given that most documentary evidence is later – in fact, post-medieval. Moreover, studies relying on historical references and place-names usually emphasise a decline in transhumant practices in the long run, with *hafod* use retreating to still higher ground in North Wales and shielings or *àirighean* to the Highlands and Islands. The conclusion of this narrative is indisputable: in all those parts of Wales and most of those in Scotland where we find late medieval or early modern evidence of transhumance, the reliance on summer dwellings was indeed gone by the mid-nineteenth century. However, in this train of thought, the decline of transhumance acquires a sense of inevitability. It becomes an expected and possibly even assumed trend in landscape history despite the fact that we still have relatively few details about pre-modern human activity in upland environments of Scotland and Wales. By the same token, there is a danger of writing off the *continued* use of shielings in the Outer Hebrides as an anachronistic outlier.

What is missing is an understanding of the actions of farmers at a local level, and their responses to wider historical trends. Unfortunately, these are not always clear from the documentary record. Thus a more interesting approach, which permits investigation of adaptation and disrupts the narrative of survival, is to examine the landscapes in which transhumance was actually practised. Archaeology has already begun to challenge assumptions, most notably at Ben Lawers in Perthshire, where excavation turned up no evidence of shieling use prior to the fourteenth century, pointing instead to it being a late medieval innovation. But greater integration of archaeological evidence with ethnographic and oral historical information, in a situated landscape context, is required to probe the agency of herders and their communities. My interdisciplinary studies of transhumance in post-medieval Ireland will therefore not only draw from existing evidence in its nearest neighbour but offer a timely source of *analogy* for the evolution and decline of transhumant mobility in medieval and post-medieval Britain.

CHAPTER 2

IMAGINING MOVEMENT: PAST AND PRESENT VIEWS OF TRANSHUMANCE IN IRELAND

PASTORAL MOBILITY IN MEDIEVAL AND EARLY MODERN IRELAND: PERCEPTION VERSUS PRACTICE

There are indications of transhumant movements taking place from the early medieval period onwards in Ireland, though historical references to that effect are few in number and sparing in detail. Two glosses (annotations) on a seventh-/eighth-century Old Irish law tract explain that it was customary to go 'out about May Day from the green of the old *senlis* [winter residence] to a summer pasture' and, about November Day, to return from the grassland to the old residence (Neilson Hancock 1865, 132). It is difficult to tell how common such practices were and what social underpinnings they had, though a more detailed later text hints that relatively long journeys could be undertaken by pastoralists.

A farmer of 100 cows named Dima is said in an eleventh-century Life of Saint Cóemgen to have brought his animals and children on a grazing circuit (*ar cuairt bhuailteachuis*) to the Glendalough area of the Wicklow Mountains, where the cows were grazed in woodland and milked by herdsmen (Plummer 1922: 153–4). With his cows lactating, it seems likely that Dima's grazing circuit took place over the summer, so as to take advantage of the seasonal pastures available in Wicklow's uplands. Dima and his 100 cows were probably not alone in undertaking this journey: an Old Irish law text cited by Kelly (1997, 44) refers to cattle grazing freely on mountain land as a general entitlement. Given that Dima is said to have come all the way from Mide, a kingdom some 40km north-west of Glendalough at its closest (and over 100km away at its farthest), the benefits of this free summer grazing must have been worth the risk for strong farmers with dairy cows.

For its unusual richness, and because it is the first documentary instance of the word *buailteachas* – now the standard term in Irish for booleying (Ó Dónaill 1977, 153) – the story of Dima stands out as the most significant historical evidence of transhumance in medieval Ireland. When other snippets of information are taken into consideration (O'Rahilly 1946, 24; Lucas 1989, 58–67), it becomes clear that summer grazing on land outside core settlements was important from at least the late first millennium AD in Ireland. The threat of wolves (Kelly 1997, 186–87; Hickey 2011) and the need to milk dairy cows would have all but ensured that *people* moved to these pastures as well.

It is only with the close of the sixteenth century that the documentary record offers more information on potential transhumant movements. The earliest of these are heavily laced with the opinions of recently arrived English planters and military figures involved in the Tudor conquest of Ireland. Most famously, Edmund Spenser notes in 1596 that the Irish were in the habit of 'keep[ing] their cattle and liv[ing] themselves the most part of the year in Bollies, pasturing upon the mountain and waste wild places, and removing still to fresh land' (Todd 1805, 363). This description conjures up images of groups of people and animals wandering, nomad-like, for most of the year, a pattern that does not entirely fit with our definition of transhumance: that is, a predictable seasonal movement between winter and summer pastures. Spenser goes on to liken the Irish habit of moving from pasture to pasture 'to the manner of the Scythians', disapproving of it as 'a very idle lyfe, and a fit nursery for a theife'. He recommends a cure – that they settle in towns and 'augment their trade more of tyllinge and husbandrye' (Todd 1805, 363).

Fynes Moryson launches a more extreme tirade, claiming that the Irish 'build no houses, but, like nomads living in cabins, remove from one place to another with their cows'. Again, this was a lifestyle that would make one 'think these men to be Scythians'; indeed, Moryson goes as far as to compare the wild (Gaelic) Irish to 'wild beasts' (Falkiner 1904, 222–32). Francis Jobson remarks in 1598 that 'so long as they may have scope to range up and down in to pasture and feed, they both can and will ever at their pleasures ... rebel and make havoc' (*CSPI* VII 445). In the same vein, Lord Deputy Arthur Chichester recommends in 1608 that the Ulster Irish be 'drawn from their course of running up and down the country with their cattle ... and settle themselves in towns and villages' (*CSPI James* III, 65).

To some degree, these accounts are exaggerations of contemporary transhumance, but they also draw on the realities of what was a very tumultuous time in the Irish political landscape. English commentators were probably influenced by what they had seen of (or heard about) another form of pastoralism known to them as 'creaghting' – a poorly defined type of nomadism that seems to have been common during the late medieval/early modern transition in Ireland. Just as international instances of nomadic and semi-nomadic pastoralism have been distinguished from transhumant pastoralism above, it is important now to highlight creaghting as a separate phenomenon, so that the present discussion of seasonal movement and settlement does not perpetuate early modern English generalisations. As previous scholars have shown, the word *caoraigheacht* is attested in Irish annals from the late fourteenth century onwards, and appears to denote the combined stock of a number of followers under one leader, often in a mobile military context (Simms 1986, 380, 389–90; Nicholls 1987, 13–14; Lucas 1989, 113–24). Although the term itself is used only in the Gaelic northern half of the country, the movements could also be led by members of the Hiberno-Norman aristocracy (Simms 1986, 379; 2015, 108, 113). From the late sixteenth to the late seventeenth century English writers pick up on the term with their anglicisations 'creaght' and 'keyraght', painting it as a nomadic phenomenon. Around Spenser's time, references to pastoralism are so vague and racially motivated that they might well be interpreted as the product of purposeful or careless conflations with transhumance.

However, in later decades there are numerous references to *caoraigheacht* or 'creaghting' that paint it as a phenomenon that certainly existed apart from transhumance. George Story recalls an incident at Mullingar in 1690–91 in which 'about 500 Creights [i.e. people in a "creaght"] came from the County of Longford, with their Wives, Children, Cattle, and everything they could bring away' (quoted by Lucas (1989), 76). Lucas (1989) and Simms (1986) agree that large-scale wanderings of this kind were products of the widespread conflict and social change that affected the country from the late sixteenth century. In her most recent discussion, Simms (2015, 114) goes further, identifying a number of specific factors that led to the growing tendency of some people to move on a large scale with herds of animals in an apparently unpredictable manner: 'The increased mobility of the lowest peasant class, the scarcity of manpower for agriculture, and the forfeiture of landed estates into the hands of the local chief from a depressed class of landowners ... fostered the growth of a semi-nomadic class of graziers.'

These developments may tie in with the issue of population decline in late medieval Europe after the mid-fourteenth-century crisis, which may in some areas have helped pastoral farming to become more popular than labour-intensive cereal cultivation (Nicholls 1987, 410–11, 413–14; Simms 2015, 107–08, 110). It is very difficult to prove that in late medieval Ireland livestock became more important relative to arable, but instances of mobile communities led by noblemen do become more frequent in the documentary sources as the period draws to a close. The pre-existing tradition of *imirce* or 'migration' in early and high medieval Ireland probably made it easier for a permanently landless class of pastoralists to emerge (Lucas 1989, 179–88; Kelly 1997, 299; Simms 2015, 109). Initially, it took the form of 'local creaghts', embedded in the fabric of Ulster society (Lucas 1989, 93–94). Only later, in the roughly one hundred and fifty years between the start of the Tudor wars and the conclusion of the Williamite War, were they transformed into longer-distance refugee movements.

Cattle may have formed the main source of wealth in the *caoraigheacht*, just as they did in transhumance; however, they were not managed in the same way. Whether in its earlier or later forms, *caoraigheacht* departed fundamentally from transhumance in that it was not tied to set land units and did not involve a fixed winter base where arable farming might have been practised. Moreover, it does not appear to have featured much, if at all, in the southern half of the country, where transhumance also took place. No more than other pre-industrial farming societies, pastoralism in early modern Ireland was not monolithic. It had more mobile offshoots, associated partly with the earlier raiding traditions of lords and displaced kin-groups and partly with the violent political and social changes of the late medieval/post-medieval transition.

For contemporary English commentators, though, distinguishing between different types of livestock management was really not the point. It was enough that Irish people were mobile. It allowed them to play up the notion that the native population was wild and unsettled, and helped to justify the conquest and plantation of Ireland under Elizabeth and James I. As Horning (2013, 32) notes, 'the emphasis upon converting the Irish from pastoralism and mobility to agriculture was inextricably linked with the colonizing and civilizing imperative.' In the context of Ireland, the association of pastoralism with a lack of civility has its origins in the writings of Giraldus Cambrensis some four centuries previously. In his *Topography of Ireland*, written after the Anglo-Norman invasion, he explains that:

> the Irish are a rude people, subsisting on the produce of their cattle only, and living themselves like beasts – a people that has not yet departed from the primitive habits of pastoral life … . The whole habits of the people are contrary to agricultural pursuits, so that the rich glebe is barren for want of husbandmen, the fields demanding labour which is not forthcoming (Wright 1863, 124).

In the genealogy of English discourse on Ireland that passage is key to understanding views of Irish inferiority: their focus on extensive systems of grazing meant that they were not making full use of the land they occupied. They were, in short, unworthy of it.

Needless to say, recent scholars have pointed out that arable crops were actually an important aspect of Irish farming landscapes during the sixteenth and, especially, seventeenth centuries (Horning 2013, 33; Gillespie 2015, 127–29). In fact, the need to spare the best land for crops and preserve grass for the winter was, ironically, what prompted many farming communities to move livestock away for the summer in the first place. The idea that the transhumant lifestyle was carried on to the detriment of arable farming is therefore a nonsense in practice as well as perception. Transhumant communities in post-medieval Ireland were essentially agro-pastoralist, albeit the balance between crops and livestock could vary greatly depending on environmental, economic and sometimes political contexts. Further analysis of the documentary record for the seventeenth century reveals a clear reliance on seasonal movement and settlement in many communities as they tried to achieve a balance that suited their own circumstances. The next section outlines that historical evidence in order to produce a preliminary distribution map of transhumant systems at the outset of the period discussed in this book. This is followed by a discussion of what modern investigations in these areas by archaeologists and geographers have revealed about post-medieval transhumance, and how their understanding of the practice has also been influenced by contemporary society and scholarship.

THE HISTORICAL BASIS FOR TRANSHUMANT SYSTEMS IN IRELAND DURING THE SEVENTEENTH CENTURY

In some areas the normality of seasonal movement and settlement is made quite obvious. Roderic O'Flaherty commented of Iar-Chonnacht (now western County Galway) in 1684 that people 'dwell for the most part next the borders of the country where commonly is the best land; and in Summer time they drive their cattle to the mountains, where such as look to the cattle live in small cabins for that season' (Hardiman 1846, 16–17). In 1698 travel writer John Dunton describes a visit to one of these 'booley' or summer habitations, 'the proper dwelling or mansion house being some miles farther neare the sea' (Dunton Letters, published in MacLysaght 1939, 344). O'Flaherty states that cows predominated because the ground in this region was most suited to pasture. Nonetheless, he does mention that several types of grain crop were also grown, and in enough quantity to be sold (MacLysaght 1939, 15). Outside Iar-Chonnacht, Counties Kerry and Cork also contain reasonably clear documentary evidence of people relying on transhumance. In 1600 Sir George Carew wrote to the Privy Council while on military campaign that the 'rebels' in County Kerry 'in the summer season … [live] on the milk and butter of their kine grazing on the mountains and in fastness, which holds this rebellion on foot longer than otherwise it would' (*CSPI* IX, 244; see Figure 2.1). In a report to the Lord Lieutenant of Ireland dated 1673 it is said generally of Kerry, as well as parts of Cork, that the people have 'no employment but the grazing of small cattle in the summer time without making any hay for the winter' (Brady 1867, 184). A reference from *c.*1682 confirms that this involved the relocation of people, at least in the parishes of Knockane and Kenmare. Thomas Kennington, a Church-of-Ireland vicar, remarks that it was 'usual for many families to remove with their cattell into ye mountains in ye summer time, often shifting their dwellings (or boolyes as they term them) for pasturage till harvest, and then return to reap their

Figure 2.1 A drawing from Thomas Dinely's *Observations* (1681) showing an Irish woman sitting outdoors on a stool and milking a cow into a wooden pail (NLI Ms. 392, 266). The cow has its two front legs spancelled with what appears to be a súgán, or straw rope. The second pail, to the right, may have been used to bring the milk home, its long shape making it easier to carry on one's back. Reproduced by kind permission of the National Library of Ireland.

corn & to their winter dwellings' (O'Sullivan 1971, 46). Here, again, one can see that grain crops were incorporated into what was an agro-pastoral system.

Transhumance is also hinted at in a letter from Colonel MacGillycuddy to his son, dated July 1679, in which the former makes the intriguing statement: 'Your wife is verie well & is com home, but goes againe when the people com from the mountaines' (Brady 1867, 133–34). A later reference, from 1758, confirms that seasonal relocation with cows continued in the south Kerry/west Cork area for at least another century. Writing from Berehaven on the Beara peninsula, the English traveller Richard Pococke says that 'The mountains have good pasturage on them, & they make huts & keep their cattle on the mountain in summer & live on new churn butter and milk' (Ó Maidín 1958, 90).

In most cases, however, seventeenth-century transhumant systems are not so easy to track. Surveys of massive amounts of land undertaken by English administrators after the Tudor and Cromwellian conquests are more reliable avenues for historical research; indeed, with close analysis, they can often yield more specific data on the geographic origins, destinations and motivations of transhumant people. For example, in south Kerry, a Down Survey barony map dating to the 1650s shows that nearly the whole south-west of Knockane parish forms one large area of 'commons', with named (though not mapped) sub-divisions capable of supporting a certain number of cows each, to which various individuals held rights of pasture (The Down Survey of Ireland, Dunkerron Barony). In a Down Survey map of northern County Waterford the Comeragh Mountains appear as the 'Commons of Clonmel', the latter a large town on the banks of the Suir, in the adjacent county of Tipperary. The exact nature of their connection is clarified by minutes of the Clonmel Corporation: an entry for 24 April 1609 states that the 'Comons of the said Towne shall have pasturing for their Cattle upon the said mountaine free from paying any thing for the same' (McGrath 2006, 25–26). Somewhat confusingly, the same entry explains that the land was to be 'set' to the merchant Edmund Prindergast that year for a sum of money, an arrangement occasionally repeated under different names. One of these was Teig o Keyly, who 'by comon consent [was] lycenced to grase with his Cattle for this present sumer in the comon mountaine remote' in the year 1610 (McGrath 2006, 35). These declarations were designed to regulate a potentially transhumant system of upland pasturing in the hinterland of a relatively important town, moreover, a town that was controlled not by the 'wild Irish' but by people of Hiberno-Norman descent.

The Desmond Survey of 1586 further attests to the importance of hill pasture in Hiberno-Norman lordships, and not simply in Gaelic areas of the extreme west. For example, in the manor of Newcastle, western County Limerick, it is recorded that 'the free and customary tenants as well as the occupiers, of every kind, of said 27 quarters of land had common pasture (*herbagium*) for their beasts and cattle on the great mountain of Slewlogher aforesaid' (The Desmond Survey 1586, 161). The 'Slewlogher' in question is *Sliabh Luachra* ('Mountain of the Rushes'), a large tract of upland occupying the Limerick/Kerry/Cork border area. At its closest, it is approximately 4km west of the Anglo-Norman-founded town of Newcastle and provides a sharp contrast with the fertile flatlands of the manor and, indeed, central County Limerick as a whole. Although the same survey does not state whether this grazing was seasonal, or if people stayed with the livestock, both seem likely. Sliabh Luachra is not very elevated, most of it lying between 200m and 300m above sea level, but is nonetheless characterised by blanket bog and poor peaty podzols that are unlikely to have sustained many cattle over a winter. Furthermore, with or without dairy cows, the relocation of herders would have been essential to protect stock from cattle raiders and wolves – the latter still being quite numerous in sixteenth- and seventeenth-century Ireland (Hickey 2011).

Other circumstantial evidence of seventeenth-century transhumance, in the Nagles and Boggeragh mountains of County Cork, has been highlighted by Costello (2016a) with the help of place-names containing the *buaile* element. The usefulness of place-names in reconstructing transhumant patterns was first exploited by Jean Graham (1954, 142–45), who drew attention to the peculiar concentration of *buaile* place-names in the low hills of Kilmaley and Inagh in west Clare, a landscape now covered by improved farmland and coniferous forestry. The variety of meanings that have been attributed to the word *buaile* over time, however, mean that place-names are not, on their own, reliable indicators of past transhumance (Costello 2016a). If seasonal settlement and grazing in these areas is to be confirmed, place-names must be used in conjunction with historical sources and ground survey.

An islandwide survey of the seventeenth century's entire documentary record has yet to be undertaken, but it is apparent from the Down Survey that intricate systems of transhumance were probably established in other parts of the country as well. In County Derry, in mid-Ulster, the parish map for Ballynascreen (or Ballinkreene) shows that most named divisions in the parish are made up of separate parcels – one or two small parcels on lower ground containing arable and pasture and one or two larger ones on higher ground containing coarse mountain pasture. One example of this is Ballyowenreagh – divided into a riverside parcel of ninety-nine acres of arable and pasture and two upland parcels of 'course mountaynous pasture', 187 and 482 acres in size each (The Down Survey of Ireland, Loghinsholin Barony). In County Leitrim, Gardiner (2015, 55) has pointed out on the Down Survey parish map of Drumreilly (then Inishmacra) that a block of 1483 acres of upland is linked with '8 cartrons of church land' some 8km away by Lough Allen. Similarly, the Books of Survey and Distribution for Killannin and Kilcummin civil parishes in Iar-Chonnacht provide unusually detailed evidence of what appear to be transhumant links. The source records numerous connections between small units of land by Lough Corrib, dominated by arable, and much larger units that contained only mountainous land (*BSD Galway*, 58–72, 82–83). Graham argues that the resulting pattern delineates a transhumant system that operated from north-east to south-west (Graham 1954, 138–39, map 30; 1970a, fig. 12.2).

In the case of Killannin the units in question lie almost 30km apart, at either end of the parish. Distances like this far surpass anything involved in nineteenth-century booleying, and they seem unusual even for the later sixteenth and seventeenth centuries. This is implied by the size of parish in which most other contemporary transhumant movements took place, such as Knockane in Kerry, Monanimy and Rahan in Cork, Maíros (containing the Carna peninsula), Drumreilly in Leitrim, Gleann Cholm

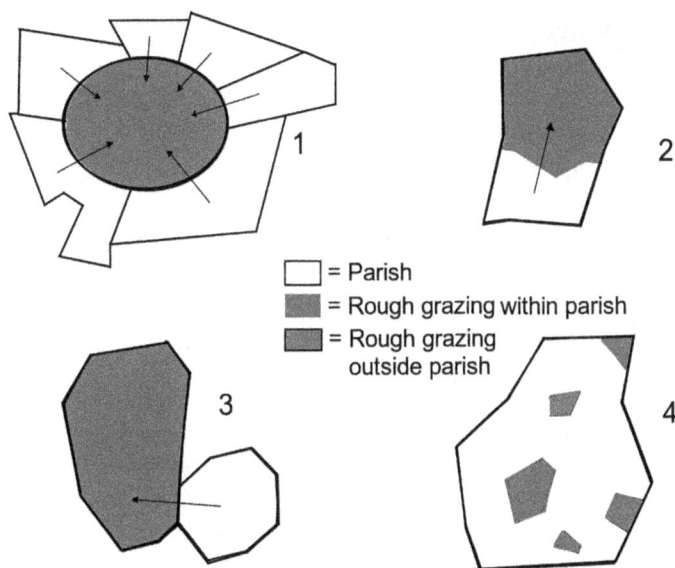

Figure 2.2 Types of transhumant movement in late sixteenth- and seventeenth-century Ireland.
1: multi-parish access to a large common.
2: common located within parish boundaries and reserved for inhabitants of that parish. 3: common reserved for one parish but not actually in the parish. 4: pockets of rough grazing scattered throughout the parish, with transhumance unnecessary.

Cille, and Ballynascreen in Derry. The extent of *these* parishes suggests that distances of more than 12km were rare. Less frequently, transhumance involved one or more parishes and a neighbouring but distinct commonage, such as west Limerick, the southern Galtees and Clonmel commons.

Even in these cases, however, 12km would seem to have been the maximum. Longer distances in the parish of Killannin are ultimately products of the large expanse of rough ground it contains and the concentration of permanent settlement almost entirely in one area. In other sparsely populated areas of the country, such as the parish of Kilcommon in north-west Mayo, similar distances may have prevailed in the early post-medieval period. Really, it should not come as a surprise that pastoral farmers did not all travel the same distances, given that the country itself varies geologically and topographically. What is most significant is that contemporary transhumance, when viewed through the available historical evidence, took place with reference to set boundaries.[1] As such, Figure 2.2 illustrates the four main types of access to rough grazing that can be attested based on all the foregoing documentary evidence. How old these arrangements were by the seventeenth century is very difficult to say in the absence of more detailed medieval records: however, as subsequent chapters will show, it is possible to gauge and find trends in their evolution over the post-medieval period.

---

[1]   The only possible exception to this idea comes down to us through a faint oral tradition recorded by Graham (1954, 27–28) from an elderly man who lived in Hilltown, just north of the Mourne Mountains. This relates that people used to come to those mountains from as far away as Hillsborough, some 30km distant and well outside the parishes in which the Mournes are actually located. However, it is not clear what time period the information refers to. Neither is it ideal that the man in question was local to the Mournes and not Hillsborough itself.

Absence of transhumance or absence of evidence?

Notwithstanding slight variations in the distances that seasonally mobile people might travel, it must be admitted that, throughout much of the country – the Midlands and Leinster especially – there is very little in the way of solid evidence for transhumance in the seventeenth century. In many areas, this is simply about historical visibility. Down Survey parish maps survive or were undertaken for only about two-thirds of the country and, even where they are available, the detail they contain is not always as informative of grazing rights as above. For example, the Mourne Mountains in south Down (Smith and Harris 1744, 125; Gardiner 2012b), the hills of Antrim (Evans 1945; Williams and Robinson 1983), the Wicklow Mountains (Aalen 1963; 1964b) and north-western County Mayo (Ó Moghráin 1943; Ó Duilearga 1947; McDonald 2014) all have at least some documentary or oral historical evidence of summer booley settlements being used in the eighteenth and nineteenth centuries. These traditions almost certainly have their origins in earlier centuries, but the documentary record offers no proof as such. Taking all later snippets of information into account, I have produced a map of the distribution of probable transhumant systems in the seventeenth century (Figure 2.3). Although it does amplify the picture, there is nonetheless a lack of coverage. The fact that transhumance was declining nationwide from the seventeenth century onwards does not help identification, as it means that some systems of seasonal movement simply did not survive long enough to be recorded either ethnographically or historically.

Furthermore, there is the question of bias towards uplands. Figure 2.3 shows that recorded systems of transhumance largely mirror the distribution of uplands across Ireland. Is this a genuine reflection of where people engaged in seasonal grazing and settlement, or are there issues with the surviving evidence? In Ireland the uplands attract attention because they can be treated as discrete blocks of rough grazing, distinct from surrounding improved land. This makes them easier to study from archaeological as well as historical perspectives. An archaeologist is provided with, if not a ready-made study area, a landscape that can be isolated without much trouble, first for inspection by satellite imagery and second for fieldwork. Similarly, upland areas stand out on historic maps, both on the Down Survey and later Ordnance Survey. An area of mountain pasture or commonage that appears on these is immediately a candidate for study, depending on its size, distance from areas of permanent settlement and recorded transhumant connections, if any, with the latter.

By contrast, efforts to identify lowland areas that might have been used in transhumance are usually frustrated. Except where raised and blanket bog prevails, it is very rare that wide expanses of low-lying marginal land (in the form of woodland, scrub, seasonally flooded or rocky land) have escaped colonisation, drainage or improvement in Ireland. This means that any archaeology associated with earlier seasonal settlement is unlikely to survive. As a result, one is disproportionately dependent on historical sources such as the Down Survey in these landscapes, and when the latter fails to provide obvious hints it becomes impossible to reconstruct transhumant movements. In one respect these difficulties are a blessing, as they waken one to the likelihood that transhumance was not relied upon by every agro-pastoral community. Figure 2.3 undoubtedly misses areas that were engaged in seasonal movements, but it would

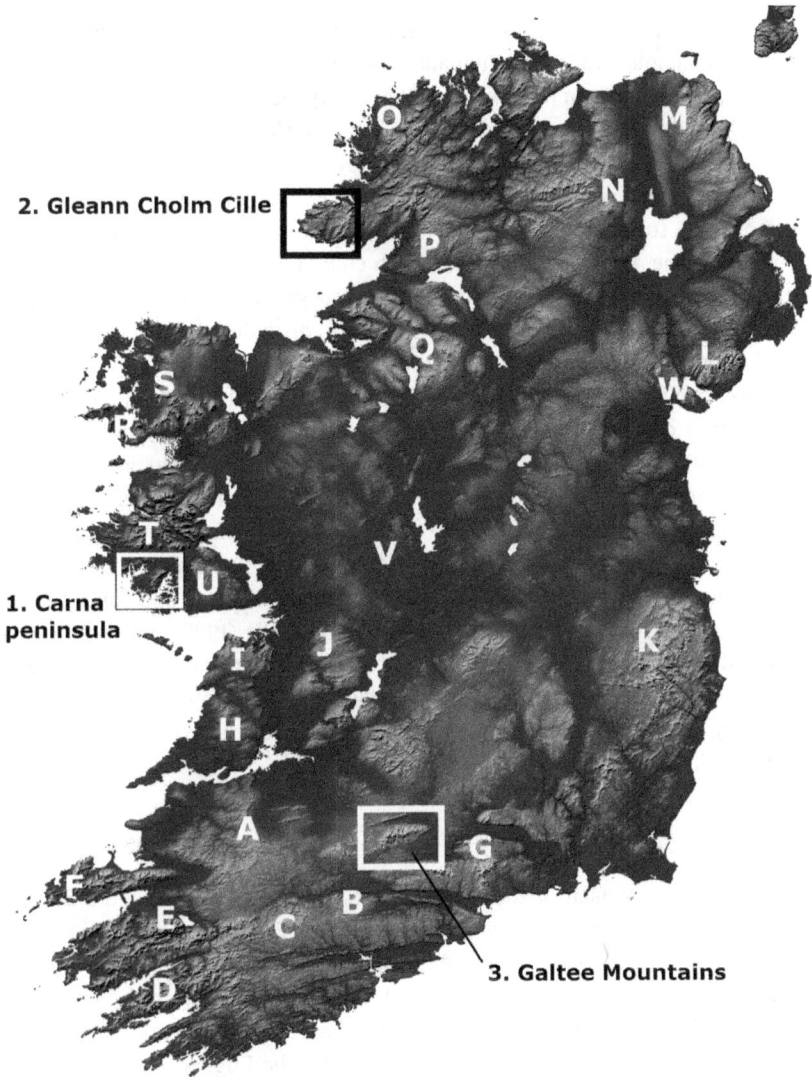

Figure 2.3 Map of Ireland showing areas with ethnographic, historical and/or archaeological evidence for transhumance during some or all of the period, *c.*1550–1900. Letters explained below.

A. West Limerick
B. Nagles Mountains
C. Boggeragh Mountains
D. Beara peninsula
E. South Kerry
F. Corca Dhuibhne
G. Comeragh Mountains/
   Clonmel Commons

H. Kilmaley and Inagh
   parishes
I. The Burren
J. Slieve Aughty
K. Wicklow Mountains
L. Mourne Mountains
M. North Antrim
N. Eastern Sperrin
   Mountains

O. North-west Donegal
P. Templecarn
Q. Lough Allen
R. Achill
S. Ballycroy
T. North Connemara
U. Killannin and Kilcummin
V. Four Roads
W. Cooley peninsula

be overly zealous to suggest that livestock rearing had to involve transhumance. In Limerick, for example, while transhumance was probably part of life at the western (Sliabh Luachra) and eastern (Galtees; see Chapter 5) ends of the county, it is difficult to imagine how it would have worked across much of the middle of the county – the fertile barony of Coshma in particular. On the Desmond Survey, as well as the later Down and Civil Surveys, profitable arable and pasture takes up the vast majority of land. Furthermore, the tower house dwellings of important freeholders and lords virtually litter the landscape, with one or more in each civil parish. Constructed between the mid-fifteenth century and the late sixteenth century, the tower houses of Limerick have been studied by Donnelly (1994; 2001), who concludes that their proliferation was 'funded by wealth generated through pastoral agriculture' (Donnelly 2001, 328). If they were, their permanence and the density of their distribution suggests that this wealth was derived from farming that was largely sedentary and controllable from fixed locations. Even where rough grazing did occur and was used seasonally on manors, it probably occurred in patches that were so small and near at hand as to render seasonal settlement unnecessary or even impractical, daily visits by herders being sufficient (Type 4 in Figure 2.2). For this part of the country, and probably other fertile lowlands in east Galway, Meath, Westmeath, Kildare and south Wexford, one therefore needs to be careful not to assume, as Delle (1999, 32) does, that 'the ordinary Irish people of the sixteenth century were largely transhumant pastoralists'. Ultimately, the most heavily settled regions, which lacked uninterrupted expanses of rough grazing even in the sixteenth and seventeenth centuries, may simply not have been involved in transhumance.

ARCHAEOLOGICAL RESEARCH ON UPLAND BOOLEY SITES

The field evidence for each of the transhumant systems shown in Figure 2.3 is not always easy to track down. In many of Ireland's lower hills (150–300m a.s.l.) the twin processes of population expansion and land improvement since about 1750 have helped to obscure nearly all evidence of earlier land use. Recent commercial plantations of non-native conifers have wreaked even more havoc, covering whole chunks of the landscape. To name but a few examples, the Nagles, the Boggeraghs and the Sliabh Luachra hills now hold very little archaeological potential for the field surveyor. Lands that reach above 400m a.s.l., and the most remote peninsulas and valleys on the western coast, offer the best hope in terms of finding evidence for transhumant-related settlement. Of course, the remains of summer settlement is not the only form of archaeological evidence one should expect to encounter when studying an extensive practice such as transhumance – droveways, grazing boundaries and the winter living quarters of herders (and perhaps livestock) all come to mind as well. Nonetheless, in terms of previous archaeological studies, by far the most attention has been paid to the seasonal habitations, or booley houses/huts, of upland herders.[2] Moreover, such

---

[2]   This book uses the term booley *house* to refer to summer dwellings that were relatively large and rectangular in plan (generally speaking, those exceeding 3m in length and 2m

Figure 2.4 Reconstructed elevation of booley house, Knocknascrow, Co. Limerick
(Ó Danachair 1945, 252, fig. 4; image owned by the Royal Society of Antiquaries of Ireland
and reproduced with their very kind permission).

studies have usually taken place only in the aftermath of isolated excavations, often
of a rescue nature. As these were not undertaken as part of larger projects or even
with the study of transhumance (initially) in mind, archaeological contributions have
usually appeared sporadically. The result has been a less than coherent evolution of
knowledge regarding the archaeological footprint of transhumance in Ireland.

The recording of oral traditions about booleying stimulated initial interest in the
ruins of buildings thought to have been occupied during summer. Working from the
memory of a former participant in booleying, Caoimhín Ó Danachair reconstructs the
appearance of a type of rectangular cabin used seasonally in the Galtee Mountains up
to the late nineteenth century (Ó Danachair 1945; Figure 2.4). However valuable, such
recording does not truly get to grips with the archaeology. Closer investigations had to
wait until excavations began in the late 1940s and 1950s. These generally took place in
east Ulster, where awareness among academics of the field evidence for booleying was
heightened by the work of E.E. Evans. Using historical and ethnographic information,
he promoted the idea that many upland house sites in North Antrim and the Mourne
Mountains must once have housed transhumant herders (Evans 1945, 29–30; 1951,

in width, internally) and the term booley *hut* to refer to smaller rectangular summer
dwellings and those that are oval/circular in shape.

129). This thinking subsequently led him and Bruce Proudfoot to interpret a partially excavated house site in the Deer's Meadow (at 335m a.s.l.) in the Mournes as seasonal in origin (Evans and Proudfoot 1958). It also encouraged Jean Graham (née Sidebotham 1950) and Humphrey Case (Case *et al.* 1969) to excavate a number of upland huts at Goodland in North Antrim, where they supposed a large group of 129 sod-built structures (between 230m and 250m a.s.l.) to represent a transhumant village.

Following a period of stagnation in the 1960s and 1970s, excavations of sites that may have been associated with summer upland settlement began once more in the 1980s. The fact that these were again concentrated in north-east Ulster suggests that Evans' earlier work on transhumance had an influence on archaeological research in this part of Ireland, but not in the rest of the country. In North Antrim Williams and Robinson (1983) carried out a survey at Glenmakeeran, near Goodland, of a cluster of three sod-built houses located below the 200m contour that was threatened by a gravel quarry. Ulster Coarse Ware from one house that was excavated (7.5m × 5.5m, plus an external annexe) shows that there was occupation in the later medieval and/ or early modern period.

The report on the survey and excavation is accompanied by a useful discussion of historical and ethnographic evidence for transhumance across North Antrim. Further south, at Ballyutoag, Williams (1984) investigated another more extensive upland settlement that he suggested may be transhumant in function. This site was dated to the mid-first millennium AD through excavation, and as such illustrates the potential depth of time that may have to be contemplated when investigating the archaeology of transhumance in upland areas. McSparron (2002) continued work elsewhere in Ballyutoag with a more recent rescue excavation of two undated hut sites (at 270m a.s.l.), the small size, paucity of finds and location of which suggested to him that their use was seasonal. One final site excavated in Antrim, Tildarg, has had such a purpose postulated for it. Here, in a large rectangular enclosure situated at 274m a.s.l., possible slots for removable cruck-roof timbers were found in a house structure dating to 1185–1375 AD (Brannon 1984, 168). This, Nick Brannon argued, may provide evidence for occupation by transhumant herders who constructed an enclosure, or *bódhún*, to protect cattle (Brannon 1984, 168).

As revealed by the improved recording techniques that had emerged by the later twentieth century, there is a considerable, in fact a puzzling, variety of form and date among the above sites. At Glenmakeeran and at MacSparron's sites in Ballyutoag there were the remains of house structures and little else, as at Deer's Meadow. By contrast, both Tildarg – with its large rectangular earthwork – and Ballyutoag – where Williams mapped a system of fields and hut sites measuring over 500m across – clearly feature much more than potential booley dwellings. Moreover, the date-range of the sites (where they have yielded dates) spans at least a millennium. Should these investigations be accepted as a sign of what great diversity the archaeology of seasonal upland settlement is likely to present? Unfortunately, closer inspection of a few of these candidate transhumant settlements may suggest otherwise.

First of all, where the early excavations at Goodland are concerned, Horning (2004) has recently argued convincingly that such a large concentration of hut sites is more likely to represent the remains of a year-round village, perhaps of marginalised immigrants from Scotland in the early modern period. At Tildarg, the form and high medieval date of the rectangular enclosure seems an uncanny echo of semi-defended farmsteads known as moated sites found elsewhere in the country (O'Conor 1998, 58–69). Parallels for large rectangular cattle enclosures of such great size have yet to be recognised. Finally, notwithstanding its location at over 200m a.s.l., the early medieval settlement at Ballyutoag seems far too elaborate to have been used only on a seasonal basis, particularly given its association with a ringfort. In her discussion of seasonality at Antrim sites Horning (2007, 365) also casts doubts on Williams' interpretation of Ballyutoag because of the presence of cultivation ridges. As I shall demonstrate in Chapters 5 and 6, however, cultivation does not necessarily rule out seasonal occupation. In general, the doubts surrounding these sites suggests that archaeologists operating in Antrim and Down may in some cases have been too enthusiastic in using transhumance as an explanation for upland settlement: inflating its archaeological legacy can only cloud scholars' view of the other uses that uplands were put to.

In Doonloughan, western Connemara, two coastal habitation sites dating to the late eighth or ninth century AD have recently been postulated as seasonal (excavated in 1997; Murray and McCormick 2012). This is one of the few excavations with transhumant associations to have taken place outside north-east Ulster, and its conclusions are strengthened by a range of detailed analyses that were not employed at the above sites. Archaeobotanical studies of radiocarbon-dated plant remains revealed no definite evidence of cereal-growing, while zooarchaeological studies showed that fishing had not been on an intensive scale. The latter, moreover, seems to have been biased towards seasonally exploited salmon, eel and (arguably) shellfish. The authors conclude, as a result, that Doonloughan – where calcareous sands are likely to have preserved an accurate record of organic remains – was probably used during the late summer and autumn for the purpose of exploiting rough grazing on the local machair plains (Murray and McCormick 2012, 18–19). While preservation of this nature is not typical of archaeological sites in Ireland, particularly not those in upland soils, the multi-faceted study of Doonloughan is a model worth following where possible in future excavations; as well, indeed, as in any revision of material from older excavations. Furthermore, the site alerts us to the possibility that summer grazing was exploited not only in uplands but in coastal, lowland areas too. Such an argument is made by both Graham (1954, 51–52) and McDonald (2014, 173) about the coastal village of Dooagh in Achill, which they hold to have been a primarily seasonal site up to the mid-nineteenth century.

Some of the most recent archaeological work on transhumance in Ireland has not necessarily involved excavation and so has had to develop a greater awareness of the landscape context of hut sites. In the Mourne Mountains Mark Gardiner (2010; 2012b) has revisited the booley huts first pointed out by Evans and revealed through extensive field-walking and total station survey that their numbers are actually higher than Evans realised. He has found that they occur in groups and are exclusively located along the north-western side of the range (Gardiner 2012b, 112, fig. 8.3). He argues that this distribution evolved because graziers who travelled long distances from the north had to stay with their livestock, in contrast to those who had their main residences close by, to the south of the mountains (Gardiner 2012b, 115). However, it is also possible that seasonal dwellings in the south have not survived because of twentieth-century dam building – leading to the flooding of valleys – and the plantation of non-native conifers.

In terms of morphology, Gardiner postulates a distinction between 'Type A' structures, which are of near circular or oval plan and occur in large groups at higher altitudes, and 'Type B' structures, which are square, have higher walls and occur in small groups not far above enclosed farmland (Gardiner 2012b, 113). Although archaeological evidence of non-elite settlement from later medieval and early modern Ireland is extremely patchy, prevailing scholarship holds that oval or circular structures with largely undifferentiated wattle superstructures were common up to the seventeenth century (see O'Conor 2002, 201–04). This is based partly on the aforementioned *Pacata Hibernia* depictions, along with others by Thomas Bartlett (Hayes-McCoy 1964), and also, as Gardiner points out himself, on the fact that the Irish parliament passed an act in 1705 forbidding the use of wattling in, among other things, cabins and houses (Anon. 1765, 87). Thus, Gardiner suggests that the circular and oval Type A structures represent the foundations of what would have been mainly wattle huts, constructed in the medieval period or seventeenth century at the latest (Figure 2.5). Higher-walled rectangular structures (Type B) are more

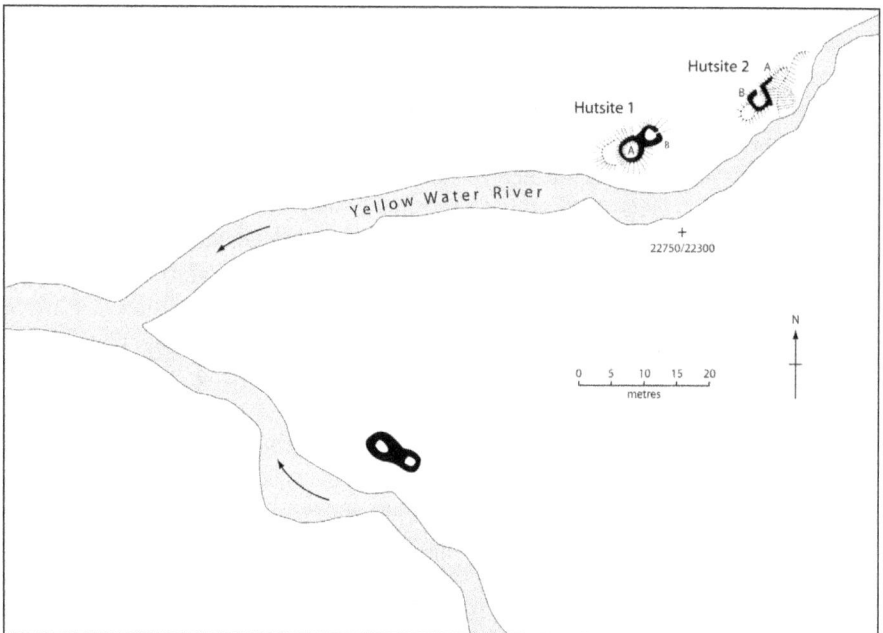

Figure 2.5 Three 'Type A' structures, Site 24, Mourne Mountains (Gardiner 2010; fig. 5). Reproduced by kind permission of the Ulster Journal of Archaeology and Dr Mark Gardiner.

likely to be later, and perhaps associated with the 'great numbers of poor people' who are said to have spent at least two months in the Mournes grazing their cattle each summer in the eighteenth century (Smith and Harris 1744, 125). This tentative chronology, and the question of its applicability outside the Mourne Mountains, is essential to the present volume's exploration of post-medieval transhumant settlements.

A contextualised approach to the archaeological evidence for seasonal settlement has also now emerged for the parish of Achill in County Mayo, thanks to Theresa McDonald's (2014) doctoral research on booley settlements in that area. Using data collected by her long-running Achill Archaeological Field School – including partial excavation of two booley dwellings and field survey of the seasonal settlements – McDonald draws together available ethnographic and historical evidence to produce the first truly in-depth local assessment of the material culture of booleying, albeit with a focus on the eighteenth and nineteenth centuries. She discusses the remains of eighty-six 'purpose-built' booley houses located in six distinct clusters around the parish (McDonald 2014, 245, Appendix 1), and places these booley houses in the following morphological categories (2014, 240–47): circular (5.8 per cent); ovoid (20.9 per cent); sub-rectangular (51.1 per cent – although McDonald admits that her interpretation of this form is not very different from 'ovoid'); rectangular (17.4 per cent); and two-roomed (4.65 per cent). Her work confirms that small-scale cultivation sometimes took place at booley settlements, that transhumance to low-lying coastal pastures could occur and that settlements could change from permanent to seasonal, and *vice versa*, over time. Although each of these conclusions had previously been suggested by various ethnographic accounts and the work of Jean Graham (1954), McDonald demonstrates this, for the first time, through archaeology. Perhaps her most original contribution is to confirm that there 'are architectural and physical differences between purpose-built booley houses and permanent houses' and, more specifically, that booley dwellings were substantially *smaller* than permanent ones constructed towards the end of the eighteenth century and in the first half of the nineteenth century (McDonald 2014, 291–96).

Furthermore, as a result of both Graham and McDonald's work on Achill the possibility that site occupation might change from seasonal to year-round and back again to seasonal highlights that archaeological evidence of upland farming and settlement may not always be tied to transhumance. Since his work in the Mournes, Gardiner (2012a) has carried out further upland survey on the now deserted Garron Plateau, County Antrim; here, he believes that evidence of human settlement is mainly associated with *year-round* occupation during prehistory and medieval/post-medieval times, rather than summer transhumance. In a major landscape archaeology project on upland valleys in the Béara peninsula, County Cork, O'Brien (2009) has recorded entire relict field systems. While two circular and sub-rectangular houses excavated in the Barees valley may be associated with early/high medieval transhumant activity (O'Brien 2009, 169–71, 257–71), in a precursor to the seasonal settlement attested in the seventeenth and eighteenth centuries, O'Brien has shown that the field archaeology in general is associated with mixed year-round farming from the late Bronze Age through to the mid-first millennium AD.

By using a landscape-wide approach O'Brien was able to show that upland land use and settlement are complex and mutable over time. This is a model which I follow, albeit for a shorter time span in which far greater documentary and oral historical material is available. As such, it moves away from the largely site-based approach that archaeologists have taken to Irish transhumance – that is, when they have studied it at all. Booleying has been seen largely in terms of the huts and houses in which herders lived, to the extent that these sites have come to epitomise the practice, and even given their name to it. In reality, transhumant people make use of not just seasonal dwellings but the landscape as a whole. Their seasonal mobility creates a physical link between intensively and extensively used land as people and livestock move regularly from one to the other, while on a notional level it leads inevitably to an interdependency of home farm and summer pasture. Booley dwellings anchor this system but they cannot be allowed to define it; neglecting the other material remains of the people who built and used them is to deny the important economic and social roles that seasonal mobility played in farming communities.

JEAN GRAHAM AND NOTIONS OF A CONSERVATIVE 'WEST'

The need for inventive use of written sources was realised at a fairly early date by geographer Jean Graham, who understood the role of alternative historical material in providing indirect evidence for transhumance. Her pioneering doctoral thesis, 'Transhumance in Ireland, with special reference to its bearing on the evolution of rural communities in the west', was completed in 1954 at Queen's University Belfast, and represents the first attempt to study post-medieval patterns of transhumance at a detailed level in the west of Ireland and to ask where the origins of such patterns might lie. Unfortunately, as it was not subsequently published (with the exception of a short preliminary article, Graham 1953), her thesis has not had the impact that might be expected of a true milestone.

Part of Graham's work, influenced by E.E. Evans, involved the collection of several surviving local traditions about the former use of summer booleys in various parts of the west of Ireland, primarily in west Mayo and Connemara. This ethnographic fieldwork, as outlined above, built on the extremely valuable accounts gathered by dedicated folklorists in other parts of Ireland and has enhanced the amount of information now at my disposal. She also highlighted the role of place-names by producing an island-wide distribution map of those beginning with a 'booley'/*buaile* element (Graham 1954, fig. 1). In the main, however, Graham, as a historical geographer, focused attention on what can be deduced from the various seventeenth-century surveys associated with the completion of the English conquest of Ireland. These – particularly the Books of Survey of Distribution – allow her to argue convincingly that certain parcels of land in less desirable areas were (originally at least) linked to other units on permanently settled ground for the purposes of transhumance – one of the more notable cases being that of Moycullen barony in County Galway (1954, 137–40). Her accompanying maps of the connections between winter bases and summer pastures form an invaluable starting point for any further research into transhumance in western baronies.

Notwithstanding Graham's accomplishment in demonstrating the usefulness of both ethnography and the documents of English conquest in gauging the presence of and need for systems of transhumance, there are also a number of aspects of her study that, in retrospect, must attract some criticism. Because she concentrates on what traditional units of land, their sizes and their links with one another say about contemporary settlement, her interpretations are inevitably quite removed from what one could argue is the reality 'on the ground': that is, the physical imprint of transhumance on the landscape and the human motivations which gave rise to it being practised at all. While Graham certainly engaged in fieldwork and provides rough plans of a few examples of booley houses and huts (Graham 1954, figs 6, 7), the archaeological evidence she encountered lies unexplored throughout her thesis. Even though they in many ways symbolise the practice of booleying, there is little appreciation of the potential of booley sites and their landscapes to inform transhumance studies. She encapsulates her dismissive stance when she says that 'the field evidence of transhumance in Ireland is scant in quantity and not entirely reliable. Since the practice is an aspect of the historical geography of Ireland, historical methods must be used to explore it' (Graham 1954, 46). Furthermore, although she draws a clear distinction between the long-distance nobility controlled transhumance of Mediterranean Europe and what she assumes was the more short-distance community-based transhumance of north-western Atlantic countries (Graham 1954, 2–6), the more relevant issue of variability *within* Ireland is not addressed.

The most serious issue with Graham's thesis, however, lies in her assumption that the west of Ireland was innately more *conservative* than the rest of the country and therefore more suited to the survival of transhumance. This is apparent in her reaction to late sixteenth-/seventeenth-century landholding divisions recorded for Donegal, Mayo and Galway. Since the tradition of joint-holding by kin groups is still partly evident here at this time, she is led to the conclusion that 'Irish characteristics increase[e] in the poorer and more westerly lands' (Graham 1954, 165). While this system of landholding may well have deep roots in the west of Ireland and elsewhere, it is dangerous to start equating 'Irish' with 'old'. Taking a case in point, Estyn Evans, in his study of surviving 'clachan' settlements at Meenacreevagh and Glentornan in north-west Donegal, championed the idea that they and their associated rundale openfields were archaeological relics or 'fossils, preserving in an impoverished way many of the characters of ancient Irish society' (Evans 1939, 24). He argued this despite knowing that these particular clachans were probably no more than 200 years old – one of their names, 'Beltany' or *Baile na Bealtaine* ('May Homestead'), even suggesting an origin as a summer booley settlement. Evans seems to have been led to this interpretation by the location of the clachans in a very remote part of the Donegal Gaeltacht (Irish-speaking region), where it was hard to imagine the way of life there being anything other than deeply traditional. It did not matter that many clachans on poor-quality soils of the west probably developed only as a result of population expansion from the mid-eighteenth century, and that little hard evidence exists for them prior to this (Simms 2000, 229); because they were in the 'most Irish' part of Ireland, continuity with settlement patterns of much earlier periods was seen as inevitable.

This reasoning pervades Graham's thesis also, and is at its most obvious when she makes the claim that 'since betaghs [unfree medieval Gaelic peasants] were in part the pre-Gaelic population of Ireland ... rundale and hamlet [must] go back with them into prehistoric times' (Graham 1954, 208). By the same token, she assumes that the potential for continuity of transhumance in the more fertile southern and eastern areas of the country was automatically less because these had seen greater Anglo-Norman settlement and were subjected to English rule sooner. She asserts that the 'disappearance [of transhumance in these areas] ha[d] been taking place since the Dark Ages (at the latest)' (Graham 1954, 204). However, evidence from Wicklow, Kerry and, in Chapter 5, the Galtee Mountains demonstrates otherwise. At the same time, post-medieval transhumance in the west is treated as an 'agricultural survival' (Graham 1954, 202), an attitude that is problematic for a couple of reasons. First of all, the relegation of recent transhumance to the status of a legacy from earlier times fails to give due credit to those post-medieval communities who continued to engage in seasonal upland settlement for reasons that were surely more complex than some vague rural aversion to change. Secondly, labelling post-medieval transhumance as a 'survival' implies that it played a much more important role among medieval farming communities. While great strides have since been made in the scholarship of medieval farming and settlement (see, for example, Kelly 1997; Lucas 1989; O'Conor 1998; O'Keeffe 2009; Murphy and Potterton 2010; O'Sullivan *et al.* 2014), details on the practice of transhumance prior to the sixteenth century are still quite scanty.

THE CONCEPTUAL BACKDROP TO EARLY STUDIES OF IRISH TRANSHUMANCE

While it is well to critique the attitude of Evans and Graham towards the west of Ireland, it is equally necessary to ask where their ideas sprang from. In so doing it may be possible to identify, and even safeguard against, unhelpful preconceptions about peoples involved in transhumance in the present book. Much of the attraction of the west as a resource for study lay in the fact that it was on the perceived periphery of the island. For Evans' school of thought in Belfast, this was much more than a cold geographical fact; it was a symptom of the cultural marginality that he claimed to observe there and which marked the region out as a store of ancient knowledge and customs that had disappeared from the east. The journey from east to west was, as Evans (1939, 207) put it himself, a journey 'into the past'.

This idea is very much rooted in the belief that the peripheral regions of a country are more conservative than the core, and found expression in academic writing in the early twentieth century among human geographers. Mark Gardiner (2011a) has summarised the evolution of these ideas and traced their subsequent influence on the work of Irish scholars. Specifically, he highlights the importance of social Lamarckianism, an approach that stresses the importance of the environment in shaping human societies (Campbell and Livingstone 1983, 269; Gardiner 2011a, 708). This was used by H.J. Fleure in formulating a theory that certain areas, or 'regions of lasting difficulty', were less susceptible to change because of their harsh environmental conditions (1919, 101;

Gardiner 2011a, 709). These, Fleure argued, could be contrasted with 'regions of effort', where more moderate difficulties could be overcome (Fleure 1919). Such thinking was developed more explicitly by Cyril Fox and Cecil Curwen in the 1930s in their division of Britain into the Highland Zone of the north and west and the Lowland Zone of the south and east (Fox 1932; Curwen 1938; Gardiner 2011a, 709–10). Within the Highland Zone, the Hebrides in particular were a 'backwater' where an 'extraordinary culture-lag' preserved traits from much earlier times (Curwen 1938, 288–89). The visible use of shielings only served to bolster these claims. In the same vein, Evans and, to a lesser degree, Graham envisaged a 'timeless past' in the 'Gaelic' west and north-west of Ireland that could be reliably studied through modern folk practice.

On the level of social attitudes, however, there existed older and more powerful factors behind the creation of a sense of timelessness in peripheral regions. In the late eighteenth and early nineteenth centuries Romantic ideals began to circulate in Europe as a reaction to the materialist and rationalist values espoused by the Enlightenment (Blanning 2012, 11–60). Romanticism found expression in numerous different ways, but in the realm of painting (e.g., Casper David Friedrich, Thomas Cole, John Constable, David Gude) and literature (e.g., the Brothers Grimm, William Wordsworth, Samuel Taylor Coleridge) it often idealised nature and the rugged beauty of landscapes that had not been tainted by the evils of industrialisation (see Day 1996, 39–63; Ferber 2010). The romanticisation of wild people and places in turn fed into evolving nationalist rhetoric in countries such as Norway (see Falnes 1933; Witoszek 1997), Ireland (see Lanters 2003; Pittock 2008), Poland and Ukraine (see Bilenky 2012), where both artists and visionaries sought to reinforce and even create cultural identities so as to distinguish them from their more powerful neighbours (Sweden, Britain and Russia, respectively). Stories of the past held a special place in such discourse, with Ireland and western Britain, for example, being painted as a 'Celtic fringe' that had survived long after the destruction of the rest of the supposed 'Celtic world' in the late Iron Age (see Dietler 1994; Sims-Williams 1998; James 1999; Ó Donnabháin 2000). Regardless of whether this 'Celtic fringe' was viewed as a cause for celebration (by nationalists) or denigration (by imperialists), one can understand how it might have provided a fertile breeding ground for later conceptions among geographers and others of a 'timeless past' in supposedly peripheral areas.

Several scholars working in Irish archaeology and geography have since bemoaned the effect these views on 'peripheries' have had. The propagation of notions of timelessness has, for example, drawn sharp criticism from Kevin Whelan, who raises the point that Gaelic areas of the west and north-west became stuck in 'an unflattering stasis' (1992, 411) where past societies' propensity for change was seriously underestimated by Evans and others. Gardiner goes further and argues that the idea of immutability has been so unhelpful as to have resulted in an under-appreciation of the quality and diversity of rural Irish houses in the period 1200–1700 (Gardiner 2011a, 714–20). Using case studies from Achill Island and southern Appalachia, Audrey Horning highlights the misleading nature of contemporary portrayals of isolation and material poverty in 'marginal' post-medieval settlements by outlining the richness of imported objects revealed by excavation in these areas (Horning 2007). Horning

(2007, 373–74) and Gardiner (2011a, 711–12) are also keen to point out that the idea of an unchanging west acted as a well for twentieth-century Irish cultural nationalists – Fianna Fáil especially – to draw upon in constructing their vision of a rural and de-anglicised Ireland. The people employed as ethnographers by the Irish Folklore Commission were certainly not tools of the Irish Free State and later Republic's agenda – they drew from their interests and enthusiasm just as much. Still, there is no doubt of the dangers of letting nationalist motives drive how and where the past is studied.

Clearly, then, recent scholars of geography and archaeology would claim to have moved on from a situation in which cultural continuity and authenticity are equated with remoteness. Yet it remains difficult to escape completely. The idea still appeals to a popular desire (in part fuelled by tourism) to see the west of Ireland as a place where things remain traditional and perhaps more Irish than elsewhere (see Nash 1993). Whether or not this is true of modern Ireland – and it may well be – is really of no moment; as students of the past it is the potential of the idea to be projected backwards in time that concerns us. If archaeologists' expectations of past societies and, in the present case, of transhumance, are biased in favour of 'peripheral' and 'marginal' regions – simply because that is how society thinks of them today – then their interpretations are equally likely to suffer from bias. Transhumance is very much an international practice and down through history has been adapted to suit a wide variety of social and environmental contexts; to view it as a symptom of certain regions' backwardness is to blind oneself to the nuances that made it relevant across a broad spectrum of farming and economic systems.

CONCLUSIONS

In Ireland, the historical importance of the cow and of pastoralism is without doubt, but during cultural encounters on the island in the late sixteenth and early sixteenth centuries it was exploited by Edmund Spenser and his contemporaries as a form of propaganda. Details mattered little as stories of wandering herds became 'proofs' of inefficient land use and mobility was equated with barbarity. Moreover, no clear distinctions were made between agro-pastoral systems of transhumance and refugee-like movements of people and cattle.

Even after this chapter's preliminary survey of early modern documents, it is obvious that the reality of moving to 'bollies' and 'pasturing upon the mountain and waste wild places' was more complicated than Spenser led his readership to believe. Booleying practices were certainly common in early modern Ireland, but they were not necessary or possible everywhere and, moreover, they tended to be embedded in local territorial systems. In recent decades, archaeological field survey and excavation have started to provide further evidence that transhumance was much more than a fleeting practice, revealing the relatively substantial remains of seasonal booley settlements.

Of course, the organised nature of Irish transhumance was recognised by historical geographer Jean Graham as early as the 1950s, but, like the oral history collected by the Irish Folklore Commission, this work went largely unappreciated. The romantic nationalist yearning for a conservative west of Ireland, where an older rural idyll was supposedly preserved, helped to generate a feeling that studying historical change in *these* places was less important; indeed, that it might spoil the image of authenticity that had been imposed on them from outside. In addition, there has been a chronic shortage of debate on everyday rural life in mainstream historical and archaeological discourses. So the valuable information gathered by folklorists and historical geographers about transhumant systems not long after they died out has never been comprehensively re-examined, and archaeological fieldwork on the material remains of seasonal settlement has been too sporadic to generate a national debate on the role of transhumance.

In recent years, various archaeologically informed studies have started to demarginalise rural communities on Ireland's western fringe in the historical and prehistoric periods (Horning 2007; O'Brien 2009; McDonald 2014; Quinn *et al.* 2018). However, if we are to address issues around the practice of transhumance that are relevant across Ireland – and overseas – landscape-based research needs to be comparative as well as detailed. Thus, while each of the following case studies has a stand-out theme, the three regional perspectives together eventually make for a stronger analysis of the book's central issues – that is, the physical and cultural manifestation of transhumance in the landscape, the adaptability of non-elite tenant communities over time and the demise of seasonal movement and settlement.

CHAPTER 3

SEASONAL SITES IN CONTEXT: SUMMER PASTURES OF THE CARNA PENINSULA

The first case study centres on the Carna peninsula of south Connemara in County Galway (Figure 3.1). The peninsula forms the majority of the civil parish of Moyrus (*Maíros*) in the barony of Ballynahinch. Known in Irish – the main language here – as *Iorras Aithneach* ('The Stormy Peninsula'), it is located in what is very much a western coastal environment. The peninsula extends approximately 14km out from the mainland in a south-western direction and is 12km across at its widest. The only terrain that exceeds 150m a.s.l. is the ridge of Cnoc Mordáin, running close by its eastern coast (highest point 354m). Hence the *vertical* element of transhumance in this first study area is not very pronounced, the practice in many instances involving a primarily *horizontal* movement to rough pastures located on various knolls and low hills in the interior. Human population today is concentrated entirely along the coast and islands, and especially at the peninsula's south-western end, east and west of the small village of Carna. Together with Cill Chiaráin in the south-east, this forms the only services centre for the local population. The interior of the peninsula, although no longer inhabited seasonally by dairy-cow herders, continues to form a minor source of income for some in the community. Farms around the coast still use it as extensive year-round grazing for small numbers of dry Aberdeen Angus and Red Shorthorn cattle, along with some mountain sheep and horses. Machine cutting of peat for household fuel also takes place on a small scale. In addition, some sections of land have been afforested with conifers in the twentieth century, particularly to the south and west of Cnoc Mordáin, though these plantations have not all thrived.

The flatter areas and sinks of the peninsula's interior are occupied by blanket bog and scattered lakes. These tracts of wet bog are unlikely to have been suitable for cattle grazing in the recent past because of the risk of heavier animals getting stuck, though younger cattle – and perhaps sheep too – may have browsed these areas. The highest ridges of Cnoc Mordáin are also unlikely to have been used as rough pasture for cattle because of relatively severe wind exposure and a steep drop along much of Cnoc Mordáin's eastern side.[1] More suitable would have been the gentler slopes leading down from Cnoc Mordáin and other slightly raised areas of the interior covered

---

[1] The place-name *Binn an Ghabhair* ('Peak of the Goat') suggests that these animals may have been grazed on the more exposed rocky locations of Cnoc Mordáin; however, the

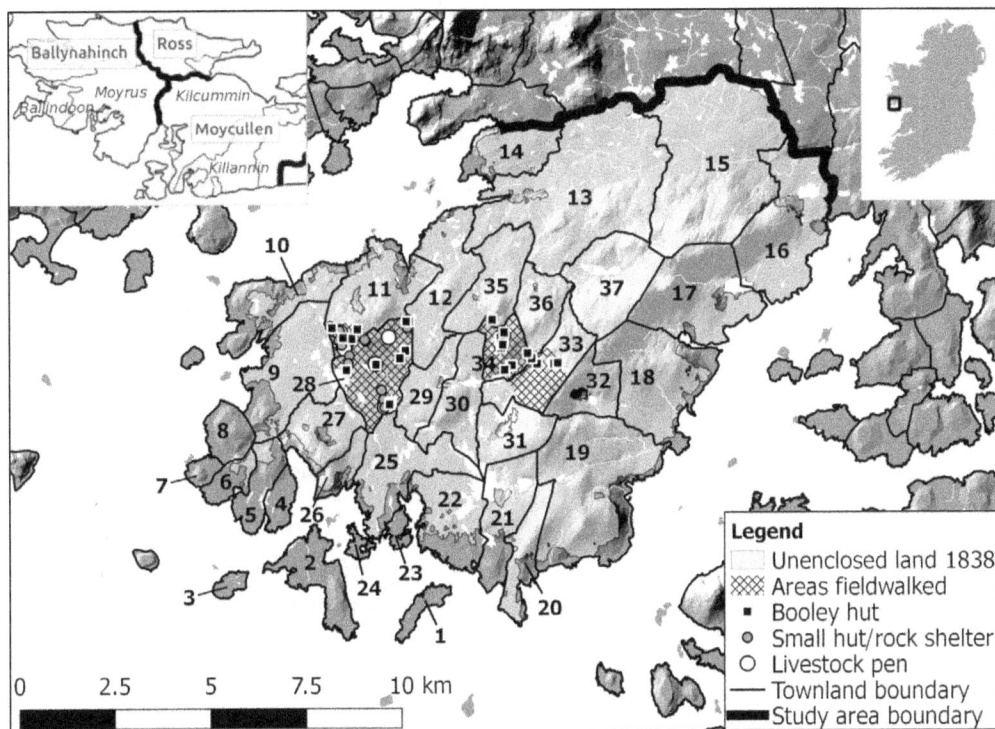

Figure 3.1 Carna peninsula, showing distribution of surveyed sites and townlands numbered 1–37. Unenclosed marginal land in 1838 is shown as a white overlay (first edition six-inch OS).

1. *Fínis*
2. *Maínis*
3. *Oileán Máisean*
4. *An Aird Thoir*
5. *An Aird Thiar*
6. *An Más*
7. *An Leathmhás*
8. *Dumhaigh Ithir*
9. *Maíros*
10. *Leitreach Ard*

11. *Glinsce*
12. *Caladh an Chnoic*
13. *Gabhla*
14. *Bun na hAbhann*
15. *An Gabhlán Thoir*
16. *Doire Iorrais*
17. *Loch Conaortha*
18. *Coill Sáile*
19. *Cill Chiaráin*
20. *An Aird Mhóir*

21. *Caladh Mhaínse*
22. *Roisín na Mainiach*
23. *Roisín an Bholgáin*
24. *Roisín an Chalaidh*
25. *Carna*
26. *Leitir Deiscirt*
27. *An Coillín*
28. *An Cnoc Buí*
29. *Dúleitir Thiar*
30. *Dúleitir Thoir*

31. *Leitir Padhbram*
32. *Gleann na Rod*
33. *Seanadh Bhuire*
34. *Gleannán*
35. *Beitheach Chatha*
36. *Seanadh Mhac Dónaill*
37. *Loch an Bhuí*

with drier blanket peat or peaty podzolic soils. The only parts of the Carna peninsula offering favourable conditions for cereal cultivation in post-medieval times are likely to have been small patches of coastal ground and the islands, where histic lithosols and acid brown podzolics are common (GSI Datasets Public Viewer). Underlying these soils as well as the blanket bog are various types of volcanic bedrock, such as granite, appinite, metagabbro, quartz and gneiss.

---

historical and ethnographic accounts of booleying in Connemara and other areas refer almost exclusively to cattle and particularly dairy cows.

This geology was and is an important influence on animal husbandry in the area. While soils on the coast and nearby islands do give better grass growth than those of the interior, they tend to lack certain minerals because of their sandy Aeolian elements. Thus, when oral historical evidence speaks of two main reasons for booleying in the Carna peninsula (one being the preservation of grass at the home farm) the second is a need for cattle to undergo a *slánú*, or recuperation, from a disease known as *galar trua*, which afflicted them after grazing by the sea for too long (Beartla King, pers. comm.; Ó Gaora 1937, 164; Ó Cathasaigh 1943, 159–60). This is probably cobalt deficiency (Costello 2016b, 69). Incidentally, the change of pasture may also have benefited cattle because there were fewer pests, or *frídeanna*, in the boggy interior (Josie Moylan, pers. comm.). At the same time, *brios brón* – possibly phosphorous deficiency – could afflict cattle if they grazed too long away from the coast (Beartla King, pers. comm.; Ó Cathasaigh 1943, 159–60). Contemporary pastoralists may not have been aware of the specific causes of these illnesses but they clearly knew how to alleviate them, and movement was their solution in this environment.

In the first section of this chapter I outline the results of archaeological survey in selected areas of the Carna peninsula's interior where seasonal grazing and settlement occurred in post-medieval times as a result of transhumance. I then reconstruct patterns in land use, demography and economy from the late sixteenth century up to the nineteenth century in order to understand why transhumance was needed in the area. This historical investigation allows me to bridge the conceptual gap between vague early modern references to booleying and the reality of the practice at a local level for people. Moreover, it allows me to trace probable changes in the practice over time and explain the geography of seasonal movement that emerges by the nineteenth century, as it is evidenced in estate records and later folk memories. In the chapter's last section I use the results of my archaeological and ethnographic research to evaluate these historical trends and understand the imprint of pastoralism on the uplands of south Connemara. Laying particular emphasis on the usage of space around booley dwellings and in summer pastures generally, I demonstrate that transhumance was not a fleeting activity and involved a high degree of familiarity with and indeed control over the landscape.

ARCHAEOLOGICAL EVIDENCE FOR SEASONAL ACTIVITY

Distribution

The remains of probable seasonal sites are widely found on rough pastures in the Carna peninsula's interior. Although walk-over survey for this book was limited to the four townlands[2] of Glinsce, An Cnoc Buí, Gleannán and Seanadh Bhuire, in-depth

---

2   The 'townland' or *baile fearainn* is the smallest administrative division on the island of Ireland, and is still used for official purposes in the Republic. The townland system is thought to have medieval Gaelic origins, but there were many different terms for and kinds of 'townland' before they began to be mapped and standardised by English administrators from the late sixteenth century onwards. The current distribution was formalised at a national level in the 1830s and 1840s by the Ordnance Survey.

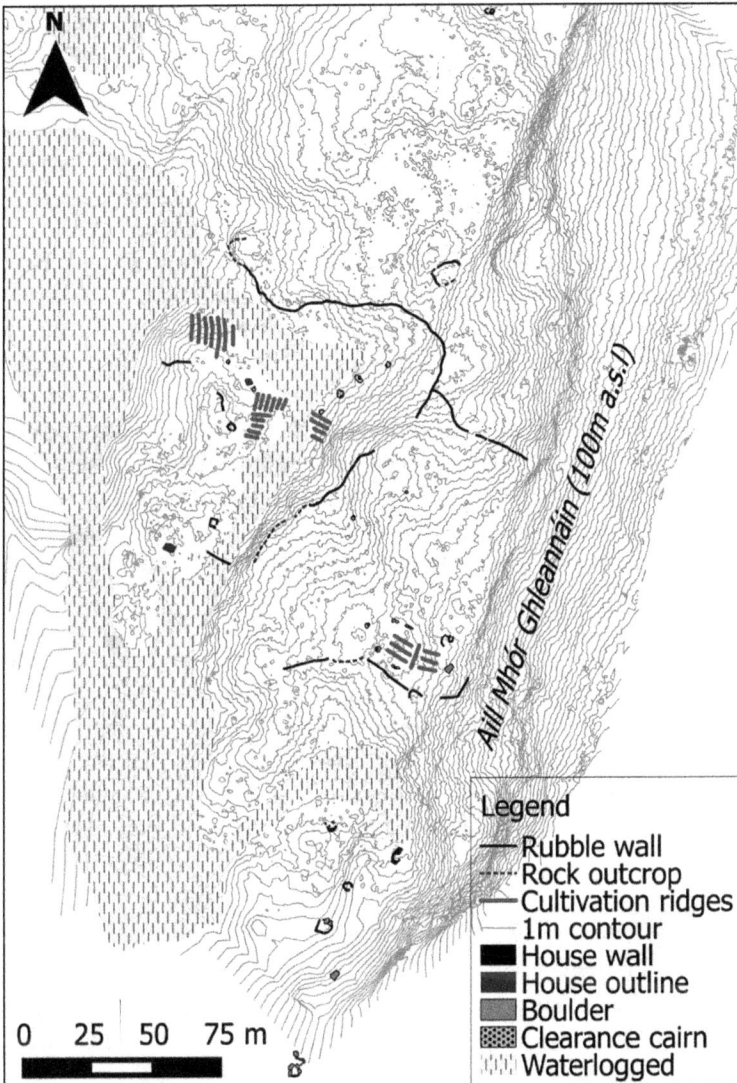

Figure 3.2 Plan of Aill Mhór Ghleannáin group in Gleannán townland.
Contours generated by Eugene Costello from an orthophotograph created
by Paul Naessens of Western Aerial Survey.

examination of satellite imagery revealed clear evidence for structures in much of
the rest of the peninsula too. Booley huts/houses are numerous and often no more
than a few hundred metres away from one another; sometimes they are as close as
twenty metres (Figures 3.1, 3.2). Site choice was not indiscriminate, however. Terrain
such as flat and quaking bogland or exposed and stony hillsides are usually bereft of
evidence for seasonal settlement. As mentioned earlier, these locations would have
been unfavourable for grazing. Instead, booley sites tend to be found on drier soils

in somewhat more sheltered locations: that is, on the sides of low hills and rises or in valleys not too far from streams. Although peat is still a major constituent of the soil in these spots, repeated manuring by livestock kept near these sites has lent the vegetation around many of them a noticeably green tinge (making them easier to identify). Bracken, a plant carcinogenic to cattle, appears to have colonised many of these green patches in recent decades, perhaps taking advantage of the lack of control around booley sites since the departure of their human occupants.

Tightly spaced clusters of huts have not been found in the study area, but they do sometimes form loose groups where the quality of pasture is best. Thus, in the west of Gleannán, at a place called Aill Mhór Ghleannáin ('The Big Cliff of Gleannán'), thirteen structures are to be found along an undulating stretch of rocky pasture roughly 500m in length (Figure 3.2). Another group of six structures is found on a slight rise in the flat south of An Cnoc Buí (Figure 3.14). The fact that both these locations offer fairly expansive views of the surrounding landscape was undoubtedly a factor in making them attractive to seasonal settlement, as cattle could be watched from a distance. In the rest of these two townlands, as well in neighbouring Seanadh Bhuire and Glinsce, structures associated with herding tend to be slightly more dispersed.

Morphology

There is a good deal of variety in the morphology of the structures identified. The simplest are small shelter-like huts, ten of which have been identified with a fair degree of confidence and a further four more tentatively. Shelters are generally not large enough for a person to lie down in comfortably and in some cases may not even have been roofed, their purpose being simply to provide herders with a temporary respite from the elements. Most are quite crude, being found beside or between boulders and

Figure 3.3 Glinsce 6, probable herder's shelter on right side of boulder.

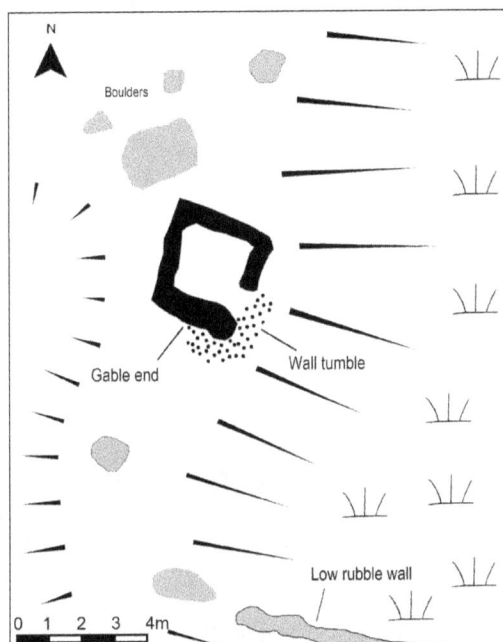

Figure 3.4 Plan of Gleannán 9.

rock outcrops where short rubble walls sufficed to close off a small patch of ground approximately 1.4m or less in internal length. Others still have little or no masonry and are effectively natural shelters – a trait making this type of site very difficult to enumerate fully (Figure 3.3).

Then there are more substantial dwellings – what I describe here as booley huts or houses, and which are known locally as *brácaí* (singular: *bráca*). These vary in size, shape and quality of construction, but all are at least large enough to accommodate two sleeping individuals. Thirty-six were surveyed during fieldwork, including nine somewhat tentative examples. Some of the uncertainty arises out of the fact that smaller booley huts, when in a collapsed state, can be very difficult to distinguish from shelters and clearance cairns. That said, where preservation is good, several construction styles are in evidence amongst the booley dwellings. The sturdiest is a small rectangular house with good drystone masonry (coursed in parts) and gabled end walls. There are only four of these and they measure an average of 3.7m × 3.2m (i.e. 11.8m²) externally and 2.4m × 1.8m (i.e. 4.3m²) internally. Three are found in that group associated with small-scale cultivation and low perimeter walls at the foot of An Aill Mhór in Gleannán (Gleannán 7, 9 and 10; Figures 3.4, 3.13).

Given that rectangular ground plans seem to have become universal in permanent farming settlements in Ireland by the eighteenth and nineteenth centuries (Ó Danachair 1972; Aalen 1997; Delaney and Tierney 2011, 165–71; Orser 2010), it is tempting to assign a similar date of construction to rectangular booley houses where they are known to have been occupied in post-medieval times. Indeed, Gleannán 9 and another

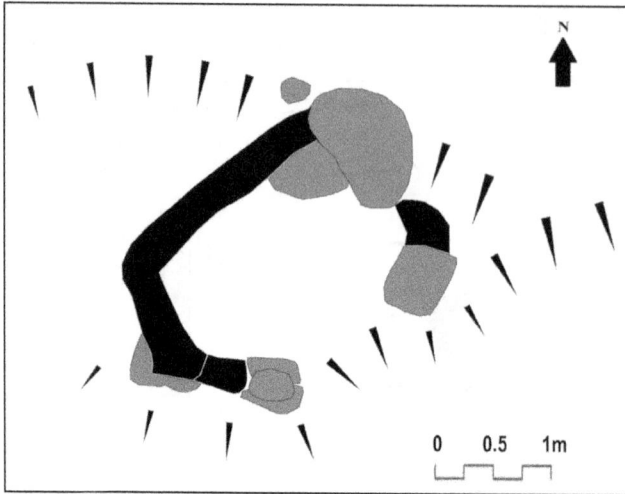

Figure 3.5 Plan of Gleannán 3.

Figure 3.6 Booley hut in Beitheach Chatha, immediately north-west of Gleannán.

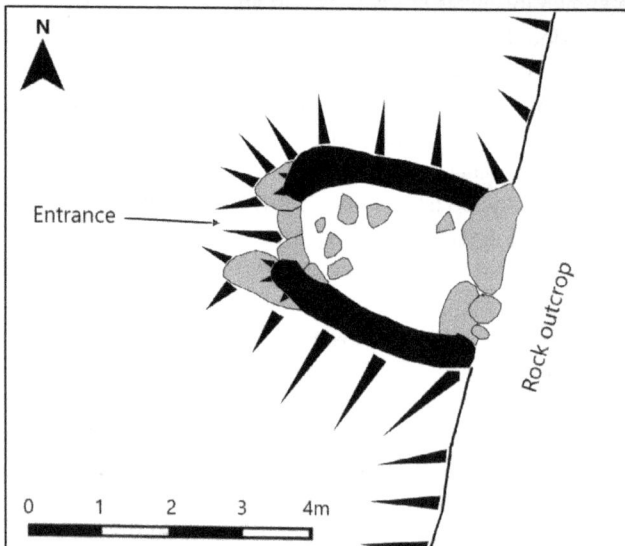

Entrance

Rock outcrop

Figure 3.7 Plan of Cnoc Buí 5.

rectangular example from Seanadh Bhuire are associated with short potato ridges, a crop not introduced to the area until the eighteenth century. Having said that, Gleannán 12, which is certainly not rectangular in shape, also has ridges next to it. Furthermore, excavation has shown that rectangular and sub-rectangular houses started to be built in medieval rural settlements in Ireland as early as the late first millennium AD (with circular and oval houses forming a co-existing tradition until the seventeenth century; Ó Ríordáin and Hunt 1942; Lynn 1994; O'Conor 2002; Comber and Hull 2010). More solid grounds for dating rectangular booley houses to the eighteenth or nineteenth centuries are to be found in the Galtee Mountains, as Chapter 5 demonstrates.

In any case, in the Carna peninsula it is much more common to find less well-constructed rubble-walled structures, often built against a natural outcrop of rock or incorporating a boulder in one or more of its walls (Figures 3.5–3.7). These structures are usually roughly rectangular in plan but sub-circular and irregular examples exist as well, in part to take advantage of the highly varied and rocky ground surface of south Connemara. In terms of size, some structures measure approximately 5.5m × 3m externally, and others as little as 2.3m × 2m. On average, they measure 3.4m × 2.7m (9.18m²) externally and 2.6m × 1.7m (4.42m²) internally – slightly smaller, therefore, than the four rectangular houses of more solid construction.

Only two out of all the ruined dwellings actually have internal divisions, which is unsurprising given the small dimensions quoted. There is no obvious evidence on the surface of hearthstones either, despite the fact that oral history collected in the 1930s repeatedly mentions the lighting of fires both inside and outside summer dwellings (NFC Ms. 62, 221; NFC Ms. 155, 54; NFC Ms. 157, 436). Indeed, the fire was a focus of activity in many stories of recreation and magic after dark at summer pastures. While future excavations should be able to locate evidence of burning, if it occurred, it is doubtful that large stone-lined hearths were constructed. In Ben Lawers in Scotland the excavation of roughly rectangular shieling huts of fifteenth- to eighteenth-century date revealed evidence for small fire pits just inside the entrance, with one or two small slabs sufficing as fireguards (Atkinson 2016, 218–19, 236–38).

As no roofs survive intact on any of the houses or huts surveyed in the study area it is likely that they were sheltered from the elements using perishable materials such as heather and sods of turf sourced nearby, as recorded by twentieth-century ethnography (Browne 1900–02, 520; Mac Giollarnáth 1941, 279; Ó Cathasaigh 1943, 159). Interestingly, these sources add that sod-walled booley structures existed as well as stone-walled ones (Browne 1900–02, 520; Mac Giollarnáth 1941, 279; Ó Cathasaigh 1943, 159; Ó Héalaí agus Ó Tuairisg 2007, 21). This conflicts somewhat with the archaeological evidence, as all structures identified in the present survey contain at least some stone. The claims in oral history may be accounted for if one considers that structures with low stone walls probably once had sods on top, the stonework simply acting as a footing (Figure 3.8). Contemporaries may well have regarded such structures as sod-walled and indeed the design has rough parallels in the peat-cased 'beehive' huts of Jura and Uig off Scotland. Having said that, it is possible that some seasonal dwellings were constructed entirely of sods and/or wattle, the latter being frequently used as a building material in Ireland before the eighteenth

Figure 3.8 Cnoc Buí 2 – the circular footing of what was probably a sod-walled hut. Another possible example of this type was found to the west in Glinsce.

century (O'Conor 2002, 201–04). McDonald encounters a similar conundrum in Achill, where all the booley houses she records are drystone, even though William Wilde in the mid-nineteenth century states that many were made of sods and wattle (McDonald 2014, 132, 246). Taken as a whole, the archaeological record is probably somewhat skewed in favour of stone-built structures. As with any other archaeological survey, the most that one may do in compensation is recognise that problems of preservation will probably prevent a totally comprehensive picture of past seasonal settlement in the Carna peninsula from emerging.

In addition to the shelters and dwellings utilised by herders, there is also archaeological evidence for livestock management. Eleven rubble-walled pens of varying sizes and shapes were found during fieldwork. Most of these are no more than 5–7m in width from wall to wall and were probably used to enclose calves or sick animals (Figures 3.2, 3.15), but a handful that measure 10–16m in length may have acted as corrals for larger numbers of adult cattle or perhaps sheep and goats. Two curving walls built on the side of small hillocks were also recorded and probably served as shelters for livestock. Aside from three small pens in the west of Gleannán, it is noteworthy that all these features of livestock management are clustered in Glinsce and Cnoc Buí – that is, the lower pastures, close to permanent coastal settlements.

LAND-USE PATTERNS AND THE ROLE OF TRANSHUMANCE, C.1580–1700

There is little one can say at a detailed local level about the organisation of non-elite human settlement and farming practices before the mid-seventeenth century. Pollen records from Maumeen Gap in the mountainous north of Connemara show that oak woodland was common up to c.1350, after which heather and grass proliferated (Huang

2002, 163). Somewhat what more relevant is a pollen profile from Dolan in Roundstone Bog, only 5km north-west of the Carna peninsula's western coast, on a neighbouring peninsula. Here the landscape's remaining woodland suffered a major decline in the early second millennium AD, with heather and later grass expanding at its expense (Teunissen and Teunissen-van Oorschot 1980; O'Connell and McDonnell 2019, fig. 8). While these changes could, in part, be linked to shifts in temperature and precipitation during the Little Ice Age, increased grazing by livestock is also likely to have been a factor in the landscape opening up, as fine-temporal resolution pollen studies at shieling sites in the Scottish Highlands have shown (Davies 2016). Even with woodland thinning out, however, the interior of Connemara was not an intensively farmed landscape. According to Roderic O'Flaherty, red deer and wolves were both still common in the Barony of Ballynahinch in 1684 (Hardiman 1846, 9).

Human settlement may have been sparser during the later medieval and early modern periods than in recent centuries, but near the southern coast of the Carna peninsula there is nonetheless a significant archaeological legacy from this time. The high medieval ecclesiastical site in Maíros, several high-status crannógs and caiseals in the lakes around Carna and Tadhg na Buile Ua Flaithbheartaigh's (O'Flaherty) sixteenth-century tower house in An Aird Thoir (Naessens 2007; 2009) all demonstrate that communal labour could be called upon from time to time by powerful secular and ecclesiastical interests. The basic organisation of people and resources that facilitated the control of communal effort becomes evident in the *Compossicion Booke of Conought* (*CBC*), from 1585. Attached to the 'Castle of Arde' at this time were six quarters of land in the 'townes of Moyrus [Maíros], Moynishfinish [Maínis and Fínis islands] and Illamashine [Oileán Máisean]' (*Compossicion Booke of Conought*, 60). 'Ardmore' and 'killkerain' (An Aird Mhóir and Cill Chiaráin) each contained a further two quarters of land, although it is not clear if they were also held by Tadhg na Buile's branch of the O'Flahertys or a neighbouring one (*Compossicion Booke of Conought*, 53, 55, 56). The number of 'quarters' ascribed to each unit reflects its carrying capacity in terms of livestock and crops. It is therefore interesting that the only units to be recorded in 1585 were along the south-west and south-east of the peninsula and its nearby islands. It has been noted that improved farmland clings mainly to these areas in the present day: the *CBC* therefore suggests that this coastal bias was even more pronounced in the late sixteenth century.

The later and more detailed *Books of Survey and Distribution* (*BSD*) allow a more incisive inspection of farming practices (*BSD Galway*, 14–17). As well as documenting changes in proprietorship between 1641 and 1670, the *BSD* estimate, for the first time, the amount of profitable, unprofitable and arable land that each unit contains. These records also name more parcels of land than the *CBC*, and most of these can be identified with later, nineteenth-century townlands. The *BSD* makes clear that arable farming was very rare in the Carna peninsula. Arable land is dominant only on Máisean island and Fraochoileán (an islet off the west of Leitreach Ard), with proportionately tiny parcels in Cill Chiaráin (thirty plantation acres), Caladh Mhaínse (twenty-eight plantation acres) and Maíros (thirty-six plantation acres). Other forms of land use are not usually specified but it is virtually certain that the rest of the 'profitable' land is good-quality pasture located around coastal settlements, and the 'unprofitable' – forming a large majority – rough grazing and bog. The farming economy of the mid-seventeenth century must therefore have been overwhelmingly pastoral in character. Roderic O'Flaherty's comments a few decades later reinforce this impression; he says that 'the greatest number of cattle in this countrey is of cows, the soil being for the most part good only for pasture and grasing ... [and] the greatest commodity [being] beefe, butter, tallow, hides ...' (Hardiman 1846, 15). He also says that corn, wheat, barley, oats and rye were produced in enough quantities for a surplus to be sold to market (Hardiman 1846, 15). Given what has been seen in the *BSD*, however, it seems more likely that subsistence was the main priority of arable farming in the Carna peninsula.

It is almost certain that transhumance was a feature of society in the Carna peninsula at this time given that O'Flaherty and Dunton attest to it in their accounts of Iar-Chonnacht, the western half of County Galway. Although the amount of land taken up by crops was insignificant in the Carna peninsula, farmers would nonetheless have found it advantageous to send cattle away to rough grazing for the summer in order to preserve grass as standing fodder at home: the more fodder there was for heifers and cows during the lean winter, the more animals that would produce milk the following year. This emphasis on dairying would, along with the threat of wolves (Hardiman 1846: 9; Hickey 2011), have ensured that overnight housing for herders and dairymaids was a necessary component of the system. Indeed, later folklore from the area contains instances of wolves approaching booley sites in remote summer pastures (NFC Ms. 155: 54–57).

The more specific question of grazing rights and the exact geographic origins of transhumant movements is more problematic, however. In the barony of Moycullen to the east, many links are recorded in the *BSD* between small units of good land by Lough Corrib and larger units of rough pasture 10–30km away (*BSD Galway*, 58–72, 82–83). This kind of implicit evidence for transhumance is unfortunately absent for the Ballynahinch barony where Carna is found. Nonetheless, as the only parts of Carna peninsula to have been organised and farmed intensively during the sixteenth and seventeenth centuries (according to the *CBC* and *BSD*) were in the south and south-west, it is assumed that transhumant movements originated here and were directed towards various rough pastures several kilometres inland to the north and north-east.

The question of grazing rights leads to an important issue in mobility: namely, that of landholding. In the sixteenth and early seventeenth centuries it was a common, albeit declining practice in Gaelic Ireland for lords to give their client farmers cattle to look after in exchange for his protecting the clients, a practice termed 'commyns' (Graham 1970a, 148). Many of the cattle involved in transhumance in the Carna peninsula may therefore have been in the ultimate possession of either Tadhg na Buile's branch of the O'Flahertys, based at An Aird Thoir, or another branch. In such a scenario, these lords would have had an active interest in where client farmers were taking their cattle to graze. Later legal records from Scotland (Gaffney 1959, 23–24; Bil 1990) demonstrate that disputes frequently arose in summer grazing uplands but it should not be taken for granted that the same happened in sixteenth-century Gaelic

Ireland. It remains an open question as to how clearly the boundaries of lordships were defined in landscapes that were used only on an extensive basis for less than half the year. Moreover, with land generally reckoned by carrying capacity rather than area before the era of agricultural improvement (Slater 2015), disputes may have centred on the *numbers* of cattle that lords and their clients sought to move as much as the question of territory.

Having said that, the potential for land-related conflict would undoubtedly have increased after the *CBC* of 1585 initiated major changes in local power structures. Wealthy Old English townsmen from Galway such as the Lynches, Martins and Blakes invested in lands to the west as the O'Flahertys were displaced or slipped down the pecking order (see Cunningham 1996; Naessens 2009, 82–86, 157–69). By the time the Cromwellian conquest and settlement was complete in the 1660s these new landlords were entirely dominant, and would remain so – in most cases – until at least the mid-nineteenth century. On the surface, a patchwork system of landed estates was a major departure from the earlier clan-based system of landholding (see Chapter 6). Yet it must be questioned, in Carna and elsewhere, whether this great shift in landholding had a major effect on transhumant movements on the ground. With the disappearance of clientship and 'commyns', the ability of the Uí Fhlaithbheartaigh to maintain ownership over large herds of cattle was undoubtedly gone, but their former clients (and themselves too, where kept on as middlemen) could have continued using inland commons. A new landlord had little reason to feel aggrieved when relatively poor grazing was used by people from outside his estate, so long as his own tenants were paying rent on the better land (see below). If the transitional decades of the early to mid-seventeenth century had any lasting impact on transhumant farming in the Carna peninsula, it is that they removed the elite in society from *direct* involvement in the practice.

HISTORICAL PROCESSES OF CHANGE AND THE PRACTICE OF TRANSHUMANCE

Population growth

When discussing settlement patterns in post-medieval Ireland it is difficult not to enter into a debate on the extent to which population was expanding into pasture land and how that may have affected transhumant movements. For instance, the presence of several 'parcells of arable' in the interior of Ballynahinch barony led Graham (1954, 136–37) to argue that mountain valleys in this area were being colonised from the coast. She argued that the same process was taking place in Moycullen barony to the east, with colonists coming from better land near Lough Corrib (Graham 1970a, 196–98). Furthermore, it has been noted above that many more place-names are mentioned in the *BSD* than in the *CBC*; were these new units created to accommodate such growth?

It has certainly been theorised that the population of Ireland as a whole grew in the decades before and after the wars and devastation of the mid-seventeenth century (Mokyr and Ó Gráda 1984, Appendix 3), but at a local level this can be very difficult to discern, mainly because there are almost no earlier documentary sources against which to compare the *BSD*. Though useful as a starting point, the *CBC* is far from a comprehensive survey of contemporary society. Indeed, there is good reason to believe that it left many parcels of land below the level of quarter (such as the cartron or *ceathrú mír*) unrecorded. It would therefore be unwise to seize upon those that appear in the mid-seventeenth century as evidence of recent land colonisation; territorial divisions in Gaelic Ireland were long-established, if not already under pressure by this time (see Duffy *et al.* 2001). In any case, for the peninsula under study there is no actual evidence in the *BSD* for pioneering arable patches in its interior. Any slow population growth that was taking place along its coast is likely to have been absorbed for much longer in this relatively large peninsula than on the narrower, richer and ultimately more congested headlands of Connemara's western seaboard.

Subsequently, however, Ireland and the west coast in particular *did* see very high rates of population growth (for causes see Connell 1950; Mokyr and Ó Gráda 1984; Kennedy and Clarkson 1993; Clarkson and Crawford 2001; Mitchell and Ryan 2001, 327–38). Between 1732 and 1821 the population of Ballynahinch grew by 301–400 per cent and in the period 1821–41 by a further 50 per cent (Smyth 2012a, figs 2 and 4). And yet, in the Carna peninsula, the impact of this phenomenal growth does not seem to have had such a detrimental impact on the overall availability of seasonal inland grazing. This is conveyed well by Ordnance Survey maps drawn up in 1838 (see the extent of rough unenclosed grazing in Figure 3.1). Although tiny new plots peppered the fringes of the peninsula's interior, the vast majority of improved land still clung to the coast and islands. Population growth over the preceding century or more was therefore a story of concentration rather than major expansion. The study area had been so lightly populated in the sixteenth and seventeenth centuries that the large-scale improvement of rough grazing was unnecessary.

Historical economy

But there was also another reason for settlement not spilling into the interior: the vast body of water that defines the study area. Put simply, the economy of south Connemara was heavily dependent on maritime resources and trade. This is implicit in the distribution of medieval archaeology across the region. Almost all high-status sites are located no more than a kilometre from the shore, while the distribution of tower houses is clearly focused on guarding approaches to harbours and bays. Fish acted as a source of food for locals and a source of enrichment, through trade, for their Uí Fhlaithbheartaigh lords (see Naessens 2009, 188–90). Moreover, as roads (other than pack-horse trails) were non-existent in the region until 1835, when Alexander Nimmo completed a highway from Galway to Clifden (Robinson 1997, 338–39), the fastest way of communicating and trading with the outside world was by boat. The closer a person was to this means of transport and its food resources, the more favourable the economic position they held.

From the late eighteenth century to the end of the Napoleonic wars the advantages that could accrue from proximity to the sea increased. People in the Carna peninsula were part of a wider market economy, reacting and contributing to it in various ways at a local level. In western County Galway as a whole five key factors are said to have driven the contemporary economy: (1) the sale of young cattle to lowland graziers further east in Ireland; (2) the sale of oats to weavers in Ulster; (3) the knitting and sale of stockings by women; (4) kelp collection and burning; and (5) fishing, especially herring (Whelan 1995b, xi–xii; 2003, 69). The last two of these 'glocal' processes ensured that population growth continued to be biased towards the coast. Moreover, two of the main ingredients for soil enrichment (at least in coastal areas) were sand and seaweed, and these could be sourced only on the beaches and rocks; a farmer in the Carna peninsula was therefore a *fear talamh is trá*, 'a man of land and strand' (Becker 2000).

Notwithstanding increased opportunities in other areas, cattle remained central to the local economy. At home, milk and butter were important dietary supplements to fish and the increasingly dominant potato (Dutton 1824, 353; Feehan 2012, 28–30), while surplus butter was also sold to market in Galway where possible (Dutton 1824, 140). In the fields outside the house, cattle manure was needed, along with seaweed, as a vital fertiliser for the cultivation of potatoes and oats, deposited mainly in the winter months after harvest and before sowing. Furthermore, with demand for young cattle high in the couple of decades before and after 1800, tenants in the Carna peninsula would have been encouraged to boost rather than reduce cow numbers, whose calves they would have sold either in late autumn or the following spring. This trade clearly benefited most tenants; in 1824 the *Statistical Survey* remarks on the relative prosperity of Connemara's coastal inhabitants, few of whom had 'less than two or three cows and many … from eight to twelve' (Dutton 1824, 353).

Effects on transhumance

It is therefore tempting to conclude that the area's settlement history is comparable to that of post-medieval Lewis in Scotland, as proposed by Alexander Fenton. That is to say, transhumant movements grew bigger as more and more of the home farms were taken up by people and their root and grain crops. Given that the population had previously been much lower, and was mainly subsistent in terms of cattle rearing, there would no doubt have been the *potential* for increased grazing in the interior (albeit currently this is impossible to quantify in the absence of livestock statistics prior to the 1851 census and the lack of fine-resolution pollen records for the locality). However, the expansion of herd sizes on the summer pastures was not possible without a matching increase in winter grass at home. Tenant farmers probably tried to sell off young cattle before winter to profit from the fattening trade, but gestating cows still had to be fed. Soil improvement with sand and seaweed would have increased the amount of winterage available to them, but not hugely. Harsh environmental realities therefore helped to limit the extent to which people in the Carna peninsula could use transhumance to exploit the economic opportunities that were unfolding in post-medieval Irish animal production.

Moreover, the vastly inflated population of tenants meant that not everyone could be accommodated in the traditional system of coast-to-inland transhumance. The landscape was now a much busier place. Aside from the many labourers and cottiers who occupied tiny plots in the core areas of permanent settlement, the first edition six-inch Ordnance Survey map of 1838 depicts several patches of improved land in the interior of the study area – probably the recently established holdings of young families who found themselves short of arable land near the coast and preferred to settle on the common pasture with which their home townland was connected. This expansion did not seriously reduce the total area of rough grazing in the peninsula,[3] but it did become a factor in the declining need for booley settlements, as these hill farmers or *fir sléibhe* were able to watch over cattle for coastal farmers instead (though probably with less emphasis on dairying; Ó Cathasaigh 1943, 160).

The increasingly uncertain basis for transhumance as the nineteenth century progresses is reflected in the somewhat truncated nature of the grazing season, according to twentieth-century ethnographic sources and oral history. In several of the accounts booleying in the Carna peninsula is said to have involved a peculiar double movement, the first in May and the second in August (Browne 1900–02, 520; Ó Cathasaigh 1943, 159; Graham 1954, 23; Ó Héalaí agus Ó Tuairisg 2007, 21). The other accounts refer variously to 'summertime', a few months or an August movement alone (Gibbons 1991, 45; Ó Gaora 1937, 164; Mac Giollarnáth 1941, 279). In addition, the same cattle may not have been present on the hills for the whole transhumant season; Finlay (1898, 68), in his description of Carna and district, says that it was normal for the cattle to be swapped at intervals between the coastal and inland pastures. While the practice of 'swapping' cattle between home farms and hill pastures is unsurprising given the inherent need for *slánú*, or recuperation from aforementioned mineral deficiencies, the other accounts are more puzzling. If there were indeed two movements, this implies a total summer grazing season in the interior of only two months, split between six weeks from the start of May to mid-June and six weeks from the start of August to mid-September (see Ó Cathasaigh 1943, 159). This was much shorter than the summer grazing seasons attested in Donegal and the Galtee Mountains for the early to mid-nineteenth century (see Chapters 4 and 5). With isolated hill farms having been established on the summer pastures and emigration reducing the numbers of young women available to tend to dairy cows at booley sites (Finlay 1898, 73; Ó Conaola 1995, 195–213), there was probably a gradual decline in the practice before booley sites were abandoned altogether in the 1900s/1910s. The extent of booleying practices in Achill, County Mayo, was also much reduced in time and space by the time they finally wound up in the 1930s and 1940s (Ó Moghráin 1943; McDonald 2014). In earlier decades 'summer' grazing is likely to have lasted longer in both Achill and the Carna peninsula. Archaeological evidence for small-scale potato cultivation at booley sites (see below) supports this interpretation, as potatoes would need to be sown in late spring and may not all have been harvested until the end of October, not to mention the earthing-up required in between.

NINETEENTH-CENTURY GRAZING RIGHTS AND THE GEOGRAPHY OF TRANSHUMANT MOVEMENTS

Somewhat ironically, it is only for this last period of flux that there is any solid information about the organisation of grazing rights. In order to understand their basis in society, some appreciation of land organisation and settlement at this time is

---

[3]   There were approximately 10,641 ha of unenclosed rough grazing remaining in 1838.

required. Although Whelan (2012, 454) asserts that a system of partnership farming known as rundale was universal on poorer lands in the west of Ireland in the century or more before the Great Famine (1845–50), it does not appear to have operated in the form he imagines here. The nucleated settlements typical of rundale (Whelan 2003, 63; 2012; Bell and Watson 2015) are absent on first edition six-inch Ordnance Survey maps of the Carna peninsula in 1838, with farmhouses instead found scattered among a complicated network of curvilinear and rectilinear fields (Figure 3.9).

This arrangement contrasts with the typical rundale layout, whereby one large infield of periodically redistributed arable strips would be found outside the nucleated settlement and held in common by its inhabitants (Whelan 1997, 79–88; 2003; 2012; Yager 2002). In addition, Martin estate rentals covering the west and south of the peninsula from 1837 to 1852 name tenants and their rents individually within the various townlands, a style not suggestive of collective tenancy (NAI M. 2429–31; M. 3440–01, 3443; see pages 157–62). Based on this mixture of cartographic and documentary evidence, it seems that the idea of common land use in the Carna peninsula was applied only to the unenclosed rough grazing found further inland. Here, most tenants are said to have enjoyed 'free grazing over very extensive mountain and bog lands as a right inseparable from their holdings' (Ruttledge-Fair 1892, 462). That access to this grazing was organised according to the townland a tenant dwelt in argues for, at most, a basic 'townland partnership' between tenant families.

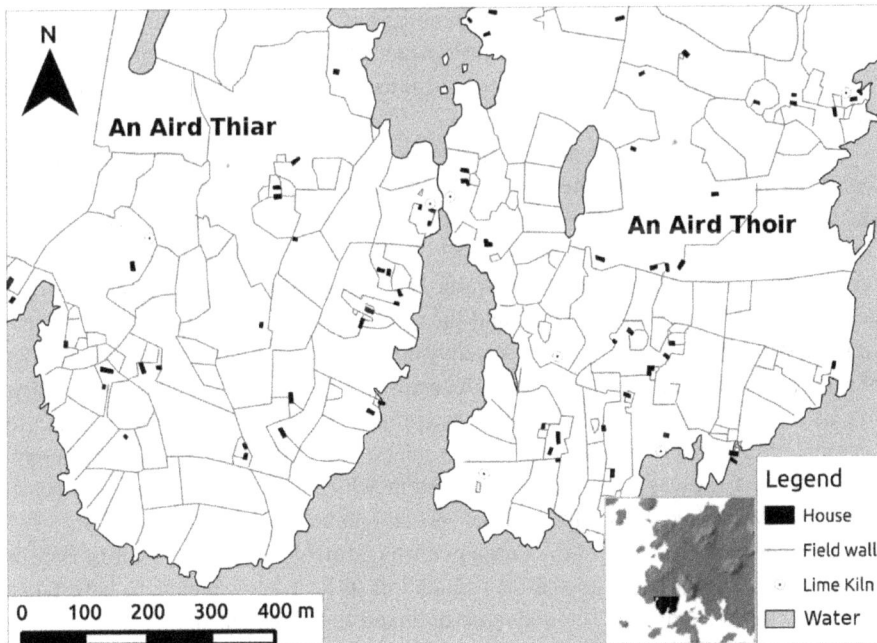

Figure 3.9 Settlement and fields in An Aird Thiar and Thoir, 1838. This is an 'old' area of permanent settlement, for it contains a ruined tower house (redrawn and adapted from the first edition six-inch OS).

Further documentation from the Martin estate confirms that two of the four inland townlands where archaeological fieldwork was carried out – An Cnoc Buí and Gleannán – had no rent-paying tenants of their own and were used as 'commonages' by two small coastal townlands in the south-west of the peninsula – An Más and An Aird Thiar, respectively (NAI M. 2429–31 PRO 1847; James Hardiman Library, Landed Estates' Court 1852). This provides unambiguous evidence of land being organised with distant grazing rights in mind, and is reminiscent of the arrangements evident almost two centuries earlier in *Books of Survey and Distribution* for the east of Connemara and in Down Survey records for Ballynascreen in Ulster. Of course, similar grazing rights must have been demanded by tenant farmers along the rest of the Carna coast and the neighbouring islands. Unfortunately, these are more difficult to track because the documentary record is incomplete for other parts of the peninsula, while oral history collected in the twentieth century contains inconsistencies as to where people from various townlands brought their cows (Mac Giollarnáth 1941, 277–79; Ó Cathasaigh 1943, 159–60; Graham 1954, 23–24; Ó Héalaí agus Ó Tuairisg 2007, 21; NFC Ms. 155, 53–54; NFC Ms. 156, 57). For example, using anonymous local information gathered in the 1950s, Graham (1954, Map 5) produces a map of nineteenth-century booleying movements in Carna and neighbouring peninsulas to the west. Here she plots Cnoc Buí as a summer pasture of An Aird Thiar and Dumhthaigh Ithir, rather than An Más, while Gleannán does not appear to have been used seasonally by anyone on the coast. This contradicts the documentary records that were drawn up while transhumance was still being practised. Nevertheless, having carried out a cross-comparison of the various oral histories, the Martin estate records and, to a lesser extent, the Griffith's land valuation, I have arrived at an interpretation of grazing patterns during the nineteenth and early twentieth centuries, illustrated on a townland-by-townland basis in Figure 3.10.

The map makes clear the general orientation of transhumant movements. Out of the whole of the study area, the islands of Fínis, Maínis, Máisean and Roisín an Chaladh and the coastal townlands around Mace Head have far more connections with land in the interior than do the other permanently settled areas around the peninsula. The reasons for this are fairly straightforward. Here, along the southern coastal fringe, permanent settlement was heaviest and the townlands relatively small. None of them contained much rough grazing and certainly not enough in proportion to the number of small holdings that appear on the Ordnance Survey 1838 six-inch and 1897 twenty-five-inch maps. This means that if all farmers in these townlands wanted access to seasonal grazing they had to travel further inland with their stock to find it. Herein, therefore, lies the essence of arrangements in which townlands (or even parts of townlands) were linked over distances of several kilometres.

Along the western coast of the Carna peninsula, townlands such as Maíros, Glinsce and Gabhla are larger and stretch far enough inland for transhumance to have taken place within their bounds. The only case of linked townlands in the west appears to have been between Leitreach Ard and Caladh an Chnoic, the former not containing much spare land and the latter being almost totally uninhabited. Around the south-east and east of the peninsula, the picture is different again. According to Graham's

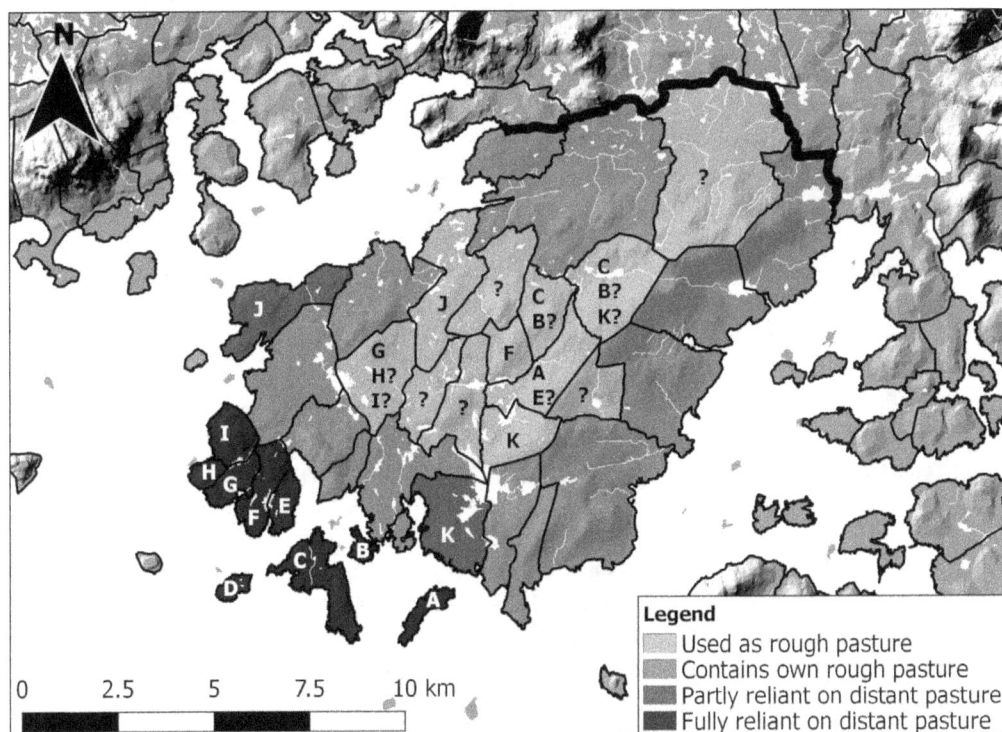

Figure 3.10 Geography of grazing requirements and transhumant links in the Carna peninsula, 1800–1920 (matching letters indicate linked townlands).

local information (1954, map 5), the inhabitants of townlands here did not practise transhumance at all because the summer grazings were so close. The high ridge of Cnoc Mordáin formed an environmental constraint, preventing easy access to pastures on the other side. (Indeed, its importance as a barrier is reflected in the number of townlands that respect it as a boundary.) Instead, farmers along the east of the Carna peninsula were apparently able to manage their cattle from a distance, without having to relocate to booley dwellings. Conversely, the south-east and east are the only parts of the peninsula where we have any indication of how much rough grazing each tenant in a townland was entitled to. In Griffith's Valuation returns (1855) for Roisín na Mainiach, Cill Chiaráin and Coill Sáile most tenants are named twice – the first time in relation to the valuation of their house and garden/fields and the second in relation to the value of rough grazing they held jointly (though not evenly) with their neighbours. The value of the second portion was in proportion to the value of land they held at home. Presumably, this was the case in the rest of the peninsula, where genuine transhumance took place (see the next chapter for a fuller treatment of grazing rights by household).

When comparing the nineteenth century to the situation that prevailed two centuries previously, two points emerge with regard to the organisation of transhumance. Firstly, the general orientation appears largely the same. The fact that permanent settlement had expanded slightly from the core areas (Mace Head in the south-west, the islands and, to a lesser extent, Cill Chiaráin in the south-east) meant that there were now additional places from which transhumance originated, such as the townlands of Leitreach Ard and Roisín na Mainiach. However, as Figure 3.10 shows, the south-west continued to provide the main impetus. The second point of comparison is landholding and the role of the elite. Somewhat remarkably, landlords are not mentioned in relation to booleying practices in any of the ethnographic accounts, suggesting that they took a somewhat laissez-faire approach towards farming practices. This view is supported when patterns of landholding are compared with the direction of transhumant movements. In the mid-nineteenth century the Lynches and Martins owned the east and west of the peninsula respectively (James Hardiman Library, Landed Estates' Court 1852, 17, MRGS 39/008; Griffith's Valuation). Yet two of the most important players in transhumance – Fínis and Maínis islands – lay under different ownership, that of Michael J. Browne and Mary Anne Nolan respectively (Griffith's Valuation). If tenants of the latter were allowed to move onto the estates of the Lynches and Martins to graze cattle each year and maintain small dwelling houses for themselves, then clearly land ownership could be circumvented where the well-being or *slánú* of cattle required a change of pasture. For example, Josie Moylan of An Áird Mhóir, who could recall much about hill farming in the decades just after booleying *per se* ceased, said that islanders would probably have struck a deal, or *margadh*, with tenants on the mainland in order to gain access to hill grazing: that is, they would make their pastures available to the mainlanders' cattle while their own were spending time on the hills (Josie Moylan, pers. comm.). The role of estate owners in this whole process, or their lack of a role, is discussed further in the first part of Chapter 6.

THE LANDSCAPE OF SEASONAL SETTLEMENT AT AN CNOC BUÍ AND GLEANNÁN

Movement and the scale of human participation in transhumance

Particular attention has been drawn to the townlands of An Cnoc Buí and Gleannán, which in the nineteenth century and probably earlier were linked to An Más and An Aird Thiar respectively. From a landscape point of view, however, it is remarkable that these units were not connected in any physical way. Even though they are separated from their coastal twins by at least 3km and 5.5km respectively, no roads or trackways can be seen to lead inland to An Cnoc Buí or Gleannán on the first edition six-inch Ordnance Survey maps. Nor could any trackways be discerned on satellite imagery or during fieldwork. In recent decades narrow metalled passageways have been laid down to help cars and machinery move inland. However, these clearly lead towards patches of peat bog that are being exploited for fuel rather than following paths that could have been used in coastal–inland transhumance. As a network of roads did not emerge in the Carna peninsula until the late nineteenth century (depicted on first edition twenty-five-inch Ordnance Survey maps in 1898), herders probably chose to move livestock through natural corridors in the landscape. For anyone making the journey from An Más and An Aird Thiar, these corridors would have presented themselves: once away from the enclosed and cultivated fields of the home townlands, herders would have had little choice but to drive their cattle along drier, rockier stretches of ground lying between the various lakes and flat boggy patches. Taking these limiting factors into account, probable lines of approach to the grazing grounds of Cnoc Buí and Gleannán are illustrated in Figure 3.11.

A landscape-based perspective also helps to gauge the *scale* of human movement in transhumance. It is particularly instructive to compare the archaeological remains of seasonal settlement with the permanent settlements on which they depended. In Cnoc Buí a total of eleven structures (two tentative) that could have been used as booley dwellings were recorded, while in An Más there was a minimum of twenty-nine permanent dwellings on the first edition six-inch Ordnance Survey map in 1838 and twenty-six on the first edition twenty-five-inch Ordnance Survey map in 1897. This simple comparison makes it obvious that not all of the inhabitants of An Más could have moved to An Cnoc Buí (Figure 3.11). It is a similar story for the other pair of townlands: Gleannán contains the remains of fourteen possible booley dwellings

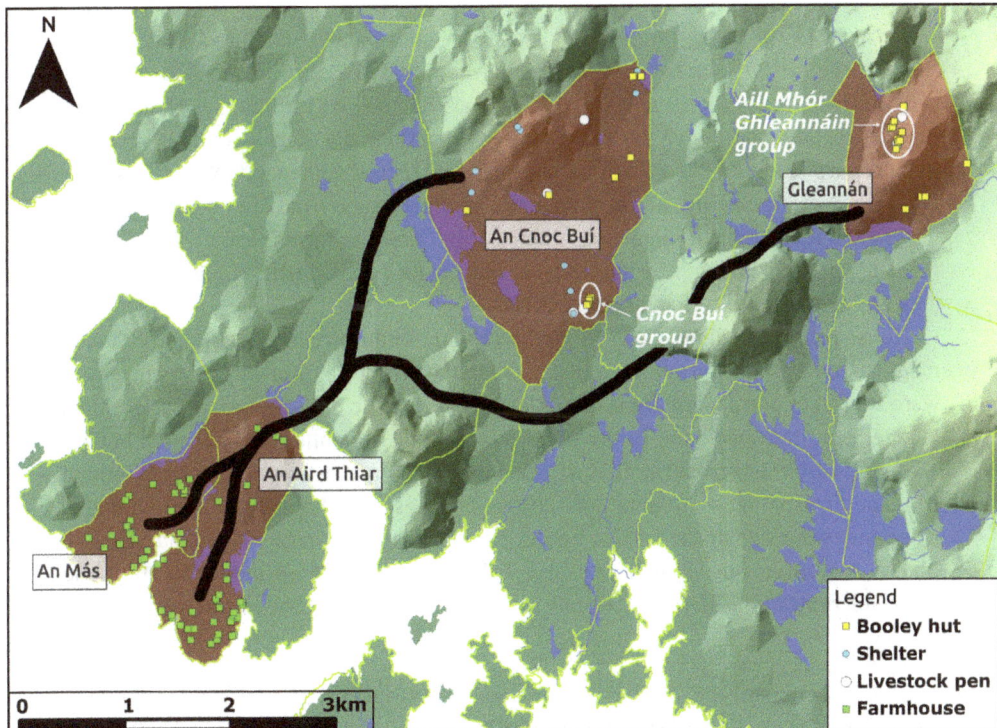

Figure 3.11 Distribution of permanent and seasonal sites in paired townlands, An Más and An Cnoc Buí, and An Aird Thiar and Gleannán. Probable natural corridors marked in black.

Figure 3.12 Ruined farmhouse in An Más.

whereas An Aird Thiar contained at least forty permanent dwellings in 1838 and thirty-three in 1897. On top of this, the permanent dwellings of tenant farmers are substantially larger than their seasonal counterparts. Two farmhouses that appear on the first edition six-inch map were inspected in the field.[4] One in An Aird Thiar has been repurposed as a shed, with its walls reconstructed somewhat. Nevertheless, it is clearly rectangular and has no internal divisions; its external dimensions are 12m x 5.2m and its internal dimensions 10.6m x 3.8m. Another farmhouse in An Más, also rectangular and lacking internal walls, is slightly longer, at 14.1m × 5.2m externally and 12.7m × 3.8m internally (Figure 3.12).

Houses of similar dimensions abound on the first edition six-inch Ordnance Survey maps, so it may safely be assumed that rectangular structures 10m or greater in length were typical of permanent areas of settlement during the decades before the Famine. Further east in Connemara, in the townland of Ogúil, Killannin civil parish, a better-surviving farmhouse from the first edition six-inch Ordnance Survey map had a gabled roof and external measurements of 12m × 5m. These farmhouses are approximately three times the size of the largest booley houses identified in Gleannán and Seanadh Bhuire. Moreover, not all of the latter are likely to have been occupied at the same time. All things considered, it would surely have been impossible for more than a

---

[4]   Mid- to late nineteenth-century reorganisation of farming and housing means that the physical remains of pre-Famine houses very rarely survive in south Connemara. This is unlike Achill, where the deserted settlements of Slievemore and Keem provide unusually comprehensive information on the size and construction of farmhouses constructed before the Famine (McDonald 2014, 179–85).

quarter of the contemporary population of either An Más or An Aird Thiar to have lived at the seasonal settlements at any one time.

This is not to say that the greater number of tenants did not participate in transhumance. On the contrary, the commons of An Cnoc Buí and Gleannán were available to all tenants in these townlands, according to the Martin rental. Similarly, although townlands in the south-east and east of the Carna peninsula appear not to have required the relocation of herders, Griffith's Valuation records that rough grazing was divided up between almost all resident tenants (in Roisín na Mainiach only seven out of twenty-three were excluded and all but one of these seems to have been a cottier). Ultimately, the most logical explanation for only a fraction of the population moving to the summer pastures is that no more than this was needed.

In the nineteenth and early twentieth centuries the system was able to operate with mainly young women or teenage girls relocating, although young men would sometimes go as well or at least pay the girls visits (Mac Giollarnáth 1941, 280; Ó Cathasaigh 1943, 159; Graham 1954, 23–24; Gibbons 1991, 45; Ó Héalaí and Ó Tuairisg 2007, 21; NFC Ms. 62, 220; Ms. 156, 54; Ms. 157, 434). The responsibility and relative freedom given to young people at summer pastures (their specific ages are not made clear) is striking and arguably formed a rite of passage in their lives prior to marriage (Costello 2017; 2018; this volume, Chapter 6). Two to five cows would be entrusted to the care of each girl, either from their own families or from neighbours as well (Graham 1954, 23), and these animals then had to be prevented from wandering back home and trespassing on arable land or meadows (Ó Cathasaigh 1943, 160). But the most important tasks were undoubtedly milking the dairy cows and either churning the milk into butter on-site or bringing it home each day (Browne 1900–02, 520; Mac Giollarnáth 1941, 279–80; Ó Cathasaigh 1943, 159–60; Graham 1954, 23–24; Gibbons 1991, 45; Ó Héalaí agus Ó Tuairisg 2007, 21). At booley sites in Gleannán it is likely that herders chose to churn the butter and bring it down periodically, rather than face a daily return journey of between 11km and 13km. Small structures located close to or forming part of some booley houses in Gleannán (e.g. Gleannán 2, 4, 5, 12) may have been constructed with precisely that in mind: that is, as cool places to store the butter. Figure 3.13 shows Gleannán 12, which contains a storage space – measuring 1.25m × 0.9m internally – on its less sunny north-eastern side. Again, this has parallels in Achill, where McDonald (2014, 246–47) has also recorded annexes. Where seasonal settlement in Cnoc Buí is concerned, the shorter journey back to the coast may have encouraged herders to bring milk home daily in a sort of relay, leaving the churning to those at home. A lack of obvious storage features in this townland supports such an interpretation.

Organisation of space at seasonal sites over time

Owing to the extremely stony nature of soils almost everywhere in the Carna peninsula – apart from flat patches of wet bogland – the clearance of stones was undertaken around many seasonal sites in order to encourage better grass growth and provide a smoother ground surface under-hoof for cows. In many cases, minor stone clearance was achieved by collecting stones for the construction of booley houses and huts. However, at locations

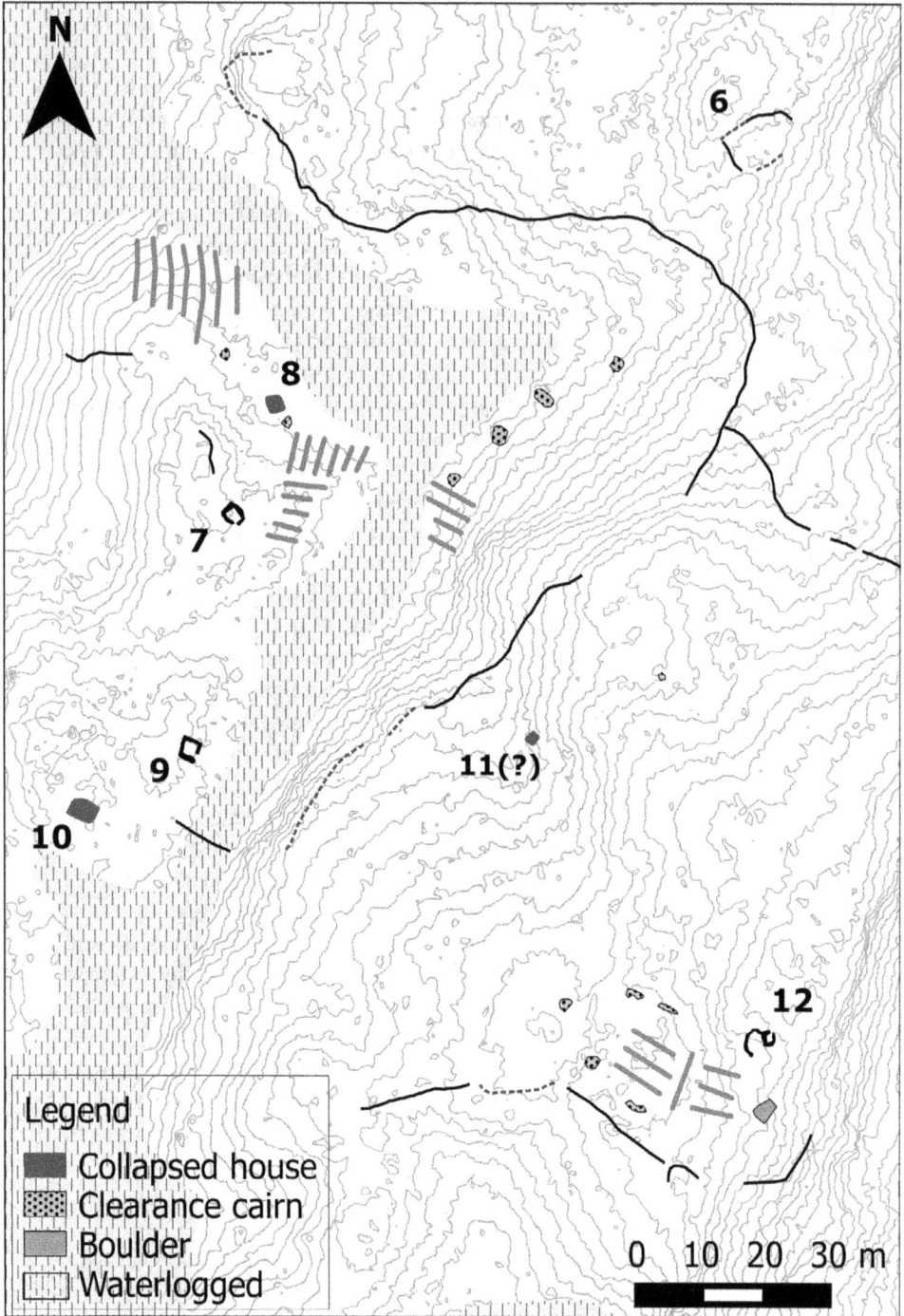

Figure 3.13 Detail of Figure 3.2 showing centre of Aill Mhór Ghleannáin group in Gleannán. Structures numbered. Note cultivation ridges and upper and lower enclosed areas; 6 is a possible pen for calves.

where settlement was denser clearance is also associated with the building of low walls marking out space. These features, rarely exceeding 0.4m in height, skirt around natural rises in the topography on which the dwellings are located, often following exposed ridges and cliffs so as to cut down on stone gathering. Two main enclosed areas can be discerned at Aill Mhór Ghleannáin, as highlighted in Figure 3.13, with some structures to the south lying outside, perhaps because the rocky topography there was naturally more restrictive. It is not entirely clear how effective the walls would have been in keeping cattle either in or out given their low height, notwithstanding recent tumbling of stone. Possibly, like some of the huts, they may once have had sods placed on top. In the south of An Cnoc Buí another loose group of booley dwellings is associated with low perimeter walls (Cnoc Buí 3–8; Figure 3.14). This group is also divided into two main areas, the lower southern area being largely free of the remains of human habitation.

It will be noticed at Aill Mhór, too, that cultivation ridges occur in small patches (roughly 5m × 7m) along the sides of the lower western space, with another patch in the south of the upper enclosure beside structure 12. While their presence at first suggests that the walls were built to keep cattle out, the apparent absence of cultivation ridges in most of the upper area and indeed at Cnoc Buí indicates that this was probably not the sole or original function of marking out space in stone. Of greater consideration is where the cows were milked. It is not stated in the oral historical evidence for Carna whether the herders brought all the cows back inside enclosed areas for milking each morning and evening, or if they milked the cows

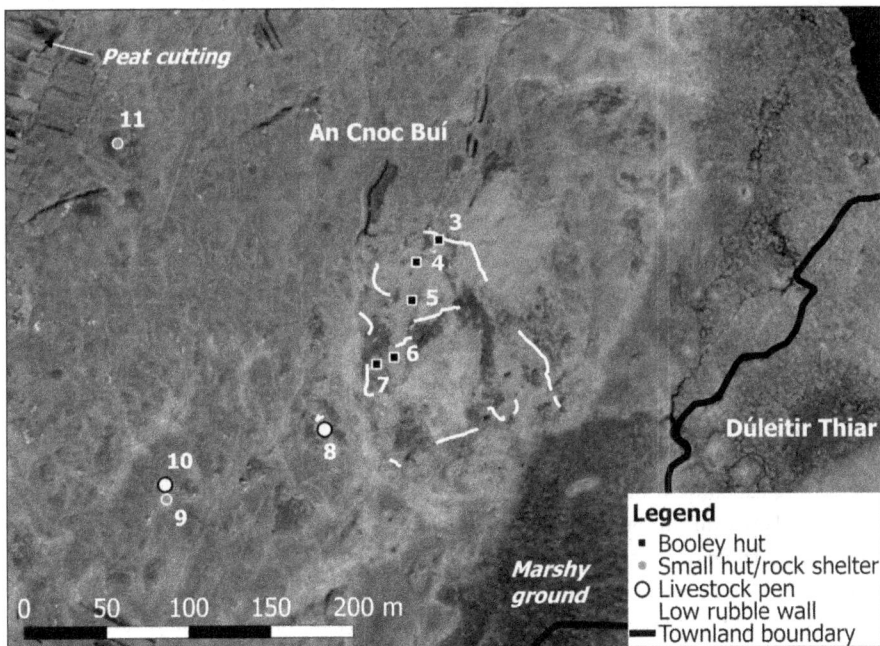

Figure 3.14 Plan of Cnoc Buí group. Satellite imagery: Google, CNES/Airbus, Maxar Technologies.

where they stood. The latter is not implausible, as milking in the field was common on Irish farms before the advent of modern milking machines, at least during the summer months. This was the experience of the present writer's grandparents in counties Limerick and Kerry. Moreover, cows that receive regular attention from people tend to become very quiet and can be milked without tethering (though their hind legs still usually need to be spancelled, or tied together). Having said that, if they were not for enclosing cows, one is left to ponder what the low walls around much of the Aill Mhór and Cnoc Buí groups were for at all – would the better grazing available within them as a result of clearance not have been an incentive for the cows to return?

An alternative scenario to the enclosed areas being used as large milking paddocks is that herders used them as meadows from which small amounts of hay were cut late in the grazing season, probably in August. The saving of hay on mountainous land is attested in 1756 for Sliabh Luachra on the Limerick/Kerry/Cork border (Smith 1756, 88, footnote 9), and also in the Uíbh Ráthach peninsula of South Kerry up to the early twentieth century (O'Sullivan and Sheehan 1992). Moreover, it will be remembered from Chapter 1 that the production of additional hay was one of the main functions of shieling-use in Scandinavian countries. Having said all that, haymaking was far from universal in Ireland prior to the nineteenth century (see Anon. 1692, 5–6; McEvoy 1802, 68; Dutton 1808, 75; Adams 1967, 69). With the country's fairly mild climate and snow rarely falling, many farmers simply let grass grow over the summer so that livestock could eat it in the fields, as standing fodder, over the winter. The rarity of haymaking in south Connemara even in the late nineteenth century is suggested by Finlay (1898, 67), who remarks, 'in a drive of five miles, along a road thickly lined with their dwellings, I saw only one pile of this kind – a dwarfed, mis-shapen hay-stack'. While the winterage system undoubtedly led to more wastage than haymaking, because cattle trample grass in wet weather, it may have been preferable on coastal farms in the Carna peninsula where male labour was vital in fishing and kelp-burning.

Thus, the preferable scenario involves cows being milked inside the enclosed areas, or at least in the larger and more open of the two enclosed areas found at Aill Mhór and southern Cnoc Buí. Indeed, given the slightly greener vegetation in these areas – surely the result of years of cow dung accumulation – it is possible that the cows were kept in overnight. Oral history from north-west Donegal and two other parts of County Galway (Joyce Country and the Slieve Aughties) does mention that cows were kept next to booley sites overnight to facilitate evening and morning milking (Ó hEochaidh 1943, 145–46; NFC Ms. 525, 83; Ms. 707, 394). This would make even more sense in the ecological context of booleying before the eighteenth century, when wolves were common. Low walls may not have stopped a wolf but they would have made it far easier for herders to keep an eye on livestock in one place. With the disappearance of the wolf, enclosure around seasonal sites perhaps lost some of its earlier importance. By contrast, where large predators are still a threat in the Cindrel Mountains of Romania sheep are still brought into rectilinear folds beside the shepherd's hut at night: not only does this make it easier to milk the sheep, it also presumably helps to prevent weaker livestock wandering towards woodland margins on lower slopes and being picked off by wolves and bears (Fieldwork by writer, July 2016).

Another form of stone clearance in the summer pastures of Carna indicates a chronology of space at seasonal settlements. Cultivation ridges have been noted at Aill Mhór, and next to them are several clearance cairns. This is somewhat peculiar, for if clearance had taken place as part of a single event one would expect most or all of the stone to have gone towards the construction of either walls or cairns – not both. As it is, the cairns – which contain significantly smaller stones than the booley houses and enclosing walls – probably belong to a later phase of stone clearance that began after potato cultivation was introduced to booley sites in the area. Although oral histories in Carna do not mention potatoes being cultivated at summer pastures, the practice is now well attested ethnographically and archaeologically as part of summer upland settlement elsewhere in nineteenth-century Ireland, such as north-west Donegal (Ó hEochaidh 1943, 139), the Galtee Mountains (Ó Danachair 1945, 250; Costello 2015) and Achill Island (McDonald 2014, 193). In view of the similar width (just under a metre) of individual ridges in the present study area and the fact that peaty upland soils are not an ideal environment in which to grow oats, it is likely that the ridges at Aill Mhór represent the efforts of herders to grow small amounts of potatoes. Small patches of potato cultivation are visible in the adjoining hill pasture of Seanadh Bhuire too but not, it seems, in Cnoc Buí or Glinsce to the west. The meaning of their absence in these areas is uncertain, although it may be associated with minute differences in soil fertility/depth and perhaps also a lesser degree of independence on the part of herders here (being slightly closer to home). At any rate, the introduction of potatoes resulted in more stone being cleared, not only in preparation for the first year of growth but also in each subsequent season as stones came to the surface through spade-digging. These smaller stones were apparently treated as waste material and piled up to form the cairns we see only a few metres away from the ridges.

Given that Roderick O'Flaherty makes no mention of potato cultivation in Iar-Chonnacht in 1684 and that the first setting of potatoes in the Carna area was within the reach of twentieth-century folk memory (apparently they were first grown on Máisean island in the south-west; Mac Giollarnáth 1941, 276), it seems probable that the clearance cairns at Aill Mhór were begun shortly after c.1700, if not slightly later. By implication, demarcated spaces that functioned as milking paddocks and night-time folds would have been laid out using larger stones at an earlier date at both Aill Mhór and Cnoc Buí – around the same time, surely, as some of the booley houses that they weave around. Whether or not the low walls fell into disrepair as wolves died out and cultivation started within parts of the enclosures at Aill Mhór is a matter for debate.[5] Ultimately, with comparable low perimeter walls absent at other booley settlements so far discovered (in the Galtees, south-west Donegal, Achill or the

---

[5] The cultivation ridges, for their part, were probably not used beyond the late nineteenth century considering the truncation of the booleying season by then and the fact that potatoes are not mentioned in connection with booley sites in the 1930s and 1940s, in Carna.

Mournes), it may be risky to dwell entirely on their functionality in terms of animal and crop husbandry. There are also important social factors and notions of community that manifested themselves in the demarcation of space. The idea that social relationships find expression in the archaeology of seasonal settlement is developed in the fourth section of Chapter 6, where their various layouts across Ireland are discussed and compared with contemporary permanent settlements.

The management of cattle in the wider pastoral landscape

The function of the smaller enclosures or pens found in the Carna peninsula is more straightforward and probably involved the enclosure of young calves. Since cows with milk are cows with calves, the latter were probably brought up to the summer

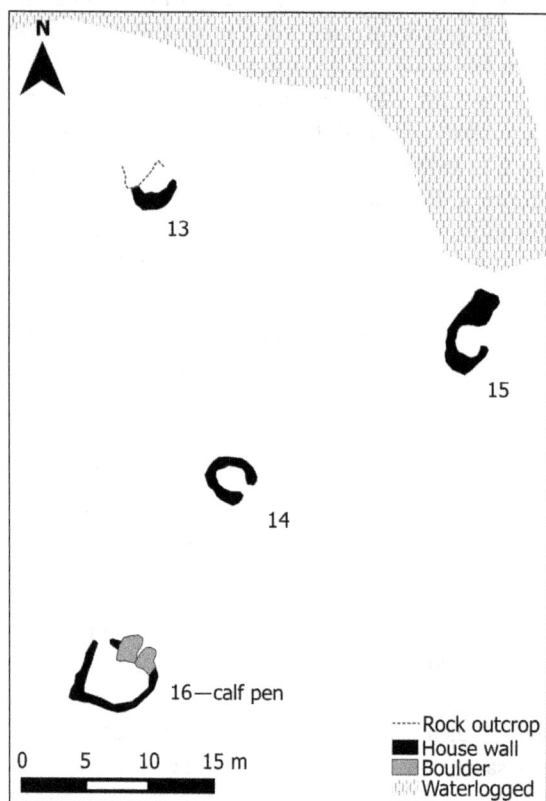

Figure 3.15 Plan of Gleannán 13–15, and small calf pen, 16. South of main enclosed areas in Aill Mhór Ghleannáin group.

pastures too. Milk would have been the main source of nutrition for them in their early months and the easiest way of fulfilling this would have been by keeping them near the source. Indeed, in his early nineteenth-century survey of farming in Galway, Dutton (1824, 142) disapprovingly relates how the calf would 'empty two teats [of the cow], whilst the dairy-maid is milking the other two', a reference that suggests that calves were weaned off their mothers only gradually. On the one hand, this would have removed the need for hand-feeding of calves with milk in the late spring/early summer (depending on calving dates). On the other, giving half of the cows' milk to their calves would have seriously reduced butter production. However, this may not have been a problem for tenant farmers in the Carna peninsula, as they relied on the butter trade less than did their contemporaries in the south of Ireland (see Chapter 5). In addition, two of the ethnographic accounts that talk about life at the *brácaí* actually remark that calves were sometimes put in folds at night-time to prevent them from wandering (Mac Giollarnáth 1941, 280; Graham 1954, 23). Bearing that in mind too, it seems likely that pens helped to regulate the amount of time young calves spent with cows before they were weaned fully (prior to being sold on later in the year). At Aill Mhór three of these structures – Gleannán 6, 16 and 19 – have been identified in varying states of preservation, while two are also present to the south-west of the Cnoc Buí group (Cnoc Buí 8 and 10). In each case, the pens are found just outside the core enclosed area of booley houses, a distribution that further argues for ground inside the low perimeter walls being reserved for the cows (Figures 3.2, 3.14, 3.15).

A cluster of slightly larger pens and enclosures in Glinsce and Cnoc Buí is less easy to explain in the context of everyday livestock management. However, it is noticeable that they are located in an area that would been crossed by transhumant herds on their way from the permanently settled townlands of An Más, An Leathmhás, Dumhaigh Ithir and Leitreach Ard (Figure 3.1). One or more of these enclosures may therefore have been used to sort livestock at the start and end of each grazing season; for example, it is not difficult to imagine a herd being divided up according to age, sex or species. Three out of the four also have relatively well-preserved walls considering their drystone rubble construction, and so continued use into the twentieth century, perhaps for sheep, is possible.[6]

Outside these pens, enclosures and the marked spaces at Aill Mhór and Cnoc Buí, the wider landscape of the summer pastures exhibits virtually no archaeological trace of livestock control. Townland boundaries have been marked on paper since the 1838 six-inch Ordnance Survey maps, but they are not always as clear on the ground. Like the corridors which livestock were moved along to reach booley sites, it seems that, rather than erect banks or walls, herders used features of the natural landscape to define different rough pastures. Straight boundaries drawn across patches of wet bog by the Ordnance Survey were probably not a reality on the ground at all, as neither livestock nor people are likely to have ventured very far across their quaking surfaces. Otherwise, the drier, more uneven land that did support cattle lent itself quite well to subtle division by eye, given that it contains numerous lakes, streams and rocky ridges. Such features would not themselves have prevented cattle from wandering into neighbouring pastures – from Gleannán into Seanadh Bhuire, for example – but with people staying at summer pastures it would have been relatively easy to keep cattle from straying beyond these natural barriers during their daytime grazing.

---

[6] Johnny Mháirtín Learaí, noted *sean-nós* singer from Leitreach Ard, told the present writer that his family would bring sheep as well as cattle up to rough pasture on Cnoc Glinsce in the early and mid-twentieth century.

The real function of these landscape features was therefore to provide herders with visible reference points and lines while watching, following and moving cattle; they allowed them to frame their workspace each day prior to the rounding up of animals in the evening for milking. Recognising and agreeing on these 'boundaries' must have been an important ongoing aspect of grazing livestock communally, and also inter-communally, as negotiation with groups of herders from other townlands was required. Social gatherings at booley sites probably helped to create an atmosphere of mutual understanding. Oral history in Carna recounts that the young female herders would occasionally come together to dance and sing, with young men sometimes visiting or watching on (NFC Ms. 156, 55). At the same time, bringing milk and butter home on a regular basis meant that herders were still answerable to figures of authority in terms of animal husbandry.

In the twentieth century, after *brácaí* ceased to be occupied, it is said that animals put on rough grazing for spells could wander freely and cross townland boundaries in the interior. With their owners coming to visit only once or twice a day and resident hill farmers being few in number and distracted by their own tasks, it is hardly surprising that the subtle controls of on-site herding were lost. Today, many pastures are fenced off with barbed wire, as nobody now lives in the interior of the peninsula and many livestock owners on the coast hold down work commitments elsewhere. Moreover, if dry cattle and sheep are being pastured on the interior at all, they are now hauled quickly along metalled roads by means of a trailer – they are certainly not walked through unmarked corridors with careful differentiation of safe and unsafe ground. With these changes, the intimate knowledge of paths and spaces that booleying required has weakened greatly.

SUMMARY AND CONCLUSIONS

It has been difficult to gauge the exact operation of transhumance in the early modern period for the simple reason that contemporary historical sources do not record any details of pastoral farming. That said, it is likely that the orientation of transhumance was much the same in the sixteenth and seventeenth centuries, as the quarters of Ard castle, the islands and Cill Chiaráin were the only areas of the Carna peninsula that were farmed intensively. The major difference between transhumance at this time and later in the post-medieval period was that society's elite had a direct involvement through the Gaelic system of clientship. After the Cromwellian settlement the relationship between landlord and tenant was a more distant one, to the extent that transhumant herders could even cross estate boundaries. Population growth in the eighteenth and early nineteenth centuries did not cause any serious pressure to be placed on the overall amount of rough grazing available, but it did swell existing areas of permanent settlement and marginalise poorer families as the Famine approached. We have also been able to reconstruct transhumant movements in the last phase of the practice in a fair amount of detail. Accordingly, the townlands that relied most on the use of booley houses were those in the south-west of the peninsula and its islands, as these had the highest population densities and the least amount of land to spare. In two cases – An

Aird Thiar and Gleannán, and An Más and An Cnoc Buí – tenants on the coast had fixed rights of commonage in detached units in the interior. Grazing rights in these units were intimately bound up with the allocation of arable land at home. As such, cattle and transhumance were integral to the system of farming that characterised pre-Famine (and immediate post-Famine) settlement in the Carna peninsula.

This chapter has shown that archaeological evidence for huts and small houses probably used in transhumance is common throughout the peninsula's interior, to an extent that implies that it formed the primary reason for human activity in the interior. While the variety of construction styles among herder dwellings suggests there was no one construction phase, the present writer believes that a substantial number of sites were at least *occupied* in the post-medieval period. This is supported by a strong correlation with ethnographic evidence from the first half of the twentieth century which mentions several booley grounds that today exhibit clear signs of seasonal settlement. With regard to the number of people who took an active part in transhumance, the archaeological evidence emphatically demonstrates that only a minority of the population can have been present at any one time on the summer pastures. This was the case from at least the late eighteenth century, when the population began to surge dramatically. Booley houses are often found singly, but two loose groups have also been identified at favourable locations in Gleannán and Cnoc Buí. These groups are intriguing insofar as there is evidence that people demarcated space in order to clear ground of surface stones and possibly keep cows enclosed at night, although implicit social factors will be discussed in Chapter 6. In Gleannán and Seanadh Bhuire the presence of potato ridges fits an emerging trend in fieldwork across Ireland and Scotland: namely, that small-scale cultivation features increasingly in seasonal settlement in the later post-medieval period. Analysis of the unusually rich surface remains of seasonal settlement in Gleannán suggests that cultivation took place after the demarcation of ground, as cultivation involved the clearance of small stones that lay deeper in the soil, which were then deposited in cairns. This finding draws attention to the importance of detailed consideration of field remains, as excavations in artefact- and ecofact-poor seasonal contexts (in acidic soils) may not always yield significant results. At the same time, some other aspects of transhumance in the wider landscape are simply not visible through field archaeology. Understanding how herders moved and managed livestock therefore requires an appreciation of the whole community and its social structures over time.

CHAPTER 4

CONNECTED PLACES: HOME AND BOOLEY IN GLEANN CHOLM CILLE OVER TIME

This book's second case study centres on the civil and Roman Catholic parish of Gleann Cholm Cille in south-west Donegal (Figure 4.1). It lies at the end of the Slieve League (*Sliabh Liag*) peninsula – Sliabh Liag being the highest point in the parish and peninsula at 595m a.s.l. Gleann Cholm Cille forms part of the Donegal Gaeltacht and its name translates into English as 'The Valley of Colmcille', Colmcille being a sixth-century Irish saint with whom an early medieval ecclesiastical site in the parish is associated. Like the rest of the peninsula, the landscape of Gleann Cholm Cille is essentially hilly. Three valleys running eastwards from the Atlantic coast cut the parish into approximately four upland blocs of varying extent, but all being 200m or greater in altitude. On the east the parish is bounded by the Abhainn Ghlinne (or 'Glen River'), which has its source in the north and its mouth at Teileann Bay in the south. At its maximum it measures 12km from east to west and 18km from north to south, and covers an area of approximately 132km².

There are two main types of bedrock in the area – psammitic and pelitic schist, marble, amphibolite and diamictite in most of the centre and along Abhainn Ghlinne, and quartzite on higher ground in the north and parts of the south. Blanket peat dominates the subsoil and soil layers of most of the parish, especially on the higher upland blocs. However, significant quantities of peaty podzols can be found on the lower slopes, along with acid brown earths and surface water gleys in the valleys, all of which have substantially greater agricultural potential than peat (GSI Datasets Public Viewer). Blackface mountain sheep predominate in the uplands, with small numbers of dry cattle found on improved farms in the valleys. Tree cover is very sparse today in the area, occurring only occasionally along field boundaries and roads. In some remote upland townlands, however, woodland scrub is beginning to regenerate as farming enters a stage of abandonment. Modern settlement is found in four main locations: Gleann village in the central valley of the parish (where most services are located), Málainn Mhór south of that, Málainn Bhig in the extreme south-west, and along Abhainn Ghlinne from the village of An Charraig northwards to Mín an Chearrbhaigh. Farming and tourism are mainstays of the local economy, while machine-cut blanket peat is still heavily relied upon for household fuel.

Whereas my study of transhumance in the Carna peninsula was used to examine the complexity of seasonal sites and the negotiation of hill pastures by herders, the

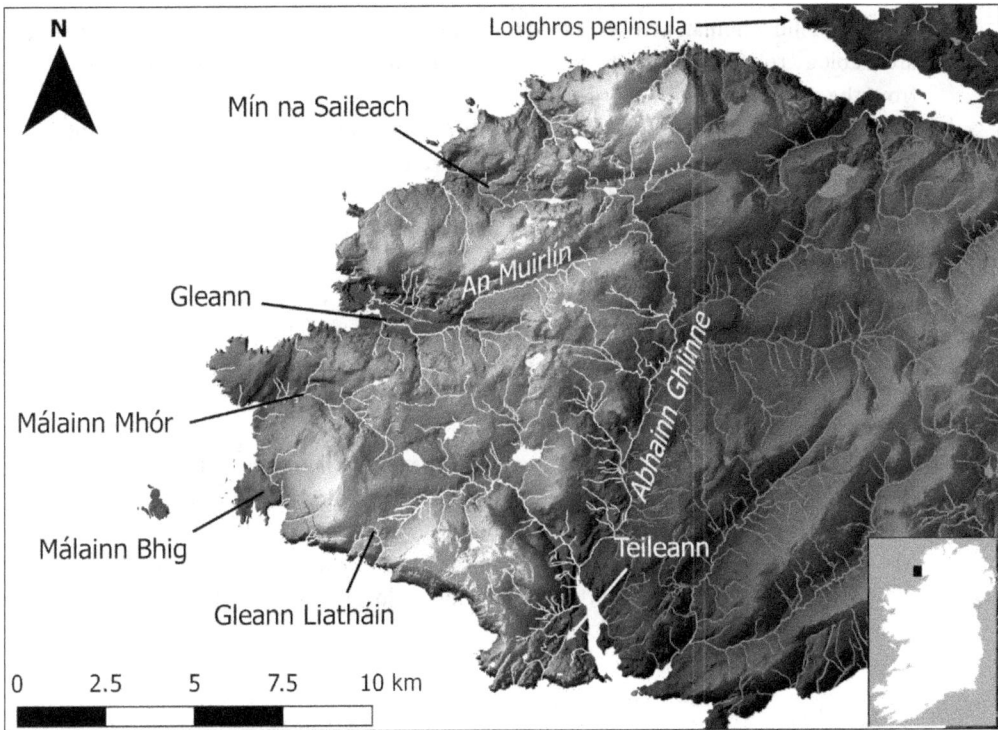

Figure 4.1 Gleann Cholm Cille civil parish, with main places and rivers (italics) labelled.

present chapter serves to emphasise the dynamic nature of *connections* between zones of permanent settlement and upland pastures. It analyses how the intensity and geography of their relationship could change over time, details the organisation and inequalities of community grazing rights by the nineteenth century and explores how transhumant links were ultimately exploited by tenant farmers as a result of demographic pressure.

ARCHAEOLOGICAL EVIDENCE FOR SEASONAL SETTLEMENT

The townland of Mín na Saileach, or 'Mountain Pasture of the Willows', lies in a short valley almost 4km to the north of Gleann, the parish's main valley. It occupies a south-facing slope, with An Port lying between it and the sea and Coillte Feannaid bordering it on the east. Bordering it on the south is a large stream that meanders along the valley bottom towards the sea. The townland can be divided into three environmental zones. The first is a slightly raised area of blanket bog along the valley bottom; the second, above a late nineteenth-century road, is an expansive and uneven area of hillside with drier soils and a mixture of grass, sedge, bracken and heather vegetation (some recent willow regeneration is also visible); and above a number of large rocky outcrops, finally, lies a plateau of eroding blanket bog. It is in the second of these zones that most human activity is evident. However, only in the west of this zone is the archaeology related to herding, much of the east being occupied by year-round farms from the early nineteenth century.

A total of fifteen structures was found through remote sensing and fieldwalking in Mín na Saileach (Figure 4.2). Of these, five were quite small and may be classified as shelters. Mín na Saileach 2 consists of a sheltering area 5.5m wide cut out from the slope and, like the sheltering walls found in Glinsce in the Carna peninsula, was built for the benefit of livestock. Two others, Mín na Saileach 3 and 4, are the remains of very small huts made from sod and stone respectively. With internal dimensions of 1.2m × 1.2m and 1.8m × 1m respectively, they are too small to afford proper dwelling space and were probably used only in passing by herders. Sites 5 and 10 are more ephemeral, with the former said by a local farmer to have been used in the past as a still for making poteen.

Another nine structures would have been large enough for one or more persons to lie down in, and, given that there is strong oral historical evidence for booleying in the area up to the early to mid-nineteenth century (Morris *et al.* 1939; Ó Duilearga 1939; NFC Ms. 991, 145–51), there is good reason to interpret them as the summer dwellings of cow herders. Moreover, nearly all of them are located within 50m of a tributary

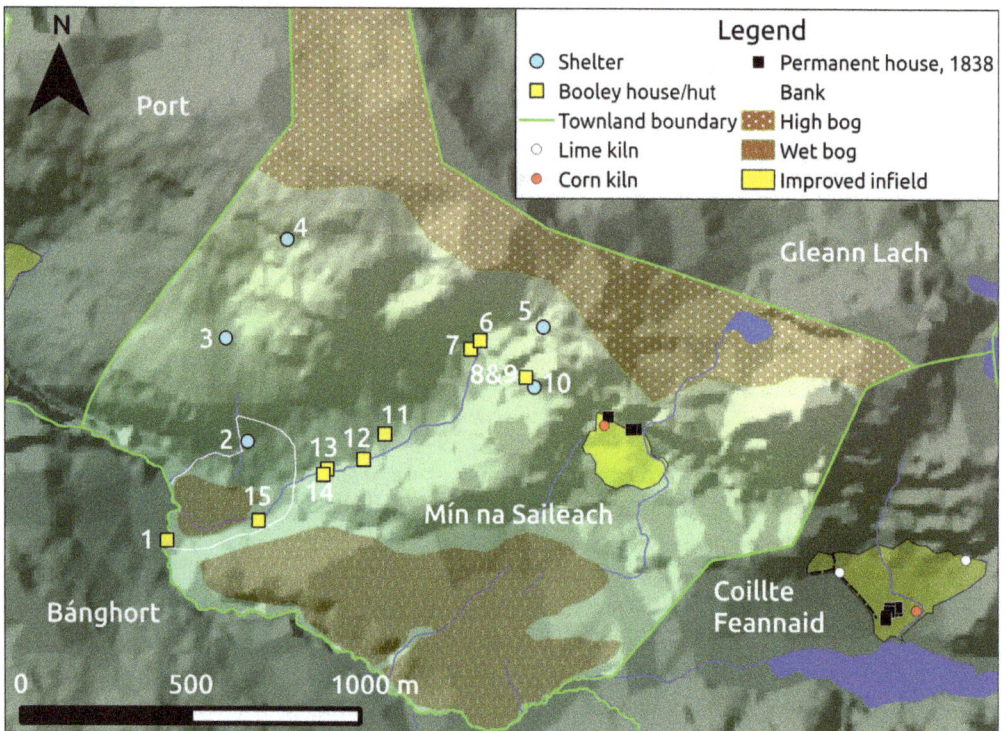

Figure 4.2 Numbered site distribution in Mín na Saileach as per fieldwork. Map also shows patches of ground colonised by 1835 (first edition six-inch OS).

stream named Sruthán na mBothóg, or 'Stream of the Huts', which runs south-west through Mín na Saileach (see O'Neill 1973). In fact, sites 13 and 14 are located only 17m from one another on opposite sides of this stream. The exceptions are site 1, which lies 90m to the south of Sruthán na mBothóg's confluence with the main stream of the valley, and site 8, which lies at a higher altitude, approximately 150m east of where Sruthán na mBothóg rises. Nonetheless, these structures still belong to the same overall drainage basin.

In view of what was found in the Carna peninsula, it will not come as a surprise that the form and dimensions of potential booley dwellings vary. Mín na Saileach 1, 12 and 13 are all well-built rectangular structures with coursed masonry and peat packing between the stones (Figure 4.3); however, their actual designs are not the same – site 1 appearing to have lean-to shelter or storage areas at both ends and site 12 consisting of two adjoining structures. Moreover, rectangular structures of mostly sod are found also (11, 14 and 15; Figure 4.4). Two oval huts made from stone and earth and a simple square hut made from large quartz blocks complete the list (6, 7 and 8, respectively). The dimensions of these nine suspected booley dwellings vary from 2.5m × 1.6m to 8.05m × 5.7m externally. On average, they occupy an area of 16.94m^2 externally and 8.32m^2 internally. No roofs survive intact on any of the shelters or booley dwellings, but judging from the lack of tumbled stone it would appear that sods of peat and/or rushes were used as roofing material.

There is very little in the way of elaboration around any of the structures. Structure 8 has a small triangular pen connected to it (structure 9, possibly for calves; Figure 4.5), but they are otherwise fairly discrete. The only obvious anthropogenic markers in their environs are green patches of vegetation that probably originated through a combination of manure from gathered livestock and spilled dairy products. Cultivation ridges could not be discerned next to any of the structures during fieldwork, but one

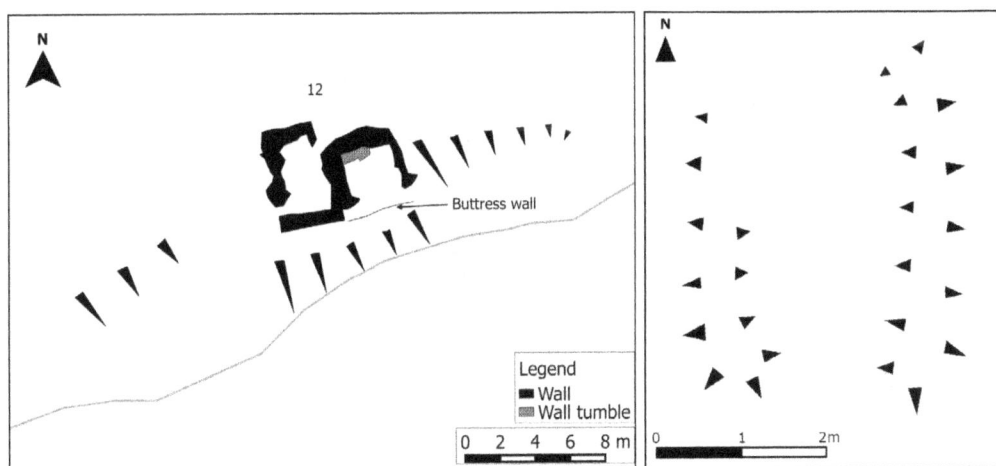

Figure 4.3 (*left*) Plan of Mín na Saileach 12, on northern bank of Sruthán na mBothóg.
Figure 4.4 (*right*) Plan of Mín na Saileach 11, roughly rectangular sod footing of structure.

Figure 4.5 Mín na Saileach 9 triangular pen with Mín na Saileach 8 hut in background.

patch, measuring approximately 15m × 15m, was subsequently made out to the north of structure 15 on satellite imagery.

THE ROLE OF TRANSHUMANCE IN EARLY MODERN TIMES

If we are to begin to understand these sites' links to areas of permanent settlement further south in the parish it is vital that we place their use in a solid historical context, and this context needs to take the environmental and societal regionality of Gleann Cholm Cille into account. It is fairly safe to say that transhumance was more commonly practised in Ulster, Ireland's northernmost province, in the early modern period than in the nineteenth century. In addition to the historical references provided in Chapter 2, a rare account of payments due to the recently fled Gaelic lord Hugh O'Neill in 1607–10 mentions that 'rent is uncertain, because by the custom of the country the tenants may remove from one lord to another every half-year, as usually they do, which custom is allowed by authority from the State' (Hill 1877, 241). This hints at seasonal transhumant movements in central Ulster and, indeed, movements that did not respect lordship boundaries. Rather than cattle being moved off O'Neill's land entirely, they may have moved between different sub-lordships under his control. It is a significant detail nevertheless and raises the question of how transhumance was organised further west, in south-west Donegal, at that time.

A different environmental context?

The answer must first address the ecological context of contemporary agro-pastoralism. In a palynological study of three sites in western Donegal – including one on Loughros peninsula, only 14km north-east of Gleann valley – Fossitt (1994) has shown that blanket bog had reached its present extent in the county by AD 500, if not earlier. After this date, the pollen data suggests that woodland was rare. If Gleann Cholm Cille has an analogous vegetation history, its landscape at the start of the post-medieval period may have had broadly similar land-use potential to today, with peaty soils and rough grazing taking up much of the parish. Place-names help to refine the picture somewhat, however. In addition to many *mín* or 'mountain pasture' townlands, several contain an element associated with woodland. Loch Dhoire Thoirc ('Lake of the Boar Oakwood') and Coillte Feannaid ('The Woods of the Flaying') are located beside one another in the east of the same valley as Mín na Saileach. Cionn na Coilleadh ('Head of the Wood') and Leathchoill ('Half-wood') are found beside one another at the eastern end of Gleann valley. Furthermore, Cruach an Chuilinn ('Round Hill of the Holly'), Mín an Draighin ('Mountain pasture of the Blackthorns') and Mín na Saileach ('Mountain pasture of the Willows') itself each contain elements that hint at the former presence of certain species of tree. These last three townlands are also in the north of the parish. Taken together, all of these place-names indicate that patches of woodland or scrubby woodland were common historically in the valleys of northern Gleann Cholm Cille.

Pinning down when wooded vegetation disappeared from the landscape is difficult without higher resolution in the pollen record. Place-names are usually quite difficult to date, so one cannot be sure what period the above examples originate in. They first appear in the historical record in 1835, on six-inch Ordnance Survey maps for the area. There is no sign of wooded areas in any of these townlands by this time, however. Ewing, indeed, writes in the 1820s that there was 'not one tree in the parish' (Day and McWilliams 1997, 64). It is probably safe to assume, therefore, that trees had not been a common sight since before the nineteenth century. But for how long exactly had the landscape been denuded? Clearly, no firm conclusions can be made, but it is likely that patches of woodland were still present in the late sixteenth century and perhaps the early seventeenth century. Woodland grazing is mentioned near Glendalough in an eleventh-/twelfth-century Life of St Coemgen, so it is certainly possible that these wooded patches were used for seasonal grazing along with the more open heathland.

Extensive grazing would not, however, have been the only activity in woodland or on peaty hillsides in the parish, which is described in the mid-seventeenth century as 'ye most Mountaine and remote parte in the Counteey of Donegall' (Simington 1934, 81). An introductory story in Manus O'Donnell's *Life of Colmcille*, compiled in 1532, hints at another activity. In Gleann Cholm Cille, Finn Mac Cumhaill is said to have let loose one of his hounds, Bran, to chase a deer. At the crossing of a river the hound spared the deer and thereafter that spot was known as 'Belach Damhain', or 'way of the deer' (Lacey 1998, 26). This tale is a reminder that red deer, as large wild herbivores, would have depended on the parish's rough grazing as much if not more than cattle brought up from the valleys for the summer. Their preservation was in the interests of local

Gaelic lords, who went on deer-hunts to reinforce their position in society (FitzPatrick 2013; see Chapter 6). At the same time, by killing off some each year, they would have ensured that herds of cattle did not have insufficient grass. After all, many of these cattle may ultimately have belonged to them, as Graham (1970a, 148–49) points out that it was common practice in west Ulster up to the early seventeenth century for Gaelic lords to distribute cattle among their followers.

The organisation of land

The other factor in determining the presence of transhumance is of course the farming system of the local population, and whether they used land in such a way that required and expected movement between pastures. Using early seventeenth-century inquisitions, Graham (1970a) produces maps of the various quarters and balliboes contained within Kilcar and Loughros (or Inishkeel) civil parishes, both of which border the present study area on the east.[1] These illustrate that most quarters in these parishes consisted of separate parcels of land – that is, one group of balliboes by the coast and another connected block of land in the hills. These divisions almost certainly speak to upland grazing rights and remind us of the situation recorded a few decades later in Ballynascreen in Derry and in the barony of Moycullen in Galway. Transhumance in south-west Donegal was therefore much more organised than the rental for Hugh O'Neill's lands would lead one to believe. Movements were predictable enough for land units to have grown up around the practice and, so far as we can tell, these movements were contained within particular parishes (Type 2 movement in Figure 2.1).

Alas, it is not possible to reconstruct transhumant links as accurately in the parish of Gleann Cholm Cille itself. Similarly detailed inquisitions into the progress of plantation do not exist for the simple reason that it was 'termon land' and so not confiscated by the English Crown as part of the Ulster Plantation. As *tearmann*, or 'church land affording right of sanctuary' (Ó Dónaill 1977), the parish belonged to the bishop of Raphoe, with the local Mac Niallais family holding the offices of 'coarb' (*comharba*) and 'erenagh' (*airchinneach*) on a hereditary basis (*Inquis. cancell. Hib. Rep.*, Appendix 5). Moreover, the area has lacked archaeological investigations of contemporary non-elite settlement and farming.

Models of the human settlement patterns and farming practices that underlay transhumance must therefore be abstracted from a small number of indirect historical sources, particularly the Civil Survey and Down Survey. In 1608 a 'Booke of the King's Lands' (undertaken for the Ulster Plantation) lists 'Carrownedromagh' and 'Carrowkilfarenet' as quarters and 'Shradd' as a half quarter (*MS. Rawlinson A 237*, 182). The first of these units was probably a precursor of the modern townland of 'Drum' or An Droim, located on the north side of the main Gleann valley. The second is probably an early name for the townland of 'Kilanned' or Cill Fhathnaid, located in the

---

[1]   Although she commits a mistake in using the modern townland system as a template – these boundaries often differing in the seventeenth century – the general pattern of the maps is reliable, as most balliboe place-names reoccur as later townlands.

south-west of Gleann, while 'Shradd' is almost certainly a forerunner of the modern townland of 'Straid' or An tSráid, which lies at the mouth of the Muirlín river. The 1608 survey appears incomplete, however, for an Inquisition from just the following year refers to 'the parish of Clancollumkill containing *five* quarters' (own emphasis; *Inquis. cancell. Hib. Rep.*, Appendix 5). The location of these other two and a half quarters is not apparent until several decades later.

By the mid-seventeenth century most of Ireland's Gaelic elite had been subdued by English forces and the Mac Niallais family were no longer in control of Gleann Cholm Cille; it was now leased from the (Anglican) bishop of Raphoe by the heirs of Archibald Askin (Simington 1937, 81), who belonged to a family of Scottish planters. However, the old structures of land organisation hung on. Just as in 1609, the Civil Survey of 1654 says that the parish contains five quarters (Simington 1934, 81), and, when the Down Survey map of 1656 is examined, one gets a more detailed idea of their distribution and the sub-divisions that they contained (Figure 4.6). In addition to '10 Balliboes of Glencollamkille arable intermix with mountainous pasture', there is the 'arrable of ye 7 Balliboes of Mallinmore' (depicted as one unit on the map). Bordering it on the south is another unit, containing 'the 3 balliboes of Malinbeg arrable intermix with mountainous pasture'. A third parcel of land is found separately in the extreme south

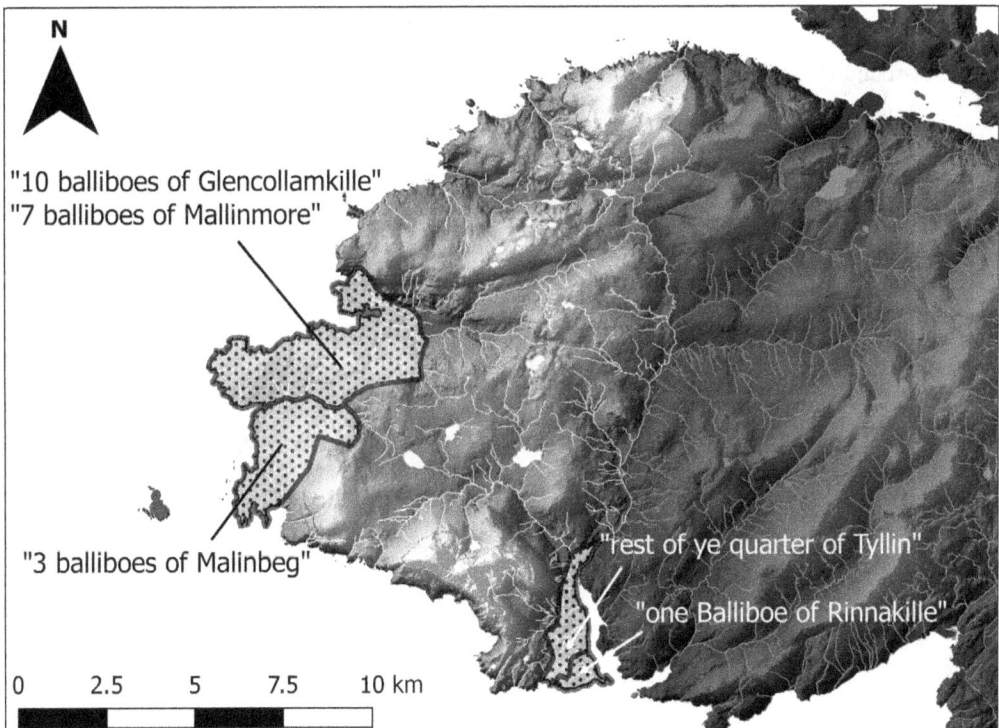

Figure 4.6 Lands recorded in Gleann Cholm Cille for the Down Survey (NLI Manuscript map 16 B. 15(14).

of the parish. It is divided into two units, the first being 'the one Balliboe of Rinnakille: good arrable' and the second 'the rest of ye quarter of Tyllin arrable and some dry Heathy pasture hardly to be distinguished from ye Arrable' – 'Tyllin' is now the locality of Teelin, or, in Irish, Teileann. Thus the Down Survey confirms the location of all five of the parish's quarters.

Unfortunately, in terms of land *use*, the Down Survey for this area does not provide an estimation of the amount of arable land versus pasture. Aside from Rinnakille, which contained seventy-eight acres of arable, it merely states that both forms of land use were present. The Civil Survey, on the other hand, does. It approximates that just over half of the land in the five quarters was 'profitable', of which seventy-five acres were arable and 250 pasture. The rest consisted of 150 acres of 'redbogg' and 150 acres of 'rockey' land (Simington 1934, 81). Clearly, this is an underestimation of the overall amount of land contained in the five quarters – the more accurate Down Survey gives their overall acreage as 1,907. All the same, if the *proportions*, at least, are reliable, they suggest that arable was relatively unimportant, occupying just 12 per cent of land and 'profitable' pasture slightly over 38 per cent.

Outside of these five quarters, however, the parish is striking for its emptiness. Its unregulated appearance is on a par with the Carna peninsula (though the absence of Down Survey maps in the latter precludes a definitive comparison).[2] One can only assume that here lay a great expanse of rough pasture. Not including the boggy or rocky land reckoned within the above quarters and balliboes, there were as many as 110km[2] of rough grazing in the uplands and few remaining pockets of woodland around the parish. With such an abundance of pasture and the comparative lack of tillable ground, it is not difficult to imagine a farming system based primarily on rearing livestock.

Reconstructing probable patterns of transhumance

But what role did transhumance play in the management of livestock? First of all, the relatively small quantity of arable would not by itself have made the practice imperative. Much more significant a factor would have been the need to preserve better-quality grassland. No matter how abundant upland grazing was in the parish as a whole, it could never be fully exploited during the summer if an equivalent amount of meadow was not preserved as winterage in the valleys – a large herd of cattle could not have made it through to the following year otherwise. A system of transhumance could allow a farmer to keep more cattle, but, as the Carna study has shown, it could not escape the land's physical limitations. There is no reason to believe, therefore, that cattle numbers in Gleann Cholm Cille were inordinately high during the seventeenth century because large amounts of rough pasture were available. In any case, from a purely subsistence point of view, high numbers of livestock were not needed. Pender's 'census' estimates in 1659 that the parish contained just 108 people, three of whom

---

2   We can be confident that all of the best land is indeed represented by these quarters and balliboes, as surveyors of the English administration were concerned with finding out the full extent and value of the country's farmland – and who its proprietors were.

were English or Scottish (Pender 1939, 47). Notwithstanding mortality in recent wars and the probable underestimation of population by a third or more (Smyth 1988; 2002, xxix), a corrected figure for the parish would still be drastically lower than the population of 4,356 recorded in 1841 (Census 1851, 105). There must have been relatively little pressure on food resources in this context.

The areas of pasture that cattle were brought to during the summer in the early modern period remain to be established. Are any of the surviving booley sites of Mín na Saileach likely to have been used as part of transhumance at this time? To be sure, the lack of uniformity we see archaeologically is only partially explicable in terms of adaptation to topography, for the ground is not nearly as rocky or uneven in Mín na Saileach as it is in Carna. The proximity of suitable raw materials was another factor, however, and arguably one that was not constant over time. For instance, it has been noted that patches of woodland or scrub were probably still a feature of Gleann Cholm Cille's landscape in the sixteenth and seventeenth centuries. This would have made construction with wattle, or even post-and-wattle, a far greater possibility than in 1820, when there was said to be hardly a tree in the parish. Thus, low structures such as Mín na Saileach 11, 14 and 15 could represent the remains of earlier booley dwellings with wattle superstructures With people after 1700 increasingly relying on sod and stone for walling material and driftwood for roof timbers, the largely stone-built (and rectangular) Mín na Saileach 12 and 13 are perhaps less likely to have been used in medieval and early modern transhumance. Yet, even if wattle construction is more likely to be early, construction with stone cannot always be seen as later. In some locales, such as the Carna peninsula, stone may always have been an obvious choice because of its abundance. Undatable opportunism of this kind is evident in Mín na Saileach at structure 8 – a small, roughly square hut – and structure 9 – a triangular pen; both have walls formed by lining up blocks of quartzite that had fallen from a small cliff directly behind them (Figure 4.5).

Thus, at least some of the surviving archaeology in the 'Mountain Pasture of the Willows' is likely to have been implicated in transhumant systems based out of central Gleann Cholm Cille during the seventeenth century or earlier. However, as a cautionary note, one should also remember that there was far less permanent settlement in Gleann Cholm Cille to restrict pastoral movements at this time. This is borne out by a comparison of land use in the upper reaches of Abhainn Ghlinne during the seventeenth and nineteenth centuries. Although 'empty' in the present writer's plot of the Down Survey, a cluster of five townlands bearing the *mín*, or 'mountain pasture', element are recorded here on the first edition six-inch Ordnance Survey in 1835. Furthermore, they all contain permanent settlement on their lower slopes in 1835. During the seventeenth century, when they appear to have been free of the latter, the farmers of some of Gleann's balliboes may have found it more convenient to bring their cattle to the east rather than over the hills to the north. Before the demise of Gaelic power the Mac Niallais *comharba* family may have played a role in determining these movements, particularly if they, like secular lords, were in the habit of distributing cattle among farmers and reserving certain areas for their own hunting pursuits. Details of such restrictions, if they ever existed, are now lost.

POPULATION GROWTH AND THE COLONISATION OF HILL PASTURES, 1700–1850

The landscape of south-west Donegal underwent a major transformation as a result of population growth in the eighteenth and early nineteenth centuries, with important implications for the practice of transhumance. As in south Connemara, permanent settlement and arable farming were quite limited in the seventeenth century. Here, however, population growth manifested itself somewhat differently, altering the dynamic of movement more noticeably. In the barony of Banagh it is estimated that population grew by over 600 per cent between 1732 and 1821; this staggering growth rate ranks as one of the highest in the country (Smyth 2012a, 15, fig. 2). The rate of increase slowed thereafter, although in the period 1821–41 Banagh's population still grew by another 20–30 per cent (Smyth 2012a, 17, fig. 4). In this study area, and neighbouring parishes, the effects of population growth can be modelled. Initially, growth took place in the areas that were already settled on a permanent basis: that is, Gleann, Málainn Mhór, Málainn Bhig and Teileann. Eventually, however, growth turned into expansion and new settlements began to spread along river valleys and, more slowly, up nearby hillsides. This is reflected in a rental of the Connolly estate dating to 1773–74 (NLI P. 6951). At this time, Gleann Cholm Cille was divided into thirteen named lots. This is more than the five and a half quarters during the seventeenth century, but far fewer than the fifty-five townlands (excluding islands) recorded by the Ordnance Survey in 1835 – indicating that land organisation was undergoing a transition. A couple of these lots, namely 'Straleele', rented by John Dobbins and partners, and 'Meenaneary', rented by Thomas Strong, represent some of the first areas of expansion outside core settlement areas. They both lie on the banks of Abhainn Ghlinne, in what would have been relatively accessible ground for people moving north from Teileann. The beginning of settlement expansion is also documented in the neighbouring parish of Loughros, where Graham (1970a, fig. 4) uses a different, but equally rare, estate survey and map to show that three of the townlands nearest to the permanently settled Loughros peninsula had been colonised by 1755.

The ongoing consequences of settlement expansion had become clear by 1835, on the first edition six-inch Ordnance Survey map. Figure 4.7 demonstrates, first of all, that the coast was not as powerful a draw for new settlements as it had been in the Carna peninsula. Although fishing was and is a very important aspect of south-west Donegal's economy (witness the Ulster Plantation Papers, which say that the bay of Teileann contained the 'fishinge of salmon and other sea fish'; Moody 1938, 292), the coast itself is difficult of access and lined with cliffs, making sand and seaweed less easy to extract for use as fertiliser. Instead, large numbers of lime-kilns are marked. Given the local geology, limestone must have been imported from outside the parish to these sites, burned and then spread as an aid to the cultivation of potatoes on poor peaty soils. At the same time, population did not expand in quite the same way as it did in the Carna peninsula. Gleann Cholm Cille's topography is less extreme, with several small areas of upland rather than one contiguous block. Instead of spreading uniformly up from older lowland farms, settlement expanded somewhat opportunistically, along a number of favourable corridors – eastwards in Gleann along the middle and upper

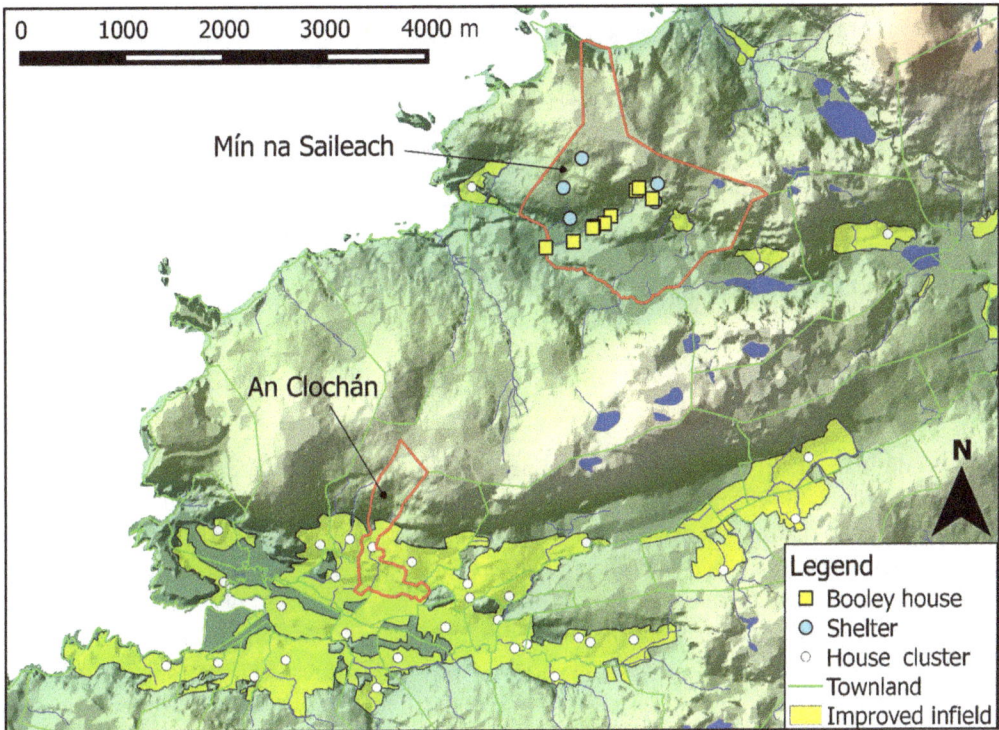

Figure 4.7 An Clochán and Mín na Saileach, 1835 (extent of infield and location of house clusters adapted from first edition six-inch OS).

courses of the Muirlín river and northwards along the Abhainn Ghlinne, invading the lower slopes of hills known as *mín*, or 'mountain pasture'. Tenants settling along the Abhainn Ghlinne corridor clearly followed the lead of Thomas Strong, who was renting land in Mín an Aoire ('Hill Pasture of the Shepherd') by the 1770s. In breaking in new land along these corridors, collective tenancy appears to have been an important vehicle. Besides the aforementioned John Dobbins in Straleele, three other lots of land in the 1773–74 rental were held by a head tenant '& partners'. By 1830, when one of the last available Connolly rentals was drawn, the number of tenants with partners had swollen to twenty-three, out of thirty-seven in the whole parish (NLI P. 6951).

However, with population continuing to grow rapidly in the core areas even after settlement had spilled into adjacent valleys and slopes, it appears that certain groups were also prepared to colonise seemingly random spots of hill pasture in the north of the parish, turning them into year-round hill farms. I have already pointed out one of these in the east of Mín na Saileach, but others are apparent in neighbouring townlands on the 1835 Ordnance Survey map. An Port, to the west, has a couple of dwelling houses situated at the centre of a patch of improved ground, while Coillte Feannaid, Loch Dhoire Thoirc and Gleann Lach to the east and north all have similar-sized patches of improved land (Figures 4.2, 4.7). Where, why and how transhumance was practised in this rapidly changing demographic environment offers a potentially fascinating insight into the flexibility of subaltern agro-pastoralists. The next section therefore takes advantage of the rich cartographic and documentary evidence for the early to mid-nineteenth century to assess what kept transhumance relevant in this landscape and, moreover, how grazing rights were organised at a communal level between different households. This, then, sets the scene for the chapter's last section, in which the oral history and archaeology are brought together to evaluate the realities of seasonal settlement in south-west Donegal during demographic pressure and how tenant farmers ultimately exploited their connections to hill pastures in order to cope.

TRANSHUMANT CONNECTIONS, 1800–1850: NECESSITY AND ORGANISATION

Mín na Saileach and the townlands neighbouring it are very interesting in relation to the rest of Gleann Cholm Cille parish. Oral history collected by Ó Duilearga (1939, 296) says that several of these upland townlands were connected to townlands further south in the main valley of Gleann. Mín na Saileach, for example, acted as hill pasture for the tenants of An Clochán, a townland over 3.5km south-west of the former. Other links are An Droim (also in Gleann) and the hill pastures of Coillte Feannaid and An Port; An Caiseal and a sub-townland area known as Sruthán Giobach; Fearann Mhic Giolla Bhríde and Gleann Lach; and Bánghort and a sub-townland area known as Mín a' Chruinne (Ó Duilearga 1939, 296).

The rights of pasturage that existed between these townlands are reminiscent of the coastal–inland connections identified for nineteenth-century Carna. In this case, however, there is only one source to rely upon, so there may have been other links that Ó Highne could not remember or was not aware of. For example, as Graham (1970a, 142, fig. 5) suggests in her work, it is probable that An Fhothair, another small townland in Gleann, was linked with Sliabh na Foithreach, to the north-west – both shared the place-name element *fothair* (meaning, in this case, a shelf or loft in a hill; Placenames Database of Ireland). Similarly, a connection between the townlands of Bíofán and Garbhros and the adjoining Sliabh Bhíofáin agus Gharbhrois seems obvious, as the latter simply means 'the mountain of Bíofán and Garbhros'. All of these links, both confirmed and unconfirmed, are illustrated together in Figure 4.8.[3]

A pattern emerges from the map. By and large, it is small and intensively farmed townlands that enjoy distant rights of pasturage in the uplands. On the 1835 six-inch Ordnance Survey map the former are for the most part taken up by swathes of seemingly undivided infield. Numerous lime-kilns dotted on the map indicate that this land was being painstakingly improved in the pre-Famine period, while the presence of 'corn kilns' suggests that most of it was under tillage. The focal point of each of these townlands is a cluster of houses that might be called a small village or 'clachan', a feature of settlement that suited the collective nature of tenancies – that is, as part

---

[3]   Three links relating to transhumance in the neighbouring parish of Inishkeel/Loughros are also mentioned by Ó Highne (Ó Duilearga 1939).

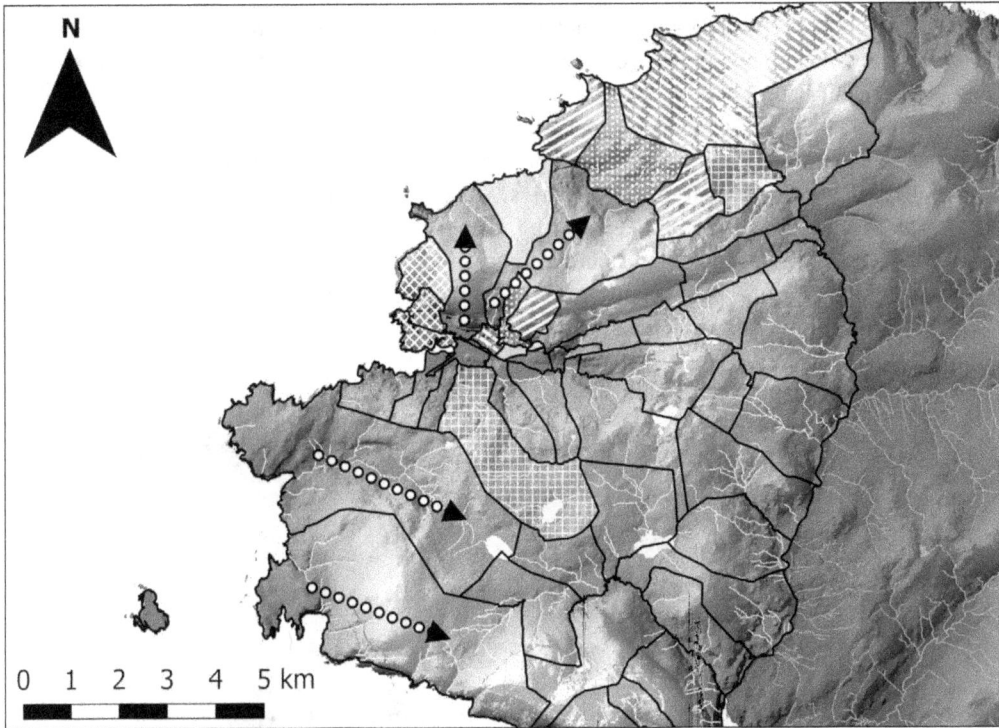

Figure 4.8 Townlands linked by transhumance (pattern-coded) and other transhumant movements within townlands (marked by arrows).

of rundale. In Gleann each townland contains just one of these clusters, but in much larger townlands, such as An Bhráid Uachtarach to the east and Málainn Mhóir to the south-west, two or even three occur. Beyond the clusters and their infields, each townland also contains an outfield of rough grazing, usually on steeper ground or in waterlogged areas. Again, this is very characteristic of rundale, a system of landholding in which all land – near and far – was held in common (Whelan 1997, 79–88; 2012; Yager 2002; Ó Síocháin *et al.* 2015). In the larger townlands mentioned, much more ground is taken up by outfield than by infield, with a ratio of rough grazing to arable of about 6:1 or greater. By contrast, outfield is under-represented in the small townlands of Gleann.

At one level, this is simply a consequence of geography. If several groups of tenants were all engaged in cultivation in a narrow valley, then grazing was not going to be available in sufficient quantity in the same location. Gleann forms the largest contiguous area of acid brown earths and surface water gleys in the parish, and was therefore too valuable as improvable arable land not to attract dense settlement in the pre-Famine period (indeed, back to the foundation of its early medieval church site). The contemporary settlement pattern therefore makes sense from the point of view of crop production, but it introduced complications for tenant farmers who wanted to keep cattle – a vital element in the local economy. For example, a farming survey of the area by Rev. John Ewing in the mid-1820s says it was mostly through the production of butter and young cattle (and flannel) that rents were paid (Day and McWilliams 1997, 65). Moreover, cattle acted as fertilisers for the infield over winter. Using An Clochán as an example, the reasons for transhumant movements outside Gleann become more tangible (Figure 4.9). The cluster of houses visible at the centre of this townland in 1835 contains fourteen medium-sized to large rectangular houses, with another four structures possibly serving as small outbuildings.[4] The total amount of land available to their occupants within the townland bounds was 46.9ha, 22.5ha of which consisted of infield.

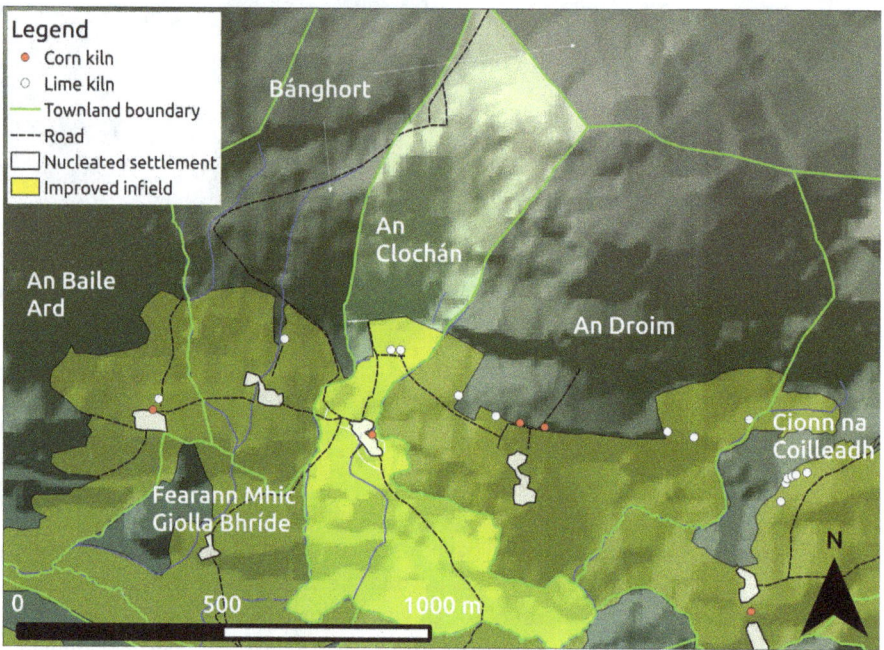

Figure 4.9 An Clochán and neighbouring townlands in Gleann in 1835 (first edition six-inch OS).

It seems from the Ewing survey that the infield was spade-dug and rotated between potatoes, barley, oats or flax, and potatoes again (Day and McWilliams 1997, 65). The other 23.4ha was an outfield of rough grazing. This would leave the fourteen households in the immediate pre-Famine period with an average of 1.6ha of infield and 1.67ha of outfield each – in other words, slightly less than the average arrived at for An Más and An Aird Thiar in the Carna peninsula. In this context, one can begin to understand the basis of An Clochán's link with Mín na Saileach: it was desirable

---

4   Fourteen dwelling houses recorded not long after, in 1841, confirms the accuracy of the six-inch Ordnance Survey map (Census 1851, 105).

because it provided tenants with much more pasture for their livestock than could be found next to their permanent settlement, and it was possible, moreover, because of the abundance of rough grazing in the hills to the north (Figure 4.7).

Some of the intricacies of the system may be examined using unusually detailed information from Griffith's Valuation. In 1857 a number of tenants are recorded as holders of 'land' in Mín na Saileach. Four of these names are of tenants who by then lived year-round in the east of the townland, but the rest are not. When checked against other Griffith's Valuation entries, it appears that the additional tenants are actually people who were based in An Clochán. This date is admittedly quite late in the lifespan of booleying, with much attendant change taking place in how the landscape was organised (see end of Chapter 6), but there remains a strong likelihood that these entries represent the grazing entitlements of tenants in the transhumance that An Clochán traditionally kept up with its partner townland. Mín na Saileach contains just over 265ha, with an improved patch of just 3.25ha recorded beside the aforementioned colonisers on the 1835 six-inch Ordnance Survey map (Figure 4.2). Even factoring in the grazing requirements of these nascent farmsteads, there is likely to have been upwards of 240ha of rough grazing for the tenants of An Clochán to use. Sixteen parties in total are recorded as having grazing rights, with each also holding land in An Clochán.[5]

All told, there were only two tenants in An Clochán who did not hold land in Mín na Saileach – these being cottiers who were not engaged in farming at all. Doubt as to the completeness of the Griffith's Valuation does arise because it occasionally fails to record every tenant in other parts of the country where rundale existed. However, the list for An Clochán seems complete: of the sixteen farming tenancies recorded, ten had houses on them, and this tallies fairly well with the population of fifty-one recorded six years earlier in the townland (Census 1851, 105). The Griffith's Valuation can therefore be taken as reliable evidence that everyone engaged in farming in An Clochán had access to distant rough pasture. In the absence of similar records dating to before the 1850s it is difficult to say whether or not this was the case in the pre-Famine period, but it seems highly likely given the communal nature of rundale-style landholding.

The grazing may have been shared by tenants; however, it was not shared equally. Valuations of the rough grazing in Mín na Saileach differ from tenant to tenant, many having as little as 3/-, others as much as 10/- or 15/- (acreages are not given because land was reckoned according to carrying capacity). When cross-checked once again against entries for An Clochán, the differences are directly proportionate to the valuation of each tenant's main holding. Thus, Condy Cannon, who possessed a house, offices and land in An Clochán valued at £3/5/-, has rough grazing worth 15/- in Mín na Saileach. This is substantially higher than most of the other tenants' shares and as such proves that land was not held equally in rundale partnerships. Later ethnographic evidence recorded by Morris *et al.* (1939, 289) implies this when it says that 'their rights

---

5   Their immediate lessor in both cases was a Rev. John Macnaughtan, who himself rented
     Gleann Cholm Cille parish from Thomas Connolly, absentee landlord.

to summer grazing over an unfenced mountain common were in strict proportion to the amount of land they held in this valley'. Interestingly, Morris relates that the system was regulated by a specially appointed 'brehon' or *breitheamh*, who saw to it at the start of May that 'each farmer got his fair share of the mountain grazing' (Morris *et al.* 1939). This was necessary because tenants did not always have the right number of cattle for the rough pasture they were entitled to. Thus, he explains, if a tenant with a right to graze thirty cattle in fact had fewer, he would be given livestock by another tenant who in that year happened to have more than he was entitled to. It is not clear if they were handed over permanently, though it must be admitted that even a temporary loan would have been a boon considering that the cattle involved in booleying were primarily dairy stock. The role of the *breitheamh* in early nineteenth-century transhumance was therefore to maintain the inequalities that already existed between tenants in the rundale system.[6]

Access to summer grazing was clearly still an important and sophisticated element in the cultural landscape of Gleann Cholm Cille in the first half of the nineteenth century, requiring the linkage of townlands 2km to 7km apart and the acknowledgement of local decision-making by a *breitheamh* so as to maintain differential grazing rights between tenants.

THE MATERIALITY OF HERDING IN AN EVOLVING DEMOGRAPHIC LANDSCAPE

Everyday life at the booley sites

The booleying season in Gleann Cholm Cille started officially on 1 May and lasted until the beginning of winter, although an exact date for the return is not given (Morris *et al.* 1939, 289; Ó Duilearga 1939, 295). This is slightly shorter than in the Galtees, and might be explained by the later onset of grass growth further north in the country (Brereton 1995, 20, fig. 3). There is no suggestion in Gleann Cholm Cille of cattle being switched or the grazing season being divided in two, perhaps because mineral deficiencies were less likely to arise in the lowland valleys where people here were based. According to Morris (1939, 289), young people of both sexes were given the responsibility of looking after the cattle at summer pasture. They were tasked with milking the cows twice a day and churning the milk into butter (Morris 1939, 289). Indeed, a historical account dating to the mid-1820s confirms that 'children are generally employed in taking care of cattle' (Day and McWilliams 1997, 65).

In terms of diet, these young herders would have lived off the milk and butter produced on-site, as well as some oatmeal brought up from home (Morris 1936, 289), while a *tuagh chuisle*, or vein-axe, would occasionally have been used to draw blood from the necks of cattle and collected in a pot to make pudding (Ó Duilearga 1939,

---

6   This tradition of having a 'brehon' may be a variant of the *Rí* or 'King' tradition found up to recent times in other parts of the west of Ireland, in which one respected individual became a sort of leader for the community, mediating difficulties, etc. (see Ó Danachair 1981).

296). Butter may not have been brought down to the home farm quite as regularly as in Carna, local information suggesting that it was sometimes buried in the bog for preservation (Francy Cunningham, pers. comm.). Presumably, this was done only when salt could not be obtained, before the nineteenth century, for example. Otherwise butter may have been stored in annexes to structures 1 and 12.

'Dancing and games' took place at the summer pastures as well (Morris *et al.* 1939, 289), as hinted by the minor place-name *Ard na nDíslí*, or 'Hill of the Dice', in Mín na Saileach (O'Neill 1973, 361). Although Morris was told that there was 'never a hint of any impropriety' (Morris *et al.* 1939, 289), it is likely that the work and play involved in transhumance had a vital role in strengthening bonds among the people of each townland, whether through eventual marriage or friendships that lasted lifetimes. Yet subtle interventions could still be made by the elders of the community. In the north-west of Donegal, where transhumance also took place up to the mid-nineteenth century, it is said that the men of the community would go up to the hill pastures sometime after St Patrick's Day in order to rebuild the booley houses or *bothógaí* that their herders – in this case just girls – would use over the summer (Ó hEochaidh 1943, 133, 136). On the one hand, this was simply an act of maintenance. However, considering the removal feasts on Lewis and other rituals associated with the start of transhumance in Scotland, Scandinavia and elsewhere (Costello 2018, 173; see Chapter 6), it is worth considering whether acts of repair at seasonal sites in Ireland contained symbolic meaning; whether they were an attempt to vouch protection and perhaps control over young people through the very architecture of the booley sites that they slept in.

The same account from north-west Donegal explains that, although booley dwellings tended to be one-roomed, some of them, at 5.5m in length and over 3m in width, had just enough interior space to allow a cow to be brought in (Ó hEochaidh 1943, 133, 134). While stalling of cows was of course not necessary during the summer months, individual heifers calving for the first time may have needed close attention. This is only to be expected given that the sharing of living space with cattle and pigs is well known in nineteenth- and early twentieth-century vernacular Irish architecture: indeed, a specific type of farmhouse known as the 'byre-dwelling' has been identified by folklife experts in the north-west and west of the country (Ó Danachair 1964; Gailey 1984; Aalen 1997). In Mín na Saileach site 13 quite possibly accommodated sick or heavily pregnant cows when necessary. It too features a one-roomed structure and has very similar dimensions to those described in the north-west of the county (5.6m × 3.9m externally, 4m × 2.7m internally); an animal could have lain down in the eastern end of the structure, with the area between the opposing entrances acting as a channel for effluent (Figure 4.10). Sites 1 and 12 are slightly more complex, but they may also have accommodated animals. At either end of site 1's main rectangular structure are two smaller annexes that could have been used to keep dairy products or livestock. Meanwhile, site 12 consists of two adjoining structures that did not communicate with each other (Figure 4.3). Since the eastern structure is less well preserved it may be an older booley dwelling that was reused as a dairy storage area or calf pen. However, if they were in contemporary use as booley dwellings they do appear large enough to have each accommodated one cow.

The rest of the cows in Mín na Saileach were probably brought close to the booley dwellings at night-time and tethered to a post of bog oak or bog deal, as oral history from north-west Donegal suggests (Ó hEochaidh 1943: 146). However, archaeological survey could find no evidence of demarcated enclosures around the booley structures, which is perhaps unsurprising given that they do not form discrete groups. That said, one very large area of irregular shape (c.500m × 300m), enclosed by an earthen bank, was identified in the south-west of Mín na Saileach. It is unclear what its use was given that, topographically, the area is quite uneven and most of the flatter ground is wet bog, unsuitable for grazing. Considering its location on the most likely route of approach from the south, it could have been associated with the sorting of livestock at the start and end of each grazing season. Alternatively, taking into account the aforementioned small patch of cultivation next to structure 15, there is a possibility that it represents an attempt at colonisation, though much less successfully than in the east of Mín na Saileach (see below).

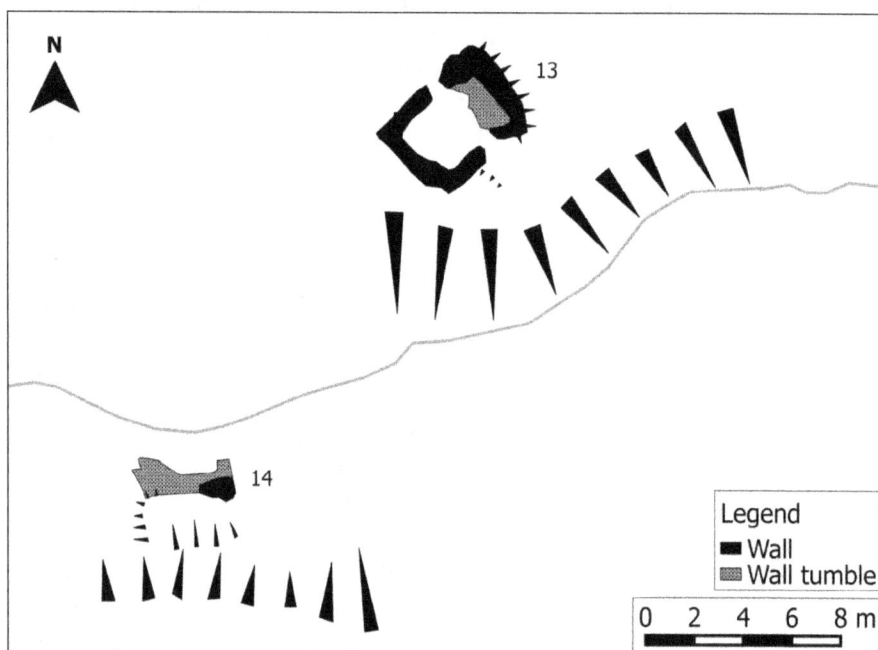

Figure 4.10 Plan of Mín na Saileach 13 and 14.

The absence of cultivation ridges on the ground – the only possible exception being that patch just north of structure 15 – and the lack of oral history relating to potatoes at booley sites in the area may suggest that cultivation was very rare or absent from the summer pastures of post-medieval Gleann Cholm Cille. However, it must be remembered that fieldwork was restricted to just one townland, so it is not inconceivable that patches of cultivation are yet to be found in other upland townlands, or indeed that cultivation took place near booley dwellings in the east of Mín na Saileach before their conversion into year-round farms. After all, even in the Carna peninsula and the Galtee Mountains ridges were found next to only a minority of seasonal sites. When it is considered that potato cultivation is attested at contemporary booley sites in north-west Donegal (Ó hEochaidh 1943, 139), as well as Achill and the other study areas, it would be surprising if it did not also feature on a small scale in Gleann Cholm Cille, especially in the first half of the nineteenth century.

The scale of human movement

The proportion of a community that travelled to hill pastures with cattle (and stayed there with them) is not possible to calculate for the seventeenth or eighteenth centuries, nor is it as clear in these earlier centuries that young people were the only ones to relocate. In Chapter 6 this problem is discussed at a national level, but at a local level it remains intractable for now. While archaeological fieldwork in Mín na Saileach provides an indication of the number of herders who could have stayed in booley houses, there are no reliable comparanda on housing and population available for its partner townland, An Clochán, prior to the 1830s. The only documentary hint comes from the 1773–74 estate rental, which records a William Blaine (a Protestant head-tenant) renting the townland together with an unspecified number of partners for £2 6s 8d per half-year. There are also no standing or visible surface remains of houses that pre-date the mid-nineteenth century.

However, when the first edition six-inch Ordnance Survey map, the subsequent national census and standing remains from other permanently settled townlands are taken into account, estimating the scale of human relocation becomes possible for the *immediate* pre-Famine period. In 1841, before the major demographic upset of the Great Famine, An Clochán's population stood at seventy-nine, divided among fourteen houses (first edition six-inch Ordnance Survey; Census 1851, Part 1, 105). The number of probable booley dwellings found by the writer in Mín na Saileach, by contrast, is nine. Even if the date-ranges for the occupation of these booley dwellings all matched up perfectly – and they almost certainly do not – there would still have been a mismatch in numbers between them and houses in An Clochán. This would indicate that transhumant movements from that townland in the decade or so before the Famine did not entail the relocation of its entire farming community. Furthermore, it must be remembered that, in terms of size, we are not comparing like with like. That is to say, it is likely that most contemporary farmhouses were larger than their seasonal counterparts. Although no above-ground remains of the farmhouses recorded in 1841 survive, approximate measurements of their external dimensions on the six-inch Ordnance Survey map show that at least ten of them are more than 10m in length and about 5m in width. Even outside An Clochán, surviving pre-Famine houses are extremely rare. That said, I have identified two probable examples in the north of the parish.

The first is located in neighbouring An Baile Ard, and was one of at least twelve dwellings in that townland's house cluster in 1835. It is a rectangular house with a gabled thatch roof and a central doorway in its south-facing side. It measures 11.5m × 5m externally (57.5m^2) and 9.7m × 3.6m internally (34.9m^2). Another example comes from the townland of An Sraith Bhuí, to the east of Mín na Saileach. It is of the same

Figure 4.11 Thatched farmhouse in An Sraith Bhuí.

design, except it is built into a natural slope at one end, and is slightly longer, at 12.5m × 5m externally (62.5m²) and 10.5m × 3.6m internally (37.8m²). Its doorway is just off-centre, with three windows in the same, south-east-facing, side (Figure 4.11). By comparison, booley sites 12 and 13 are the only seasonal dwellings in Mín na Saileach that approach these dimensions. The latter has an internal and external area of 10.8m² and 21.84m² respectively, while neither of site 12's two structures have external areas exceeding 21m².

The considerably smaller dimensions of these booley dwellings provides additional evidence that a substantial number of people stayed in the home townland during transhumance. Based on an average internal booley house area of 8.32m², with each adolescent requiring a living space of 1.5–2m² (at most), and the rest given over to dairying equipment, butter and perhaps a cow or calf, three is taken as the average number of sleeping individuals that a summer dwelling could accommodate. This means that there would have been at least twenty-eight people stationed in Mín na Saileach at any one time. In 1841 this would have equated to 35.4 per cent of the total population of An Clochán – or slightly more than estimated for nineteenth-century Carna.

From seasonal removal to permanent relocation
Having said that, it will be remembered that year-round farmhouses in the east of Mín na Saileach (Figure 4.2) seem to be of recent origin. The origins of this isolated patch of year-round settlement were, rather remarkably, remembered in local oral

history. Séamus Ó Híghne – then an inhabitant of Mín na Saileach – claims that his grandfather was the first person to come and live permanently in that part of the hill pasture (Ó Duilearga 1939, 297). Given that Séamus was born around 1880, his grandfather is likely to have settled Mín na Saileach no earlier than the 1820s or early 1830s. Colonisation was rapid, for it had a resident population of eighteen by 1841, split among three houses (Census 1851, 105). Although soil improvement and more recent construction has covered the original Ó Híghne farmstead and any earlier archaeology, there is good reason to believe that this spot had been used as a booley site. Ó Híghne's grandfather would probably have preferred such a place over 'virgin' ground because its soil had already been fertilised on a small scale through years of dairying and incidental manuring. Furthermore, pre-existing booley sites would have offered architecture and raw materials that might be repurposed, especially stone. With the arrival of Ó Híghne and others after him as a result of population growth, a small number of booley houses and the rough grazing beside them were thus lost to An Clochán. Before this colonisation, when overall population was lower and seasonal structures still existed in the east of Mín na Saileach, one can only assume that a greater proportion of people took part directly in transhumant movements. However, with continuing uncertainty as to how many of the surveyed booley dwellings were still in use at the time in question, it would be foolish to attempt exact calculations.

Of course, these upland townlands were still also in use as summer pastures during the first half of the nineteenth century. The establishment of year-round farms in most of them did not drastically reduce the amount of grazing available, but it must have complicated other issues in transhumance. For example, did conflict arise when booley dwellings were taken over by certain families? And did these families come from connected lowland townlands, or others? The Ó Híghne surname, for example, does not appear among Griffith's Valuation entries for An Clochán. This could indicate that Séamus Ó Híghne came from a different lowland townland, like An Droim (where the name *is* recorded as 'Heena'). Alternatively, it may be that the Ó Híghne surname had simply died out in An Clochán by the time of the Valuation in 1857. This point is of essence to the whole process of colonisation. If Ó Híghne did not have an existing right to graze in Mín na Saileach, or at least a marriage connection with a family who did, it is difficult to imagine how he could have established a new farm there without alienating tenants from An Clochán who held customary grazing rights.

Luckily, tenant families on other colonised summer pastures can be traced back to their home townlands. In the Griffith's Valuation, the surnames Gillespie and McGinley are recorded in Port, while Gillespie, Byrne and Gara are found in Coillte Feannaid. Their home townland, Droim, also contains these surnames. Likewise, Gleann Lach had one tenant in 1857 – a McCunnigan – whose namesakes lived in the home townland of Fearann Mhic Giolla Bhríde. The repetition of surnames in this way suggests that colonisers came from lowland farms that were already connected to these pastures, not from random areas of the parish. Having said that, the new hill farms in Mín na Saileach, Coillte Feannaid and Gleann Lach all have at least one other tenant family in 1857 who do not have relations bearing a surname from the home townland. It is therefore proposed that permanent settlements were founded in the first instance

Figure 4.12 An area of rough pasture in An Port (immediately west of Mín na Saileach) which was colonised in early nineteenth century. Now largely abandoned.

by the sons and daughters of families who had a right to engage in transhumance. However, as the nineteenth century wore on and the system became weaker, hard-pressed tenants from other townlands – with marriage connections perhaps – found it possible to join them. The relatively substantial archaeological footprint of the hill farms, which were subsequently abandoned over the course of the twentieth century, confirms that they were occupied by more than one family. Typically, they feature the remains of more than one farmhouse, along with outbuildings and improved fields defined by substantial drystone walls (Figure 4.12).

SUMMARY AND CONCLUSIONS

This chapter has examined the evidence for transhumance in the parish of Gleann Cholm Cille between approximately 1550 and 1860, when the practice ceased. Relatively little is known about how transhumance operated within early post-medieval society. Palaeoenvironmental evidence from comparable areas of western Donegal suggests that a largely open, peat-covered landscape had become established in Gleann Cholm

Cille by the early medieval period, with woodland surviving in patches thereafter. Population would have been much lower at this time, and permanent settlement much more limited. The only areas that appear to have had any intensive farming – that is, the cultivation of oats and good pasture – are Gleann, Málainn Mhór, Málainn Bhig and Teileann. The rest of the parish would have been left as semi-natural heathland for domestic cattle and wild deer to graze, the latter perhaps hunted occasionally by the Mac Niallais *comharba* family. It has been noted that, since permanent settlement covered less ground at this time, the orientation of transhumant movements may not have been the same. For example, a conspicuous grouping of *mín* place-names in the east of the parish may have been used by some inhabitants in the two and a half quarters of Gleann.

From the mid-eighteenth century onwards this area and others were affected by population growth. Using an eighteenth-century rental, the first edition six-inch Ordnance Survey maps, Griffith's Valuation and what was already known about population growth in this region between 1732 and 1841, I have proposed a model in which permanent settlement gradually snaked its way out along the valleys from the 'older' areas of the parish. Increased numbers of people meant that farming practices took more from the land in terms of resources; thus, the last patches of woodland were felled, leaving their only trace in townland names, and areas of very poor peaty soil were taken into cultivation using lime and the revolutionary new potato crop. Even the remotest parts of the parish had a use now, whether for the extraction of fuel or the sustenance of livestock over the summer. The extension of farming of one kind or another into all areas of the parish by the nineteenth century may have led to transhumant movements becoming more regularised, forcing townlands in Gleann to focus on set areas of rough pasture to the north, as opposed to the east, where land had been colonised. Of the northern hill pastures, Mín na Saileach was used exclusively by tenant farmers from An Clochán during the first half of the nineteenth century. It was necessary for these agro-pastoralists to relieve pressure on their own land by sending cows to separate areas of rough pasture during the summer. In terms of organisation, summer grazing in the nineteenth century was shared, just like arable land. However, it was not shared equally. The rundale system and its local *breitheamh* sought to maintain existing inequalities between the tenant farmers of each townland. It was only later, as the rundale system was taken apart indirectly by inflated population and directly by landlords, that this balance was upset and transhumance lost its social framework (see Chapter 6).

Field survey in Mín na Saileach has shown that potential seasonal sites are frequent on upland pasture, albeit they are somewhat biased towards grassier locations by streams. Furthermore, it is clear that there was no one template for constructing a booley house or hut. In addition to a number of smaller shelters, booley dwellings can be rectangular, oval, irregular, made with coursed stone, made of rubble, or made out of sods. Adaptation to micro-topography and nearby raw materials is occasionally a factor in their design but not to the extent seen in south Connemara. Temporal variation was probably a stronger factor in the diversity – after all, historical sources show that transhumance was practised at least as far back as the late sixteenth century in Ulster. Thus, oval and sub-rectangular structures defined by sod or rubble walls may have their origins in that time or earlier. These buildings could have been weather-proofed with wattle superstructures, which would not have been possible by the nineteenth century, given the complete disappearance of the parish's last scrubby patches of woodland. By contrast, a form of well-built (i.e. mostly coursed) rectangular stone structure found at three sites in Mín na Saileach may, given its similarity in shape (if not quite size) to later post-medieval farmhouses in the area, represent a late type of booley dwelling. Crude comparison of surviving seasonal sites with document-derived numbers of permanent dwellings demonstrates that only a minority of An Clochán's population can have relocated to summer pasture during booleying's last phase – these were the young people, who were required to make butter and bring home what they did not eat themselves so that it could be used to pay rents.

Historical landscape analysis has also shown that transhumance facilitated different forms of human movement over time. From the 1820s onwards links between permanent settlements in the valley of Gleann and corresponding hill pastures in the north were effectively used as routes for a final phase of population expansion. In the east of Mín na Saileach an isolated patch of upland pasture was colonised from An Clochán, as were other patches in neighbouring pastures. These were probably established at pre-existing booley dwellings and, in the early days, by tenants who had a right to graze in the area. This model may help to understand processes of upland colonisation not only elsewhere in Ireland but also in Highland Scotland, where many shielings began to be settled on a year-round basis in the late eighteenth century, and in the English/Scottish Borders area and parts of Wales, where some seasonal sites are known to have transitioned into hill farms in the early modern period (Chapter 1).

The present case study suggests that, while seasonal removal of livestock made it easier for people to cope with geographical constraints at home, these traditions of movement were also ripe for exploitation when some in the community tried to navigate their way out of the demographic pressures that steep population growth caused. Individual agents exploited transhumant linkages that the rest of their agro-pastoral community relied upon, using them as routes in the process of colonisation. This amounted, effectively, to a cannibalisation of the practice from within. In this way, the material culture of seasonal settlement not only influenced but became part of a new phase of permanent settlement in the uplands, sharing the same distribution pattern and perhaps – as future excavations may investigate – having some of their fabric reused in the walls of new permanent houses.

CHAPTER 5

ALTITUDE AND ADAPTATION: EVOLVING SEASONAL SETTLEMENT IN THE GALTEE MOUNTAINS

The Galtee Mountains (Irish: *Na Gaibhlte*) are located in the south-western province of Munster and feature a long central spine of mountain peaks – the highest of which, Galtymore, reaches 919m a.s.l, making it the highest in the country outside County Kerry. As such, this is the only case study in the book that deals with seasonal settlement in a *mountain* environment, albeit not in an Alpine sense. The entire range stretches approximately 23km from east to west and 10.4km north to south ·at its maximum. Along its northern flank is the Glen of Aherlow, while along the south is a wider plain, hemmed in on the south by the Knockmealdown Mountains. The Galtees are drained by valleys that meander away from the central spine towards these northern and southern lowlands (Figure 5.1).

Soil cover on the lower slopes consists of peaty podzols, with blanket peat occupying the higher plateaus and peaks (Gardiner and Radford 1980). Most of the Galtees' vegetation consists of either grass- and sedge-dominated pasture or heather moorland. The livestock roaming this ground today are predominantly Blackface mountain sheep, who have a year-round presence. Some cattle – suckler cows, bullocks and heifers – also occasionally graze on the unenclosed commonage, but for the most part bovines are now limited to the improved pastures of privately owned farms in the foothills. Substantial parts of the lower slopes in the east and north of the Galtees have recently been afforested with non-native conifers for commercial purposes, along with valleys in the south, such as those containing the Attychraan and Burncourt Rivers. This land-use change has probably destroyed many archaeological features, some of which probably related to pastoralism. Generally speaking, however, the Galtee Mountains have experienced the ravages of coniferous planting to a lesser extent than Ireland's other inland uplands.

The nature of the soils varies considerably in the surrounding lowlands: the east and north-east is mainly covered by minimal grey brown podzolics with the rest falling under the categories of brown podzolics and gleys (Gardiner and Radford 1980). Most of this land is currently utilised intensively as enclosed cow pasture, with some tillage farming present in the more free-draining soils of the east and south-east. Today, settlement around the Galtees is characterised by dispersed farmsteads and an extensive network of small roads. Caher, in the east, and Mitchelstown (County Cork), to the south-west, are the only towns, with small villages located at Galbally, to the north-west, and Ballyporeen and Clogheen, in the south.

This final case study considers an area of Ireland in which transhumance was practised under substantially different conditions, where there was earlier and more direct control over estates by the landlord class and greater opportunities for people to interact with capitalist systems of food production. I examine the impact of these trends on the uplands that were used in transhumance and ask to what extent the archaeology of seasonal settlement has been shaped by the adaptive strategies of tenant farmers. Moreover, the Galtees present an environmental variable that was not as strong in Carna or south-west Donegal: namely, altitude. In the last third of this chapter I examine how tenant farmers exploited it as they sought to cope with both rapidly changing socio-political circumstances and new economic opportunities.

ARCHAEOLOGICAL EVIDENCE

Remote sensing and fieldwork was conducted in the Galtees on rough grazing above the limit of enclosed farmland and year-round settlement, as they appear on first edition six-inch Ordnance Survey maps drawn up around 1840. All told, the examination of satellite imagery, walk-over survey and consultation with hill farmers allowed me to identify a total of thirty-two archaeological sites with evidence of pre-twentieth-century occupation or stock management (Figure 5.1). Four of these

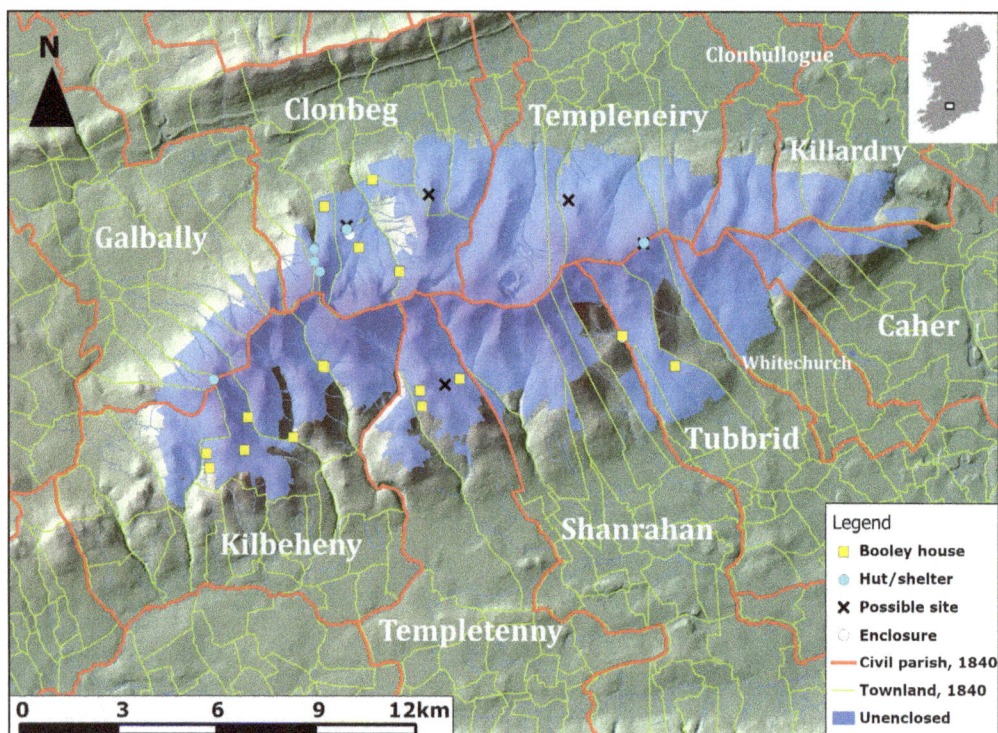

Figure 5.1 The Galtee Mountains in *c.*1840, showing site distribution.

had been on the Record of Monuments and Places at the time of survey, but the rest were not. It should be noted, however, that fieldwork was not carried out in the easternmost townlands of Templeneiry or Tubbrid, or in the civil parishes east of them, because large sections of their valleys have been afforested and are therefore likely to present a biased record of post-medieval pastoral activity.

As the Galtees rise steeply from approximately 100m to 900m a.s.l., there is a much greater vertical dimension to the distribution of sites here than in the Carna peninsula or south-west Donegal. Three-quarters of sites identified in the Galtees are located between 250m and 550m a.s.l., with only three occurring below this range and five above it (Figure 5.2). In terms of horizontal distribution, sites are most common on the Galtees' southern flank, although there is a significant number of sites in and around the Glencoshabinnia/Drumleagh basin in the north-west of the range. The lack of sites further east along the northern side may be due to recent afforestation of the lower slopes and of one mountain valley in particular (just east of the aforementioned basin). These tracts of ground would otherwise have been prime candidates for walk-over survey.

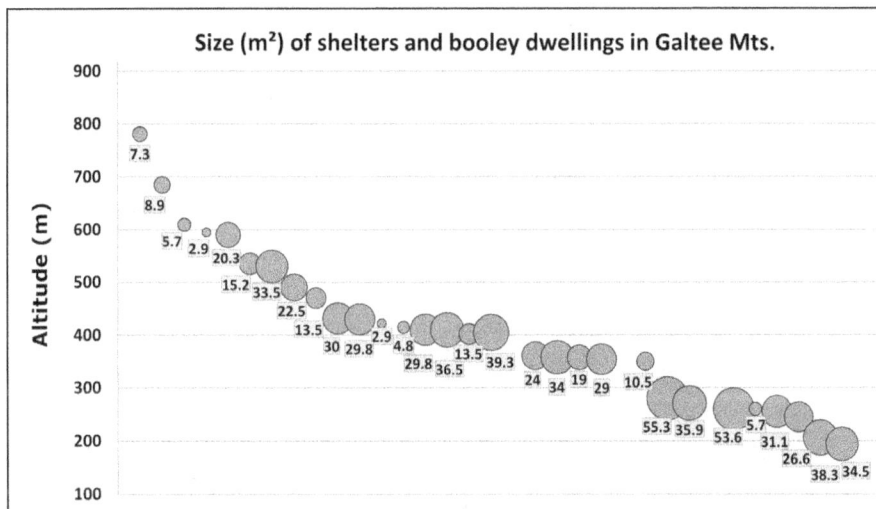

Figure 5.2 Altitudinal site distribution, showing total area (m²), excluding two enclosures.

Notwithstanding problems with preservation, the overall site distribution is far less dense than in the other two study areas. Sites in the Galtees are usually separated from one another by anything from several hundred metres to a couple of kilometres. While two discrete livestock enclosures were identified, the other thirty sites are structures formerly used for human shelter and/or habitation. In terms of form, these vary from simple circular huts and shelter-like structures approximately 1.5–2.7m in diameter externally to more substantial roughly rectangular houses measuring in the region of 5m × 7m externally. Their average area is 23.8m² externally and 10.9m² internally. Most structures are drystone with peaty material packed between the stones; sods form an important building material in a small number of examples.

Taking into account a number of different factors, such as the size and appearance of a structure, nearby features, landscape context and altitude, it becomes possible once again to make a distinction in the archaeological record between temporary shelters (blue dots in Figure 5.1) and larger dwellings that could have been lived in for extended periods (yellow squares). In the Galtees the former not only offer rather cramped internal space but are also found in very exposed locations and/or on extremely steep ground with no nearby source of water. It is much more likely, therefore, that they functioned as occasional shelters for herders and perhaps sheep in bad weather. Bohernarnane 1 and Longford 1–3 all fall into this category, while Knocknascrow 6 and Moneynaboola 1 may have been used as unroofed shelters (Figure 5.3). Some of these structures probably continued to be used until quite recently, with Longford 1 reputed by locals to have been used as a look-out by local IRA commander Dan Breen during the Irish War of Independence (1919–21). Others are still used as shelters by mountain sheep.

The majority of sites feature the remains of larger cabins or house-like structures, and are located on more hospitable ground rarely more than 50m from running water of some sort (if one includes small bog streams). These structures were probably built to be occupied for longer spells and by several individuals (Figures 5.4, 5.10, 5.11). Indeed, Costello (2015) argues that most of these larger structures, being

Figure 5.3 Bohernarnane 1 – a rubble-walled shelter just below the summit of Laghtshanaguilla.

rectangular and built with coursed stone, date to quite late in the post-medieval period, perhaps the late eighteenth or nineteenth centuries. While rectangular and roughly rectangular forms have been found in the Carna peninsula and south-west Donegal, as well as in Achill (McDonald 2014) and the Mourne Mountains (Gardiner 2012b), they are not quite as large as those in the Galtees. This could, in part, be due to the length of time that people spent at summer pastures here, the cows being brought up to the mountain in April and kept there until the end of October (Ó Danachair 1945, 250). This is slightly longer than in Donegal and significantly longer than in Achill, the Mourne Mountains and the Carna peninsula (in the last phase of seasonal settlement, at any rate).

Another reason for assigning a late date of construction to the Galtees' large rectangular booley houses is their relatively high location. On the southern side of the mountain range, and in Knockascrow especially, they are generally found above 250m or 300m a.s.l., with recent hill farms occupying the lower, improved slopes. Pointing out similarities in form between the dwelling houses on these farms and the large rectangular booley houses, Costello (2015; 2016c) makes the case that the latter were established only after *older* herding sites in the foothills were lost to the expansion of permanent settlement. As such, the vertical location of sites associated with herding has a bearing on not only the interpretation of transhumance but also the interpretation of population history in the whole area. Indeed, the process by which people engaged with altitude over time in both seasonal and permanent settlement is a key theme of this chapter.

Figure 5.4 Knocknascrow 1 well-built rectangular booley house. Note rubble reconstruction of right end wall (for sheltering sheep). The sunlit hillside in the left background is Coolagarranroe.

THE ENVIRONMENTAL AND HISTORICAL BASIS FOR SUMMER UPLAND GRAZING

Long before the post-medieval period, the middle and upper slopes of the Galtees – that is, where most of the above archaeology was recorded – offered a relatively open environment conducive to the grazing, movement and supervision of significant numbers of livestock. According to pollen analysis of a core taken at 476m a.s.l. in Borheen Lough – a corrie lake nestled in the centre of the Galtees – grass, heather and hazel have been dominant over more woody species such as oak, pine and elm since roughly 2000 BC, and especially since AD 400 or so (Hawthorne 2015, fig. 6.1.5). In addition, analyses of charcoal deposits in the Borheen Lough core and another taken at 554m a.s.l. from Diheen Lough, one kilometre to the west, show that burning events became more common in their catchment areas as the medieval and post-medieval periods progressed (Hawthorne 2015, figs 4.5, 6.1.6). These fires may have been started by pastoralists in an attempt to improve upland pastures, although it is not clear that they actually succeeded, as heather appears to have increased slightly at the expense of grass (as a result of wetter conditions in general).

No explicit references to transhumance in the Galtees are available prior to the nineteenth century. However, it has been noted in Chapter 2 that grazing cattle in the mountains for the summer was a common practice during the seventeenth century in neighbouring parts of Munster, such as the Comeragh Mountains in County Waterford and the Nagles and Boggeragh Mountains in County Cork. Furthermore, the famous early seventeenth-century religious writer and historian Dr Seathrún Céitinn, raised only a few miles south-east of the Galtees, likens our impermanent life here on Earth to transhumance, with the old home, or *seanbhaile*, our real, heavenly destination: 'Dá chor i gcéill nach fuil acht buailteachas san bheathaidh se, agus gurab é flaitheas Dé is sean-bhaile ré síor-chomhnaidhe againn' ('Making clear that this life is mere booleying, may the Kingdom of God and the old home be our perpetual rest', my translation; Osborg Bergin 1931, 87). Céitinn may have drawn inspiration for this metaphor from his own observations of *buailteachas* or transhumance in south Tipperary. Indeed, he would hardly have cited the practice if it were not a well-known aspect of life for his seventeenth-century Irish-speaking audience.

Some aspects of the organisation and basis for summer grazing in the Galtees emerge with an examination of the Civil Survey and slightly later maps of the Down Survey, which cover most of the region in detail (Down Survey Limerick; NAI QRO/ DS/1/27; NLI Manuscript map 20D: Simington 1931, 362–70, 373–76; 1934, 15–31; 1938, 228–30). The only exception is the south-west, where Templetenny civil parish (then the western half of Shanrahan), County Tipperary, and most of Kilbeheny civil parish, County Limerick, were already under the Protestant English ownership of Sir William Fenton, Mitchelstown, later Kingston (Power 2000, 4).

In the first place, these sources suggest that in the mid-seventeenth century tillage played a far more significant role in the faming economy of this region than in either the Carna peninsula or south-west Donegal. Contemporary estimates in the Civil Survey suggest that arable land predominated in most townlands around the Galtees Mountains,

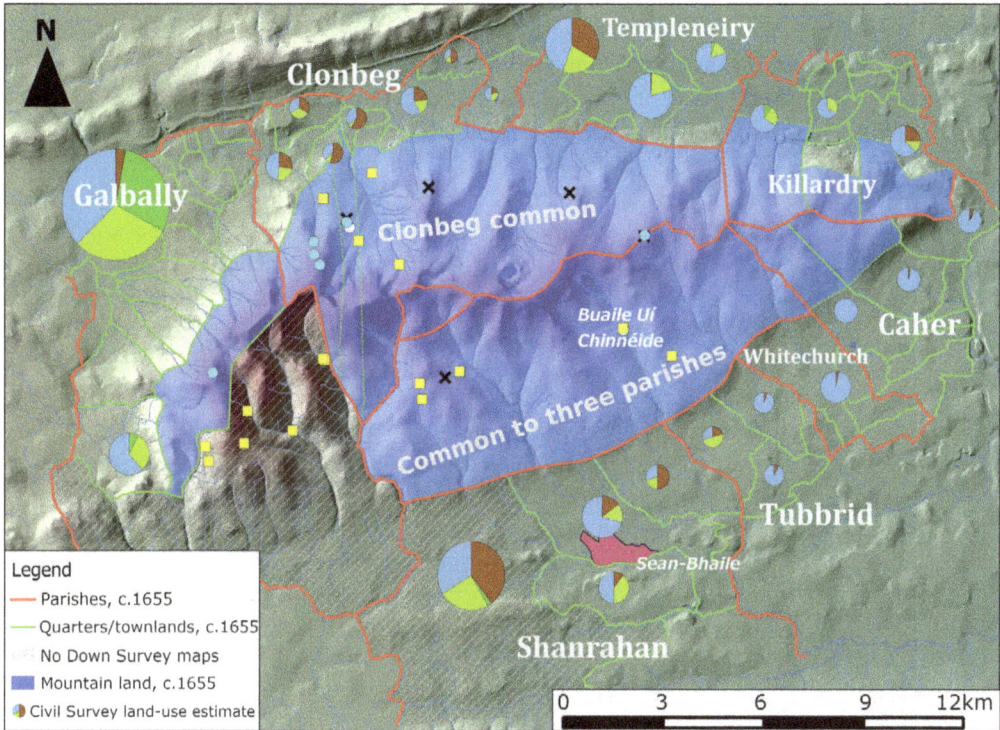

Figure 5.5 The Galtee Mountains in *c.*1655, showing land-use and boundaries recorded in Civil and Down Surveys. Blue = arable; light green = pasture; dark green = meadow; brown = forest (moorland excluded).

and the south-east especially (Figure 5.5). The significance of arable cultivation is also implied in the early seventeenth-century text *Pairlement Chloinne Tomáis*, which describes the plain of Cashel, little more than 10km to the north-east, as being under a *lear cruithneachta* or an 'ocean of wheat' (Williams 1981, 14). Widespread tillage would have left a lot of ground unavailable to cattle and other livestock from the time the crops were sown until their harvest near the end of summer, so here lay an added incentive for farmers to send livestock to the mountains. Accessing summer grazing there would have allowed them to keep more cattle than they would if just using the pasture around their main settlement.

Where available, the maps of the Down Survey also provide a fairly accurate guide to townland and parish boundaries in the early modern period (Figure 5.5). Comparing them with nineteenth-century townland and parish boundaries in Figure 5.1, it is clear that they differ in two main respects: first, the recorded units are fewer in number and larger, possibly because of smaller population densities; and, second, very few units extend upwards into the mountains, giving the latter a rather open appearance.[1]

---

[1] The extent of mountain land mapped in the Down Survey must be taken as an absolute minimum, as the Civil Survey makes mention of other, smaller areas within some townlands on the lower slopes that are not depicted on the Down Survey.

Much of the southern Galtees form one large block shared by the parishes of 'Shancreheene [Shanrahan], Whitechurch, and Raghill [Rehill, i.e. Tubbrid]' according to the Down Survey map of 1656. Considering that this was not due to any uniformity of ownership at the time (each parish had a different landowner; Simington 1931, 362–70, 373–76), the map may be hinting at some degree of mutual understanding between the three parishes. This probably amounted to a system of commonage in which the inhabitants of all three parishes were free to graze their animals on this block of mountain, akin, perhaps, to the situation in west Limerick in the 1580s, where the manor of Newcastle's 'free and customary tenants as well as the occupiers, of every kind' had common pasture in Sliabh Luachra (Chapter 2). Of course, within this large block, people would have in reality gravitated towards certain pastures year after year through tradition and the inevitable hefting of livestock. The steep valleys that divide up the southern side of the Galtees would, in any case, have hindered free movement of livestock. A similar situation prevails today among hill farmers who keep sheep on the mountain: although common grazing technically stretches all the way from Caher to the western extreme of the Galtees (Patsy King, pers. comm.), any one farmer will generally graze his sheep only on the section of mountain ground nearest his own farm.

The argument for a historic system of transhumance in the southern Galtees is lent support by a number of place-names. A recent article has discussed their role in reconstructing past transhumant systems in the south of Ireland and, while it found that their meaning can vary over time and space, they do form an important body of supporting information when the wider landscape history of an area is taken into account (Costello 2016c). Most significant here is the 'shanbally', or *sean-bhaile* place-name mentioned in 1667 and surviving as a modern townland in Shanrahan civil parish (*Abstracts of Grants and Lands*, 91; Figure 5.5). Meaning 'old home', *sean-bhaile* is a term that as early as the seventh and eighth centuries (Kelly 1997, 44) could be used to denote one's winter or permanent habitation. It is the rough equivalent of *hendref* in Wales – the opposite of *hafod*, or 'summer dwelling', in that country's system of medieval transhumance (see Davies 1984–85). The location of this *sean-bhaile* just over 2km south-east of the lower limit of seventeenth-century commons may point to the former existence here of a winter/permanent base for people in Shanrahan who were involved in seasonal movement to the mountains.

One valley that they or others south of the Galtees probably used is Boolakennedy, the original Irish form of which – *Buaile Uí Chinnéide* or 'O'Kennedy's Booley' – hints at a seasonal transhumant presence before permanent settlement becomes evident on the nineteenth-century map. Moreover, the stream running down Boolakennedy is referred to in the mid-seventeenth century as the 'brooke of Glaunary' (Simington 1931, 363), which may be an anglicisation of *Gleann Áirí*, or 'Valley of the Summer Milking-place'. Indeed, as discussed below, the remains of a hut and livestock pen near this stream may form the remnants of a phase of seasonal settlement and livestock management by or for the eponymous O'Kennedy. Furthermore, the Civil Survey calls the next valley to the east, at the eastern edge of Tubbrid civil parish, Glounbuollyneheneihy (Simington 1931, 363). This has been interpreted as an anglicisation of *Gleann Bhuaile na hInnighthe*, meaning 'Valley of the Booley of Retribution' (see Boolakennedy entry, Placenames Database of Ireland). However, it is much more likely to be an anglicised form of *Gleann Bhuaile na hAon Oíche*, 'Valley of the One-Night Booley' (Prof Nollaig Ó Muraíle, pers. comm.). In Scotland's Hebrides, the tale of the One-Night Shieling (*Àirigh na h-Aon Oidhche*) is very common in the body of oral tradition surrounding transhumance, and generally involves supernatural beings tricking and then murdering the occupants of a newly constructed summer shieling (Kupiec 2016, 394). Similar stories have been recorded about booleying in Connemara and west Mayo, though the present writer has not found any indication as yet that newly constructed sites attracted particular attention. This peculiar early modern place-name in the Galtees may therefore be explained as a relic of the story in Ireland, and as such it offers a rare insight into transhumance's role in the cultural landscape *before* the era of ethnographers. In any case, the 'buaile' element strongly suggests that Glounbuollyneheneihy was also used seasonally in the seventeenth century or earlier (although commercial forestry has destroyed any possible archaeological evidence of the 'one-night booley').

There are other indications of access to summer grazing in the Galtees at this time. Across the northern side of the range the Down Survey shows a large tract of common within the boundaries of one parish, Clonbeg, leaving smaller adjacent parishes to the east without an obvious means of accessing the mountain. The distribution of archaeological evidence suggests that seasonal relocation, if it took place, was mainly focused on the Drumleagh/Glencosh basin, which was within easy reach of permanent settlements in the west of the Glen of Aherlow. If people from Clonbeg decided to graze cattle further east along the common, as the Down Survey implies was their right, they may have done so in daytime, returning at night to the aforementioned basin where they were based. An alternative scenario is that they did not need to graze any further east. Costello (2015, 60) suggests that, because of the prevalence of woodland in the Glen of Aherlow in early modern times, there may in fact have been little need for people to engage in transhumance on this side of the Galtees. The Civil Survey makes clear that woodland was quite prominent in the 1650s (Simington 1931, 365–66, 374–76; 1934, 20, 21; 1938, 229), and in the late sixteenth century the area was estimated by English officials to contain over 12,000 hectares of forest (McCormack 2005, 35). Contemporary population levels to the north of the Galtees may therefore have been quite low, with the few agro-pastoralists in the area possibly making do with summer grazing in the woods, or the aforementioned basin. However, as shown above, there is evidence for possible anthropogenic fire events on the middle and higher mountain slopes at this time. The lack of an archaeological imprint remains a problem, but it would not be surprising if modern tree-planting on the more fertile lower slopes and along the western side of one particularly suitable valley leading up to Borheen Lough has now obscured the summer dwellings of these hypothetical herders. If people from adjoining parishes in the north, such as Templeneiry, had been able to access 'Clonbeg common' through some lease agreement, or if they did so freely before the mid-seventeenth century, they would probably have chosen to set up their summer dwellings in these more accessible areas.

COMMERCIALISED PASTORALISM AND THE 'IMPROVEMENT' OF UPLANDS

From the seventeenth century onwards the pastoral economy of the Limerick/Tipperary/Cork border area in mid-Munster seems to have developed stronger connections to international markets than did either south Connemara or south-west Donegal, where livestock rearing was primarily associated with the supply of local or national markets, such as the sale of young cattle to farmers in the midlands and east. Tenants and well-off graziers in the fertile lowlands around the Galtees were slightly better placed in terms of geography and environment, and, with cattle prices surging as a result of demand from Europe's cities and New World colonies, they now sought to give over more land to pasture (Cullen 1972, 52–56; Smyth 1985, 107–08; Whelan 2000, 191–94). It is clear that this shift came partly at the expense of arable farming. By the late 1770s Arthur Young (1780, 55) was able to declare that tillage in the Kingston-owned parishes of Kilbeheny and Templetenny 'extends no farther than what depends on potatoes, on which root they subsist as elsewhere', while neighbouring County Cork was described by Coquebert de Montbret in 1790 as *'presque tout en pâturage'* ('almost all in pasture'; quoted in Dickson 2005, 283). Although cattle production waned somewhat in the last two decades of the eighteenth century as a result of war-time demands for cereal and the Corn Laws (Dickson 2005, 283–88), the export of cattle recovered in the 1820s and a renewed decline in tillage is seen across the country (Jones 1995, 28–32).

In addition to a rise in beef prices, records show that the value of butter grew massively from the seventeenth century; indeed, the value of its annual export from Ireland to British America rose from only a few thousand pounds in 1683 to over £70,000 in 1777 (Nash 1985, table 1). Having the most suitable land in the country for large herds of dairy cows – that is, fertile soils slightly too heavy for intensive arable – and benefiting from a long grass-growing season, farmers in south Munster pivoted towards butter production. As a result, coastal urban centres such as Cork city and Youghal, situated 50km south of the Galtees, became major points of export in the trans-Atlantic provisions trade, while Limerick city, 50km to the north-west, controlled exports of butter to northern Europe (Rynne 1998; 2014, 25–28; Dickson 2005, 143–47; Downey 2014). Although the popularity of dairying peaked between 1750 and 1770 (Nash 1985, 193), the butter trade remained very important to the Irish and especially the Munster economy thereafter; in 1799–1803 it still accounted for some 45 per cent of all exports of farming produce (Crotty 1966, 279).

Farmers around the Galtees were deeply embedded in this system. In a practice that may have roots in earlier distributions of cattle (the so-called 'commyns'), head tenants and other middlemen would let out dairy cows – 'the chief stock' – to sub-tenants known as 'dairymen' (Young 1780, 56). These dairymen had to give the owner a hundredweight (just over 50kg) of the butter produced by each cow and also provide twelve to fifteen shillings' worth of labour or 'horn money' each year; but for every twenty cows the dairyman and his family looked after he 'had a privilege of four collops [the grazing of four cows], and an acre of land and cabbin' (Young 1780, 56). This system was already declining in the late 1770s as part of a wider 'democratization of cow ownership' across south Munster (Dickson 2005, 234–25); yet the importance of the cow remained. Sheep were kept 'in very small numbers' around the Galtees, although on the mountain itself there was apparently a small breed hardy enough to graze on furze and heath in winter as well as summer (Young 1780, 56). Their presence on rough pastures is generally less easy to track than that of cattle, but with the Civil Survey recording a tucking mill (for wool) in Rehill, to the south-east of the Galtee Mountains (Simington 1931, 374), it is likely that sheep had long formed an important, albeit secondary, component of grazing systems in the region. Indeed, two minor place-names in the far north of Kilbeheny civil parish suggest that the highest slopes were grazed by goats (*Binn Ghabhar* and *Gleann na nGabhar*; Costello 2016a, 203, 208–09).[2]

The commercialisation of beef and dairy production around the Galtees had mixed implications for common grazing in the mountains. On the one hand, the declining extent of grain crops in the late seventeenth and eighteenth centuries arguably made it less critical to remove cattle from the lowlands during the summer months. On the other, one could hypothesise that, as farmers were now involved in a system that expected surplus creation, they would have tried to make even *greater* use of mountain pasture in summer, as it would have allowed them to close off more ground as meadow (and therefore winter more animals). Incidentally, haymaking seems to have been more common in south Munster by the eighteenth century than in either Connemara or Donegal; however, as dedicated winter housing for cattle was rare (Young 1780, 57; Dickson 2005, 233) the cattle were probably fed outdoors with hay cut from a large rick.[3]

Of course, the complex reality of the post-medieval landscape means that commercial production was not the only influencing factor. It was accompanied, first, by demographic change. Population growth was not quite as high in the Galtees area as in Carna, and it was certainly not as extreme as the growth experienced by communities in south-west Donegal. The wider extent of permanent human settlement in Munster's lowlands prior to the eighteenth century probably had a role in limiting subsequent expansion. Nonetheless, in the barony of Coshlea, County Limerick, there was an estimated increase of 100–200 per cent in the period 1732–1821, while Iffa and Offa West and Clanwilliam, County Tipperary, both saw increases of 201–300 per cent (Smyth 2012b, 15, fig. 2). These barony-level statistics probably mask higher growth rates locally around the Galtees: for instance, the population of Shanrahan civil parish is known to have trebled between 1766 and 1815 (Smyth 2012a, 385). Population growth eventually contributed to the expansion of permanent settlement, although this does not seem to have begun in earnest until the 1770s.

---

[2] Again, this echoes the evidence from Carna and also the MacGillycuddy's Reeks in Kerry (Weld 1807, 164).

[3] The practice of building one large conical rick of hay, or sometimes a long rectangular *síog*, in the haggard next to a farmhouse continued up to the mid-twentieth century in County Limerick on farms that did not have hay barns (Joyce 1949). In the previous century it would have been almost universal on haymaking farms given the absence of hay barns on tenant farms before the 1890s (Bell and Watson 2008, 54, 165).

When it did it was strongly linked to estate-driven improvement, which started over a century earlier than on the Connolly estate of south-west Donegal, and 150 years earlier than the Congested Districts Board's interventions in south Connemara. Improving measures were initially limited to low-lying farmland, perhaps in association with more intensive grazing and livestock management; in 1727, for example, head tenants on the Kingston estate in Templetenny and Kilbeheny civil parishes were required to fence all the outbounds of their farms, with quicksetting to follow (Smyth 1976, 37). In subsequent decades, according to the famous agriculturalist Arthur Young (1780, 60), who visited the Kingston estate in the late 1770s, trees were given to the tenantry for free in order to encourage planting. Young's writings capture the beginnings of organised improvement on mountain ground. Although he remarks of the area that 'the population is very great ... [and] the cabbins are innumerable' (Young 1780, 58), it is implied that the Galtee Mountains themselves were still free of permanent human settlement. Thus, he began a programme of soil improvement on a section of mountain that had been 'commonage to the adjoining farm', marking out several enclosures, clearing the ground of stone, paring and burning it, liming it and building two cabins (Young 1780, 173). His perspective on the labourers who carried out these works is revealing. Blaming them for the collapse of some of his banks, Young (1780) explains that 'the men, instead of knowing how to make a ditch were mountaineers, who scarcely knew the right end of a spade'. In other words, these people had no experience of tillage farming and probably knew the mountain as a pastoral landscape where they herded cattle and sheep. Following his advisor's lead, the landlord Kingston forced his tenants to 'take in' other parts of the mountain:

> The adjoining farms being out of lease, he had a power of doing what he pleased; I marked a road, and assigned portions of the waste on each side to such as were willing to form the fences in the manner prescribed, to cultivate and inhabit the land, allowing each a guinea towards his cabbin, and promising the best land rent free for three years, and the worst for five (Young 1780, 176).

Key here is the direction that they not only *cultivate* mountain land but *inhabit* it as well. Thus began a process in which year-round settlement and farming crept up the contours of the south-western and southern Galtee Mountains for approximately seventy years, gathering pace in the first few decades of the nineteenth century. Smyth (1976, 41) argues that a spike in the number of trees being planted in the barony of Iffa and Offa around 1815 can be equated with the most intensive period of field enclosure. In the same ground-breaking article, he showed that landlord policy in the early 1800s deliberately sought to deflect population pressure onto the poorest land in the Galtees so as to foster a burgeoning class of strong Catholic farmers in the lowlands (Smyth 1976, 43–46).

Comparing the extent of unenclosed mountain in the 1650s with what remained in 1840 (Figure 5.1 vs Figure 5.5),[4] I estimate that out of 16,200ha approximately

---

4   Calculating the total area of unenclosed mountain land for the 1650s required speculation for much of the south-west, which was not mapped at all in the Down

4000ha had been improved and/or enclosed. While the proliferation of tenants on what the Down Survey and later Arthur Young deemed 'unprofitable' mountain land would have boosted the rental income of Kingston and other landlords (especially now that they were circumventing the cow-owning middlemen with direct leases; Young 1780, 58–9; Smyth 1976, 41), it also clearly had implications for transhumance. In the first instance, permanent settlement expanded onto the most accessible and fertile areas of common pasture. People took advantage of the relatively fertile peaty gleys on lower slopes and the sides of valleys, improving their properties with liming and potato cultivation to such an extent that even soils between 200m and 300m a.s.l. are now today classified as acid brown earths (GSI Datasets Public Viewer). As these tenants in Kilbeheny, Templetenny and Shanrahan civil parishes pushed the limit of permanent settlement up the contours, transhumant herds would have had to be grazed at still higher altitudes, where the vegetation on peaty podzolic soils and blanket peat was less favourable. There is a noticeable contrast with lands outside the improving Kingston and O'Callaghan estates; here, the lower slopes and valleys have retained their peaty gley soil cover as a result of the less extensive and short-lived nature of upland colonisation.

Moreover, upland improvement would have greatly complicated pre-existing arrangements for accessing the mountain. In addition to there being 4000ha less common pasture, there were now, theoretically, a lot more potential claimants to what remained. Did new tenancies usurp the rights of older farmsteads in the lowlands to use the remaining mountain pasture, or did grazing rights accumulate? Smyth (1976, 38) and Dixon (2005, 243) both argue that the enclosure of common land – initially within lowland townlands and subsequently on the mountain – was one of the main aggravating factors in the emergence of Whiteboy violence in mid-Munster during the early 1760s. The seriousness of their reaction reflects the genuine loss that cattle-owning farmers on low-lying ground felt as a result of the disruption to transhumance. The exact details of their transformation to a more sedentary form of pastoralism are now irretrievable given that there is no detailed documentation about their previous use of summer upland commons. It may be that lowland farmers tried to offset the loss of distant rough grazing by switching entirely from winterage to haymaking, as that would have allowed more efficient use of grass at home (with the necessary extra labour provided by the herders, who were now staying put). At the same time, some lowland farmers may also have decided to pay the new tenants on the hills to take in dry cattle for them. From a documentary standpoint, then, the story of post-medieval pastoralism in south-west Tipperary and south-east Limerick is one of intensification linked to market trends and sedenterisation linked to enclosure and upland improvement.

Survey. A hypothetical border was followed along the base of the mountain range, meeting the attested borders at both ends.

TENANT AGENCY AND ADAPTATION

This last section refines and corrects the trends that I and others have discerned by means of documentary research. It uses a combination of oral history, archaeology and nineteenth-century cartographic evidence to show that the new generation of small hill tenants were *also* agents of landscape change, and even developed a form of seasonal movement and settlement that was specific to their changing environment.

Making a new upland

The extent of agricultural improvement becomes clearer if we look at Knocknascrow and the townlands immediately south of it in 1840 (Figure 5.6). Over the previous eighty or ninety years the boundary of mountain pasture had been pushed gradually upwards. The name of a low hill in Carrow, almost a kilometre south-west of that townland's boundary with Knocknascrow, bears witness to this changing landscape. Known as Knockawhannia, an anglicisation of *Cnoc an Bhainne* ('Hill of the Milk'), it was clearly once part of the open mountainside where summer dairying took place. Moreover, the Tithe Applotment Books of 1831 do not include an entry for Knocknascrow as they do for Carrow and its other neighbours to the south, an omission that probably indicates that it had yet to be officially organised into a townland because it had so few year-round inhabitants. Further east in the Galtees most leases in the mountainous north of Templetenny date back only to *c.*1810 (Landed Estates' Court, Kingston). The lack

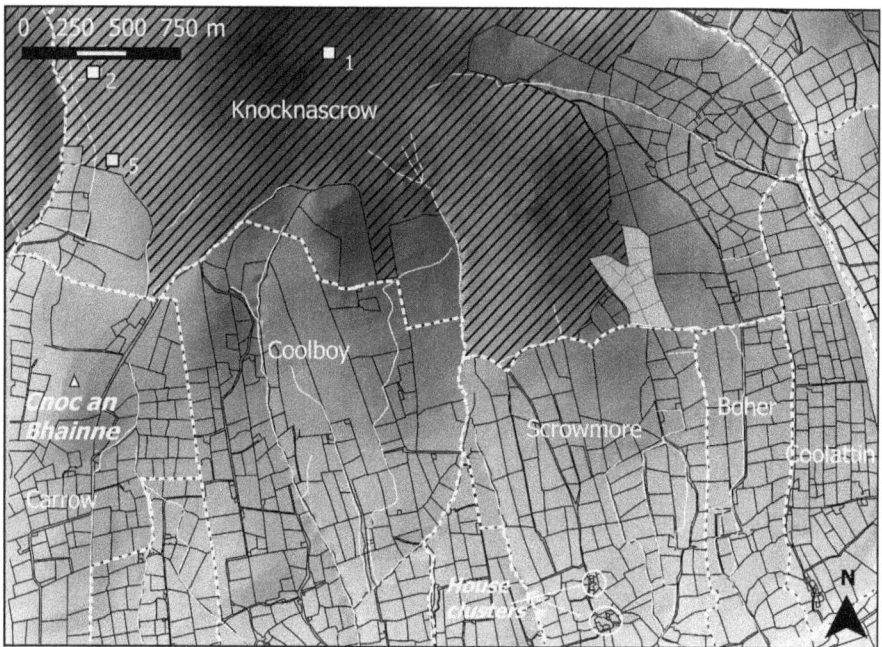

Figure 5.6 Field patterns associated with upward expansion of permanent settlement in Kilbeheny civil parish. (Basemap adapted from first edition six-inch OS, 1841).

of references in the place-name record to human settlement (other than that related to herding) supports the idea that year-round habitation was recent. As Smyth (1976, 45) has pointed out, the townland names of the Galtees instead tend to describe topographic or ecological aspects of the landscape, such as Cullenagh/*An Chuileannach* ('The Place of Holly'), Carrigeen Mountain/*Sliabh an Charraigín* ('Mountain of the Little Rock') and Knocknagalty/*Cnoc na nGaibhlte* ('Hill of the Galtees').

Landlord-encouraged expansion into these areas meant that tenants had to alter their view of the mountains from that of an open pastoral landscape to one where they now had to live on a permanent basis within fields that could be cultivated. Renegotiating the meaning of these landscapes in reality involved a lot of back-breaking work: digging ditches, hauling limestone up from lower ground, building lime kilns to burn and spread the lime, beginning potato cultivation and, of course, setting up house. In this last respect they had to deal with pre-existing booley sites that lay in the path of improvement. These are very difficult to identify archaeologically, for obvious reasons, but a few candidates have been identified. The aforementioned 'O'Kennedy's Booley' area was encroached upon significantly in pre-Famine years, with various houses and planned fields marked on the 1840 Ordnance Survey sheet (see Figure 6.2). Field survey in this landscape led to the discovery of two unmarked structures at the confluence of Gleann Áirí and another stream. One is a small rectangular house structure, stone-built (but without visible coursing) and measuring 5.4m × 3.5m externally and 3.9m × 1.7m internally (Boolakennedy 2). A roughly rectangular enclosure (10.3m × 3.4m) was found under a bluff near the smaller tributary stream (Boolakennedy 1); it may have acted as a pen for mountain sheep or for calves that needed to be separated from their mothers at night. This isolated pair of structures may represent all that is left of an earlier (seasonal) occupational phase in the Boolakennedy/Glengarra valley. Similarly, the Carrigeen Mountain 1 site is found at 402m a.s.l. in a remote valley colonised for a few decades in the nineteenth century (see Figure 5.9). Considering it is just 3.3m × 1.6m internally, and made of coursed stone, rubble and sods, it may be a booley hut that fell out of occupation (or was reused briefly as a year-round house) when this stretch of valley was improved.

On the open, unenclosed mountainside only two sites are likely to pre-date the larger, well-built booley houses found in Knocknascrow, Coolagarranroe and the Drumleagh/Glencosh basin. These are the oval and sub-rectangular sod-and-stone structures of Knocknagalty (discussed in Costello 2016c, 93–94; see Figure 5.7) and possibly also a sub-rectangular sod hut in Cloheenfishoge measuring 2.6m × 1.4m internally (Cloheenfishoge 1, Tubbrid civil parish). An earlier construction date is suggested for Knocknagalty 1–3 because of the low height of their mainly sod walls, which, again, may have been to allow for an undifferentiated wattle superstructure; their curved form is also clearly at odds with eighteenth- and nineteenth-century houses attested in permanent settings (see next section). Finally, it is significant that they occur in a small group, as nucleation is not a feature of rural settlement around the Galtees during the nineteenth century (but may have been in preceding centuries; see Chapter 6). It is not clear how far into the era of improvement, if at all, these structures were occupied.

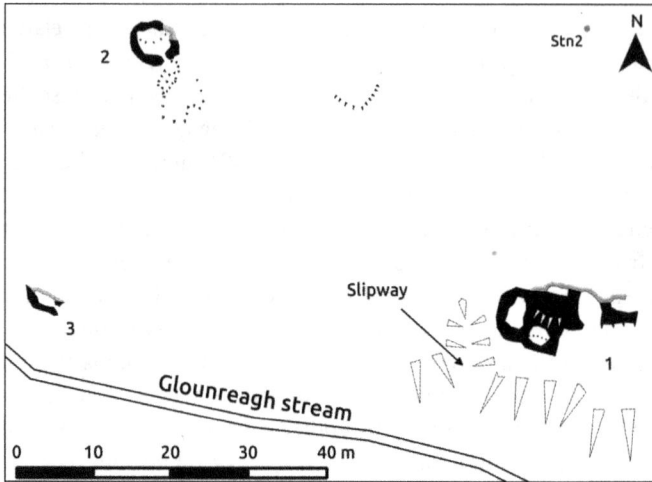

Figure 5.7 Plan of Knocknagalty 1–3.

Peat and butter: a final phase of summer settlement, 1770–1860

As hard-pressed tenants repurposed the landscape with the help of landlord rental incentives, they also expressed a degree of innovation. Encouraged by their own recognition of economic trends, they began to exploit the resources now at their doorstep. One non-agricultural resource was the blanket peat that covered the plateaus above 500m and 600m in the Galtees. Today, many disused trackways run up the slopes towards these bogs, where peat-cutting was continued by hill farmers until the middle of the twentieth century (Lewis 1985, 36; Patsy King, pers. comm.; Figure 5.8). Given that these tracks are often deeply rutted into the landscape and adopt a zig-zag course on reaching steeper ground, their main function seems to have been to aid the transportation of heavy loads of peat downhill.[5] After being left to dry *in situ* over summer, peat could have been used as fuel in the household and for burning limestone in kilns, and sold to tenant farmers on lower ground who no longer had a reliable supply of timber fuel. The fact that Young does not mention turbary in his description of the area suggests that this minor industry did not take off until a permanent tenant population had become established in the uplands. Of course, cattle, sheep and goats may also sometimes have walked along the peat tracks, but only on an opportunistic basis – restricting them to such well-defined paths would not have served a purpose for herders when they were already on the open mountain.

Where grazing of the livestock was concerned, hill farmers were clearly excluded from the best land within their landlords' estates. Specialisation in bullock rearing for beef was unfeasible on their small lots. Dairying, however, was something that they would have been involved in in any case as part of subsistence. Seasonal exploitation of the rough pastures that were still to be found higher and deeper in the Galtees

---

[5]   In the twentieth century, and probably earlier, batches of peat were dragged down the steepest slopes by donkeys pulling wooden sleds (Lewis 1985, 36).

Figure 5.8 Trackway in Rossadrehid townland, Templeneiry civil parish. Note modern afforestation.

allowed them to keep enough cows to produce surplus milk, which could then be churned into butter and sold for cash. This situation was exploited by tenants through a new system of small-scale booleying, of which, rather unusually for the south of Ireland, living memories were recorded (Ó Danachair 1945, 250). Michael Cunningham, from Knocknascrow in Kilbeheny parish, relates that he participated in booleying in Knocknascrow as a child and passed on an invaluable account of the practice as it operated just before its final demise. Among other things he says that, until *c.*1875, cattle were driven up to the mountain pasture (known as the *buaile*) of Knocknascrow each year around the middle of April, and that young – or occasionally old – people would stay in houses at the *buaile* until the start of November to look after the herd, milk the dairy cows and churn the milk into butter. This butter was brought down from the mountain in firkins every now and then so that it could be sold in Mitchelstown, County Cork.

   The archaeological remains of four of these *buaile* houses are found in the peaty northern reaches of Knocknascrow. They were located with the help of Michael Cunningham's grandson, John (who also recognised them as former summer dwellings). There is also one roughly circular drystone-walled structure at the summit of Temple Hill in the far north of the townland (Knocknascrow 6), though its very isolated location at 781m a.s.l. and its small internal diameter of 1.5m suggest that it was used as a shelter rather than a booley house. The distribution pattern of sites found during fieldwork confirms the oral historical evidence that Michael Cunningham gave Ó Danachair (1945, 250): namely, that the booley houses were widely spaced,

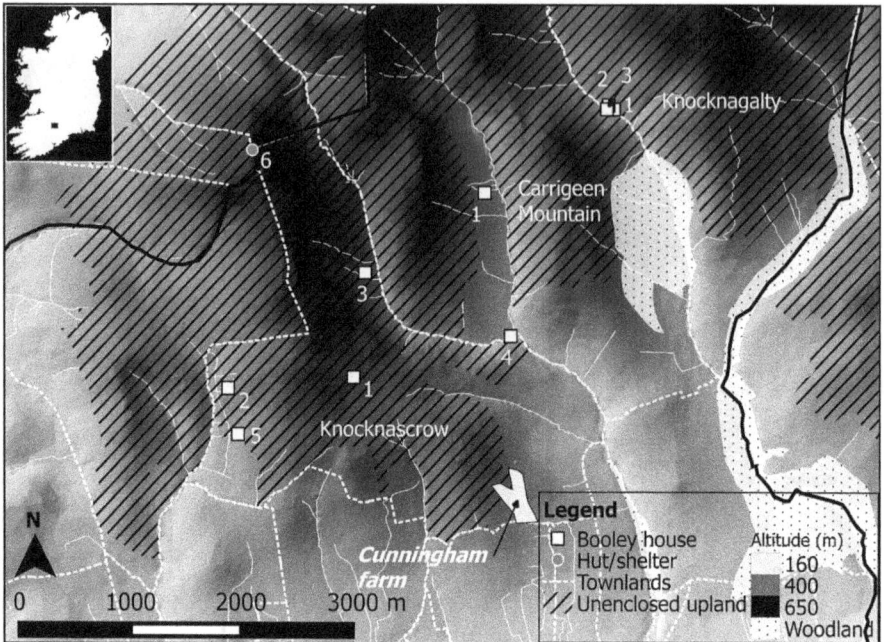

Figure 5.9 Map of south-west Galtees *c.*1840 showing sites identified in Knocknascrow, Carrigeen Mountain and Knocknagalty townlands (numbered accordingly).

leaving the young herders stationed at them feeling 'kind of lonely sometimes' (Figure 5.9). The significance of this distribution in contrast to other distribution patterns in Irish seasonal settlement will be discussed in Chapter 6, as it has implications for how we interpret pre-modern social organisation across the country. Nevertheless, communality was certainly still a feature of nineteenth-century booleying in the Galtees, Michael Cunningham remembering that he and the others would meet up 'to have a dance or some other fun'.

With the exception of Knocknascrow 5 – which survives only on the first edition six-inch Ordnance Survey map – all of Knocknascrow's booley dwellings are clearly of the well-built, coursed-stone rectangular type mentioned earlier in the chapter. Knocknascrow 1, 2 and 4 are roughly the same size, ranging from 5.4m × 3.7m to 6.4m × 3.4m internally (Figures 5.4, 5.10), while Knocknascrow 3 is slightly smaller, at 4.6m × 2m internally (Figure 5.11). Other examples of this well-built rectangular type are found a few kilometres east of Kilbeheny, still in what would have been the Kingston estate, on the upper slopes of Coolagarranroe townland, while the north-western basin of the Galtees contains at least two more – Drumleagh 1 and Glencoshabinnia 1. Two out of the nine houses listed feature a second, smaller room *within* their overall rectangular plan and another two have external annexes, possibly dedicated to butter storage.

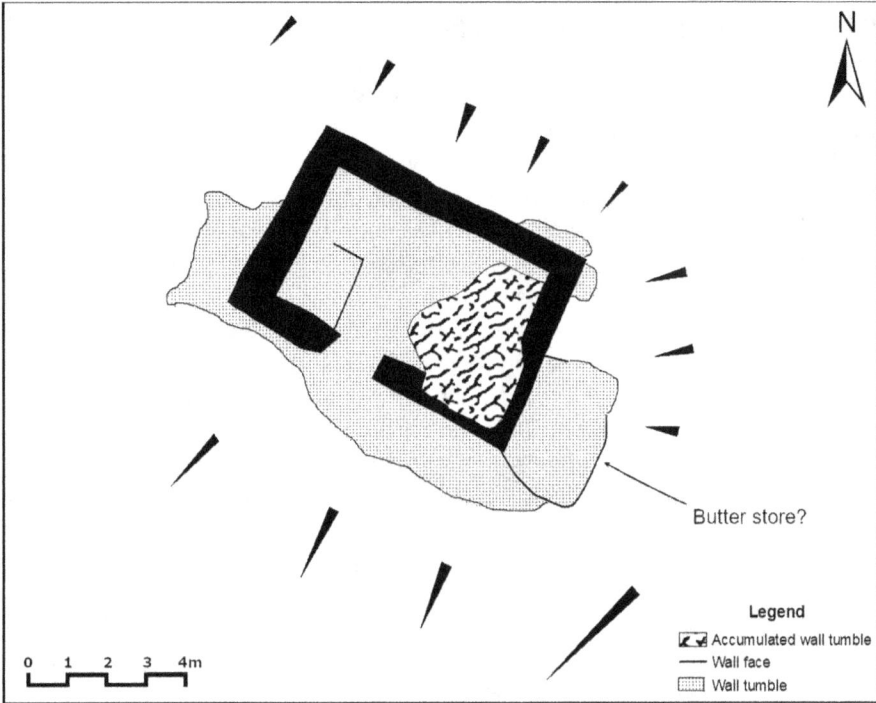

Figure 5.10 Plan of Knocknascrow 2, with possible butter store at the south-east end.

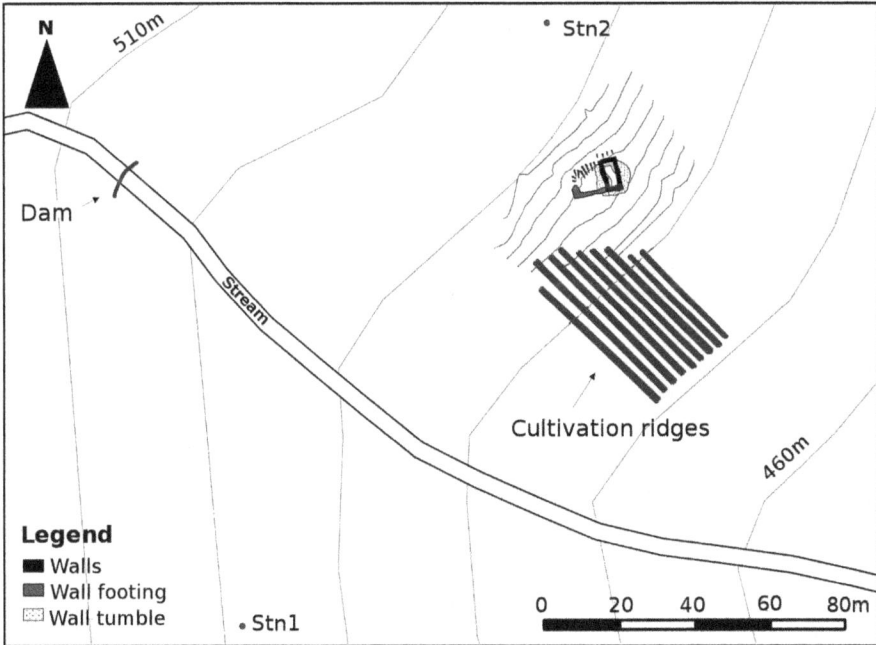

Figure 5.11 Plan of Knocknascrow 3 and its landscape.

Dating and distinguishing late booley houses

These substantial rectangular structures are relatively small in number compared with huts found in the Carna peninsula, Achill and the Mourne Mountains. However, this is an essential part of their story. They represent a late and short-lived phase of seasonal settlement that was designed to take full advantage of the butter trade, and, as peat became an important fuel, they may also have been frequented by adult males on their way to and from the bogs. As excavation has not taken place at any of the Galtees' probable seasonal sites, it is not possible to support this claim of late construction with absolute dates. Nevertheless, the structures just described undeniably share basic similarities with the farmhouses of hill tenants, which we know were built in either the late eighteenth or the early nineteenth century. Both forms of dwelling are rectangular in plan and both are fairly well built in that they contain coursed masonry and pointed corners. In addition, the presence of small patches of cultivation outside four of these ruined *buaile* houses – Knocknascrow 3, Coolagarranroe 1 and 2 and Drumleagh 4 – all but confirms *occupation* in the eighteenth and nineteenth centuries. As Cunningham recalls, 'they used to plant potatoes up on the mountain near the buaile [in May] ... and it would be nearly November when they dug the last of the potatoes on the mountain' (Ó Danachair 1945, 250).

At the same time, there are features that allow us to distinguish between the well-built rectangular booley houses and their permanent counterparts. Individual stones are more precisely cut and fitted in farmhouses, and lime mortar is often visible in their stonework, whereas it is never seen in booley houses and huts. There are differences in size, too. The Cunningham house in Knocknascrow – occupied since the first edition six-inch Ordnance Survey map was drawn in 1841 – has overall dimensions of 13.5m × 5.5m and internal dimensions of 11.5m × 3.8m (Figure 5.13). An abandoned farmhouse established before 1841 in the south-east of Knocknagalty measures 12m × 5.5m overall and contains two rooms (see Costello 2016c, Plate II). Hundreds of other pre-Famine farmhouses survive on the slopes of the Galtees, and measurements of how they appear on six-inch maps and Digital Globe satellite imagery show clearly that they were nearly all 10–14m in length – that is, at least 2m longer than the largest booley houses.[6] A tiny number of permanent dwellings, located near the upper limit of improved land, are as small as booley houses. One example is found in the west of Knocknagalty (only 200m south-east of Knocknagalty 1–3). However, even this house is fairly easy to pick out as occupied on a year-round basis. The structure measures only 5m × 5m overall, but its walls survive to a height that would be abnormal at a seasonal site: this is the result of lime mortar and well-dressed stones being used in its construction (Figure 5.12). Moreover, it is associated with a small outhouse, rectangular enclosures, a tall, planted tree and at least one sizeable area of cultivation ridges (70m × 30m). The larger farmhouse in south-eastern Knocknagalty is contained within a large rectangular enclosure outlined by

---

[6] This excludes small cottages, which would not have been involved in transhumance. In any case, these were found to be a rarity on the slopes of the Galtees compared with the surrounding lowlands, where they occur frequently on roadsides.

Figure 5.12 The core of a small isolated farmstead in Glounreagh valley, Knocknagalty.

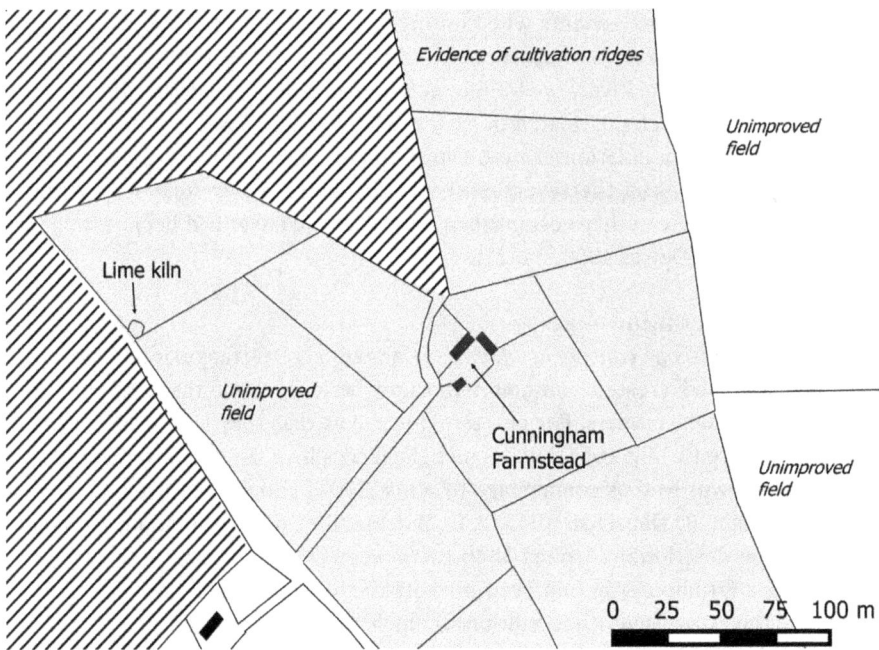

Figure 5.13 Cunningham farm, Knocknascrow. (first edition six-inch OS; Griffith's Valuation).

tall coniferous trees, with a very large area of ridges in the adjoining fields (300m × 100m, at least), while the Cunningham farmhouse has a similar level of complexity, as well as two outhouses. Lime kilns are also located within a few hundred metres of most upland farmhouses (Figure 5.13).

The construction and landscape context of pre-Famine farmhouses permit their distinction from booley houses, therefore. At the same time, it remains true that those booley houses greater than 5m in overall length, rectangular in shape and constructed with coursed masonry have no closer parallel in the local archaeological record than these farmhouses. It is speculated here, therefore, that booley houses of this type were built not only in the post-medieval period but probably in the period after c.1770 and before the Great Famine: that is, just as these farmhouses began to appear on the Galtees' slopes. This would make sense in the context of contemporary settlement expansion. It is not implausible that, as rough pasture was encroached upon across the southern Galtees, many pre-existing booley sites fell out of use or were converted into permanent dwellings. This has already been highlighted in the context of relict place-names (in Boolakennedy and south-west Clare), but in Counties Galway and Donegal there are even stronger parallels for the replacement of seasonal settlement with permanent settlement during the eighteenth and nineteenth centuries (see Chapter 6). For the Galtee Mountains I hypothesise that in the seventeenth and early eighteenth centuries, there were seasonally occupied structures at lower altitudes than today. A rare survival of that phase is possibly to be found in Knocknagalty, where sites 1–3 seem at odds with most of the rest of the archaeological evidence. After a tide of settlement expansion had subsumed much of this landscape, those tenants who continued to engage in transhumance would have needed to construct new seasonal dwellings at higher altitudes; these may be represented by the relatively well-built rectangular stone structures discussed. A similar model has been postulated in Wales, where place-names and historic maps both indicate that population growth caused many *hafod* sites to be colonised on a permanent basis from the seventeenth century onwards; *lluestau* sites found at higher altitudes were perhaps established only after the latter had been turned into year-round farms (Davies 1980, 24–25).

Flexibility of commonage

The evolving landscape context in which the Galtees' large rectangular booley houses were required and created contains important lessons about the adaptability of marginalised tenant farmers. For one thing, it shows that they kept their notion of common pasture flexible over time. Cunningham recalls of the 1850s and 1860s that 'the mountain was held as commonage by a number of people who lived at the foot of the mountain' (Ó Danachair 1945, 250). But the 'foot of the mountain' makes for quite a vague description. Around 1840 there were fourteen separate tenant farms (containing a farmhouse) in improved pockets of the south-east and south-west of Knocknascrow townland (first edition six-inch Ordnance Survey map; Griffith's Valuation, 1848–64). Of these, judging from the Griffith's Valuation of 1852, seven meared on the open mountain – one being the Cunningham's own 8.5ha holding

(Figures 5.6, 5.9).[7] However, there were at least four occupied holdings in Carrow, Coolboy and Scrowmore immediately to the south that also shared a boundary with 'the mountain' – and that is not to mention dozens of other small farm units on former rough pasture in these townlands, which by then had been locked into an enclosed farmscape thanks to continuing upland improvement at higher altitudes. How many of these tenants had grazing rights on 'the mountain' of Knocknascrow, given that only four booley houses could be found archaeologically? The only concrete conclusion to be drawn from the sparse available evidence is that only tenants such as the Cunninghams, who were mearing on the open mountain, had guaranteed access.

In addition, other tenants may have been able to graze their livestock there through agreements with their neighbours. This is not implausible given the herd sizes Cunningham mentions: 'from twenty to forty cattle each one would have on the mountain' (Ó Danachair 1945, 250). Even the relatively decent-sized hill farm of the Cunninghams in Knocknascrow was too small to over-winter a herd of that magnitude, notwithstanding the probable slaughter or sale of some young cattle at the end of autumn. Moreover, the relatively large internal areas of Knocknascow 1 ($20m^2$), 2 ($23m^2$) and 4 ($18.6m^2$) could have slept between eight and eleven adolescents each; and even Knocknascrow 3's $9.2m^2$ could have accommodated as many as four young individuals.[8] This raises the possibility that each booley house contained children from several different farms, bringing with them cows and calves in order to form larger herds of twenty to forty cattle. How these numbers were decided in the Galtees is far from clear, not least because there is no evidence of rundale farming here during the nineteenth century. It is possible that the landlord or his representative acted as a mediator in these situations, as the local brehon did in Gleann Cholm Cille. Regardless, Cunningham's repeated use of the word *comaointeas* – a local variant of *comaoin*, meaning 'favour' or 'recompense' (Ó Dónaill 1977) – to describe booleying strongly suggests a basic mutual understanding among tenants (Ó Danachair 1945, 250). Its use also hints at the fact that Irish was the vernacular of at least 83 per cent of the population of Knocknascrow electoral division in 1845 (FitzGerald 2003, 236), and probably all the tenant farmers and herders who were concerned with booleying. Thus the renegotiation of commonage and summer settlement during the late eighteenth and early to mid-nineteenth centuries must have been played out to some degree in informal verbal situations that went unrecorded at an elite, English-speaking level.

Yet the informality that characterised *comaointeas* also facilitated tenants who wished to mark off certain parts of the mountain as their own private pastures. Detail available

---

[7]   Although this survey post-dates the Great Famine – an event that caused population in the Knocknascrow Electoral Division (Knocknascrow and adjoining southern townlands) to drop by 31.56 per cent by 1851, compared with 1841 levels (Famine Atlas and Historical Population Statistics) – the effect on farm boundaries does not seem to have been nearly as disastrous. Most holdings still contained no more than one house in the Valuation, which suggests that, if some had been abandoned and taken over by other tenants, their boundaries were preserved.

[8]   As with Mín na Saileach, this calculation is based on a sleeping space of $1.5–2m^2$, leaving additional space for a hearth and storage of dairying equipment.

in Griffith's Valuation and its accompanying maps give a glimpse as to how this was achieved. They show that unoccupied sections of mountain along the southern boundary of Knocknascrow were being enclosed by adjacent tenants, in some cases jointly. Among these are 16ha just west of the Cunningham farm that were held by the latter and two neighbouring tenants; this land was subsequently marked off with an earthen bank, as the first edition twenty-five-inch Ordnance Survey map illustrates. This process is even clearer in the townland of Glencoshabinnia in Clonbeg civil parish. Several sections of mountain pasture in 1851 were held by adjacent tenants, sometimes jointly by brothers and sometimes individually. For example, one small chunk of twenty-two statute acres valued at five shillings was being rented by John Shea from the landlord Rev. John Dawson. Its upper boundary is still marked off today by a straight earthen bank. These claims differed from enclosure of the lower mountain slopes in that improvement and colonisation were not the goals – now, tenants simply wanted exclusive access to the rough grazing nearest them, and presumably paid rent directly on this land for the luxury. Their doing so undermined the long-standing idea of mountain being 'held as commonage' (Ó Danachair 1945, 250) and contributed to the abandonment of summer dairy houses that depended on co-operative herding and use of pasture. Moreover, in Glencoshabinnia, Coolagarranroe and perhaps even Knocknascrow, the need for overnight stays at summer houses would have been negated at this stage by the very close proximity of the newest tenant farms (less than a kilometre). The end of Chapter 6 discusses the final cessation of seasonal pastoral movements in the Galtees and elsewhere in Ireland.

SUMMARY AND CONCLUSIONS

This chapter has focused on a mountain range in the south of Ireland that, up to the late nineteenth century, attracted seasonal settlement from the surrounding area. It has been shown that booley houses were used from April to October by children tasked with looking after their families' dairy cows on the mountain. Although these sites were not very far from tenant farmhouses of the nineteenth century, relocation was still deemed necessary because of the need for milking and churning, important activities providing butter that could be sold to the advantage of the families involved. Food supplies were bolstered in at least a few cases by the growing of potatoes at booley sites.

While seasonal relocation is remembered only in Knocknascrow, structures identified elsewhere seem likely to have been used in transhumant movements that came to a halt earlier, perhaps only a few decades previously. They are mostly found on the south-facing side of the Galtees and can be described as roughly rectangular drystone houses, occasionally with internal divisions. Other more ephemeral hut sites in exposed locations are interpreted as temporary shelters. With the exception of the Drumleagh/Glencoshabinnia basin in Clonbeg, there is little evidence to suggest that seasonal settlement took place in the valleys in the north of the Galtees – perhaps because of the prevalence of dense forest along the lower slopes and in the Glen of Aherlow up to the middle of the seventeenth century, but modern commercial forestry may also have played a role in obscuring archaeological evidence.

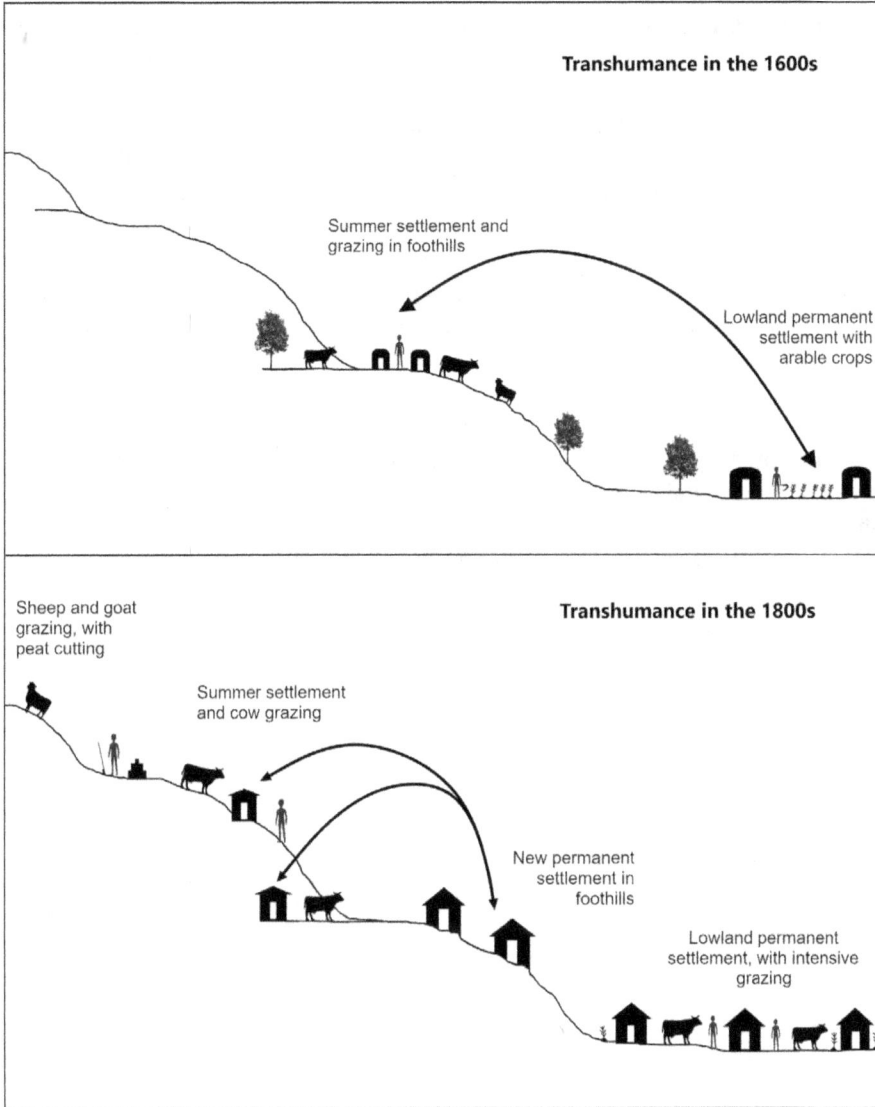

Figure 5.14 Representation of landscape and settlement in the Galtee Mountains during the seventeenth and nineteenth centuries.

While there is no direct historical data on transhumance in the study area prior to the nineteenth century it is very likely that the roots of small-scale booleying by tenants in Knocknascrow and other townlands lie in earlier centuries. This is based partly on the fact that transhumance was commonly practised in similar areas of the country before the nineteenth century and partly on place-names and the nature of land boundaries and land use in the mid-seventeenth century. Much more of the Galtee

Mountains was available for common grazing at this time and farmers needed to use it as a result of the popularity of tillage. In turn, this arrangement may have allowed lowland farmers to rely on winterage rather than labour-intensive hay, a form of fodder that was uncommon until the nineteenth century.

This whole system, however, experienced major changes over the following two centuries. The altitude of the Galtees was exploited by landlords over the course of the eighteenth and nineteenth centuries, first as a release valve for demographic pressure in fertile lowlands and secondly as a means of generating more rent income from butter production. But the people who actually improved the slopes with their spades and maintained malleable systems of commonage were participants in this change. They took advantage of rental incentives when they painstakingly altered the physical properties of mountainous soil and built new permanent dwellings; and, as those incentives expired, they expressed their own agency in landscape change by exploiting the untouched higher ground. Tenants in Knocknascrow and neighbouring townlands broke in and maintained upland routes to the high-altitude peat bogs and, through a short-lived final phase of seasonal settlement, developed a means of maximising their income from dairy cows and the butter trade (Figure 5.14).

CHAPTER 6

HERDERS AND HISTORICAL
FORCES, 1600–1900

This chapter discusses the evolving nature of seasonal movement and settlement in the three study areas in the context of major social, demographic and economic trends that set in from the seventeenth century. It examines the role of elites, first of all, and demonstrates how their level of concern with the management of upland pastures and cattle not only changed over time but varied across Ireland. In doing so, it provides a timely regional characterisation of the socio-political power structures in which subaltern peasant farmers practised transhumance over the course of the post-medieval period. With that in mind, it is possible to explore their adaptive capacity as population and land-use pressures became more noticeable in the Irish landscape. The (re)organisation or cessation of seasonal movements and the encroachment of farmers on upland commons all provide subtle indicators of interaction with these trends, and above all how people dealt with and contributed to them at a local landscape level.

Yet transhumance in this period does not simply echo wider historical processes. It also contains a hidden history of non-elite rural society. Thus the chapter examines the pragmatic approach to dwelling shown by herders as they made a seasonal home out of the hills, considering environmental as well as chronological factors in the morphology of booley sites and comparing their layout with that of contemporary permanent settlements. Furthermore, it highlights the role of transhumance in reproducing the socio-cultural structure of rural communities from generation to generation, particularly through delegation of upland herding tasks to young girls and women. The gender- and age-specific nature of participation in seasonal removals by the nineteenth century was, however, partly related to changes in market demand that tenant farmers became cognisant of. I therefore examine how the currents of capitalism changed livestock farming in uplands – in some cases conflicting with the idea of transhumance, in others encouraging it. The chapter's last section reveals how the disruption of customary grazing rights and elite-induced reorganisation of estates contributed to the final decline of seasonal movement.

THE ROLE OF THE ELITE IN CHANGING RURAL SOCIAL STRUCTURES

The Gaelic and Hiberno-Norman elites exerted significant influence over how transhumance operated before the mid-seventeenth century. For the Carna peninsula, the local Uí Fhlaithbheartaigh lords would have been more concerned with where cattle were taken than were later landowners because of the practice of 'commyns' (from *commaín*, meaning 'equal wealth'), in which Gaelic lords had their subjects mind cattle in return for protection (Graham 1970b, 148; Nicholls 1987, 415). The significance of cattle ownership to the Gaelic elite is highlighted by a nickname given to one of the Uí Fhlaithbheartaigh: Murchadh na mart, or Murchadh 'of the cattle', who was dispossessed after the 1641 rebellion (Naessens 2009, 82, 270). Even in Hiberno-Norman areas, lords seem to have held large numbers of cattle: in June 1580 John Fitz Edmonds of Cloyne, Co. Cork, had '3,000 head of great cattle' taken from him by rebels aligned with the earl of Desmond (*CSPI* II, 226).

Hunting associations

But there was another practice that may have drawn lords into contact with transhumance: hunting. This activity was an indicator of high status in both medieval Gaelic and Anglo-Norman society (Murphy and O'Conor 2006; FitzPatrick 2013; Beglane 2015) and, with red deer and wolves taking refuge in areas of low population density, it is likely that they were pursued in similar landscapes to those used for extensive summer grazing. For example, Roderic O'Flaherty refers in 1684 to the quality of hunting in the Carna peninsula (Hardiman 1846, 9, 95). An account from the very end of the century, but probably applicable to pre-Cromwellian times, reveals how transhumance and hunting may have been connected through the contemporary lifestyle of the elite. In 1699 John Dunton visited a 'booley or summer habitation' in the east of Iar-Chonnacht that he says was set up by an O'Flaherty whose 'proper dwelling or mansion house [was] neare the sea' (MacLysaght 1939, 344). Treated to a feast of various meats and drink, as well as brought out to hunt deer, Dunton appears to have stayed in some sort of elite booley house-cum-hunting lodge. Archaeological evidence for such sites has not been identified in this study. Some booley houses are larger than others, of course, but excavation is really required to uncover evidence of high-status feasting.

All the same, Dunton's association of the 'booley' with elite hunting practices is fascinating, as it raises the question of governance. Did lords exercise control over transhumant movements when hunts took place in the same marginal areas? Did they reserve certain tracts for game, or were hunts integrated with the seasonal movements of people and stock? In the eastern Cairngorms, and in other parts of Scotland, some mountainous ground was reserved exclusively for hunting up to the eighteenth century (Dixon 2009, 39–40). Anglo-Norman parks established in Ireland during the thirteenth century had well-defined boundaries too, although, owing to scarcities in fallow deer – a species introduced by the Normans – it seems that many were used for the pasturing of livestock rather than actual hunting (Beglane 2015, 69–72, 116–19). Ultimately, large hunting reserves were not a success in the Irish landscape. There are no documented parks in Anglo-Norman territory around the Galtee Mountains, and most of those found in Leinster became defunct during the fourteenth century (Beglane 2015, 161–62). This is what led Fynes Moryson and Arthur Young to remark at the start and end of the seventeenth and eighteenth centuries, respectively, on the scarcity and smallness of Irish deer parks (Falkiner 1904, 222; Young 1780, 236–37).

In parts of Ireland that *had* remained under Gaelic control in the later medieval period there is no evidence that enclosed parks were ever created. Instead, FitzPatrick (2013, 95–118) argues that hunts of native red deer took place across the open countryside, terminating at bare-topped hills associated with a valley or plain. These hills often bear the toponym *formaoil* or *formáel*, one of which occurs as a townland name in the civil parish of Kilcummin, County Galway. Recorded in *BSD Galway* (65) as 'Two Cartrons of Mountain ... belonging to the ½ Qu^r of Tullybreda', it was probably used in the seventeenth century as a summer pasture by distant farms to the north-east, like most of inland Kilcummin. Here, then, it seems that elite hunting of wild animals took place at or very near a location that was important for transhumant pastoralism. Similar categorical examples are lacking in this book's study areas because of the unpredictability of both place-names and historical sources; however, some sharing of the landscape was inevitable given the tendency towards hunting in the open countryside (eventually practised by Hiberno-Norman noblemen too; Beglane 2015, 72). As such, the hunting prerogatives of elites in Ireland do not seem to have stood in opposition to grazing rights as they did in late- and post-medieval Scotland (Dixon 2009).

At the same time, having established that elite hunting took place in uplands and other 'marginal' landscapes, there are barriers to teasing out the exact nature of its influence on summer grazing. For one thing, hunting can take place during the winter as well as summer; and transhumant herds were obviously not going to be disturbed if it were the former, Furthermore, no one hunt could have lasted longer than a day, and either long breaks or fresh hunting grounds were required to give deer populations a chance to recover. Dunton's account, for all its richness, is therefore somewhat frustrating. It does not state how long the house was occupied for apart from the fact that it was a summer habitation, and it makes no reference to herders or lower-class booley sites in the vicinity. At best, it hints that the presence of elites on rough hill pastures was more pronounced and formalised in native lordships than on later landed estates. Elite hunting did not cease in the eighteenth and nineteenth centuries, but there were serious declines in numbers of red deer and wolves as a result of deforestation and the expansion of farming and settlement (Harris and Yalden 2008, 424, 579). The extinction of these wild mammalian fauna in most or all of the island undoubtedly contributed to the situation that prevailed by the Famine period, wherein marginal landscapes had become the domain of small tenant farmers pasturing their (own) livestock seasonally and cutting peat for use as fuel. There was no longer any hint of elite association with these activities.[1] Thus, when competition for space and resources in uplands and boglands became a factor in Ireland, it was farming and the growing rural population that unquestionably won, at the expense of the country's remaining large mammalian fauna and the tradition of large-scale hunts in the open countryside.

---

[1] Indeed, as early as 1744, booleying was being described as poor people's practice in County Down (Smith and Harris 1744, 125).

The emergence of the landed estate

A monolithic system of landlordism became established over the whole country during the seventeenth century, replacing dynastic lordships that had their own identities and styles of rule (Jones-Hughes 1965; Whelan 1993, 205; Smyth 2006, 4–5). This did not simply represent a change in the people who held the land and wealth of the country; it was a clash of 'a privatised concept of landownership, on the one hand, and a family/clan-based concept of landownership, on the other', an ideological barrier that ultimately exacerbated the levels of violence associated with the ethno-religious wars of the mid-seventeenth century (Smyth 2006, 127). In terms of transhumant patterns, it is doubtful if this ideological shift had a major impact on where people brought their livestock to graze seasonally. Excepting instances of population displacement or *caoraigheacht*, the Desmond Survey hints and the Down Survey shows that transhumance had a structure to it before landlordism was firmly established. There is no reason to believe that new landlords in the three study areas set out to tamper with these grazing rights in the *immediate* aftermath of the English conquest.

However, the establishment of the landed estate did bring about a subtle change in the relationship between small farmers and people higher up in society. For one thing, it turned the former (either individually or in groups) into lease-holding and rent-paying tenants (Cullen 1986, 166–67; Gillespie 1991, 25–27). The transition to this state of affairs had started earlier, with the MacWilliam Burkes of Mayo extracting money as well as in-kind payments from their followers in the late sixteenth century (Ó Raghallaigh 1926–29) and Hugh O'Neill, earl of Tyrone, extracting what was almost entirely a money rent from his many subjects at the start of the seventeenth century (see Hill 1877, 240–55). Nonetheless, the disappearance of most inter-regional conflict from the country after the 1650s helped complete the process by rendering provisioning and protective responsibilities largely unnecessary. It was primarily an economic relationship that prevailed between tenants and landlords from the mid-seventeenth century on.

Estate management and transhumance in the west of Ireland

In order to consider how this change affected the social environment in which transhumance operated it is crucial to bear in mind that landed estates were not run in the same way across the country. In some places, such as Gleann Cholm Cille, landlords became very removed from the realities of everyday farming life. It has been seen that written rentals survive here, which points to some formal recognition of the estate by the powerful Connolly family, but in general they seem to have taken little interest in the actual running of their south-western Donegal lands. From the time of their arrival in 1706 until the 1830s (see Mac Cuinneagáin 2002, 56–62) they were represented primarily by an agent, the family itself residing in Kildare, in the east of Ireland. This policy was not without its consequences. In the summer of 1778 a number of letters to Connolly from the then agent, Henry Major in Ballyshannon, related that he was finding it difficult to extract rent from tenants, leading him to temporarily confiscate nearly all their cattle (Mac Cuinneagáin 2002, 63). He says that this was due to the poor market for black cattle and yarn, but one might also speculate that the *laissez-faire* attitude of the Connollys reduced the efficiency of rent collection. Clearly, they did not regard the rough terrain of their south-west Donegal estate as worthy of great attention. The presence of just one agent for the whole of it, an area several parishes in size, reinforces that impression.

In this context, the 1773–74 rental is instructive. The whole of Gleann Cholm Cille contains the names of just twelve tenants, four with 'partners'. The named tenants are obviously middlemen, who filled the void left by an absentee landlord. What is more, only two of them – Mc Loughlin and Cunningham – have surnames that suggest they belong to the native Gaelic Irish population. The vast majority of the parish was leased by middlemen with British surnames who were almost certainly Protestant (Mac Cuinneagáin 2002, 81–82). The latter's prevalence as head tenants or middlemen is not surprising given the plantation of Scottish settlers in Ireland's northernmost province of Ulster during the seventeenth century. Although their presence in south-west Donegal was far from heavy – the 1659 'Census' records just three English or Scots in Gleann Cholm Cille (Pender 1939, 47) – those who did settle were clearly favoured by landlords. In the context of Ireland's recent conquest, this is potentially quite significant. Almost two centuries after Edmund Spenser and others had complained of Irish people moving around with cattle, here were Protestant farmers of English or Scottish descent living in an area where the ability of tenant farmers' ability to pay rent depended on transhumance. As middlemen, they would have dealt directly with tenant families who took part in seasonal movements, and may indeed have grazed their own cattle on the hill pastures in summer. Having said all that, the situation in Gleann Cholm Cille had changed by the 1830 Connolly rental, when Catholic head-tenants were quite numerous (Mac Cuinneagáin 2002, 267). The emergence of strong Catholic farmers at the expense of Protestant ones is a trend found across early nineteenth-century Ireland (Smyth 1976, 41, 44; Whelan 1995a, 61–64).

On other large estates that lacked close attention from their proprietors native Irish Catholic gentry were able to maintain a strong foothold. Kevin Whelan has eloquently described how these families stayed on as head-tenants or middlemen in south Kerry and other western areas after the Cromwellian settlement (Whelan 1995a, 12–13). Some of the best-known examples, indeed, come from western County Galway, as Dunton's account of an elite booley in 1699 already hinted. At the western extreme of the county, in the maritime parish of Ballynakill, the Blake family left the Uí Fhlaithbheartaigh (O'Flahertys) of Renvyle in effective control of 13,000 acres. This had been purchased by Henry Blake in 1680 but, as late as 1811, Anthony O'Flaherty was 'the acknowledged chief' in those parts (Blake Family of Renvyle 1995, 12–13; Whelan 1995a, 22–23). Although 1811 was to be the year that the Blakes decided not to renew the O'Flahertys' long-standing lease, the arrangement does demonstrate that the old Gaelic aristocracy had hitherto managed to retain their local prestige and power. A similar situation obtained on the small peninsula of An Cheathrú Rua (Carraroe), just east of the Carna peninsula, where Máirtín Mór Ó Máille is said in 1794 to have operated a large smuggling enterprise and maintained an armed guard of forty men – all while a tenant of Richard Martin (Whelan 1995a, 23). It was even claimed that the latter, who had a reputation for profligacy, had borrowed large amounts of money from Ó Máille (Robinson 2011, 303–04). Situations like these are likely to have facilitated a degree of continuity in rural society into the later seventeenth and eighteenth centuries, perhaps even where transhumance is concerned.

In the Carna peninsula itself there do not appear to be any detailed historical accounts or records on landlord–tenant relations. In the Lynch-owned east of the peninsula – that is, Cill Chiaráin and neighbouring townlands – written estate records may never have been kept. Evidence taken in June 1844 for the Devon Commission from the director of the Irish Waste Land Improvement Society (which entered into said estate in 1841 on a temporary basis) comments that there was 'no rent roll or returns of the tenants, or of anything connected with them or their holding' (Devon Commission 1845, 2). Although the Lynches were originally a family of Galway townsmen who had Anglo-Norman ancestry, they seemingly did not take an active role in managing the lands that they had acquired in the west. This might explain their apparent leniency with regard to patterns of transhumance attested by ethnographic evidence, which show that islanders from the south customarily moved onto parts of the Lynch estate to graze their cattle.

As to the Martins and their role in the Carna peninsula, they owned the larger western and southern sections of the peninsula from the first half of the seventeenth century up to the 1850s. Unlike the Blakes and Lynches, they were not absentee landlords, and based themselves at Ballynahinch Castle, close to an island tower house that had previously been the seat of another branch of the Uí Fhlaithbheartaigh. Moreover, Ballynahinch Castle is no more than 10km north-west of the Carna peninsula and lies in the same parish. Consequently, the Martins were probably more aware of what was going on in their lands than other landlords in Connemara. Still, it is very difficult to say if this amounted to anything more than rent collection. The irregular and often curvilinear field boundary patterns visible on the first edition six-inch Ordnance Survey maps for the study area have a look of organic growth about them that suggests that macro-planning by a landlord did not take place here. There are signs that this began to change in the early nineteenth century, as 'landlords [across Ireland] developed a heightened sense of seriousness' (Whelan 1995a, 63). On an 1819 map of County Galway a solitary road reaches less than halfway into the peninsula (Larkin 1819, sheet 7); nineteen years later, on the first edition six-inch Ordnance Survey sheet, it goes as far south as Maínis island, a sure sign of ongoing construction. This minor infrastructural development reflects a belated concern with estate management and improvement on the Martins' part, another indicator of which is their recording of individual tenants from the 1830s (NAI M. 2429–31, M. 3440–01, 3443). Their efforts in this direction are not unique: the Connolly estate took steps to reorganise rundale farms in Gleann Cholm Cille in the period 1835–48 (see below).

Gentle or not, these attempts to exert greater influence over their estates do not hide the fact that landowners in certain parts of Connemara and Donegal had generally shied away from altering rural society over the preceding century and a half or more. With rents based primarily on land, and landlords now neither distributing nor receiving cattle, they were effectively removed from direct participation in farming and transhumance. In this regard, the commutation of dues and services (ultimately) to a money rent has social as well as economic significance. Landowners such as the Connollys and the Martins may have had legal title to vast amounts of land, but they did not influence local people directly. This role was filled by middlemen, some of whom were notable enough to find their way into history, and others, under the Martins and Lynches perhaps, who are now lost to us. Unfortunately, so little documentary evidence survives from the late seventeenth and eighteenth centuries in south-west Donegal, and south Connemara particularly, that it is impossible to describe exactly how strong tenants in these areas mediated between the landlord and his lowest tenants. It also means that it is very difficult to assess how transhumant movements were regulated by them. One obvious possibility is that middlemen prolonged the Gaelic tradition of commyns by having lesser tenants mind their cattle, though historical evidence for 'dairymen' could not be found in either Donegal or Connemara. Ultimately, economic and demographic factors were to have greater significance for the development of transhumance in these areas during the eighteenth and nineteenth centuries. Indeed, there is a long-standing belief among historical geographers that economic and demographic trends overrode other factors in shaping the Irish landscape (Andrews 1970, 11; Maguire 1972, 107–82; Smyth 1976, 47). However, their studies have tended to underplay the role of poorly documented tenant farmers as agents and mediators of these trends.

Landlord control in the Galtees: consequences for traditional grazing

Before they can be given a voice, a contrast must be drawn with the Galtees region, where landlords were not as removed from the realities of estate management. Based in Mitchelstown, County Cork, the Kingstons owned the civil parishes of Kilbeheny and Templetenny up to the 1850s, as well as a few townlands in adjoining Shanrahan and Galbally. The O'Callaghan landlords based at Shanbally came to own almost all of Shanrahan, increasing their share between 1721 and 1805 (Smyth 1976, fig. 2). Thus, between them, they controlled of most of the southern side of the Galtees, where archaeological indications of seasonal upland settlement are most prevalent.

As Chapter 5 has shown, these landlords were exercising a degree of control over the landscape from as early as the 1720s, ordering lowland farms to be fenced and later also incentivising tree planting and improvement of the mountain slopes. Indeed, they were making these interventions despite the presence of Protestant middlemen (Smyth 1976). The measures of the Kingston and O'Callaghan estates influenced the development of field systems in a way that is not evident in either the Carna peninsula or Gleann Cholm Cille. Straight ditches, often orientated on a north–south axis, were laid out in many townlands and are evident on the first edition six-inch Ordnance Survey maps. During the eighteenth century, this had meant the enclosure of common land first of all in the lowlands and then on the fringes of the mountain. Smyth (1976, 38) links this trend to the emergence of Whiteboy agrarian disturbance, which was orchestrated by tenants unhappy with the disruption of traditional grazing rights and possibly also the displacement of native Catholic middlemen by Protestant ones. A precursor of this conflict is attested in Shanrahan in 1717–18, which saw three smallholders accused of driving cattle belonging to the descendant of a Cromwellian grantee off a former townland common (Smyth 1976, 38). In east Tipperary, planned enclosure of the landscape by the Barker estate of Kilcooly has also recently been demonstrated for the period 1748 to 1840 (Clutterbuck 2015, 170).

In terms of landlord–tenant relations, then, it appears that in the Galtees region changes in landownership during the seventeenth century were followed by greater reorganisation of the rural landscape. This sprang from the notion that the landed estate was a unit deserving of control and improvement, and it had consequences in turn for how other social, economic and demographic trends were played out over the course of the eighteenth and nineteenth centuries. Even on the Kingston and O'Callaghan estates, however, there seems to have been no actual elite involvement in transhumance. One is forced to take this view given the lack of detailed agricultural records from outside the demesne and the undeniable contemporary decline of transhumance within wider society. If the Protestant middlemen had a role in seasonal movements – for example, as the owners of dairy cows that minor tenants looked after on the mountain – it did not last. The dairymen system was being deconstructed in the 1780s (Young 1780, 56) and by the time one gets a genuinely clear understanding of transhumance in the nineteenth century (not just in the Galtees) seasonal movement survived only as a practice of the tenantry, particularly of smallholders, who hovered above the cottier and labourer classes.

I have now described the basic landlord–tenant frameworks in which transhumance operated after the 1650s, and have surmised that direct elite involvement in transhumance disappeared gradually everywhere, while increasing indirectly around the Galtees as a result of landlord-driven changes. It remains now to discuss how people responded – through patterns of permanent and seasonal settlement – to these elements of continuity and change as they coalesced with demographic and economic forces.

DEMOGRAPHIC TRENDS AND THE EVOLUTION OF TRANSHUMANT PATTERNS

Types of population expansion

Each of the three study areas show a large increase in population between the seventeenth century and the beginning of the Great Famine in 1845. Most of this growth took place from c.1750 onwards and involved the expansion of permanent settlement onto land that had not previously been subject to intensive use. The unevenness of the process allows us to discuss regional trends in population expansion, which in turn are crucial to understanding the different patterns of change and decline in transhumance after the seventeenth century. Broadly speaking, there were three types of population expansion into the uplands of post-medieval Ireland, each of which are represented in Figure 6.1.

The first is most apparent in the Galtee Mountains and involved the improvement of relatively large amounts of common pasture, moving steadily up from the limits of seventeenth-century farmland. This was purposeful and involved a degree of

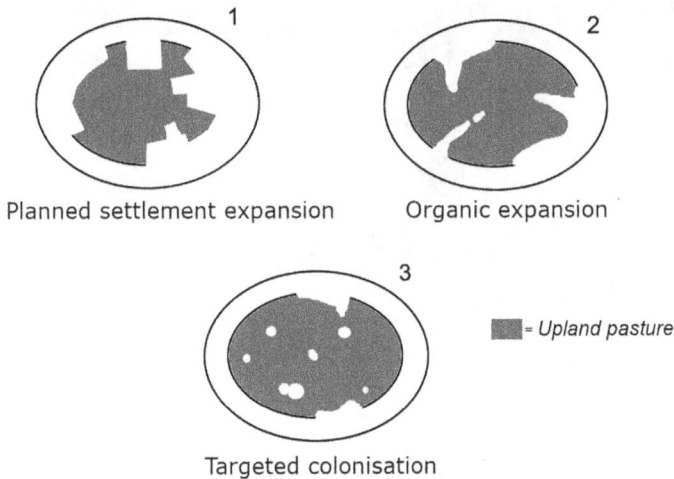

Figure 6.1 Types of permanent settlement expansion in Ireland, *c*.1700–1845.

organisation. Boolakennedy and Glengarra is the most extreme example. Straight boundaries run up either side of this wide valley for almost two kilometres, with perpendicular banks marking out each tenant's holding irrespective of topography – as if planned, on a map, to be one large-scale reclamation (Figure 6.2). However, the lack of sub-division and other improvements in these holdings suggests that they were not occupied for very long before all the tenants were evicted by the earl of Glengall in early 1847, at the height of the Great Famine (Smyth 2012a, 392).

In other parishes and townlands to the west, encroachment on common pastures started earlier and was more piecemeal. Nevertheless, field patterns here display an element of planning. Looking once again at Kilbeheny, it is clear that many field boundaries in the townlands of Coolboy, Scrowmore and Coolattin run upslope in straight lines (Figure 5.6). They divide the upper reaches of these townlands into strips of similar widths, with each being sub-divided and improved at somewhat different paces. The more accessible slopes of Coolattin had all been sub-divided by 1841, whereas that was yet to happen on the highest land in Scrowmore and Coolboy. On the Primary Griffith's Valuation map from the 1850s the long sides of these strips form boundaries for many holdings, although holdings rarely occupy their entire length. Originally, each of the strips was probably established by one family or extended family, with a proliferation of houses along their length thereafter. The landlord, Kingston, may have had a role in encouraging their improvement, perhaps making allowances on rent, as O'Callaghan did on mountain land in Shanrahan (Smyth 1976, 37). Whether or not the straight layout was also stipulated by the landlord is impossible to prove. It could have been an innovation among tenants, but then it would have to be explained why fields in a few nearby townlands display less regularity. For example, deeper into the mountain range, in Knocknascrow, Carrigeen Mountain and Knocknagalty, the shape and size of individual fields is not determined by any boundaries laid out

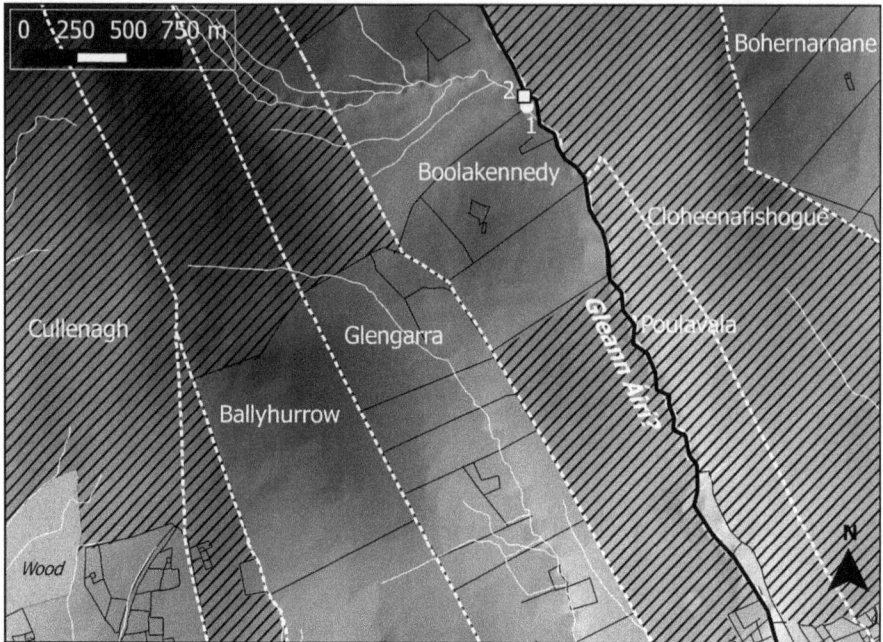

Figure 6.2 Planned pre-Famine encroachment on the mountain commonage (which is striped) on the border of Shanrahan and Tubbrid parishes, showing pre-existing booley site Boolakennedy 1 and 2. Organic expansion visible in Cullenagh. (Basemap adapted from first edition six-inch OS, 1841).

in advance, and farms do not advance upslope quite as evenly. These holdings were some of the last and most vulnerable to be carved out of the mountain commons and probably did not receive the same attention from estate management because of their remoteness from the demesne. But on the majority of lower hill farms, created between 150m and 350m a.s.l., planning is evident.

The second type of population expansion also involved steady growth out from areas of older, seventeenth-century settlement; but in this case it happened more organically, following the most favourable topographical corridors. This is especially evident in the Carna peninsula and Gleann Cholm Cille. Instead of pre-Famine settlement advancing upwards onto hill pasture in a fairly even manner, it clearly follows the coast in the Carna peninsula and, in Gleann Cholm Cille, a number of long valleys that cut through the parish (Figures 3.1, 4.7). The former has a very long coastline owing to its many inlets, and these are excellent for the collection of sand and seaweed – not to mention their importance as harbours for inshore fishing boats. Thus, as population density was increasing around Maíros, Mace Head, Maínis and Cill Chiaráin, permanent settlement was spreading tentatively along the coast out from these core areas. By the time of the 1838 six-inch Ordnance Survey map this pattern of expansion had left a thin veil of tenant holdings all along the coast of Leitreach Ard and Glinsce in the west of the peninsula and around the south-east between Áird

Mhóir and Loch Conaortha. In Gleann Cholm Cille the coast is less accessible and so had less of a pull for people. This deflected settlement growth inland, where it spread over what relatively flat ground was available before climbing up the narrower valleys. In both of these western study areas the pre-Famine improvement of land appears to have been more opportunistic than in the Galtees. Individual fields in the Carna peninsula and the larger infields of Gleann have little regularity to them; they simply extend into the ground that offered the most immediate advantages in terms of resources and/or offered the least resistance to cultivation. All of this suggests that population expansion was managed in both of these areas by the tenants themselves, whose intimate knowledge of the local landscape found expression in patchier, but ultimately more nuanced, encroachment on rough grazing.

The third and final type of population expansion might be termed 'targeted' expansion, insofar as it involves permanent settlements popping up in isolated locations, separate from the main body of improved farmland and settlement. A few minor instances have been encountered in the Galtees, but they do not form a major pattern by any means: in the main, it is characteristic of the western study areas. Figure 4.7 showed how prevalent the phenomenon was in the north of Gleann Cholm Cille, with all upland townlands containing an isolated patch of improved ground supporting between one and three small farmhouses. It was concluded that this phase of population expansion was the last to take place in south-west Donegal before the Famine. Targeted expansion also occurred in the Carna peninsula, with clear examples to be found on the first edition six-inch Ordnance Survey maps and on the ground today. Thus, several kilometres inland, Seanadh Mhac Dónaill contains

Figure 6.3 'Targeted' permanent settlement in Seanadh Mhac Dónaill dating to 1830s.

one marked house and a small associated field in 1838. This targeted settlement grew subsequently so that, by its abandonment in the mid-twentieth century, it contained two relatively large dwelling houses and a complex of field walls (Figure 6.3). Another established on the border between Dúleitir Thiar and Thoir (Dooletter West and East) also grew successfully. This was not always the case, however. The remains of smaller and relatively short-lived targeted settlements may be found in the south-east of Seanadh Bhuire and by Loch Buaile in Cnoc Buí. Overall, those in Gleann Cholm Cille, particularly around Mín na Saileach, proved more resilient throughout the nineteenth century. A couple of these continue to be farmed and occupied to this day, unlike on the Carna peninsula.

Effects on transhumant movements

These three forms of tenant expansion into upland pastures up to the mid-nineteenth century had different implications for the direction of cattle movements and the sites that herders could use as summer dwellings. Most dramatically, it has been argued in the Galtees that a wave of land improvement on the southern side of the range led to the construction of a new generation of booley houses on higher slopes. This is unlikely to have occurred any earlier than 1750 because of the slow initial rate of population growth. Indeed, sites such as Knocknascrow 1 and 2 and Coolagarranroe 1, 2 and 3 may not even have been built until the 1790s or the early decades of the following century, since that was when encroachment upon upland commonage really set in. At the same time, the proximity of structures such as Coolagarranroe 1 and 2 to the highest farmhouses in that townland (less than 700m) suggests that construction of this hypothesised second generation was well completed by the 1840s, when the last mountain farms were established; otherwise, farmers would not have built the booley houses in locations that were so close as to defeat the purpose of summer relocation. The eventual realisation of the latter is an indicator of how short this last, small-scale phase of booleying must have been.

But there is another feature of nineteenth-century booleying in the Galtees that underlines the fundamentally altering effect of population expansion on transhumance. Looking at patterns of *permanent* settlement at this time, it is quite obvious that the permanent bases of transhumant movements had changed over the previous 200 years. No longer was booleying a parish-wide or multi-parish strategy upon which lowland farming settlements could depend; it was a minor farming activity based in small upland farms that were decades-old at most. Thus had the locations of both permanent *and* summer settlements – the foci of any transhumant system – shifted. As such, population growth seems to have led to the development of a new pattern of transhumance, for however short a period of time.

Just east of the Carna peninsula in County Galway, in the civil parishes of Kilcummin and Killannin, an even more emphatic reorientation took place in the post-medieval period. Along most of their southern coastline, between An Spidéal and An Cheathrú Rua, settlement of a permanent nature appears to have been very light, if not entirely absent, during the seventeenth century. No 'profitable' land was recorded here in the mid-seventeenth century (*BSD Galway*, 58–72, 82–83), while the present-day Record of Monuments and Places contains very few archaeological sites that might safely be dated to the early post-medieval period. A tower house, church and house of indeterminate date on the bay of An Trá Mhór probably represent the remains of a small contemporary settlement, but by and large such evidence is lacking (Naessens 2009, 220–22). As noted in Chapter 3, these areas were mainly used for rough grazing in a system of relatively long-distance transhumance (Graham 1970a, 196–97). These links did not survive into the nineteenth century, however. By the time the area was mapped by the Ordnance Survey in 1838, it contained a dense network of small farms and fields, the product of decades of organic population expansion along the coast from neighbouring areas and probably also the targeted colonisation of booley settlements by people from the direction of Lough Corrib.

Indeed, a twentieth-century folk story from the area mentions booleying between tenant farms in Indreabhán and the inland hill of Formaoil to the north (Mac Giollarnáth 1934, 105). This movement would have run in nearly the opposite direction to seventeenth-century rights of pasture mapped by Graham (1970a, fig. 12.2), and so indicates that here, too, population expansion (albeit of a different kind) could give rise to new forms of transhumance at the same time that it disturbed old grazing rights. Regardless of how much input landlords had in the process of expansion and improvement, tenant communities in the foothills of the Galtees and in this part of County Galway displayed great adaptability in managing to change their grazing and wintering strategies in concert with the widespread alterations to the landscape that their many hands and spades were making. Their reorientation of transhumance is all the more remarkable when compared with the fate of the practice in much of the rest of the country. Several examples of probable transhumant systems in the sixteenth, seventeenth or eighteenth centuries simply disappear in the nineteenth century, suggesting that population expansion more often than not squeezed out elements of seasonal settlement in pre-Famine landscapes.

In the other two study areas, relatively inaccessible from the outside and containing small populations to begin with, organic expansion did not result in the improvement of large areas of rough grazing. This facilitated greater continuity in transhumant patterns. In the Carna peninsula the spread of permanent settlement along the coast would have restricted grazing lands only slightly, with little direct impact on where people relocated to and only minor changes to where they originated from. In Gleann Cholm Cille the impact on seasonal settlement seems to have been a little more serious; as pointed out, several townland names containing *mín* in the east of the parish were affected by organic growth that came from the Gleann and Teileann directions. This may have led to the reorientation or even discontinuation of some transhumant movements, though not on the scale described in the south of the Galtees or in Killannin parish in Galway. While transhumance would have been complicated, its main winter bases continued to lie in areas of seventeenth-century settlement – namely, Gleann and other pockets of good land in Málainn Bhig and Teileann. A comparable situation developed in the Loughros peninsula, which lies to the north-east of Gleann Cholm Cille and has more historical data. By comparing early seventeenth-century inquisitions with an estate survey from 1755, Graham (1970a,

140–41, fig. 4) is able to show that three minor sections of mountain land with which the peninsula was connected had been settled on a permanent basis by the mid-eighteenth century. Nevertheless, the primary impetus for using summer pasture continued to come from the well-settled but small peninsula of Loughros. Gleann valley occupied a similar position in that it had increasingly little rough grazing of its own as the eighteenth century wore on and therefore even more reason to rely on summer pasture. Settlements that eventually stretched out organically from it were not significant enough to disrupt where the system was rooted.

Targeted expansion in Gleann Cholm Cille and the Carna peninsula on the face of it produced a similar result to expansion in the Galtees, in that it led to some seasonal sites being replaced by permanent ones. However, in Gleann, as oral tradition and Griffith's Valuation have shown, most targeted settlements were effectively colonisations; they were drawn to particular places in the landscape because they had a tradition of habitation as booley sites. This was probably also true of farmsteads established at Seanadh Mhac Dónaill and Loch Buaile in the Carna peninsula. Although Griffith's Valuation fails to offer comparable lines of evidence for Carna, it is known from oral history that the locations in question were grazed in summer. Furthermore, the archaeological record contains indications of previous occupation. Five hundred metres to the west of Seanadh Mhac Dónaill farmstead, on a slope in the same townland, are the remains of a sub-oval structure that has a wall footing constructed of rubble stone and earth (3m × 1.5m internally). Because it is not marked on any map and is quite unlike other ancillary buildings near the farmstead, it could be a pre-existing booley dwelling (Figure 6.4). Near the small farmstead established at Loch Buaile in Cnoc Buí is a poorly preserved squarish hut measuring only 2.6m across (Cnoc Buí 13) – again, this is possibly the remnant of an earlier seasonal phase.

By contrast, the relatively even advance of permanent settlement up the Galtees would suggest that seasonal sites on its lower slopes were generally not singled

Figure 6.4 Possible, pre-existing sub-oval booley hut in Seanadh Mhac Dónaill on left, compared with oval booley hut, Mín na Saileach 6, in south-west Donegal.

out for improvement. Some older (sixteenth-/seventeenth-century?) booley sites may have been repurposed as farmsteads, but only on an incidental basis; in other words, encroachment was not structured around them. Again, for the pre-Famine period, this meant less continuity in the Galtees than in the western landscapes of Connemara and Donegal.

Seasonal activity and landscape learning in the uplands

Yet what we have learned about booleying from documentary evidence and oral history encourages a bit more thought on how transitions to year-round occupation actually occurred at seasonal sites, and particularly about the agency of individuals. Whether we are talking about uplands in the west of Ireland or the Scottish Highlands in the post-medieval period or certain parts of England in high medieval times, it seems rather unambitious to write seasonal sites off as an 'obvious choice' for year-round occupation. What role did herders play in the establishment of hill farms during periods of population-related land-use pressure? Is it possible to talk about processes of landscape learning and environmental knowledge which facilitated upland colonisation? Certainly, it was hypothesised some time ago for late prehistoric Norway that the initiation of seasonal pastoral activity formed a key step in the establishment of permanent settlement in the country's inland valleys (Hougen 1947). Since then, a lot of archaeological and palaeoecological evidence has come to light in the outlands of eastern Norway and western Sweden, allowing several scholars to argue that a 'farm–shieling package' gradually opened up the Boreal forests to permanent human settlement from the early first millennium AD onwards, and especially during the Viking Age (Pettersson 2018, 30, 33, 37; Svensson 2018, 17–20). Similarly, shielings have been recognised as an important element of Norse colonisation on islands in the North Atlantic (Sveinbjarnardóttir 1991; Lucas 2008). Indeed, there is a growing body of literature in archaeology generally on the issue of landscape learning in environments of which humans – or at least certain cultural groups – had no prior experience (e.g. Rockman and Steele 2003).

Of course, the hills and mountains of Ireland were not 'virgin' lands, there being a long history of anthropogenic impacts on vegetation over 200m and, in some areas, significant archaeological evidence of Bronze Age, Iron Age and early medieval settlement (Moore 1995; O'Brien 2009; Gardiner 2012a, 20–24). Nor were Ireland's uplands anywhere near as extensive as the Boreal forests of inland Scandinavia, where recurrent summertime dairying and hay-cutting around *fäbod* sites gave rise to distinct human 'niches' in the ecology; these survive today as species-rich meadows in the forest clearings (see Eriksson 2018). All the same, there are subtle indications of transhumant-driven niche construction in this book's study areas. Patches of purple moor grass (*Molinia caerulea*) and other palatable grasses are often found immediately outside former booley dwellings, where presumably surplus buttermilk – a by-product of dairying – would have been thrown out and where cows would have lain down and deposited dung. At some sites, the decades since abandonment have also seen soft rush (*Juncus effusus*) and bracken (*Pteridium acquilinum*) colonise their semi-anthropogenic soils. These 'niches' were created and recognised by herders and, as they began to try out the cultivation of potatoes in the late eighteenth or early nineteenth centuries, they would have gained even more familiarity with the ground and its potential to support cultivation.

Moreover, their experiences had an obvious route of transmission back to the rest of the family and community through transhumance. This is at its most obvious in Gleann Cholm Cille, where there is solid documentary evidence not only for the grazing rights held by specific tenant families in hill pastures but also for the establishment of new farms on these pastures by some of the families. With their intimate knowledge of soil, plant growth and shelter, the adolescent sons and daughters of tenant farmers undoubtedly played a role in site choice. They would have recognised the anthropogenic niches created by seasonal pastoralism at booley sites and 'targeted' them for colonisation. It is even possible that, after marriage, they actually led this process. For example, there are indications in Sweden that *säter* or *fäbod* sites could be used as year-round farms by young couples waiting on a farm of their own (Svensson 1998, 104). In the Galtees, the local 'mountaineers' contemptuously referred to by Arthur Young undoubtedly also had an intimate understanding of terrain and pasture; however, there is less evidence here for the specific targeting of booley sites because landscape macro-management by landlords proved to be an overriding factor in the expansion of population.

Targeted upland colonisation in Connemara and Donegal involved a *replacement* of seasonal activity, and gave rise to a definite new phase of architecture in many hill pastures in the early nineteenth century. However, their occupants did not break grazing links with the home settlements totally. According to local tradition in the Carna peninsula, it was customary for hill farmers (*fir sléibhe*) to take in cattle from coastal farmers and give some back in return; this was because a seasonal change of pasture was still a necessary part of maintaining a nutritional balance in their diet (known as *slánú* or 'recuperation'; Ó Cathasaigh 1943; Beartla King, An Más, pers. comm.). Interestingly, at Seanadh Mhac Dónaill in the 1930s cattle were taken in from a related family who owned a small farm in An Aird Mhóir (Ciarán Moylan, pers. comm.). This is an isolated instance of familial ties facilitating the continuation of grazing practices (if not actual transhumance); in general, local tradition maintains that such ties were not necessary for targeted inland settlements to receive cattle from the coast (Beartla King, pers. comm.). In Gleann Cholm Cille solid local information on how older farms adapted to the establishment of targeted upland settlements is harder to come by. That said, a vague story about a hill farmer in Gleann Lach lighting a fire every May as a signal that livestock were to be brought up (Francy Cannon, pers. comm.) possibly hints at his inheritance of some roles that booley herders once fulfilled. It could be argued, then, that some of these targeted hill settlements helped ease the final transition into a sedentary farming society that no longer partook in transhumance *per se*.

THE MORPHOLOGY OF SUMMER DWELLINGS

Time and the physical environment

In Chapter 5 morphological variation between booley houses in the Galtees was explained in terms of tenant farmers beginning a new, if short-lived, phase of seasonal settlement in the mid- or late eighteenth century. The fact that most upland farmhouses involved in nineteenth-century booleying pre-date the Famine by only a few decades means that this should be a *terminus post quem* for the construction of the smaller but similar booley houses above them. In the Carna peninsula and south-west Donegal it is not as easy to invoke landscape history as a factor in the development of new forms of summer dwelling as there is more continuity in transhumant patterns over the post-medieval period. That is to say, there is no obvious geographical shift in summer pasturing to higher altitudes, as occurred in much of the southern and south-western Galtee Mountains. It has been suggested that within Mín na Saileach in Donegal there was a move away from building booley dwellings with mainly wattle superstructures after woodland scrub vanished from the landscape in the eighteenth and early nineteenth century. This would have led to a greater reliance on stone construction, perhaps using permanent rectangular dwellings in the valleys as design templates, as tenants did in the Galtees.

As to the Carna peninsula, aspects of the material evolution of seasonal settlement over time have been discerned thanks to stone clearance activities at two complex sites in the south of Cnoc Buí and the west of Gleannán. For individual booley dwellings, however, it is difficult to distinguish older structures of one design from newer structures that might have a different design. While there are four small but fairly well-built rectangular booley houses in Gleannán and Seanadh Bhuire, the vast majority of structures do not conform to a particular style. Although they are generally made of rubble stone, their shape can be sub-rectangular, sub-circular or slightly irregular. They also vary in overall size from 2.3m × 2m to 5.5m × 3m. Consequently, it is very difficult to place them in a neat morphological category. The only trait that seems to tie them together is their unpredictability. In this context, another explanation of morphology is required, one that takes into account the agency of seasonally mobile people across space as well as time.

Considering the physical environment in which booley dwellings are found, local stone is clearly an important variable in their construction. Load-bearing walls are not as easy to construct when using uncut granitic and schist stones of differing sizes, as these are difficult to fit in place and interlock. Thus, when trying to build a house with straight sides and ends, rubble walls need to be relatively wide at the base. However, if large amounts of stone were not available in the immediate vicinity (or there was insufficient time or manpower to fetch them) builders would have had to settle for structures with less substantial walls. In this case, one or more curving sides may have helped to strengthen otherwise frail rubble walls. They would also have found it convenient to adapt the form of the buildings to natural micro-topographies. In many cases, boulders form part of the walls (Figures 3.5, 3.6) while a few structures utilise rocky outcrops as end walls (Figures 3.7, 6.5). Using exposed bedrock and hillocks in this way usually meant that standardised shapes and dimensions were impossible to implement. As such, the builders of booley huts in the Carna peninsula made strategic decisions about construction at each new building site. Similar architectural compromises and innovations are visible in the design of some herders' huts constructed out of stone on the Isle of Eigg in Scotland, the Bernese Alps, the French Pyrenees and the Cantabrian Mountains in north-west Spain (Rendu *et al.* 2016, 68–74; Andres 2018, fig. 11.2; Dixon 2018, fig. 5.3; Fernández Mier and Tente 2018, fig. 15.6).

Figure 6.5 An Cnoc Buí 17, trapezial-shaped hut with far end built against rock outcrop.

This shows that the builders did not operate solely with reference to socially acceptable forms but used their individual capacity to mediate between themselves and the realities of the physical environment in which seasonal settlement took place. In this regard, their building style speaks to the rather fluid relationship that human agents involved in transhumance maintain with traditional social 'structures' (see Giddens 1981, 27; Hodder 1982; Barrett and Fewster 2000, 31; Barrett 2001). Indeed, it could be argued that ideas of structuration and *habitus* (Bourdieu 1977; Reckwitz 2002) are slightly too rigid for discussions of seasonally mobile people, who move between environmental niches that had potentially different cultural meanings, and therefore different expectations around human action. Moreover, these theories were developed in sociological contexts in which scholars were usually concerned with human agency in metaphysical social structures, certainly not as part of a landscape. Even Actor–Network Theory (Latour 2005), which provides a looser conceptual mesh, was not necessarily developed for a physical setting.

Ultimately, this is one of the problems of applying sociological and anthropological theories to the study of *past* social practice – they do not always fit the historical and archaeological records on which we rely. For my part, I argue that the agency of people involved in farming, and certainly semi-mobile pastoralism, must be scrutinised from a spatial perspective, with their social and cultural practices being understood in the context of the landscape. Thus, in the foregoing examples from Carna there was little attempt to adhere to a socially expected form of summer dwelling. Instead, people preferred to adapt to the more obvious *physical* form of their environment – the extremely stony topography of Carna's inland pastures. This was facilitated by transhumant herders' situation in the contemporary cultural landscape. At the end of the day, these seasonal zones of human activity were not open to the same social scrutiny from peers and elite groups that people living in densely settled areas had to deal with. The consequences of this for day-to-day herder behaviour are discussed later in this chapter.

In her discussion of booley house morphology in Achill, County Mayo, McDonald also argues for environmental factors playing an important role in construction, but in a rather different way. With sixty-two booley houses in the parish classified as either ovoid or sub-rectangular – that is, 72 per cent of the total surveyed by her and the Achill Field School – she rightly seeks an explanation for the prevalence of curved end walls (McDonald 2014, 243). Provoked by the remarks of Caesar Otway, who claimed (incorrectly) in the late 1830s that the islanders 'had not yet arrived at the art of making a square quoin, or erecting a gable end', and Edward Newman, who in 1838 described their houses generally as 'miserable wigwams ... all built without gable ends', she is keen to highlight that the people here were not 'backward' or 'stubborn[ly] intransigen[t]' (McDonald 2014, 236–37). Citing O'Conor (2002, 201–02), she consequently goes on to argue that booley houses were constructed with round ends because that design made them 'less susceptible to wind damage in comparison to straight-sided, gabled ended houses' (McDonald 2014, 236). This seems improbable, however. Wind might well 'funnel' around 'curvilinear ends in a very efficient way', but this cannot be why the design was favoured. For one thing, wind speeds would not be anywhere near strong enough to cause serious damage to a small stone dwelling, even if it had four quoined corners and a gabled rather than hipped roof. Mean annual speeds in Achill are between seven and eight metres per second, with maximum gusts of forty-nine metres per second exceeded only once every fifty years (Wind Mapping System SEAI).

In any case, there are a number of other aspects to McDonald's argument that do not stand up. First of all, if protection against wind damage was really the main concern of builders, one would expect oval or circular houses – that is, houses lacking straight sides – to be much more common than they are. Whatever strength was gained through having rounded ends or corners in a structure would have been negated by retaining straight sides: when viewed in plan, the *middle* is always the weakest point of a structure that is longer than it is wide, regardless of what shape its ends are. As it is, at least 73.2 per cent of the houses in Achill's six 'purpose-built' booley settlements have straight side walls (McDonald 2014, 243–45). Secondly, the positioning of houses is not always ideal for wind protection: for example, at Bunowna two structures – Bun 11 and Bun 12 – that have one curved and one straight end each have their less 'aerodynamic' straight ends facing downslope *into* prevailing winds (Figure 6.6). Thirdly, there are plenty of instances both locally and nationally of post-medieval houses without curved walls being constructed in upland environments. Aside from examples encountered by the writer, there are ten rectangular (with pointed corners) and two square booley houses among those surveyed by McDonald (2014, 244–45). It goes without saying that these booley houses had to withstand the very same wind speeds that curved forms did. Another telling comparison is provided by McDonald's investigations at the permanent settlement of Slievemore. This location is also exposed to relatively high wind speeds, yet most of its houses are clearly rectangular with gabled ends, a construction style that McDonald has shown dates back to the mid to late eighteenth century (Wind Mapping System SEAI; McDonald 1998, 80–81; McDonald 2014, 257–58, 262).

If environmental conditions played any role in the prevalence of rounded corners and curved end walls in Achill, I maintain that micro-topographical features were far more significant than the wind. This is borne out by a re-examination of structures

Figure 6.6 Roughly rectangular booley houses (15 & 16) at Bunowna, Achill, facing south-east.

A1–A4 in the small booley settlement of Annagh, located close to the north-western extreme of the island (Figure 6.7). These conjoined stone structures are found in a line, nestled between two low ridges. The two eastern structures, A3 and A4, are rectangular, while A1 and A2 appear to be slightly curved externally. Based on excavation and careful cleaning of the location of the wall joints, McDonald (2014, 217) argues that all four were constructed at more or less the same time. This brings the slight variation evident in their design into sharp focus. Although it is not highlighted by McDonald, the slightly curved nature of A1 and A2's northern and western walls is plainly the result of their being built up against the aforementioned ridge on the west. Indeed, fitting A1 into the sequence meant that it had to be built slightly to the south of the others. If the rectangular shape had been persisted with on the north and west of A1 and A2, the slope would have been impacted and much more labour would have been required to fit the structure in. Internally, however, A1 and A2 are both still roughly rectangular. Their external design was therefore a compromise – an adaptation to the local micro-topography.

In a similar way, the appearance and landscape context of booley sites in the Carna peninsula suggest that transhumant people frequently acted upon the challenges of building in this stony environment by varying the ground plans of their huts and using naturally occurring stones where possible. In short, they innovated. The idea of innovation gains credibility if we consider that booley dwellings were not major undertakings. The smaller among them in Carna would probably not have taken more than a day or two to construct, depending on how many hands were available.

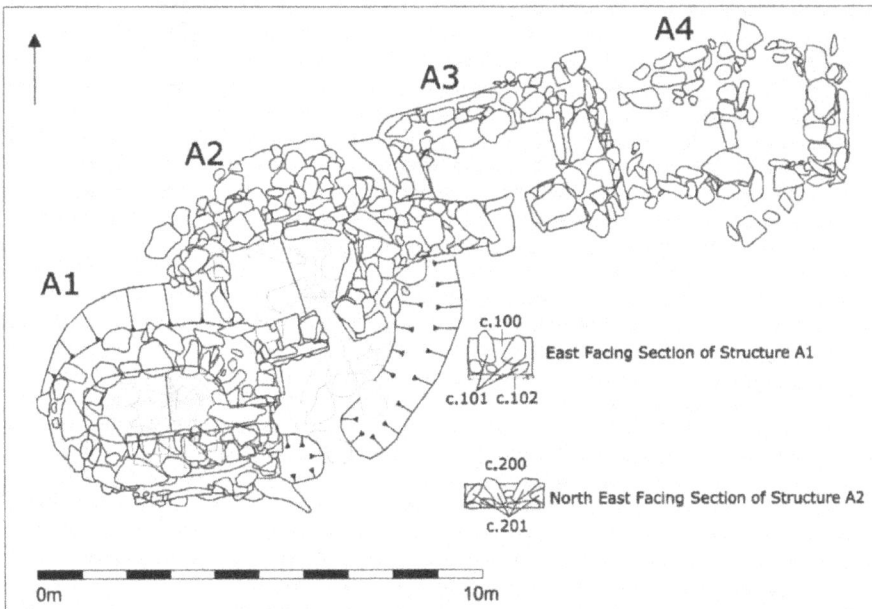

Figure 6.7 Plan of Annagh 1–4, Achill (McDonald 2014, fig.72, reproduced by her kind permission).

Innovation ought to be a more important consideration for archaeologists and historians of rural landscapes, who, despite their best intentions, often look beyond the role of individuals in long-term human–environment interactions.

The size of summer dwellings versus permanent houses

Still, there remains the question of exactly *how* small booley dwellings were in relation to the houses in which tenant families were based, and how far back in time this size contrast existed. Outside Ireland there is a well-documented size difference between the seasonal and permanent dwellings of transhumant communities in the post-medieval period and possibly also in the medieval period. In the Scottish Highlands field survey of 1129 shieling huts probably late medieval or post-medieval in date has revealed a mean internal breadth of 4m × 2m (Dixon 2018, 63), which is far smaller than not only eighteenth-century houses excavated in Lochtayside but also twelfth- to thirteenth-century buildings in Lochtayside and Pitcarmick-type houses from the late first millennium AD (Atkinson 2010; Atkinson 2016, 91–94, 127–57). Notwithstanding their shape, shieling huts in the Hebrides are also clearly smaller than the 'blackhouses' occupied by tenant families in post-medieval times (Symonds 2000; Moreland 2011; Raven 2011). At *säter/fäbod* sites in western and central Sweden the remains of late medieval and post-medieval log-timber cabins are much smaller than the wooden houses found in hamlets and villages (Emanuelsson *et al.* 2003, 32–41, 122–23; Andersson *et al.* 2011, 18). Similarly, in Iceland, many late medieval *sel* sites and certainly most eighteenth- and nineteenth-century *sel* sites could be described as miniature versions of the parent farmhouses (Sveinbjarnardóttir 1991; Sveinbjarnadóttir 1992, 23–24; Gísladóttir *et al.* 2012, 79–82; Costello 2018, 174).

Clearly, it is essential to establish the size of permanent dwellings before attempting a contrast with any associated seasonal dwellings. In the Carna peninsula and Connemara generally, the size of permanent year-round houses in the early nineteenth century tallies roughly with the remains of those surveyed at Slievemore and Keem on Achill Island. In these two settlements, occupied on a year-round basis up to the mid-nineteenth century, houses 10m in total length are common and more than two-thirds have an internal area of greater than 20m^2 (McDonald 2014, 262–63; Appendix, 121–92). This is slightly less than the average sizes in Carna, Gleann Cholm Cille and the Galtee Mountains, where I relied on first edition Ordnance Survey maps that probably left out some smaller cottages and labourers' cabins. However, since these people – the poorest in rural society – would not have had the cattle to partake in transhumance, it is appropriate to exclude their dwellings. For the same reason, it is likely that houses with internal areas of less than 20m^2 at Slievemore and Keem were occupied by individuals or families who were too poor to own cattle and make use of booley sites.

The permanent houses of those who *did* take part in booleying during the late eighteenth and early nineteenth centuries have now been shown by both this book and Theresa McDonald's PhD thesis to be larger than booley dwellings. In the Carna peninsula and Gleann Cholm Cille, they occupied three or four times the area, and in the Galtees between one and a half and two times the area. Meanwhile, McDonald's (2014, 266) detailed analysis in Achill has shown that only 7 per cent of 'purpose-built' booley houses are over 20m² in internal area, compared to 70 per cent of houses in permanent settlements. These size differences are significant and should aid in the identification of seasonal sites elsewhere in Ireland, though some caution needs to be shown. The validity of the size contrast at earlier times in the post-medieval and medieval periods remains uncertain because of our patchy understanding of non-elite *permanent* housing prior to the late eighteenth century in Ireland. At least in Connemara, there seems to have been an appreciable difference in size between booley dwellings and permanent houses from the late seventeenth century, with Roderic O'Flaherty referring in 1684 to the '*small* cabins [used by cattle herders] for that season' (own emphasis; Hardiman 1846, 16–17).

Need for absolute dating of archaeological sites in seasonal contexts

Eventually, trial excavations will be needed in order to trace the chronological relationship between booley sites and houses in permanent settlements back into the medieval period. But an initial insight on the occupation date range of post-medieval booley dwellings has emerged from Achill Island, where two structures at the aforementioned site of Annagh – A1 and A2 – have been excavated (Figure 6.7). The floors of both appear to have been formed by slabs, and finds of creamware, spongeware and whiteware confirm that they were occupied during the nineteenth century and possibly the late eighteenth century – creamware production beginning around 1750 in Staffordshire, England (McDonald 2014, 206–19; 220). Overall, the most significant find was a single piece of creamware from *below* the floor of A1, which would suggest that the structure was constructed sometime after the mid-eighteenth century. If it is accepted as reliable[2] this date is highly significant, as it means that A1, and A2–4 by extension, were all constructed at some stage in the period *c*.1750–1900. The construction of booley houses in Achill as late as this lends support to the writer's own argument for continued or renewed construction of booley houses at this time in other parts of Ireland. Critics might point to differences between well-built rectangular forms in the writer's study areas and the slightly curved external walls of A1 and A2. However, as argued above, the external shape of A1 and A2 was influenced by the low ridge nearby. Abutting them on flatter ground to the east, after all, are two rectangular structures that appear older in the sequence of construction.

Excavations in other parts of Ireland would help researchers to establish whether or not a chronology of site types can be formulated at a national level, though the difficulties of getting absolute dates from artefact-poor upland sites must not be taken lightly. The booley houses at Annagh revealed only a handful of sherds (McDonald 2014, Appendix 3), while at Glenmakeeran, County Antrim, a large sod-built

---

2   Unfortunately, McDonald (2014) does not provide a plan, section drawing, illustration or photograph of either the context (C104) or the creamware sherd.

sub-rectangular house (perhaps too large to be a seasonal dwelling) turned up only six sherds of Ulster coarse pottery (Williams and Robinson 1983, 33). One major inhibiting factor in the accumulation of material culture at seasonal sites was surely the removal of useful objects as people returned home. Scant artefact evidence is a challenge even for archaeologists working at low-status sites in lowland contexts, at least before the influx of mass-manufactured pottery towards the middle and end of the nineteenth century. In Moyveela, County Galway, a partially excavated nucleated settlement abandoned by 1838 was very poor in artefacts, especially when compared with a nearby farmstead at Lavally that continued to be inhabited up to the early twentieth century and was littered with glass, metal, pottery and clay pipes (Delaney and Tierney 2011, 165–71). To frustrate matters further, radiocarbon dating may not always be an option because of the poor survival of organic material in acidic soils and the likelihood that people removed any substantial timbers from the roofs of booley houses after they ceased to be occupied.

Researchers need to be mindful as well that construction was an ongoing process at seasonal sites. This is true of most dwellings in use over a long period, but is more the case in seasonal dwellings, which by definition are abandoned for at least half a year. Partial collapse and rotting of peat- or heather-covered roofs over wet winters was inevitable in these structures; poorly secured stones may have fallen from the tops of walls, and sods of peat lying on top of stone footings may have suffered erosion. Repairs at the start of each summer were crucial to making booley sites habitable again. These repairs are attested in oral history from Carna and north-west Donegal (Gibbons 1991, 45; Ó hEochaidh 1943, 133, 136) and, if parallels with Scotland and Sweden are to be believed, they may have had implicit symbolic power too (see below). But here, from the point of view of dating, annual repairs are vital to bear in mind, as decades or even centuries of remedial work would gradually have led to alterations in the design of booley dwellings. Structural renewal may even have caused them to diverge from one another in terms of appearance and been a contributing factor in the diversity we see today in field remains.

Certainly, excavations in Scotland have shown that sites can contain several phases. For example, investigation of a raised shieling hut on Skye's Vaternish peninsula revealed three major – though undated – phases of building (MacSween and Gailey 1961), leading Dixon (2018, 67, 71) to suggest that tell- or mound-like shielings are probably an indicator of repeated occupation. The much more detailed Lochtayside excavations have revealed several occupation horizons within the structure of early modern shieling huts at Edramucky Burn, while hut T8 at Meall Greigh clearly changed in appearance from the fifteenth to the eighteenth centuries – its external turf batter slipping gradually and two stone slabs being placed at its entrance late on (Atkinson 2016, 232–38). Archaeologists must therefore recognise that the seasonality of transhumance manifested itself physically in the gradual evolution of herders' dwellings, and not simply in the movement of people and ivestock.

THE ORGANISATION OF SEASONAL SETTLEMENT VERSUS PERMANENT SETTLEMENT

Having surmised that farmhouses visible on the first edition six-inch Ordnance Survey maps acted as templates for well-built rectangular booley houses in the late eighteenth and early nineteenth centuries, it is worth asking whether the layout and distribution of permanent settlements influenced how people organised associated seasonal settlements in the hills. There are indications of this in the Central Scottish Highlands, where shieling huts usually occur in small groups, like the houses in eighteenth-century townships or *bailtean* (Atkinson 2016), and also in Iceland, where both *sel* sites and farmsteads tend to occur singly (Sveinbjarnardóttir 1991; 1992), though the idea has not been teased out explicitly by other scholars. With the results of detailed field survey and landscape analysis now available from several different areas, Ireland offers a sort of testing ground. However, it is not a straightforward task. With little solid dating evidence in Ireland, it is risky to attempt a simple comparison between the organisation of permanent farm settlements around the year 1840 and booley sites as they appear now in archaeological survey. Neither type of settlement will have remained static in its overall layout over the course of the post-medieval period, especially given what has been learned regarding population expansion.

Achill

Keeping that variable in mind, the writer returns to Achill, County Mayo, where a clear pattern is evident in the early nineteenth century. Each of the six 'purpose-built' booley settlements surveyed here can be described as clusters, with none occupying an area greater than approximately 240m in length and 100m in width (McDonald 2014; Figure 6.8). Unusually, four of them are depicted on the first edition six-inch Ordnance Survey map, illustrating that their composition has hardly changed since 1838. When compared with permanent settlements on the same map, the similarity in layout is obvious: year-round houses at Dooagh, Keel and Slievemore form clusters too, albeit in much larger numbers (Figure 6.9). The nucleation of dwelling houses in pre-Famine Ireland is, of course, a phenomenon associated with rundale (Whelan 2012; Bell and Watson 2015), a system of partnership farming that dominated the landscape of Achill. The fact that booley settlements within rundale mirror the layout of their parent settlements has important socio-cultural implications that McDonald overlooks. It not only implies that transhumant farmers in Achill accepted nucleation as a 'normal' settlement layout but strongly suggests, moreover, that they brought a notion of communality with them to the summer pastures.

When this pattern of settlement originated is uncertain. It has already been explained that the four conjoined booley houses at Annagh were probably built after 1750, but this does not extend the chronology of clustering very far back for seasonal sites. Clustering of permanent settlement is not easy to trace either, given that most of those present in 1838 are now overlain by modern villages, and therefore unsuitable for archaeological investigation. Two, however, have been abandoned since that time: Keem and Slievemore. An excavation of one house at Keem by McDonald (2014, 231)

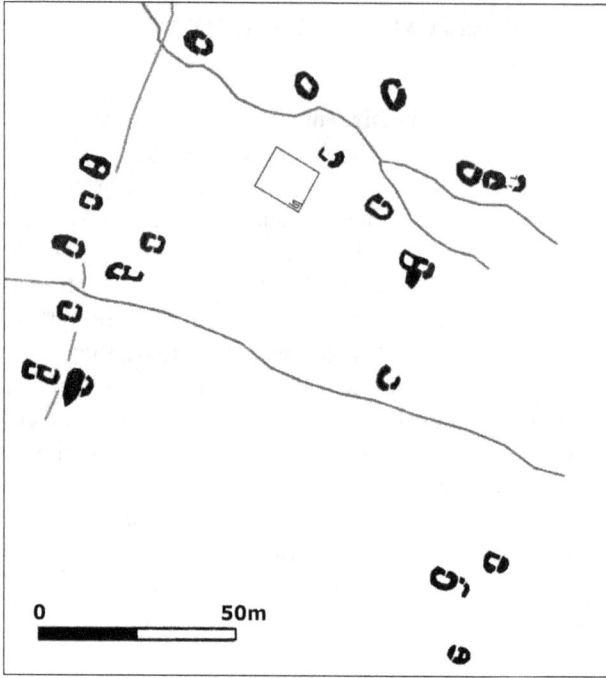

Figure 6.8 Dirk booley settlement, Achill (redrawn after McDonald 2014, 159, fig. 49).

0   50m

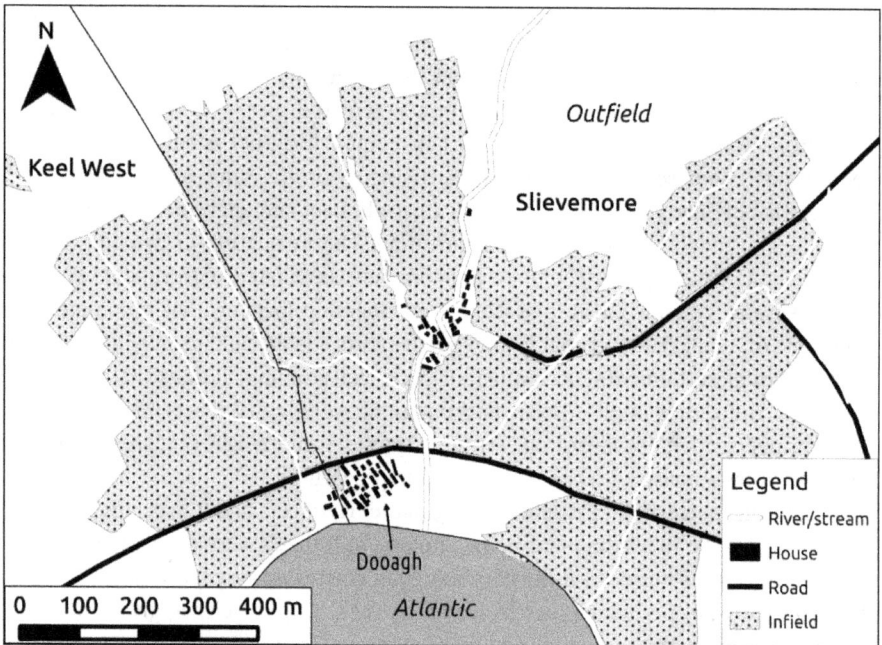

N

Keel West

Outfield

Slievemore

Dooagh

Atlantic

Legend

River/stream

House

Road

Infield

0   100   200   300   400 m

Figure 6.9 Dooagh and Tonregee villages in 1838, located at centre of large infield (adapted from first edition six-inch OS). Typical of contemporary permanent settlement in Achill.

failed to turn up any datable material related to its construction or occupation, but detailed investigations at Slievemore have been more fruitful. Thousands of artefacts have been recovered from Houses 23 and 36 and their adjoining gardens, dating their origins to the late eighteenth and early nineteenth centuries (with occupation of a seasonal nature continuing thereafter up to early twentieth century). In addition, a few sherds of North Devon ware from contexts underlying potato ridges attest to activity at Slievemore during the seventeenth or early eighteenth centuries (Database of Irish Excavation Reports 2004, 1154; 2005, 1133; 2006, 1471). The layout of the settlement at this earlier time cannot be described on current evidence, though with North Devon ware recovered from two separate locations it may be that there was a minor clustered settlement at Slievemore in the seventeenth century that was subsequently swollen by population growth.

Galtee Mountains

Are there similarities in patterns of permanent and seasonal settlement in other post-medieval landscapes? The answer in the Galtee Mountains is a resounding 'yes'. Virtually all tenant farmhouses in the foothills follow a dispersed pattern on the first edition six-inch Ordnance Survey maps, each forming the nucleus of a small holding. This pattern is replicated in the distribution of booley houses – albeit, owing to small numbers, the booley houses often lie a kilometre or more apart. Permanent dwellings, while still clearly separate, have a much denser distribution – the results of intense population growth on the margins of the mountain range.

Notwithstanding the mismatch in numbers between permanent and seasonal sites (a trend seen elsewhere), it is obvious that tenants involved in transhumance during the nineteenth century transferred the idea of living in discrete dwelling houses to the open mountain where they pastured cattle. This reinforces the impression given by the Kingston rentals for Kilbeheny in 1840, which record individual tenancies rather than partnerships, demonstrating that the last phase of booleying in the Galtees did not operate within a rundale system of landholding as it did in Achill (NLI Ms. 3276). This conclusion is a firm one for the nineteenth century because of the clear picture that Ordnance Survey maps provide, but earlier in the post-medieval period it is much less certain how permanent settlement manifested itself in the landscapes of south-east Limerick and south-west Tipperary. In 1780 Arthur Young observed of the Kingston estate that 'great tracts are held in partnership' (Young 1780, 54). If he is correct, it contrasts with the situation sixty years later, when only mountain pasture could be described as commonage (and even then Griffith's Valuation shows that it was nominally owned by the major landlords).

The question that needs to be asked is whether partnership farms involved a different pattern of *settlement* to that shown on the first edition Ordnance Survey map in 1840. Smyth (1976, 38) has examined two townland maps dating to the early nineteenth century that were commissioned by the neighbouring O'Callaghan estate in Tipperary: they depict surviving partnership farms, but without any nucleation of settlement. In the 1650s Civil Survey records for the area mention a few instances of 'cabbins', but it is usually impossible to tell if they are nucleated or dispersed. However, two definite instances of nucleation do occur in Shanrahan parish: in Reaghill – an old manorial centre – stood 'a castle and some thatcht houses and a Bawne about them [as well as] some thatcht houses and cabins without the sd Bawne'; and in Ballyshichane there were 'some cabbins within a bawne' around Sir Richard Everard's mansion house (Simington 1931, 374). There is no trace of these settlements by the nineteenth century. Does this suggest that rural house clusters were once more common around the Galtees? Perhaps, but it is not possible to say on current evidence if nucleation was ever the *dominant* form of settlement.

Only one case of a *nineteenth*-century cluster of farmhouses could be found. In the townland of Scrowmore, just south of Knocknascrow in Kilbeheny, two small groups of buildings are visible on the first edition Ordnance Survey map (Figure 5.6). Given that they are located between 145m and 180m a.s.l., within what may have been seventeenth-century common land, their antiquity is debatable. Nevertheless, the nature of landholding around them hints that they perpetuate an earlier tradition. According to the Griffith's Valuation, some of the tenants living in these two house clusters held fields that were scattered throughout Scrowmore, a pattern that might fossilise a system of partnership farming akin to rundale in which the whole townland was held communally, with fields regularly redistributed among tenants.

If this is a remnant of the partnership farms that Young mentions it could mean that nucleation featured in pre-nineteenth-century landholding. The booley structures of Knocknagalty 1–3 may be associated with this older communal system. They have already been noted as distinctive because of their construction style; however, their proximity to one another and the conjoined layout of Knocknagalty 1 are also unusual (Figure 5.7). Such features are, conceivably, derived from permanent settlements that were nucleated and required more daily interaction and co-operation than that needed between tenant farmers who were based in farmhouses dispersed across numerous individual holdings. In order to substantiate this claim it would have to be proved that the Knocknagalty group was established at a time when partnership farming was common – that is, before the nineteenth century – and that nucleated settlement was actually a common sight at that time. These are big questions that preclude a comparison of the layout of permanent and seasonal settlements any further back in the post-medieval period. Nonetheless, the available evidence does hint at a greater degree of communality in farming around the Galtees than is evident by the time of the Ordnance Survey.

Carna peninsula

There are broad similarities between the layout of permanent settlements as they appear in 1838 and the seasonal settlements identified by the writer. Tenant farmhouses are densely distributed on the islands and coast, though there is no actual clustering of settlement as on Achill. Similarly, even though booley houses and huts are relatively numerous in those areas surveyed they are very rarely found within 10m of one another. On favourable rocky pasture in Aill Mhór Ghleannáin and the south of Cnoc Buí booley houses do occur in greater numbers than normal, but they still cannot be described as anything other than loose groups. Curvilinear walls that divide and partially enclose these groups have been discussed functionally as milking paddocks that facilitated stone clearance, but division of space also contains an implicit social meaning. Arguably, it was a concept that transhumant herders derived from areas of permanent settlement. Here, instead of land being held communally (as was the case along much of Ireland's western seaboard), each tenant held his own farm either from year-to-year or under a three-year lease (NAI M. 2429–31, M. 3440–01, 3443). In such a context, divided space was expected and found material expression in the proliferation of irregular field boundaries around increasing numbers of farmhouses in the pre-Famine period (Figure 3.9).

Although currently it is impossible to confirm that low marker walls visible at Aill Mhór and to the south of Cnoc Buí are contemporary with these field systems, the fact that they are associated with booley dwellings occupied during the nineteenth century is strongly indicative of a connection. It is tentatively concluded, therefore, that they were laid out by transhumant herders who were familiar with the idea of enclosure and sought to replicate it in locations where seasonal settlement was dense enough to rival the social complexity of home.

This did not occur in Achill, even though seasonal settlements on that island are clearly larger and contained more people. Aside from pathways and natural streams, there is no division of space within Achill's booley settlements. While walled livestock enclosures *are* found at Bunowna and Dirk (Figure 6.8), just as they are sometimes found on the Carna peninsula, they are discrete and occupy fairly insignificant areas of ground. In other words, they do not indicate social divisions among the herders. Banks of earth constructed along the high cliffs near both Bunowna and Dirk were, as McDonald (2014, 154) thinks, probably intended to keep cattle away from the cliff-edge. The lack of divided social space in the archaeological record in Achill may be explained by its lack in home settlements on the island. Other than people's farmhouses and any tiny gardens they might have maintained, all land in Achill was held communally from the landlord, regardless of whether it was used as tillage or pasture. As long as this system of landholding was maintained, with people living in communal clusters both at home and in the hills, there was simply no need for the enclosure of ground on a fixed, permanent basis. Neither was enclosed social space a necessity around the later booley sites in the Galtee Mountains, as they were relatively few in number and relatively far removed from one another.

Gleann Cholm Cille

An Clochán and Mín na Saileach are the only pair of land units in this book in which there is a stark contrast in the layout of permanent and seasonal settlement. Farmhouses in An Clochán in 1835 are found in a tight cluster, while the booley dwellings in Mín na Saileach are spread out. The different distribution patterns may be associated with the more intensive nature of land use at home, and the convenient nexus that a centrally located settlement offered. Herders in Mín na Saileach, by contrast, had to range more widely in their daily routine. Given, however, that the clustering of dwellings did not hinder booleying in Achill, this argument is not sufficient by itself. If indeed the spatial organisation of booley settlement does mirror that of permanent settlement, there may be another explanation as to why they do not appear similar in the townlands surveyed.

None of the house clusters shown on the first edition six-inch Ordnance Survey map of Gleann are particularly large; in fact, An Clochán is one of the largest, with fourteen houses. Nucleated rundale settlements in other parts of the west of Ireland dwarf this: Keel in Achill, Barn Hill in Magheramore, County Galway, and Mionlach, just north of Galway city, for instance, all contain dozens of houses on the same set of maps. Considering that population in south-west Donegal rose rapidly from a low base during the eighteenth and early nineteenth centuries, it is tempting to regard much of the clustering in Gleann as a development which started only in the late eighteenth century. This is all the more plausible if we consider that some of the targeted settlements established in the early nineteenth century had attracted up to six houses by 1835. Thus, farmhouses in Gleann may previously have been more isolated and, with that, more comparable to the distribution of booley huts and houses. There is only so far that this argument can be pushed, however, without a distribution map of seasonal sites in the whole parish and without absolute dating evidence for both them and the farmhouses.

HUMAN PARTICIPATION IN SEASONAL RELOCATION

The question of how many people in a farming community relocated to summer pastures has been emphatically answered for the early to mid-nineteenth centuries. The archaeology of seasonal settlement in the Carna peninsula and Gleann Cholm Cille shows that little more than a third of the population could have been accommodated at summer pasture at any one time. In the Galtee Mountains it is more difficult to arrive at estimations because the extent of the transhumant community is difficult to define. However, even if it were just those tenant families who meared on the mountain common that engaged in transhumance it can only have been a small minority of this population who physically relocated with cattle by the mid-nineteenth century given that the farmhouses greatly outnumber surviving booley huts and houses. The size differences between them across Ireland confirm, too, that the seasonal sites cannot have accommodated as many people. Furthermore, the oral histories repeatedly indicate that adults tended to stay at home.

Before the nineteenth century, however, a greater percentage of people within Irish rural communities may have been seasonally mobile. This is plausible because populations in areas of permanent settlement were lower, and it is suggested by a number of historical references. In 1821 a statistical report on the parishes of Ballynascreen, Desertmartin and Kilcronaghan in mid-Ulster claimed that, up to about 1760, every family would move in May up to the 'woody glens and upland heights' of the Sperrin Mountains, bringing with them their 'flocks and herds' (Day and McWilliams 1995, 119). These movements probably represent a continuation of the transhumant links identified on Down Survey maps for Ballynascreen in Chapter 2. Meanwhile, in east Ulster, Harris' account of the Mourne Mountains in 1744 stated that 'great Numbers of poor People resort in the Summer Months to graze their Cattle [and] bring with them their Wives [and] Children' (Smith and Harris 1744, 125). This is supported by that somewhat vague folk memory of whole families coming from Hillsborough to the Mournes in the late eighteenth century (Graham 1954, 27–8). Earlier again, in 1682, Thomas Knox remarked that a sacred building near the ruined parish church of Templecarn in south-east Donegal was 'of old' used by locals to store valuable goods while they were away in summer pastures with their cattle, implying that nobody stayed at home (Leslie 1932, 84). The only other obvious reference to whole families relocating before the eighteenth century comes from the extreme south-west of the country in County Kerry (see Chapter 2).

Notwithstanding these sources, it would be overly simplistic to conclude that transhumance involved the movement of everyone in a community during the seventeenth and eighteenth centuries. For one thing, there is a chance that they contain a degree of exaggeration. A telling example of such comes from Sir William Wilde, who, in 1847, claimed that 'during the spring, the entire population of several of the villages ... in Achill, close their winter dwellings ... drive their cattle before them, and migrate into the hills ... ' (Wilde 1847, 775). Of course, McDonald's analysis shows that this cannot have happened. Exaggeration is even more likely to have crept into non-contemporary accounts such as those relating to the Sperrins, Hillsborough and Templecarn. The distribution of the references is also problematic. With Wilde discounted, Kerry is the only part of the country outside Ulster for which movements of all age groups are attested. Historical evidence for the west of County Galway in 1684 paints a different picture: O'Flaherty, who was actually from this area, strongly implies that only some people relocated to the summer pastures, 'where *such as look to the cattle live in small cabins*' (my emphasis; Hardiman 1846, 16–17). In south Connemara, adult men who stayed behind were probably involved in fishing.

It could be argued that arable farming also required people to stay at home. Even before the potato became popular the production of oats or barley would have been necessary to supplement the dairy products in the diet. Oaten bread and oatmeal, sometimes mixed with butter, were important constituents of the diet of non-elite Irish people in the sixteenth and early seventeenth centuries, according to references collected by Lucas (1989, 108–09). The production of cereals around the home settlements of contemporary transhumant farmers is suggested in all three study areas by the estimations of arable land found in the *BSD*, Civil Survey and Down Survey (albeit these are quite low in the Carna peninsula and Gleann Cholm Cille; see also Nicholls 1987, 411–12). In subsequent centuries, oats remained an important dietary supplement for transhumant people, including those transhumant families in the Sperrins, who are said to have lived 'on a scanty supply of oatmeal, but abundance of butter, curds, cream' (Day and McWilliams 1995, 119). With transhumant communities involved in tillage throughout the post-medieval period, it is therefore unlikely that they abandoned their home settlements completely. Grain crops needed to be checked regularly to ensure that they were not trampled by wandering livestock from non-transhumant communities or families, and a large workforce would have to be around in August and September to actually harvest the crops and dry the corn in kilns.

Thus, even if there was a tendency in some areas for adults to relocate with young people, there were good reasons for maintaining a presence at home. In other areas, where tillage was for more than subsistence (south and east of the Galtees), and where coastal fishing drained manpower (the Carna peninsula and Gleann Cholm Cille), home settlements must have retained a sizeable proportion of their population throughout the summer and early autumn.

THE SOCIO-CULTURAL ROLE OF TRANSHUMANCE AND THE PERCEPTION OF UPLANDS

The fragmentation of rural communities for the purposes of seasonal labour is not uncommon around the world, even up to the present day, and is well-attested in Ireland during the nineteenth and early to mid-twentieth centuries. For example, thousands of *spailpíní* and 'tattie hokers' are known to have left the west of Ireland in summertime to work on farms in the east and south of the country or in Britain, sometimes as a means of gaining cash for permanent emigration to America (O'Dowd 1990). While small-scale transhumance such as booleying cannot really be described as *migratory* labour, which was a cash-service performed for external parties at long distances from home, it nonetheless involved a removal of people that divided the community in a spatial sense for part of the year. This is what makes booleying and shieling practices across north-west Europe so significant from a socio-cultural point of view.

In two recent articles I have asked what seasonal spatial fragmentation as a result of transhumance meant for the cohesion of rural communities in post-medieval Ireland and north-west Europe as a whole (Costello 2017; 2018). Where the nineteenth and early twentieth centuries are concerned, it clearly afforded young people, and adolescent girls especially, a degree of freedom from the regular social constraints of home. In the evening they were able to enjoy themselves and spend time with members of the opposite sex. As one account in 1935 in Carna remembers:

> … bu geal le fuiseogaí iad ar maidin ⁊ trathnóna; ⁊ tharnuídís go leór go na fir óga bhí thart tímpull na háite amach ag éisteacht leothab a fonnadóireacht ⁊ a' casa poirt ⁊ a'damhsa, ⁊ a' déana chuile shórt spóirt. Ach tá an aimsir sin caite ⁊ níl tada gon spórt sin ar bun anois (NFC Ms. 156, 55).

> As bright as larks they [the young women] were morning and evening; and they used to draw many of the young men who were around the place out listening to them playing music, singing songs, dancing and making all sorts of fun. But that time is gone and there's no fun like that going on anymore.

Similarly, an elderly man in north-west Donegal says that when his mother was at the booley she and the other girls would have a small *céilí* (social evening) when the day's work was done, with the boys from home sometimes coming up as well and spending much of the night with the girls. Moreover, his mother apparently acquired much of her repertoire of songs during her time as a dairymaid in the hills (Ó hEochaidh

1943, 148); in this regard, the presence of different age groups ('young girls', 'girls', 'young women') at booley sites probably facilitated the learning process (Costello 2017, 197). Indeed, the Irish proverb 'Thug sí an damhsa ó bhuaile léi/She was well-schooled in dancing' literally means 'She brought the dance from the booley' (Ó Dónaill, 1977, 152–53).

Seasonal isolation in the hills thus afforded young women an opportunity not only to hone their skills as dairymaids but also to exchange knowledge of music and dance and gain experience in the performance of that knowledge among their male peers. Taking place in a largely unsupervised environment, booleying was a rite of passage that helped to socialise new generations of young people. This was beneficial for the whole community in the long term, as the sustainable exploitation of common-pool resources depends on regular dialogue between interested parties in case of, for example, disputes over grazing. Meetings at booley sites normalised interaction between members of different tenant families from an early age, providing a strong social basis for future negotiation in adulthood.

It is less clear from the accounts given by elderly people whether socialisation went so far as to involve pre-marital sexual activity, as seems to have been a strong possibility in Scandinavian countries during post-medieval times according to folk material, and in the medieval period according to Icelandic sagas (Kupiec 2016, Table 7.1; Costello 2018, 169–70). Nevertheless, there are a couple of very subtle hints that romantic encounters could take place at seasonal sites in Ireland. In south-west Donegal, for instance, the emphatic stress on there 'never [being] a hint of any impropriety' raises more questions than answers (Morris *et al.* 1939, 289), while an account of booleying in Gaoth Dobhair in north-west Donegal maintains that many marriages resulted from the meeting of young people in the hill pastures (NFC Ms. 1453, 110–11). Things did not always end positively, though. In a very interesting folk song that is known to this day in parts of western Ireland, a married woman now living in a town curses both the priest and her husband for taking her away from the summer pastures (Ó Duilearga and Ó Gallchobhair 1940, 257–58). She plaintively remembers the older calves bawling at the booley (' … géimneach na ngamhna 'san mbuailí') and wishes she could watch them from her little green summer hut (' … b'fhearr liom i mbothóigín glas Samhraidh'). She also adds that it was not town life that she knew in her youth, but the life of dancing on upland pastures with the calves. As an eminent folklorist has speculated, the woman is possibly alluding here to romantic dances with members of her own species (Professor Mícheál Briody, University of Helsinki, pers. comm.).

The reticence to speak out more directly must be understood in the context of Irish society in the 1930s and 1940s. By this time, when living memories of Irish transhumance were finally being recorded, the Irish Catholic Church was at the height of its powers both politically and spiritually and in such a climate it is highly unlikely that the Folklore Commission's fieldworkers would have committed explicit information about 'fornication' to paper even though it might have occurred several decades beforehand. Moreover, most of the elderly people interviewed by the Folklore Commission were men, so they may not have been willing or able to talk about the issue of female sexuality in booleying. The potential role of the Catholic Church in changing views on the morality of booleying is a fascinating issue worthy of further exploration in future. While local clergy probably adapted their stance on the seasonal independence of herders, the beginnings of a negative theological position are evident in the Counter-Reformation writings of Fr Seathrún Céitinn (already quoted in relation to the Galtee Mountains). By associating *buailteachas* with the fleeting mortal world and the more permanent *sean-bhaile* with everlasting life in heaven, he arguably casts transhumance in a sinful light. In a sermon written in Louth in 1797, Fr John Heely goes further and denounces *buailteachas* as a vice alongside drunkenness, prostitution and thievery (RIA Corpas, Seanmóirí John Heely, 141). With the expansion of the Catholic Church's clergy and infrastructure in the late nineteenth century (Larkin 1972) it is possible that this thinking permeated rural communities and households and contributed to the decline of booleying as a socio-cultural force.

However, these negative views were not entirely new. To some extent, they drew on the pre-existing perception of hills and mountains as liminal spaces where strange or even supernatural events were more likely to occur. In addition to accounts that provide first- and second-hand memories of seasonal settlement, there are in west Mayo and south Connemara a number of longer folk stories associated with booleying (see Costello 2017). These describe encounters with hags who curse people at the booley huts and transform into hares to steal milk from cows; mention harassment by wolves who sometimes turn out to be young men; and recount the attempts of bands of strange men to 'abduct' girls as brides. Such events usually take place at night and the hero or heroine in almost all cases is a young woman or girl, sometimes helped by her younger brother. Many of these themes – particularly shape-shifting and the danger of strange men – are also found in folk tales about shielings in the Outer Hebrides and Iceland (Kupiec 2016, Tables 7.1, 7.2). While rural communities in north-west Europe did have a number of genuine fears about outland and upland environments, such as the possibility of injury in poor weather, the loss of livestock to bogs and cliffs and the sexual assault of female herders, the folk stories almost certainly exaggerate and invent some of the dangers in order to warn young people into more watchful behaviour.

At the end of the day, transhumant herders in post-medieval north-west Europe were often only 2–6km away from the main settlements and could keep in fairly regular contact with their families. The return of butter and cheese would have taken place at least every few days, and adult males would probably have walked through summer pastures on their way to cut peat and undertake charcoal and/or iron production (Costello 2018, 176–78). Indeed, when male repairs to booley huts are considered in the light of male-controlled fire rituals that renewed or inaugurated shieling sites in Scotland's Western Isles and the Boreal forests of Sweden, it can be argued that there was a degree of adult male control over the architecture of summer huts and houses (Andersson *et al.* 2011; Costello 2017, 197–98; Costello 2018, 173–74).

Moreover, many seasonal settlements were undergoing a process of domestication in later post-medieval times, and the organisation and use of space within them tends to echo the layout of permanent settlements. This pattern suggests that people were – consciously or otherwise – transposing ideas about home to the hills. So a degree of tension and ambiguity ran through the experience of transhumant herders in uplands. While the liminality evident in folk stories did throw up some risks and facilitate freedoms – making it a 'rite of passage' for young people – there were clearly limits to that independence and also to the perceived dangers when the archaeology and geographic reality of seasonal settlement are taken into account.

THE CURRENTS OF GLOBAL CAPITALISM IN LIVESTOCK HUSBANDRY

If internal changes in Irish society and settlement played a key role in the development and decline of transhumance, deepening economic ties with the rest of the world had important concurrent effects. As the post-medieval period progressed Irish farmers increasingly interacted with the growth of capitalism, altering, as they did, the number and kinds of livestock they kept. This in turn had an influence on whether or not the seasonal relocation of significant numbers of people with livestock continued to be required.

Beef production and its visibility in the zooarchaeological record

One major change over the course of the seventeenth century was the great increase in Irish beef production. This was a departure from earlier livestock husbandry. As a result of farming's mainly local orientation, extant records from the sixteenth century show that it was by-products of slaughter, such as cattle hides and sheep skins, that dominated the contemporary Irish export trade (along with fish; Nicholls 1987, 416–17, 421; Simms 2015, 103; Gillespie 2015, 122). Furthermore, commenting on his experience of Ireland at the very start of the seventeenth century, Fynes Moryson says that the wild Irish 'seldom kill a cow to eat', living for the most part on 'white meats' (Falkiner 1904, 230). The slaughter of calves 'that [the people] themselves may have more abundance of milk' emphasises that cattle were farmed primarily as dairy animals (Falkiner 1904, 230). The analysis of faunal remains from urban excavations supports this historical evidence. In excavated contexts from the late medieval town of Galway the examination of mandibles, tooth-wear and epiphyseal fusion on cattle remains – the dominant species – suggests that it was principally adults and elderly individuals that were brought into the town, having been raised for dairying/breeding or traction (Murray 2004, 575–76). Similarly, faunal analysis from excavations in Cork city in the south shows that over 60 per cent of cattle remains – 57 per cent of all identified fauna – were fully mature individuals: indeed, many may have been as old as seven when slaughtered – clearly, therefore, they had been raised for dairying or traction (McCarthy 2003, 377).

However, this was true only of the medieval period, with later contexts from Cork turning up more young individuals that were presumably raised solely for beef (McCarthy 2003, 377). An increasing human population would have helped to drive this shift in the assemblage, but there was also a growth in overseas demand that may not be represented in local zooarchaeological evidence. By 1616–17 Gillespie (2015, 122) calculates that 'almost 50 per cent of all [of Ireland's] external trade was in cattle and cattle products [mainly beef], [and] 11 per cent in sheep and wool, with grain representing less than 6 per cent'. If cattle were being exported *en masse* as live animals or even joints of meat, then a substantial proportion of cattle bones from Irish beef stock would never have made it into the urban archaeological record in Ireland. This may partially explain why there is no rise in younger cattle in the post-medieval assemblage from Galway. Although the western port town dominated Irish beef and hide exports in the early seventeenth century (Gillespie 2015, 122), it had a smaller human population than Cork and would not have registered the same growth in local consumption. Increased numbers of cattle being raised for export in its supply region – including the Carna peninsula – would therefore not be represented in the town's archaeological record.[3]

Neither would a historical rise in cattle numbers be expected to show up at rural sites. At Glanworth Castle, County Cork, the faunal remains recovered from seventeenth-century features demonstrated the presence of sheep (44 per cent), cattle (29 per cent) and pigs (27 per cent) (Crabtree and Ryan 2010, 119). However, as these are a record of on-site slaughtering only, any cattle sent to urban centres or abroad would have been invisible to the excavator. This problem is compounded by the fact that bone preservation is poor in acidic soils and/or because faunal analysis is simply not prioritised in post-excavation. For example, Orser's book on the nineteenth-century tenant farms of Ballykilcline, County Roscommon, was published before the (admittedly scanty) animal remains had been properly identified (Orser 2006b, 173). His subsequent article contextualising Ballykilcine with two other excavations in Sligo and Donegal does not mention faunal remains (Orser 2010). All in all, targeted and fully published research excavations are rare in post-medieval rural contexts, and certainly there are no faunal studies from the present study areas that might shed light on local slaughtering practices.

The rise of dry cattle and the decline/survival of transhumance

For now, it has to be inferred from historical information that cattle raised solely for beef were becoming more common in the Irish landscape. Gillespie (2015, 122–24) shows – again through trade records – that live cattle exports to England grew massively until they were banned by the Cattle Acts of 1663–67, with exports continuing in the form of processed meat thereafter. The early seventeenth-century grazing leases for cattle in the Comeragh Mountains (see Chapter 2) are possibly a manifestation of the push among farmers towards dry stock, while the expanding presence of Galway townsmen as landowners in Connemara during the late sixteenth and seventeenth centuries (Ó Bric 1974; Naessens 2009, 169–70, 180) was probably also born out of a desire to capitalise on the profitability of rearing cattle for beef.

Notwithstanding fluctuations in market demand – too numerous to outline here[4] – later historical evidence implies that dry cattle retained an important place

---

[3]   Owing to an inadequate number of mandibles, Galway's post-medieval cattle record is less clear-cut than that of the later medieval period, although Murray (2004, 575–76) does argue that adults aged from three to four years continued to dominate.

[4]   For example, the mid- to late 1680s saw low prices for high exports of Irish farming goods, only to be followed by disastrous cattle murrain – all factors that contributed to

in livestock farming, at least in the west of Ireland. Thus, non-payment of rent in south-west Donegal in 1778 was partially down to the poor prices that black cattle (i.e., for beef) were fetching for tenant farmers (Mac Cuinneagáin 2002, 63), while at Ballinasloe, County Galway, a large fair was held each year for 'fat cattle, to which the buyers from Cork, Limerick, all parts of Leinster, and frequently from England and Scotland, repair[ed] in October' (Dutton 1824, 118).

The implications of a new beef sector for existing systems of transhumance were serious. In Ireland, with summer grazing rarely more than half a day's walk from permanent areas of settlement – even in the seventeenth century – the only reasons for herders' presence overnight would have been to milk cows and ward off wolves and thieves. Given that wolves and warfare both became less common in the landscape after the 1650s, dairying would have been left as the main if not only reason for continued human occupation of booley sites. An increase in the number of dry cattle pasturing marginal land would not have been matched by an increase in numbers of transhumant herders; in fact, seasonal settlement may have entered a phase of abandonment in areas where rearing or finishing of dry cattle began to take priority. These animals may have required checking only once a day and, where wolves and rustlers remained a threat, they could have been accompanied by a small number of herdsmen at most. The rise of dry beef cattle seems to have been even more widespread in the Scottish Highlands, with increasingly large numbers of 'black' cattle being driven southwards to urban markets from the late seventeenth century (Haldane 1952; Adamson 2014). Indeed, in Lochtayside the trend of specialisation in black cattle is positively correlated with the abandonment of primarily dairy-focused shieling sites in the mid-eighteenth century (Atkinson 2016, 104, 211, 272–73).

Yet the growing attraction of rearing dry cattle does not work as a blanket explanation for transhumance's decline. Behind it was a lot of local complexity and farmers would have had to consider several factors concurrently when making decisions about what kind of livestock they wanted to rear and how to manage them. For instance, shieling sites on the Isle of Skye remained in use into the early nineteenth century despite the export of black cattle from the island from as early as the sixteenth century (MacSween 1959, 81–82), and in south-west Donegal and Connemara booleying continued even though the sale of young cattle had attained great local importance by 1800. In both of these areas it was the expansion of settlement (in both organic and targeted ways), followed by the reorganisation of farms and fields, that ultimately had the most serious effects on local transhumant systems.

Why do these areas form exceptions? Like many other aspects of transhumance, the answer lies ultimately in the land and how it was used. In the mid-seventeenth century proportionately tiny amounts of ground are estimated as arable in Gleann Cholm Cille and the Carna peninsula, so there can have been little pressure on pastures from this direction. However, the landscape changed as potatoes became a staple and the population grew. With good soils very limited in extent, it remained a necessity for

an emerging contemporary political crisis (Gillespie 2015, 137–38). For a price history of Irish farming produce after the mid-eighteenth century see Kennedy and Solar (2007).

at least a minority of the community to bring dairy cows elsewhere for the summer. By contrast, in districts where there was a greater area of productive land and (slightly) less population pressure farmers were able to accommodate limited numbers of dairy cows close to home for subsistence purposes while larger herds of dry cattle were fattened further away. This is a simplified comparison, but it helps to explain the differential survival of transhumance between regions of poorer or richer soils, even as both were drawn into the commercial world of beef production. Examples of upland pastures that were (mostly) given over to dry cattle by the nineteenth century include the hills around Athea in west Limerick (Danaher 1998, 40) and the Slieve Aughties in south-east Galway (Kevin Cunningham and Christy Cunniffe, pers. comm.), both of which have wide expanses of fertile lowlands nearby. Meanwhile, the karstic limestone hills of the Burren in north-west Clare, which may once have facilitated a rare system of *winter* transhumance, came to be dominated by sheep and, in more recent times, by non-dairy suckler cows – neither of which required the relocation of herders to seasonal accommodation (Dunford 2002; O'Rourke 2005).

The role of dairying

In other areas, dairying actually *intensified*. The aftermath of the Cattle Acts of the 1660s saw Ireland's victualling trade with the Continent and New World take off, leading to substantial growth in not only beef exports but butter too (Whelan 1993, 206). Better internal distribution of imported salt through Ireland's proliferating fairs and markets (O'Flanagan 1985, 367–68) facilitated the preservation of both types of food over long journeys. In terms of the butter trade, Whelan (1997) and Dickson (2005) have now established that it had a particular role in the farming practices of south Munster, where soils gave better year-round grass growth and Cork city was well positioned to take advantage of trans-Atlantic trade routes.

It was shown in Chapter 5 that high prices for butter were exploited down to the level of the minor tenant farmer, and they arguably provided such producers with an incentive to continue keeping numbers of dairy cows that went well beyond their subsistence needs.[5] For hill farmers along the south of the Galtees with little improved land, this meant that mountain pasture and the overnight occupation of booley houses continued to form part of life up to the mid-nineteenth century. The fact that new booley houses seem to have been constructed at a higher altitude after encroachment testifies to the importance that seasonal upland activity retained in the face of settlement expansion, if only for farms lying in the mountains' shadow. The relative inaccessibility of much of the Galtees – compared with other upland areas in or near the Munster dairying zone – joined with economic circumstances to help keep transhumance relevant in people's lives.

---

[5]   Interestingly, it has been argued that, although butter was being produced in greater quantities in post-medieval Ireland, *per capita* consumption actually decreased, leading to a greater reliance on oatmeal and especially potatoes (Clarkson and Crawford 2001, 21). Herein lay one of the reasons for Ireland's astonishing population rise, for potatoes could feed far more people per hectare than milk and butter from a grazing cow.

Without a strong regional emphasis on butter production it is questionable whether tenant farmers in the Galtees would have considered it worthwhile to rely on booley sites in the nineteenth century. After all, the mountain ranges of Leinster – most noticeably the Wicklow Mountains – have no recorded oral traditions relating to the occupation of booley sites (though in a few cases cows were still grazed on mountain land during summer; Aalen 1964a; NFC Mss. 1453–4; 1565; 1669; 1831). Thus, by the mid- to late nineteenth century the south-west of the Galtees could be described as an anomaly in livestock farming systems of southern and eastern Ireland, as at that time transhumance was generally practised only by land-starved communities along the western seaboard, which lay at the fringe of the butter trade.[6]

THE FINAL DEMISE OF SEASONAL MOVEMENT AND SETTLEMENT IN THE LANDSCAPE

Customary rights questioned and Blackface sheep introduced

Several additional factors coalesced in the mid- to late nineteenth century to render the continued removal of people to booley sites either impractical or unnecessary. The first is the weakening of commons where summer grazing and settlement took place. Arthur Young (1780, 176) asserted that the improvement of waste land was easy in Ireland compared with England because 'there are no common rights to encounter'. However, this is clearly an exaggeration. He himself describes the patch of mountain he adopted for improvement in the Galtees as 'a commonage to the adjoining farm' (Young 1780, 172). What his declaration really speaks to is a disinterest in non-written assumptions and traditions maintained by the peasantry of a 'backward country' (Young 1780, 222). Grazing rights on marginal land may have been *recorded* from time to time in documents of conquest such as the Desmond Survey and the Down Survey and in later rental rolls, but these were not legal documents that non-elite people in Ireland could cite, or even wanted to cite.

Their customary rights of pasture were upheld through practice and verbal discussion. In the Carna peninsula, common grazing in particular parts of the interior was a 'right inseparable' from the holdings of tenants, in south-west Donegal people from the townlands of Gleann had grazing rights for certain numbers of cattle in blocks of shared hill pasture (overseen by a local decision-maker) and in Knocknascrow the common grazing of cattle on the Galtees was inherent in the system of *comaointeas* that tenants maintained among themselves. In north-west Donegal the grazing rights of booleying families in Cloch Cheannfhaola over an area that stretched 8km from Mount Errigal to the village of Gaoth Dobhair are remembered in much the same way (Ó hEochaidh 1943, 133):

---

[6] By the end of the nineteenth century, the Congested Districts Board reports for both Gleann Cholm Cille and the Carna peninsula that very little butter was being sold (Gahan 1892, 5; Ruttledge-Fair 1892, 3).

A dh'aindeóin go rabh siad ceangluighthe thíos anseo ag na cladaigh, bhí ceart acú ó na tighearnaí a gcuid eallaigh a chur ar inghilt ar na sléibhte i bhfad ar shiubhal.

Although they were tied to the coast down here, they had the right from the lords to graze their herds of cattle far away on the mountains.

Moreover, there is an assumption that such customary rights of pasture came free from higher authority. Dickson (2005, 243) refers to the commonly held idea in Munster that certain tracts of mountain grazing were reserved by the crown for the poor and their livestock. Thus, regarding Slievegrine area north of Ardmore, County Waterford, Ryland (1824, 321) records 'a favourite notion among the common people is, that it was reserved by Queen Anne for the relief of the poor of Ireland'. Although the seasonal relocation of people to booley sites was perhaps less likely on the hills of Slievegrine, because of their proximity to surrounding permanent settlements, the tradition of free grazing by royal decree echoes the eighteenth-century justification for booleying in the Mournes. When Smith and Harris (1744, 125) remarked on the poor people who brought their cattle to those mountains in summer they note that they used a large area of pasture called 'by some, the *King's Meadow* (because people have their grazing in it free)'.

But the verbal traditions of non-elite peasant farmers were strong only when everyone concerned – including the landed elite – was more or less in agreement about free grazing. This came into question when landlords sought to claim ownership of those large blocks of 'unprofitable' common land that are depicted on Down Survey maps. Large tracts of rough grazing that had not formed part of any one territory in the seventeenth century now held potential in the eyes of improvers as well as offering small farmers a means of coping with population pressure and exploiting broader economic trends where possible. From the early nineteenth century nation states across Europe sought to document and measure land in unprecedented detail for a range of nationalistic and economic reasons (e.g. Konvitz 1987; Hansen 2015) – for Ireland, the government of the United Kingdom wanted a basis for accurate land and building valuation (Andrews 2002). In this climate, landowners gradually woke up to the fact that, of anyone in rural society, they were best-placed to assert ownership of unclaimed land, particularly when they adopted the attitude of Arthur Young and paid little attention to customary rights. For instance, the beliefs of poorer people regarding Slievegrine are noted by Ryland in the 1820s only because the earl of Grandison had claimed the title of those uplands in 1733, creating a long-running legal dispute between squatters, graziers and the landowning class (Dickson 2005, 243, 573).

In the mid-nineteenth century the commons of some upland areas were subjected to increased pressure. As Griffith's Valuation attests, *all* of the uncultivated rough grazing used by communities in Gleann, Carna and Kilbeheny as part of transhumance was recorded as being 'in fee' of the local landlord by the 1850s. This had not been the case in the seventeenth century and, with the bankruptcy of many landlords in

Ireland after the Great Famine, outside speculators with little regard for non-written customary grazing rights could now take advantage (Lane 1996; Nolan 2012, 570–72). After the bankrupt Kingston estate was sold in 1851 (Power 2000, Appendix A) a rent of £3 is supposed to have been placed on every head of cattle that tenants possessed, an action that defeated the purpose of grazing extra cattle on the (rent-free) mountain pasture of Knocknascrow (Ó Danachair 1945, 250). Local tradition holds that Scottish sheep were then brought in by a new Manchester-based landlord Nathaniel Buckley to replace the dairy cattle of tenants on mountain pastures (Lewis 1985; Michael Kearney, pers. comm.). Similarly, in Gaoth Dobhair, County Donegal, hillsides traditionally used as summer pastures in booleying were fenced off as private sheep-runs by the new Lord Hill between 1854 and 1856, forcing tenants to sell off their cattle (Mac Suibhne 1995, 559). These changes were so rapid and shocking that tenants reacted violently in both areas, eventually regaining the right to use their upland pastures.

Even if it was temporary, however, the exercise of landlord proprietorship in the hills and mountains served to disrupt the dairy- and cattle-based booleying system. In line with estate policy across much of the Scottish Highlands from the late eighteenth century (Bil 1990, 309; Whyte and Whyte 1991, 167–69; Bangor-Jones 2002, 181), the Blackface sheep was introduced in large numbers to Irish uplands, as they were seen to offer the most efficient use of rough ground in the gradually depopulating landscape of post-Famine western Ireland (see Jones 1995, 106–10). Indeed, sheep became dominant in Gleann Cholm Cille as well: in 1892 its three electoral districts contained 4,665 sheep versus 1,148 cattle (Gahan 1892, 4). This may be compared with overall statistics for south-west Donegal in 1851, when sheep numbered 19,172 and cattle 22,826 (of which 12,624 were aged two and a half year or more; Agricultural Returns 1851, 641). A few decades later the local Congested Districts Board inspector advocates the improvement of local flocks 'with good well-bred Scotch rams' (Gahan 1892, 4), while today it is only the Blackface that grazes the open hill pastures of Gleann Cholm Cille. Seemingly, the Scottish breed came to be recognised as the most suitable animal for grazing difficult areas where labour was perhaps lacking after the Famine, and, whether such flocks were owned by tenants or their landlords, their dominance ultimately rendered seasonal relocation unnecessary. These hardy (and less valuable) animals did not require constant attention and, as they were raised for their meat and wool rather than dairy products, there was now no need for a significant human presence on rough pastures.

A weakening social basis for co-operation and the emergence of emigration

Customary grazing rights were not interfered with as dramatically in the south-west of Donegal or in the Carna peninsula, however, and in the latter cattle have retained a presence on rough pastures. In these two study areas it was the reforming measures of landlords and the Congested Districts Board in tenants' *home* settlements that undermined the traditional basis of transhumance. A few short years before the Famine the Connolly estate's attitude towards land organisation in south-west Donegal changed – a shift that reflects the increasingly negative thoughts of external commentators on rundale-style partnership farms (Knight 1836, 47; Bell and Watson 2008, 108). In line with developments elsewhere in Donegal, such as in the barony of Tirhugh (Anderson 1995) and on the Hill estate prior to the conflict over upland grazing in the 1850s (Mac Suibhne 1995), landlord policy now forced the abolition of rundale.

Ideologically, the notion of collective holdings was replaced with individual tenancy, and, physically, house clusters and their infields were taken apart in favour of 'striped' holdings. In 1844, when giving evidence to the Devon Commission, James Cunningham, a tenant in Fearann Mac Giolla Bhríde of the middleman Hume, says that 'Colonel Conolly will assist you and give you 40 shillings and slates and timber for the house' (Devon Commission 1845, 156). This is presumably a reference to the tenants' construction of new houses after they were forced to demolish their nucleated settlements. By 1848, when updated six-inch maps were completed (and used in the subsequent Griffith's Valuation), the process was well under way in several parts of Gleann Cholm Cille. For example, most houses in An Droim, Cill Fhathnaid and An Dumhaigh were now spread out, with narrow rectangular fields dividing up the old communal infield. That said, a majority of townlands, including An Clochán, still seem to have had largely intact rundale landscapes, perhaps because the Great Famine had retarded the process of reorganisation (Figure 6.10). Nonetheless, the striping of farms

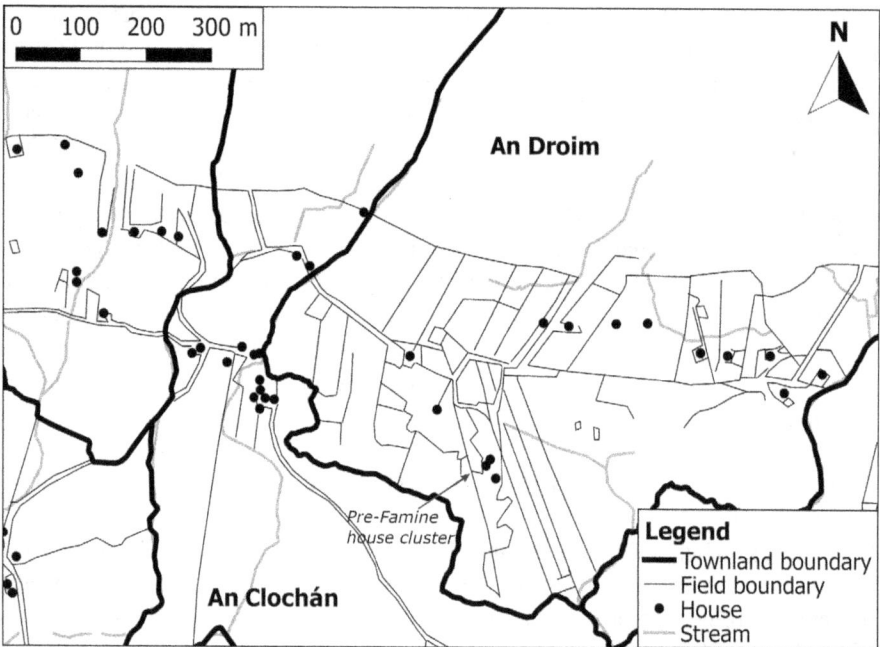

Figure 6.10 Detail of Gleann in 1848, redrawn from the (updated) six-inch OS maps used in Griffith's Primary Valuation. In An Droim, most of the houses are now spread out, with new striped holdings overlaying most of the older communal infield. An Clochán to the west is still almost untouched, however.

proceeded apace after that crisis had left its mark and, by the time of the first edition twenty-five-inch Ordnance Survey map in 1907, every valley and area of permanent settlement in the parish was divided up into separate holdings. Ribbon settlements are visible along newly constructed roads, but they no longer form true clusters.

This rearrangement of the landscape from above is a powerful reminder that the agency of tenants had limits. Landlords could exercise power over their estates at any time and, when it eventually happened in south-west Donegal, Connolly's improvements fundamentally disturbed the social structures of transhumance. The dispersal of home dwellings and division of infields weakened the co-operative basis that had characterised rundale, leaving areas of upland grazing open to the highest bidder. Thus, the aforementioned James Cunningham complained to the Devon Commission in 1844 that he had recently given up his rent of 2,231 acres of mountain grazing because of the high price – £21 – that Mr Hume was charging for Cunningham's *home* farm of twenty acres (Devon Commission 1845, 155–56). The figure of 2,231 acres equates exactly in size to the townland of Gleann Lach, which oral history confirms was traditionally linked with Fearann Mhac Giolla Bhríde – Cunningham's townland (Ó Duilearga 1939, 296). In the Devon Commission report Hume retorts that the lease of Gleann Lach was actually only £16 and was now being keenly sought by other tenants (Devon Commission 1845, Supplement to Minutes of Evidence, 9).

This dispute is symptomatic of the competition that was emerging between strong tenant farmers and the increasing disruption to customary grazing rights that resulted. Certain individuals realised their ability to lease large swathes of mountain pasture as rundale came under pressure, and in doing so undermined the principle of communal use of summer pasture. Tenants may have continued to help one another out at various times at home – in, for example, the *meitheal*, or working party – but, strictly speaking, the end of collective tenancies meant that co-operation was no longer a social obligation. A reflection from local man Pádraig Ó Beirn in the 1930s captures the situation's essence: 'the people still send their cattle to the mountain in summer, but there's no one now to see that there is any equation. The poor send what they can, and the rich eat up the grass the poor are unable to graze' (Morris *et al.* 1939, 289). The practice of transhumance was already being complicated as a result of massive population growth; the even quicker reorientation of the system's social basis between 1840 and 1860 was a fatal blow to its successful operation in Gleann Cholm Cille.

In the Carna peninsula an early attempt was made to reorganise the landscape in 1844 by the Irish Waste Land Improvement Society. They entered into an agreement with the Lynch estate to take over the management of their land in the east of the peninsula (Robinson 1990a, 89–90), but, owing to poor timing, their encouragements to drain and improve moorland failed, and the Lynches retook possession. Population decline of 32.5 per cent between 1841 and 1851 (Famine Atlas and Historical Population Statistics)[7] presented a better opportunity for reform

---

[7]   This was a major change, but not as severe as the interior of Connemara or other parts of the west of Ireland, where the drop was sometimes over 50 per cent. In the Carna

from the 1850s onwards. The encumbered Martin estate was sold in 1852 to the Law Life Assurance Society, and afterwards to Richard Berridge of London, while the Lynch estate was eventually sold in 1869. On the Valuation maps of 1855, holdings in a number of townlands were already being depicted with straight red lines; by the time the twenty-five-inch Ordnance Survey was drawn in 1897 much more of the older fieldscape had been divided up, creating a sort of 'ladder' field pattern with many new houses, roads and laneways. The Congested Districts Board, established in 1891 to alleviate poverty and congestion in much of Ireland's west, played a major role in completing these changes to Connemara's farming landscape (Ruttledge-Fair 1892; Breathnach 2005; Arrowsmith 2008, 210–11).

The creation of long, straight fields that cut across the small, irregular fields that had grown up organically over time, and the construction of new farmhouses on many of these reorganised holdings, did not immediately prevent tenants from continuing to engage in transhumance, as the oral history and ethnography in Chapter 2 attest to. After all, the change in the Carna peninsula was not as dramatic as Gleann Cholm Cille's, where actual rundale infields and house clusters were replaced in the mid-nineteenth century. Nonetheless, the relatively rapid reorganisation of farm boundaries did weaken the tradition of co-operation within and between townlands that had provided for the allotment of grazing rights. Ongoing changes in land ownership after the Famine did not help the situation, either. For example, the frailty of tenants' grazing rights after the break-up of the Martin estate was demonstrated in 1889, when Berridge gave most of An Cnoc Buí to the government for a forestry experiment to be run by the Congested Districts Board (Robinson 1990, 90). In so arbitrary a way were tenants in An Más (and possibly other townlands) deprived of their traditional booley grounds. Furthermore, it seems that a growing class of credit-rich shopkeepers was gradually displacing smaller tenants in the use of rough pasture, as they were taking their cattle as payment and then grazing them on the hills themselves (Finlay 1898, 71–72).

The informal social structures that transhumance had depended on were thus loosening. However, it took other factors to bring a final cessation to the seasonal occupation of *brácaí* in the Carna peninsula. The colonisation of small patches of the interior – probably on former seasonal sites – by marginalised tenants before and after the Famine seems to have fundamentally changed how stock were looked after. An ethnographic source from 1943 explains that it was by then prevailing practice for hill farmers (*fir sléibhe*, 'mountain men') to take in cattle from coastal farmers, who no longer relocated seasonally themselves (Ó Cathasaigh 1943, 160). The transition to this state of affairs began in the nineteenth century, and made sense for both parties. Hill farmers were well-positioned to make up for their geographical disadvantage by carrying out herding duties, for which they were presumably reimbursed with cash or a service-in-kind (such as provision of fish, shellfish or seaweed). Coastal and insular farms would have been equally ready to discontinue or phase out seasonal settlement with the emergence of emigration as a form of economic relief (see Hatton and Williamson 1993; Ó Conaola 1995, 195–213; O'Rourke 1995; Ó Gráda and O'Rourke

---

peninsula fishing probably alleviated famine conditions somewhat. See Ó Conaola 1995.

1997). They actively encouraged younger people, their would-be herders, to leave; of Carna and district in 1898 it is remarked that 'all the girls of these large families who are not married at eighteen ... are despatched to America' (Finlay 1898, 73). Ultimately, the cash that tenant families received from their emigrant sons and daughters outweighed any loss resulting from the cessation of dairy-based transhumance. This pattern repeated itself in Achill Island in subsequent decades as summer labour in the Scottish Lowlands (see Dunn 2008) proved a more lucrative activity for young people and their families than being able to keep a small number of extra dairy cows at the booley. Their adaptation was effectively emigration.

Worsening living conditions on a number of fronts forced their hands in this regard. By the end of the nineteenth century ownership of more than a couple of cows had become a rarity in Carna – the price per head sometimes reaching thirty shillings in the locality – while prices in the once-lucrative kelp trade were much reduced (Finlay 1898, 67–69; Browne 1900–02, 520). Furthermore, with the reorganisation of farms, rents appear to have been unfairly inflated (this, apparently, as a result of a local expert naively overestimating the value of poor land in 1885; Finlay 1898, 72–73). At the same time sheep became more common, with their numbers in Ballynahinch barony rising from 10,139 in 1851, to 42,606 in 1891 (Agricultural Returns 1851, 650; Agricultural Statistics 1891, 64). Although they did not replace cattle to the extent seen in the Galtee Mountains, an increased reliance on sheep inevitably meant that a human presence on rough grazing was less necessary. In the last years of booleying valuable dairy cows were probably sent in fewer and fewer numbers, until eventually a situation obtained in the 1910s where only dry stock and sheep were kept on the Carna peninsula's inland heaths, watched over by the isolated hill farmers or an occasional visitor from the coast.

Whether it was permanent emigration of to America, seasonal migration to Lowland Scotland or – on the Isle of Lewis – the departure of young men for war, the pull of external forces on local labour was a critical factor in the discontinuation of transhumant movements. These forces are well documented by historians, and emigration is obviously emotive and eye-catching in an Irish context. However, the landscape-level case studies in this book have also revealed the importance of preceding events, such as landlord claims to commons and the disruption of traditional settlement patterns. Where these changes from above occurred quickly, they acted as shocks to the local community, making them more pliable and likely to abandon transhumance, which is an inherently complex practice because of the need for movement as well as land and labour. Where they occurred more slowly or later in the nineteenth century, economic and political forces on a global stage triggered the final abandonment of seasonal sites in Ireland and the Western Isles of Scotland.

CONCLUSION

In spite of disparaging and vague remarks on Irish pastoralism by English commentators in the late sixteenth and early seventeenth centuries, there is now good reason to believe that, throughout the post-medieval period, transhumance was a stable, well-organised form of cattle farming. It was not long-distance or unpredictable; rather, it took place over distances that rarely exceeded 12km (frequently less in the nineteenth century) and with reference to set units of land – such as between smaller internal units within a parish, from one parish to an adjoining area of commonage outside the parish, or from several parishes to one large shared commonage. That seasonal movements of livestock are always grounded in political, economic and environmental realities is implicit in the distribution of transhumant systems in the sixteenth and seventeenth centuries: even then, farmers in the most productive expanses of lowland do not seem to have practised transhumance at all, their landscape being too densely settled and rough pasture occurring in patches that were too small and disparate for seasonal settlement to be a necessity.

THE VISIBILITY OF TRANSHUMANCE IN UPLAND LANDSCAPES

Where seasonal pastoral movements were necessary they are most clearly attested in today's cultural landscape by the remains of small houses and huts that both published and unpublished oral history indicate were occupied in summertime by herders who tended to and milked dairy cows. Many of these structures were in use up to the nineteenth century, and later still on rough pastures in the Carna peninsula and Achill Island. While they had a number of regional names, this book has chosen to refer to individual summer dwellings as either 'booley' houses or 'booley' huts (depending on their size), which stems from the Irish-language word *buaile*, meaning a milking place in summer pasture, or simply summer pasture.

The archaeological remains of booley dwellings are generally found on unenclosed and unimproved rough pasture between an altitude of 50m and 550m a.s.l., depending on the regional topography – the Carna peninsula containing examples of the former and the Galtee Mountains having examples approaching the latter elevation. All of them are located within a few hundred metres of a water source. However, in contrast to booley settlements previously surveyed in the Mourne Mountains, and the well-known example at Bunowna in Achill, it is only a small minority of the seasonal sites surveyed for this book that are found less than ten metres from a stream (most notably in Mín na Saileach, Donegal). The examination of a range of topographical settings within the 'upland' spectrum indicates that shelter, availability of building materials and quality of pasture could in fact be just as important as access to water in terms of site location.

Furthermore, fieldwork in each study area has shown that booley dwellings are usually accompanied by smaller numbers of shelters; these are crudely constructed and probably afforded no more than temporary respite to individual herders or animals. In the Galtee Mountains, where weather and soil conditions become noticeably more difficult with altitude, these shelters tend to be located on the highest or steepest slopes, where goats or sheep may have grazed. Shelters have less distinctive distribution patterns in the other two study areas, although the location of some suggests that access to water was, naturally, not a priority.

The construction style of booley dwellings ranges from sod- and rubble-walled huts of various shapes to larger rectangular 'houses' with coursed walls. Although examples of each were found in all three of this book's study areas, there is a noticeable trend towards larger rectangular examples in the Galtee Mountains. These are the largest individual booley dwellings surveyed so far in Ireland, measuring between 5m and 8m in length externally. Owing to similarities in shape with tenant farmhouses found on lower slopes, it is hypothesised that these rectangular booley houses date to the same period – that is, the second half of the eighteenth century or the nineteenth century. Likewise, the larger rectangular shielings that stayed in use on Lewis until the 1940s, and even had interior wallpapering, seem to have taken their form from the 'blackhouses' that predominated in permanent settlements during the eighteenth, nineteenth and early twentieth centuries. That said, even these larger booley and shieling dwellings are still smaller than the farmhouses in question; in the Galtees, for instance, they contain only half the square meterage in terms of area. Smaller but still fairly well-built rectangular structures in the Carna peninsula and Gleann Cholm Cille are also tentatively assigned a later post-medieval date owing to similarities with tenant farmhouses constructed before the Famine.

On the whole, however, huts with rubble stone walls are much more common in the Carna peninsula, and these contain few features that might provide a date of construction. While the shape of these huts is usually roughly rectangular, circular and irregular examples are found as well and, given that many of them incorporate boulders or natural outcrops in their wall fabric, in reality no two are the same. It is argued that the variety they exhibit is the result of adaptation to the Carna peninsula's very uneven and stony ground surface. As such, they attest to the innovative capabilities of their builders, who were able to mediate between social norms and the practical reality of making a summer dwelling in a difficult environment. The idea that people in marginal upland landscapes of Ireland did not always implement designs that were favoured in wider society is a new concept, and has important implications for how archaeologists interpret the morphology of seasonal settlements elsewhere.

Adaptation to topography cannot explain all of the variety evident in the morphology of booley dwellings, however, as apparent in areas with less challenging topographies, such as Mín na Saileach, Achill and the Mourne Mountains. Here, there are surely chronological factors behind the presence of different forms of booley dwelling. Whether this means that structures consisting of low, curving wall foundations really are older than square and rectangular forms will remain unresolved until datable finds are retrieved from exemplary sites through future excavation. However, it is a strong possibility that construction in stone became more common in many areas of post-medieval Ireland after the last significant patches of older woodland were either cut down or over-grazed as a result of the increasingly commercial nature of livestock rearing.

SEASONAL SETTLEMENT AND THE ADAPTABILITY OF RURAL COMMUNITIES

Seasonal sites and the landscapes in which transhumance took place speak to the complexity of livestock rearing in Ireland and much of north-west Europe before the homogenising effects of improvement. They open up a window onto the agency of subaltern farming communities who have been left out of mainstream narratives in agrarian history. In the first place, transhumant herders were agents of landscape learning in north-west Europe. Young family members participating in transhumance for the first time would have experienced this more keenly than others as they drove cattle along suitable corridors to the pastures, sometimes without any obvious markers to delineate the journey, and met other novice herders who were on their way to neighbouring pastures in the hills. On arrival at the actual booley sites, more senior figures would have assessed the building repairs necessary after winter winds and rains. Returning to the pastures every year cemented the knowledge of the uplands among these novices, making transhumance an iterative process. Indeed, their activities could also act as a source of transformation over time in upland landscapes. As pressures on food and land became an issue among tenant farmers in the late eighteenth and early nineteenth centuries a whole new engagement with the landscape emerged in some uplands as people sought to exploit the familiar anthropogenic niches that had been created. Thus a minority of booley sites were taken in as secondary areas of cultivation using the innovative potato crop, leading to targeted colonisation in some cases. The gradual domestication of these places through transhumance demonstrates that summer pastures were not as wild or dangerous as many folk stories from the west of Ireland, the Scottish Hebrides and Iceland would suggest. This is not to say that the view of uplands as liminal was not genuine. However, it may have been a mutable concept depending on the story-teller and who they were trying to warn.

In this regard, the number of people who actually relocated to summer sites is highly informative of social organisation within rural communities. A comparison of the size and number of structures present on summer pastures with the houses occupied year-round in coastal or lowland areas demonstrates that little more than 30 per cent of the total farming population that still depended on transhumance in the early nineteenth century can have relocated with livestock. In many areas, full relocation may never have occurred because of the importance of fishing and/or tillage farming at home, but, with the growth of population, particular age and gender roles seem to have become more clearly outlined – young and/or female generally being equated with the herding and milking of cows, adult and/or male with the home and heavy labour. This was a crucial characteristic of transhumance not only in the last 150 years (if not more) of its practice in Ireland and the Scottish Hebrides but also going back to the later medieval period in Iceland, Norway and Sweden. Having received practically no analysis before, the role of young people in tending to dairy cows and in 'manning' seasonal settlements amounts to a hidden history not just of Ireland's uplands but of rural life generally in the country.

Of course, it should be stressed that removal to booley and shieling sites in post-medieval times did not mean genuine isolation for young people, as there was still fairly regular contact with people at the home farms faciliated by the return of butter and cow's milk and the occasional presence of men who came to cut and stack peat in the hills. Moreover, there were subtle reminders of home at the booley sites owing to the aforementioned domestication of space, which could involve potato cultivation, stone clearance, demarcation of ground and – in some cases – the replication of farmhouse design on a miniature scale in the summer dwellings. At a more symbolic level, the sometimes ritualistic repair of summer dwellings across north-west Europe at the start of each grazing season suggests that the community, and adult men in particular, were keen to maintain a claim over the sites and their surrounding pastures.

Despite these moderating factors, it is clear that the care of dairy cows several kilometres from home did afford unmarried young people and unmarried young women in particular a degree of freedom. They had space to exchange cultural knowledge and meet members of the opposite sex without supervision. Instead of dismissing this practice as a form of deviancy, or a quirk of 'remote' rural landscapes, I believe we should see it as central to the reproduction of social practice in these families and communities. Yes, it was a compromise based on the need to spread labour across two spheres of activity, and may have involved some risk (note the 'abduction' and 'wolf' stories), but it also came to serve a purpose by giving children and teenagers what was effectively an apprenticeship in animal husbandry and socialising them in communities that depended on the common use of resources.

Yet 'uplands' were not the same everywhere and neither were the communities who used them. It is perhaps unsurprising, then, that we find evidence of adaptation to regional topography and society in the layout and distribution of seasonal settlements. In the Galtee Mountains, the Carna peninsula and Achill there is a pretty clear correlation between the seasonal settlements and permanent settlements as they appear in c.1840. That is, some core characteristics of the latter are found in the archaeology of seasonal settlement. In Achill both the permanent houses of tenant families and their booley houses are found in tight groups or clusters, with no evidence for division of space within them by walls. In the Carna peninsula booley dwellings are located apart from one another, but still within shouting distance and, in two significant cases, in loose groups that contain low rubble walls; this layout appears to imitate the dense but non-clustered settlement found in their home townlands. In the Galtees most booley houses are deliberately isolated, and as such reflect the separation of tenant farmhouses established on lower slopes from the middle of the eighteenth century.

These patterns reveal much about the attitudes of transhumant farmers' and herders' towards their neighbours as settlement and landholding evolved. Thus, in Achill's rundale system all space outside the actual dwelling and the occasional small garden was held communally by tenants. The lack of division within both booley settlements and their parent villages, even as the latter grew to contain hundreds of people, points to the resilience of this idea. In the Carna peninsula rough pasture was also accessed communally (on a townland basis). However, permanent and seasonal settlements here have a degree of division within them. As population density increased in the home townlands small curvilinear fields seem to have multiplied. The idea of divided space was therefore valued between farmhouses, and recreated at summer pastures where booley dwellings occurred in loose groups. In the Galtee Mountains seasonal settlement was not dense enough to make division of space necessary on the open mountain, even though the trend towards individual holdings is even stronger in this region. It is less clear how permanent and seasonal settlement would have manifested itself in the landscape of the Galtees before landlord improvement and tenant encroachments, but the proximity to one another of older-looking booley dwellings in Knocknagalty, coupled with some historical references in the lowlands to clustered houses, does suggest that communities were once more tight-knit. This, along with the targeted colonisations attested so well in Gleann Cholm Cille, serves as a reminder that rural settlements were not static, and neither were the ways in which transhumant farmers distinguished between one another while continuing to share an area of rough pasture.

WIDER HISTORICAL TRENDS AND THE PRACTICE OF TRANSHUMANCE

The advent of the landed estate had an important transformative effect on the role of elite society in transhumance. Before the seventeenth century lords probably had reason to take an interest in transhumant movements because of their involvement in hunting and, in Gaelic lordships at least, their ownership and distribution of cattle to followers. However, the new monetised relationship that developed between most landlords and tenants, coupled with a decline in large wild mammals across much of Ireland, meant that elites no longer involved themselves directly in the practice during the eighteenth and nineteenth centuries. In Connemara and south-west Donegal landlord policies were quite *laissez-faire*, and facilitated a degree of continuity in rural settlement patterns. When permanent settlement eventually expanded beyond core areas as a result of population growth, it did so organically. In Gleann Cholm Cille this probably led to minor renegotiations of transhumance as the upper reaches of its two longest valleys were deforested and settled on a year-round basis. Significantly, however, the main impetus for the practice continued to come from the core areas. In the Carna peninsula the strong coastal bias of population expansion ensured that the direction of transhumant movements had changed even less by the nineteenth century. The organic expansion of settlement by tenant farmers could have a variety of effects on transhumant patterns, therefore, depending in each case on the amount of land available and the density and distribution of pre-existing populations.

There is no evidence that landlords took an active interest in how transhumance operated in the Galtee Mountains either, but improving policies on two estates in the region did have a more definite effect on the manifestation of population growth in the uplands, which in turn influenced the practice of transhumance indirectly. From the mid-eighteenth century small tenant farmers were encouraged to improve land on the margins of the extensive mountain common rather than continue to sub-divide lowland farms. This, of course, hindered access to mountain pasture for older farms in the lowlands, but landlords overcame this obvious source of conflict in the long term through the break-up of partnership farms and, presumably, the erasure of their members' claims to mountain commonage (who, in any case, were now giving over less ground to cereals than in the seventeenth century). In the foothills of the Galtees settlement expanded in a more even fashion than in the other study areas owing to the topography and the macro-planning of field patterns, probably ordered by the landlords who had encouraged improvement in the first place. This created a relatively stable social environment in which a spirit of *comaointeas* was preserved and hill tenants could agree on the construction and shared use of new booley houses at higher altitudes – in effect, a short-term, smaller-scale phase of seasonal settlement that allowed them to maximise their dairy production and therefore exploit the major trans-Atlantic trade in butter which had emerged.

That major encroachment onto common mountain pasture in the Galtees could be mitigated by the development of a new system of booleying at higher altitude and the (largely) peaceful cessation of an older system attests to the long-term adaptability and innovation of non-elite farmers when faced with major landscape change. This change was influenced by wider demographic and economic currents and driven by the actions of both local landlords and tenant farmers. In the Carna peninsula and Gleann Cholm Cille, where there was no formal planning of the landscape and no estate reorganisation until the 1840s or later, the majority of livestock-owning tenant farmers seem to have relied on transhumance up to the time of the Great Famine (1845–49). This *could* happen because of low pre-existing populations, and *did* happen because of the extraordinary spatial restrictions that emerged in the coastal/valley townlands where permanent settlement and tillage farming was concentrated – productive soils being at a premium compared with the Galtees region. Dairying of cows also factored in the west of Ireland's continued tradition of seasonal settlement, but was generally not as important to surplus creation as the sale of young cattle, which had emerged as a strong regional trend by the early nineteenth century.

THE FINAL DEMISE OF SEASONAL UPLAND SETTLEMENT

In the nineteenth century various pressures from within and without caused the abandonment of transhumance in the areas where it had survived. The colonisation of booley sites began to render the relocation of herders unnecessary, as the new hill farmers could be paid to look after cattle and dairy cows sent to them. Not long after, the Famine caused much indirect damage to the tradition of booleying. In the aftermath of that cultural and humanitarian disaster spatial limitations became less severe, as fewer people were competing for the best tillage land. The pressures they faced in setting land aside for winterage or hay-making – important reasons for sending dairy cows to the mountains – were thus reduced for those who remained. Small-scale tillage production also declined as Ireland entered the twentieth century, so that, overall, more cattle could now be kept at a convenient distance from the home farm. At the same time, the reorganisation of landholding, which had already led to great change around the Galtees, now took place on the western seaboard in Connemara and Donegal. This had the crucial effect of weakening co-operative bonds between tenant families.

Furthermore, in both Gleann Cholm Cille and the Galtee Mountains the introduced Blackface sheep became a more common sight on distant hill pastures. They required much less supervision, although occasionally the sheep might take shelter in the ruins of the booley houses, encouraged by the occasional rebuilding of windward walls by careful hill farmers. The onset, finally, of rural economic decline (interrupted briefly by the boom of the First World War) and the availability of opportunities abroad for young people eventually robbed many smallholdings in each of the study areas of a future. The declining fortunes of their inhabitants underscore the human presence in transhumance and the obsolescence of the practice without it.

FUTURE DIRECTIONS FOR RESEARCH

The study of transhumance in Ireland had until recently advanced quite slowly since Jean Graham completed her doctoral thesis in 1954. Gardiner's study (2010; 2012b) of the Mourne Mountains, followed by in-depth analysis of booley settlements in Achill (McDonald 2014), and now the present, more wide-ranging study of post-medieval transhumance have changed this by paying greater attention to the archaeological record.

Yet there remains much room for progress. First and foremost, it is now clear that more excavations of probable booley sites are needed. Rectangular forms with coursed masonry appear to date to the eighteenth or nineteenth centuries and, if excavation were to take place at such sites, it might be possible to retrieve small amounts of material culture such as pottery and/or stratified organic remains that could be radiocarbon dated. Geoarchaeological techniques such as soil micromorphology and loss-on-ignition could also be applied in order to gain a detailed picture of stratigraphic development. This would either confirm or deny the reasoned speculation offered here. For the same reason, it is necessary to undertake excavation at sites that have been assigned older dates of construction and sites at which the topography appears to have been the main factor in how a booley dwelling was constructed. In advance of such detailed (and expensive) investigative techniques, more field survey ought to be undertaken so as to gain a fuller picture of the distribution of possible booley sites at a regional and national scale. Time is of the essence in this regard given the spread of coniferous plantations across many uplands now viewed as unproductive for the purposes of modern intensive farming. The problem of recent unplanned forestry has been hinted at throughout the book as one that prevents a full evaluation of upland cultural landscapes, in effect by destroying and/or obscuring from view the archaeological features.

Furthermore, given that much of the discussion of seasonal settlement has relied on comparisons with permanent settlement, it would be beneficial, if somewhat ambitious, to initiate a programme of excavation at the permanent dwellings of transhumant families and communities. Although a great deal is known about tenant housing from the early nineteenth century onwards, it is less clear what kind of permanent houses non-elite people built before this, not only in Ireland but in much of Scotland and Wales too. A better understanding of how nucleated or dispersed settlements were during the later medieval and early post-medieval periods would also allow for a more anchored discussion of the layout and distribution patterns of booley dwellings. Put simply, one cannot understand how summer settlements worked if their parent settlements continue to go understudied.

Considering the difficulties in obtaining solid dating evidence from the acidic soils on which evidence for booley settlement is usually found, it would also be useful if more palaeoenvironmental studies were carried out in former transhumant landscapes. Few published pollen studies were available in this book's three study areas and in areas where they are available it is often the case that prehistoric or early medieval farming is the object of study. Perhaps because of the perception that historical records and maps are available from the sixteenth century onwards, the same attention has rarely been paid to the last 1000 years of environmental history. If more pollen samples from recent layers of peat were analysed, provided they survive intact, and more cores extracted from lakes and bogs in upland or otherwise 'marginal' contexts, then researchers would gain a better insight into how vegetation changed over time in the very landscapes that were used for seasonal grazing. How extensive really was woodland, and could it have been used as open woodland pasture? Are there any indicators of grazing intensification or lulls from the medieval period through to the post-medieval, and can those changes be linked to phases of construction or abandonment in excavated booley houses? Did the continued growth of blanket peat adversely affect grazing quality? How widespread were grasses in uplands compared with the situation today? These are some of the questions that need to be answered.

With excavation and palynology added to the researcher's toolset, meaningful examination of transhumant landscapes could be pushed back into the medieval period. This is ultimately where studies of transhumance in Ireland and elsewhere will have to go, as the origins of the practice clearly lie in the medieval period, or even earlier. This book has shown that the practice existed in both Anglo-Irish and Gaelic areas of Ireland during the sixteenth and seventeenth centuries, but was this the case in the thirteenth and fourteenth centuries? Is it safe to assume that transhumance was a natural response to the need for a balanced agro-pastoral economy, or might it have had negative cultural connotations for Anglo-Norman settlers after the invasion of Ireland in 1169? Place-names, references to livestock in Anglo-Norman manorial accounts and further landscape research may shed light on these questions. And, finally, given the proposed shift towards arable farming in parts of Ireland in the mid- to late first millennium AD (McCormick 2008; Kerr et al. 2009; McClatchie et al. 2015), is it possible that the eleventh-century story of Dima and his one hundred cows travelling to the Wicklow Mountains bears witness to an increased value of uplands for lowland farmers – that is, a grazing resource more extensive than anything they could find at home? What role might transhumant movements have played in the evolution of medieval territories and land units as a result?

Finally, returning to the post-medieval world, this book has highlighted capitalism as a process that had important effects on livestock farming within Ireland and the ongoing need for transhumance. The experience of transhumant communities in post-medieval Ireland is therefore a good barometer of interactions with international capitalism. In the future it would be worth comparing the experience of Ireland with that of other countries, such as Scotland. As a farming practice, transhumance is extremely sensitive to wider economic trends. At the same time, the fact that capitalism emerged in what was primarily an agro-pastoral world means that its development, at least initially, was linked to the success or failure of farmers. If ever there was a major project for historical archaeology to tackle, therefore, it is that dynamic relationship between pastoralism and capitalism – a relationship of international significance, but rooted ultimately in the day-to-day decision-making and seasonal rhythm of farming lives.

BIBLIOGRAPHY

PRIMARY DOCUMENTARY SOURCES

Boole Library Special Collections, University College Cork
Down Survey Limerick = Down Survey Parish Maps and Terriers, 1657, Limerick (Microfilm of N.L.I. Ms. 718).

James Hardiman Library, National University of Ireland, Galway
Gahan, F.G.T. 1892. Congested Districts Board for Ireland report no.15, District of Glencolumbkille. Dublin: Her Majesty's Stationery Office (microfilm copy).

Landed Estates' Court (O'Brien) rental and particulars of the Martin estate, 14 July 1852, Volume 17, MRGS 39/008 (microfilm copy).

Landed Estates' Court (O'Brien) rental and particulars of the Kingston estates, 17 June & 1 July 1851, Volume 9 (1, 2 & 3), MRGS 39/004 (microfilm copy).

Ruttledge-Fair, M. 1892. Congested Districts Board for Ireland report no. 50, District of Carna. Dublin: Her Majesty's Stationery Office (microfilm copy).

National Archives of Ireland (NAI)
M. 2429–31. P.R.O. Particulars, valuation and report by W.W. Simpson on the estate of T.B. Martin in Co. Galway, 1837. Particulars of the Martin estate in Galway City and Moycullen Barony, and Ballynahinch Barony, c.1847.

M. 3440–01, 3443. P.R.O. Rentals of the estate of T.B. Martin in Ballynahinch and Moycullen Baronies, Co. Galway, 1849, 1852.

QRO/DS/1/27. County Tipperary Down Survey tracings.

National Folklore Collection (NFC), University College Dublin
Mss. 62, 155–57. Various materials recorded in Iorras Aithneach.

Mss. 1452–53, 1565, 1669, 1831. Milk and Milk Products Questionnaire, 1955–58.

National Library of Ireland (NLI)
Manuscript map 16 B. 15(14). Part of the barony of Boylagh and Bannagh in the County of Donegal. Traced from Down Survey map by Aeneas Higgins. Oblong sheet (17th c.?).

Manuscript map 20D. Composite map representing the Down Survey, 1655–8, for County Tipperary superimposed on the Ordnance Survey sheets of 1839–43. Drawn by R. Johnston, 92 folio sheets, 1955.

Ms. 392. Dineley, T. 1681. Observations in a Voyage through the Kingdom of Ireland. Being a Collection of Several Monuments Inscriptions draughts of Towns Castles &c. 328pp.

Ms. 1740. Rent-ledger of the O'Callaghan estate at Shanbally, Co. Tipperary, 1810–28.

Ms. 3276. Rental of the estates of the Earl of Kingston in counties Limerick, Tipperary and Cork, 1841–42.

Ms. 5671. Day book in respect of the estate of Lord Lismore at Shanbally, Co. Tipperary, 1803–06.

P. 3767 (microfilm of Ms. 2a.2.6 P.R.O.). Books of Survey and Distribution, Co. Cork, 1641–1701.

P. 3768 (microfilm of Ms. 2a.2.7 P.R.O.). Books of Survey and Distribution, Co. Londonderry, Co. Donegal, Co. Tyrone, 1641–1701.

P. 3770 (microfilm of Ms. 2a.2.11 P.R.O.). Books of Survey and Distribution, Co. Kerry, Co. Waterford, 1641–1701.

P. 3772 (microfilm of Ms. 2a.2.15 P.R.O.). Books of Survey and Distribution, Co. Limerick, 1641–1701.

P. 3774 (microfilm of Ms. 2a.2.19 P.R.O.). Books of Survey and Distribution, Co. Tipperary, 1641–1701.

P. 6951. Rentrolls and rentals relating to the estates of the Conolly family in Co. Donegal, 1680–87, 1726, 1728, 1774, 1782–6, 1800, 1831.

PUBLISHED PRIMARY DOCUMENTARY SOURCES

Abstracts of Grants and Lands = Anon. 1825. Appendix I – Abstracts of Grants of Lands under the Acts of Settlement and Explanation, A.D. 1666–1684, in *The Fifteenth Annual Report from the Commissioners of Public Records of Ireland*, 45–280.

AFM = O'Donovan, J. (ed.) 1848–51. *Annála Ríoghachta Éireann; Annals of the Kingdom of Ireland by the Four Masters, from the Earliest Period to the Year 1616*, 7 vols. Dublin: Hodges and Figgis.

Agricultural Returns 1851 = Anon. (ed.) 1892. *The Census of Ireland for the year 1851, Part II: Returns of Agricultural Produce in 1851*. Dublin: Her Majesty's Stationery Office.

Agricultural Statistics 1891 = Anon. (ed.) 1892. *The Agricultural Statistics of Ireland, for the year 1891*. Dublin: Her Majesty's Stationery Office.

Anon. 1692. *A Brief Character of Ireland. With Some Observations of the Customs, Etc. of the Meaner Sort of the Natural Inhabitants of that Kingdom*. Dublin.

Anon. 1765. *Statutes at Large Passed in the Parliaments held in Ireland, Volume 4 (1703–1719)*. Dublin.

Blake Family of Renvyle, 1995. *Letters from the Irish Highlands of Connemara, 1823/4* (reprint). Clifden: Gibbons Publications.

Brady, W.M. (ed.) 1867. *The McGillycuddy Papers: a selection from the family archives of 'the McGillycuddy of the Reeks'; with an introductory memoir.* London: Longman, Green, and Co.

Browne, C.R. 1896–98. The Ethnography of Ballycroy, County Mayo. *Proceedings of the Royal Irish Academy* 4, 74–111.

Browne, C.R. 1900–02. The Ethnography of Carna and Mweenish, in the Parish of Moyruss, Connemara. *Proceedings of the Royal Irish Academy* 6, 503–34.

BSD Galway = Mac Giolla Choille, B. (ed.) 1962. *Books of Survey and Distribution, Volume III: County of Galway.* Dublin: Irish Manuscripts Commission.

Carmichael, A. 1884. *Grazing and Agrestic Customs of the Outer Hebrides, The Report of the Royal Commissioners of Inquiry on the Condition of Crofters and Cottars in the Highlands of Scotland*, Appendix A, xcix, 451–82.

Census 1851 = Anon. (ed.) 1852. *The Census of Ireland for the year 1851, Part I.* Dublin: Her Majesty's Stationery Office.

Clesham, B. 1994. A voyage into the Kingdom of the Joyces in 1756. *Journal of the South Mayo Family Research Society* 7, 2–5.

Compossicion Booke of Conought = Freeman, A.F. (ed.) 1936. *The Compossicion Booke of Conought.* Dublin: Irish Manuscripts Commission.

CSPI = Hamilton, H.C, Atkinson, E.G. and Mahaffy, R.P. (eds) 1860–1912. *Calendar of the state papers relating to Ireland in the reigns of Henry VIII, Edward VI, Mary, and Elizabeth, 1509–1603*, 11 vols. London: Her Majesty's Stationery Office.

CSPI James = Russell, C.W. and Prendergast, J.P. (eds) 1872–80. *Calendar of the state papers relating to Ireland in the reign of James I*, 5 vols. London: Her Majesty's Stationery Office.

Day, A. and McWilliams, P. (eds) 1995. *Ordnance Survey Memoirs of Ireland, Volume Thirty-one: Parishes of Co. Londonderry XI, 1821, 1833, 1836–7.* Belfast: Institute of Irish Studies.

Day, A. and McWilliams, P. (eds) 1997. *Ordnance Survey Memoirs of Ireland, Volume Thirty-nine: Parishes of Co. Donegal II, 1835–6.* Belfast: Institute of Irish Studies.

Devon Commission 1845. *Evidence taken before Her Majesty's Commissioners of Inquiry into the state of the law and practice in respect to the occupation of land in Ireland, Part II.* Her Majesty's Stationery Office, Dublin.

Dutton, H. 1808. *Statistical survey of the County of Clare.* Dublin: Dublin Society.

Dutton, H. 1824. *A statistical and agricultural survey of the county of Galway.* Dublin: Royal Dublin Society.

Falkiner, C.L. (ed.) 1904. *Illustrations of Irish history and topography, mainly of the seventeenth century.* London: Longmans, Green & Co.

Finlay, T.A. 1898. The Economics of Carna. *New Ireland Review* 9, 65–77.

Grene Barry, J. 1897–1904. The Cromwellian Settlement of the County of Limerick. *Limerick Field Club* 1, 16–33; 2, 43–49, 211–16, 257–68; 3, 18–24, 58–63, 160–65, 230–37.

Hardiman, J. (ed.) 1846. *A chorographical description of West or h-Iar Connaught, written A.D. 1684 by Roderic O'Flaherty.* Dublin: Irish Archaeological Society.

Hayes-McCoy, G.A. (ed.) 1964. *Ulster and other Irish maps, c. 1600*. Dublin: The Stationery Office.

Hill, L.G. 1971. *Facts from Gweedore; compiled from the notes of Lord George Hill: a facsimile reprint of the fifth edition (1887) with an introduction by E. Estyn Evans*. Belfast: Queen's University Belfast.

Hill, R.G. 1877. *An Historical Account of the Plantation in Ulster at the Commencement of the Seventeenth Century, 1608–1620*. Belfast: McCaw, Stevenson and Orr.

Inquis. cancell. Hib. Rep. = Anon. 1829. *Inquisitionum in Officio Rotulorum Cancellariae Hiberniae Asservatarum Repertorium, Vol. II*. Dublin: His Majesty's Commissioners of the Public Records of Ireland.

Kay, G. 1794. *General View of the Agriculture of North Wales, Caernarvonshire*. Edinburgh: Board of Agriculture.

Knight, P. 1836. *Erris in the Irish Highlands and the Atlantic Railway*. Dublin: M. Keene and Son.

Lacey, B. (ed.) 1998. *The Life of Colum Cille by Manus O'Donnell*. Dublin: Four Courts Press.

Laffan, T. 1911. *Tipperary's Families: Being the Hearth Money Records for 1665–67*. Dublin: Duffy.

Larkin, W. 1819. *A map of the county of Galway*, 16 sheets. London: S.J. Neele.

MS. Rawlinson A 237 = Anon. 1931. MS. Rawlinson A 237, the Bodleian Library, Oxford. *Analecta Hibernica* 3, 151–218.

McEvoy, J. 1802. *Statistical survey of the county of Tyrone*. Dublin: The Dublin Society.

Mac Giollarnáth, S. (ed.) 1941. *Annála Beaga ó Iorrus Aithneach*. Baile Átha Cliath: Oifig an tSoláthair.

McParlan, J. 1802. *Statistical survey of the county of Donegal*. Dublin: The Dublin Society.

Moody, T.W. 1938. Ulster plantation papers, 1608–13. *Analecta Hibernica* 8, 179–298.

Neilson Hancock, W. (ed.) 1865. *Ancient laws of Ireland, volume 1*. Dublin: Alexander Thom.

Newte, T. 1791. *Prospects and Observations on a Tour in England and Scotland, Natural, Oeconomical and Literary*. London.

Ó Cathasaigh, S. 1943. Buailíochaí in Iarthar Chonamara. *Béaloideas* 13, 159–60.

Ó Danachair, C. 1945. Traces of the Buaile in the Galtee Mountains. *Journal of the Royal Society of Antiquaries of Ireland* 75, 248–52.

Ó Duilearga, S. 1939. Varia. Nóta ar shean-nós: buailteachas. *Béaloideas* 9, 35.

Ó Maidín, P. 1958. Pococke's tour of south and south-west Ireland in 1758. *Journal of the Cork Historical and Archaeological Society* 63, 73–94.

Ó Moghráin, P. 1943. Some Mayo Traditions of the Buaile. *Béaloideas* 13, 161–72.

Ó Raghallaigh, T. 1926–29. Seanchus Búrcach. *Journal of the Galway Archaeological and Historical Society* 13, 50–60, 101–37; 14, 30–51, 142–67.

O'Sullivan, W. 1971. William Molyneux's Geographical Collections for Kerry. *Journal of the Kerry Archaeological and Historical Society* 4, 28–47.

Osborn Bergin, D.D. (ed.) 1931. *Trí Bior-Ghaoithe an Bháis: Séathrún Kéitinn do sgríobh/ The Three Shafts of Death by Geoffrey Keating*, 2nd edn. Dublin: Hodges, Figgis, & Co.

Otway, C. 1839. *A tour in Connaught: comprising sketches of Clonmacnoise, Joyce country, and Achill*. Dublin: William Curry, Jun. and Company.

Otway, C. 1841. *Sketches in Erris and Tyrawley*. Dublin: William Curry, Jun. and Company.

Pacata Hibernia 1633 = Anon. 1633. *Pacata Hibernia; or, a history of the wars in Ireland, during the reign of Queen Elizabeth*, 2 vols. London.

Pender, S. (ed.) 1939. *A Census of Ireland, circa 1659, with supplementary materials from the poll money ordinances (1660–1661)*. Dublin: Irish Manuscripts Commission.

Pennant, T. 1776. *A Tour in Scotland and Voyage to the Hebrides; 1772. Part 1, Second Edition*. London: Benjamin White.

Pennant, T. 1810. *Tours in Wales, Vol. II*. London: Wilkie and Robinson.

Petty, W. 1685. *Hibernia Delinatio*. London.

Plummer, C. (ed.) 1922. *Bethada Náem nÉrenn. Vol. I, Introduction, Texts, Glossary*. Oxford: Clarendon Press.

Ryland, R.H. 1824. *The History, Topography and Antiquities of the County and City of Waterford*. London: John Murray.

Simington, R.C. (ed.) 1931. *The Civil Survey. A.D. 1654–1656: County of Tipperary, vol. i, eastern and southern baronies*. Dublin: The Stationery Office.

Simington, R.C. (ed.) 1934. *The Civil Survey. A.D. 1654–1656: County of Tipperary, vol. ii, western and northern baronies with the return of crown and church lands for the whole county*. Dublin: The Stationery Office.

Simington, R.C. (ed.) 1937. *The Civil Survey. A.D. 1654–1656: Counties of Donegal, Londonderry and Tyrone, vol. iii, with the returns of church lands for the three counties*. Dublin: The Stationery Office.

Simington, R.C. (ed.) 1938. *The Civil Survey, A.D. 1654–1656: County of Limerick, vol. iv, with a section of Clanmaurice Barony, Co. Kerry*. Dublin: The Stationery Office.

Smith, C. 1750. *A new and correct map of the county of Cork*. Dublin: Ridge.

Smith, C. 1756. *The Antient and Present State of the County of Kerry*. Dublin.

Smith, C. and Harris, W. 1744. *The Antient and Present State of the County of Down*. Dublin.

Todd, H.J. (ed.) 1805. *The Works of Edmund Spenser, Volume the Eighth*. London: F.C. & J. Rivington and others.

Trench, W.S. 1869. *Realities of Irish life*. London: Longmans, Green, & Co.

Weld, I. 1807. *Illustrations of the scenery of Killarney and the surrounding country*. London.

Wilde, W. 1847. Irish Rivers – no. 5: The Boyne – second article. *Dublin University Magazine* 29, 764–83.

Williams, N.J.A. (ed.) 1981. *Pairlement Chloinne Tomáis*. Dublin: Dublin Institute for Advanced Studies.

Wright, T. (ed.) 1863. *The Historical Works of Giraldus Cambrensis*. London: Bohn.

Young, A. 1780. *A Tour in Ireland: with general observations on the present state of that kingdom: made in the years 1776, 1777, and brought down to the end of 1779. Volume II*. London: T. Cadell, in the Strand.

SECONDARY SOURCES

Aalen, F.H.A. 1963. A Note on Transhumance in the Wicklow Mountains. *Journal of the Royal Society of Antiquaries of Ireland* 93, 189–90.

Aalen, F.H.A. 1964a. Clochans as Transhumance Dwellings in the Dingle Peninsula, Co. Kerry. *Journal of the Royal Society of Antiquaries of Ireland* 94, 39–45.

Aalen, F.H.A. 1964b. Transhumance in the Wicklow Mountains. *Ulster Folklife* 10, 65–72.

Aalen, F.H.A. 1997. Buildings, in Aalen, F.H.A, Whelan, K. and Stout, M. (eds), *Atlas of the Irish Rural Landscape*. Cork: Cork University Press, 145–79.

Aalen, F.H.A, Whelan, K. and Stout, M. (eds) 1997. *Atlas of the Irish Rural Landscape*. Cork: Cork University Press.

Adams, G.B. 1967. Work and words for haymaking. *Ulster Folklife* 13, 29.

Adamson, D.B. 2014. Commercialisation, change and continuity: an archaeological study of rural commercial practice in the Scottish Highlands. Unpublished PhD thesis, Department of Archaeology, University of Glasgow.

Alizadeh, A. 2008. Archaeology and the Question of Mobile Pastoralism in Late Prehistory, in Barnard, H. and Wendrich, W. (eds), *The Archaeology of Mobility: Old and New World Nomadism*. Los Angeles: UCLA Cotsen Institute, 78–114.

Anderson, J. 1995. Rundale, rural economy and agrarian revolution: Tirhugh 1715-1855, in: Nolan, W., Ronayne, L. and Dunlevy, M. (eds.), *Donegal History & Society*, 447–69.

Andersson, J., Elfwendahl, M., Gustafson, G., Hägerman, B.M., Lundqvist, R., Lönnquist, U.S., Ulfsdotter, J. and Welinder, S. 2011. Visible Men and Elusive Women. *International Journal of Historical Archaeology* 15(1), 10–29.

Andres, B. 2016. Alpine huts, livestock and cheese in the Oberhasli region (Switzerland): medieval and early modern building remains and their historical context, in Collis, J., Pearce, M. and Nicolis, F. (eds), *Summer Farms: Seasonal Exploitation of the Uplands from Prehistory to the Present*. Sheffield: J.R. Collis Publications, 155–82.

Andres, B. 2018. Alpine settlement remains in the Bernese Alps (Switzerland) in medieval and modern times: the visibility of alpine summer farming activities in the archaeological record, in Costello, E. and Svensson, E. (eds), *Historical Archaeologies of Transhumance across Europe*. Themes in Contemporary Archaeology 6. London: Routledge, 155–70.

Andrews, J.H. 1970. Geography and government in Elizabethan Ireland, in Stephens, N. and Glasscock, R.E. (eds), *Irish Geographical Studies in Honour of E. Estyn Evans*. Belfast: Department of Geography, Queen's University Belfast, 178–91.

Andrews, J.H. 1997. *Shapes of Ireland: Maps and their makers, 1564–1839*. Dublin: Geography Publications.

Andrews, J.H. 2001. The mapping of Ireland's cultural landscape, 1550–1630, in Duffy, P.J., Edwards, D. and FitzPatrick, E. (eds), *Gaelic Ireland, c.1250-c.1650: land, lordship, and settlement*. Dublin: Four Courts Press, 153–80.

Andrews, J.H. 2002. *A paper landscape: the Ordnance Survey in nineteenth-century Ireland*. Dublin: Four Courts Press.

Arbos, P. 1923. The Geography of Pastoral Life: Illustrated with European Examples. *Geographical Review* 13, 559–75.

Arrowsmith, A. (ed.) 2008. *The Complete Works of J. M. Synge*. Ware: Wordsworth Editions.

Aston, T.H. and Philpin, C.H.E. 1985. *The Brenner Debate: Agrarian Class Structure and Economic Development in Pre-Industrial Europe*. Cambridge: Cambridge University Press.

Atkinson, J.A. 2010. Settlement form and evolution in the Central Highlands of Scotland, c 1100–1900 AD. *International Journal of Historical Archaeology* 14(3), 316–34.

Atkinson, J.A. 2016. *Ben Lawers: An Archaeological Landscape in Time. Results from the Ben Lawers Historic Landscape Project, 1996–2005*. Scottish Archaeological Internet Reports, 62. Available at <http://archaeologydataservice.ac.uk/archives/view/sair/contents.cfm?vol=62>.

Austin, D., Faith, R., Fleming, A. and Siddle, D. 2013. *Cipières: Landscape and Community in the Alpes-Maritimes, France*. Oxford: Windgather Press.

Bain, J. (ed.) 1894. *Calendar of Border Papers*. Edinburgh: HM General Register House.

Baldwin, J.R. and Whyte, I.D. 1985. *The Scandinavians in Cumbria*. Edinburgh: The Scottish Society for Northern Studies.

Bangor-Jones, M. 2002. Sheep Farming in Sutherland in the Eighteenth Century. *The Agricultural History Review* 50, 181–202.

Barker, G. 1995. *A Mediterranean valley: landscape archaeology and annales history in the Biferno Valley*. London: University of Leicester Press.

Barnard, H. and Wendrich, W. (eds) 2008. *The Archaeology of Mobility: Old and New World Nomadism*. Los Angeles: UCLA Cotsen Institute.

Barrett, J.C. 1994. *Fragments from Antiquity: An Archaeology of Social Life in Britain, 2900–1200 BC*. Oxford: Blackwell.

Barrett, J.C. 2001. Agency, the duality of structure, and the problem of the archaeological record, in Hodder, I. (ed.), *Archaeological theory today*. Cambridge: Polity Press, 141–64.

Barrett, J.C. 2012. Agency: a revisionist account, in Hodder, I. (ed.), *Archaeological theory today*, 2nd edn. Cambridge: Polity Press, 146–66.

Barrett, J.C. and Fewster, K.J. 2000. Intimacy and structural transformation: Giddens and archaeology, in Holtorf, C. and Karlsson, H. (ed.), *Philosophy and archaeological practice: perspectives for the 21st century*. Göteborg: Bricoleur Press, 25–33.

Barth, F. 1961. *Nomads of South Persia: the Basseri Tribe of Khamseh Confederacy*. Boston: Little Brown and Co.

Barth, F. 1962. Nomadism in the Mountain and Plateau Areas of South West Asia. *The Problems of the Arid Zone. UNESCO Arid Zone Research* 18, 341–55.

Bar-Yosef, O. and Khazanov, A. (eds) 1991. *Pastoralism in the Levant: Archaeological Materials in Anthropological Perspectives*. Madison: Prehistory Press.

Beaudry, M., Parno, M.C. and Travis, G. (eds) 2013. *Archaeologies of Mobility and Movement*. New York: Springer.

Becker, H. 2000. *Seaweed Memories: In the Jaws of the Sea*. Dublin: Wolfhound Press.

Beglane, F. 2015. *Anglo-Norman Parks in Medieval Ireland*. Dublin: Four Courts Press.

Bell, J. and Watson, M. 2008. *A history of Irish farming, 1750–1950*. Dublin: Four Courts Press.

Bell, J. and Watson, M. 2015. Farm Cluster: Clachans, in Ó Síocháin, S., Slater, E. and Downey, L. (eds), *Rundale: Settlement, Society and Farming* (*Ulster Folklife* 58). Cultra: Ulster Folk and Transport Museum, 33–39.

Beresford, G. 1979. Three deserted medieval settlements on Dartmoor: a report on the late E. Marie Minter's excavations. *Medieval Archaeology* 23, 98–158.

Bil, A. 1989. Transhumance economy, setting and settlement in Highland Perthshire. *Scottish Geographical Magazine* 105, 158–67.

Bil, A. 1990. *The Shieling, 1600–1840: The Case of the Central Scottish Highlands*. Edinburgh: John Donald.

Bilenky, S. 2012. *Romantic Nationalism in Eastern Europe: Russian, Polish, and Ukrainian Political Imaginations*. Stanford: Stanford University Press.

Blache, J. 1934. *L'homme et la montagne*. Paris: Librairie Gallimard.

Bladé, J.F. 1892. Essai sur l'histoire de la transhumance dans les Pyrénées françaises, *Bullétin de Géographie historique et descriptive* 7, 301–15.

Blanning, T. 2012. *The Romantic Revolution*. London: Weidenfeld and Nicolson.

Bourdieu, P. 1977. *Outline of a Theory of Social Practice* (translated edition). Cambridge: Cambridge University Press.

Bradburd, D. 1994. Historical Bases of the Political Economy of Kermani Pastoralists: Tribe and World Markets in the Nineteenth and Early Twentieth Centuries, in Chang, C. and Koster, H.A. (eds), *Pastoralists at the Periphery: Herders in a Capitalist World*. Tuscon: Arizona University Press, 42–61.

Bradley, R. 1972. Prehistorians and pastoralists in Neolithic and Bronze Age England. *World Archaeology* 4, 192–204.

Brady, N. and O'Conor, K.D. 2005. The later medieval use of crannogs in Ireland, in Klápště, J. (ed.), *Water Management in Medieval Rural Economy (Ruralia 5)*. Turnhout: Brepols, 127–36.

Brannon, N.F. 1984. A Small Excavation in Tildarg Townland, near Ballyclare, County Antrim. *Ulster Journal of Archaeology* 47, 163–70.

Braudel, F. 1972. *The Mediterranean and the Mediterranean World in the Age of Philip II*. Volume I, translated by S. Reynolds. London: Collins.

Braudel, F. 1980. *On History*. Chicago: University of Chicago Press.

Breathnach, C. 2005. *The Congested Districts Board of Ireland, 1891–1923: Poverty and Development in the West of Ireland*. Dublin: Four Courts Press.

Brereton, A.J. 1995. Regional and year to year variation in production, in Jeffrey, D.W., Jones, M.B. and McAdam, J.H. (eds), *Irish grasslands – their biology and management*. Dublin: Royal Irish Academy, 12–22.

Brigand, R., Tencariu, F.A., Weller, O., Alexianu, M. and Asăndulesei, A. 2018. Ovine pastoralism and mobility systems in Romania: an ethnoarchaeological approach, in Costello, E. and Svensson, E. (eds), *Historical Archaeologies of Transhumance across Europe*. Themes in Contemporary Archaeology 6. London: Routledge, 245–63.

Briody, M. 2007. *The Irish Folklore Commission 1935–1970: history, ideology, methodology*. Helsinki: Finnish Literature Society.

Browman, D.L. 1997. Pastoral Risk Perception and Risk Definition for Altiplano Herders. *Nomadic Peoples* 38(1), 22–36.

Burri, S., Py-Saragaglia, V. and Cesarini, R. 2018. Moving up and down throughout the seasons: winter and summer grazing between Provence and Southern Alps (France) AD 1100–1500, in Costello, E. and Svensson, E. (eds), *Historical Archaeologies of Transhumance across Europe*. Themes in Contemporary Archaeology 6. London: Routledge, 135–54.

Campbell, E. (ed.) 2014. *The Field Names of County Louth*. Dundalk: Louth County Council.

Campbell, J.A. and Livingstone, D.N. 1983. Neo-Lamarckism and the Development of Geography in the United States and Great Britain. *Transactions of the Institute of British Geographers* 8, 267–94.

Canny, N. 1970. Hugh O'Neill, Earl of Tyrone, and the changing face of Gaelic Ulster. *Studia Hibernica* 10, 7–35.

Carrer, F. 2013. Herding Strategies, Dairy Economy and Seasonal Sites in the Southern Alps: Ethnoarchaeological Inferences and Archaeological Implications. *Journal of Mediterranean Archaeology* 28(1), 3–22.

Case, H.J., Dimbleby, G.W., Mitchell, G.F., Morrison, M.E.S. and Proudfoot, V.B. 1969. Land Use in Goodland Townland, Co. Antrim, from Neolithic Times until Today. *Journal of the Royal Society of Antiquaries of Ireland* 99, 39–53.

Caseldine, A. 2006. The environment and deserted rural settlements in Wales: potential and possibilities for palaeoenvironmental studies, in Roberts, K. (ed.), *Lost Farmsteads: Deserted Rural Settlements in Wales*. York: Council for British Archaeology, 133–53.

Champion, T.C. 1990. Medieval archaeology and the tyranny of the historical record, in Austin, D. and Alcock, L. (eds), *From the Baltic to the Black Sea*. London: Unwin Hyman, 79–95.

Chang, C. and Koster, H.A. (eds) 1994. *Pastoralists at the Periphery: Herders in a Capitalist World*. Tuscon: University of Arizona Press.

Chang, C. and Tourtellotte, P.A. 1993. Ethnoarchaeological Survey of Pastoral Transhumance Sites in the Grevena Region, Greece. *Journal of Field Archaeology* 20, 249–64.

Chaniotis, A. 1995. Problems of 'Pastoralism' and 'Transhumance' in Classical and Hellenistic Crete. *Orbis Terrarum* 1, 39–89.

Childe, V.G. 1936. *Man Makes Himself*. London: Watts and Co.

Clarkson, L. and Crawford, M. 2001. *Feast and Famine: Food and Nutrition in Ireland 1500–1920*. Oxford: Oxford University Press.

Cleary, M.C. 1987. Contemporary Transhumance in Languedoc and Provence. *Geografiska Annaler* B 69, 107–13.

Clutterbuck, R. 2015. Rural Landscapes of Improvement in Ireland, 1650–1850: An Archaeological Landscape Study. Unpublished PhD thesis, School of Geography and Archaeology, National University of Ireland, Galway.

Coll, F. and Bell, J. 1990. An account of life in Machaire Gathlán (Magheragallan), north west Donegal, early this century. *Ulster Folklife* 36, 80–85.

Collis, J., Pearce, M. and Nicolis, F. (eds) 2016. *Summer Farms: Seasonal Exploitation of the Uplands from Prehistory to the Present*. Sheffield: J.R. Collis Publications.

Comaroff, J. and Comaroff, J. 1992. *Ethnography and the Historical Imagination*. Boulder: Westview Press.

Comber, M. and Hull, G. 2010. Excavations at Caherconnell Cashel, the Burren, Co. Clare: implications for cashel chronology and Gaelic settlement. *Proceedings of the Royal Irish Academy* 110 C, 133–71.

Comeau, R. 2019. The practice of 'in rodwallis': medieval Welsh agriculture in north Pembrokeshire, in Comeau, R. and Seaman, A. (eds), *Living off the Land: Agriculture in Wales c. 400–1600 AD*. Oxford: Windgather Press, 130–52.

Connell, K.H. 1950. The Colonization of Waste Land in Ireland, 1780–1845. *The Economic History Review* 3, 44–71.

Costello, E. 2012. Post-medieval Settlement in Ireland and the Practice of Transhumance: a Case-Study from the Galtee Mountains. Unpublished MA thesis, Department of Archaeology, University of Sheffield.

Costello, E. 2015. Post-medieval upland settlement and the decline of transhumance: a case-study from the Galtee Mountains, Ireland. *Landscape History* 36, 47–69.

Costello, E. 2016a. Feirmeoirí faoi cheilt: dul chun cinn agus dúshláin sa taighde faoi ghnás an bhuailteachais. *Béaloideas: Journal of the Folklore Society of Ireland* 84, 192–211.

Costello, E. 2016b. Seasonal management of cattle in the booleying system: new insights from Connemara, western Ireland, in O'Connell, M., Kelly, F. and McAdam, J.H. (eds), *Cattle in Ancient and Modern Ireland: Farming Practices, Environment and Economy*. Newcastle: Cambridge Scholars Publishing, 66–74.

Costello, E. 2016c. Seasonal settlement and the interpretation of upland archaeology in the Galtee Mountains, Ireland. *Landscape History* 37(1), 87–98.

Costello, E. 2017. Liminal learning: social practice in seasonal settlements of western Ireland. *Journal of Social Archaeology* 17(2), 188–209.

Costello, E. 2018. Temporary freedoms? Ethnoarchaeology of female herders at seasonal sites in northern Europe. *World Archaeology* 50(1), 165–84.

Costello, E. and Svensson, E. (eds) 2018a. *Historical Archaeologies of Transhumance across Europe*. Themes in Contemporary Archaeology 6. London: Routledge.

Costello, E. and Svensson, E. 2018b. Transhumant pastoralism in historic landscapes: beginning a European perspective, in Costello, E. and Svensson, E. (eds), *Historical Archaeologies of Transhumance across Europe*. Themes in Contemporary Archaeology 6. London: Routledge, 1–14.

Coyne, F. 2006. *Islands in the Clouds: An Upland Archaeological Study on Mount Brandon and the Paps, County Kerry*. Tralee: Kerry County Council.

Crabtree, P. and Ryan, K. 2010. Faunal Remains, in Manning, C. (ed.), *The history and archaeology of Glanworth Castle, Co. Cork: excavations 1982–4*. Bray: Wordwell.

Crawford, B.E. 1995. *Scandinavian Settlement in Northern Britain Thirteen Studies of Place-Names in their Historical Context*. London: Leicester University Press.

Cribb, R. 1991. *Nomads in Archaeology*. Cambridge: Cambridge University Press.

Crotty, R.D. 1966. *Irish Agricultural Production: Its Volume and Structure*. Cork: Cork University Press.

Croucher, S.K. and Weiss, L. (eds) 2011. *The Archaeology of Capitalism in Colonial Contexts: Postcolonial Historical Archaeologies*. New York: Springer.

Crowley, J., Smyth, W.J. and Murphy, M. (eds) 2012. *Atlas of the Great Irish Famine, 1845–52*. Cork: Cork University Press.

Cullen, L.M. 1972. *An economic history of Ireland since 1660*. London: Batsford.

Cullen, L.M. 1986. Economic development: 1750–1800, in Moody, T.W. and Vaughan, W.E. (eds), *A New History of Ireland. Volume IV: Eighteenth Century Ireland 1691–1800.* Oxford: Clarendon Press, 159–95.

Cunningham, B. 1996. From Warlords to Landlords: Political and Social Change in Galway 1540–1640, in Moran, G.P. (ed.), *Galway: History and Society.* Dublin: Geography Publications, 97–130.

Cunningham, B. and Gillespie, R. 2003. *Stories from Gaelic Ireland: microhistories from the sixteenth-century Irish annals.* Dublin: Four Courts Press.

Curwen, E. 1938. The Hebrides: a cultural backwater. *Antiquity* 12, 261–89.

Dalglish, C. 2003. *Rural Society in the Age of Reason: An Archaeology of the Emergence of Modern Life in the Southern Scottish Highlands.* New York: Kluwer.

Danaher, K. 1998. *Folktales of the Irish Countryside*, reprint. Cork: Mercier Press.

Darvill, T. 1986. *The archaeology of the uplands: a rapid assessment of archaeological knowledge and practice.* London: Royal Commission on the Historical Monuments of England.

Daugstad, K. and Schippers, T.K. 2016. Moving up and down. Two cases of seasonal family dwellings in mountainous areas: mid-Norway and the southwestern Alps, in Retamero, F., Schjellerup, I. and Davies, A. (eds), *Agricultural and Pastoral Landscapes in Pre-Industrial Society: Choices, Stability and Change.* Oxford: Oxbow Press, 289–304.

Davies, A. 2016. Flexibility in upland farming: pollen evidence for the role of seasonal pastures in the Scottish farm economy from *ca.* 1600–1900 CE, in Retamero, F., Schjellerup, I. and Davies, A. (eds), *Agricultural and Pastoral Landscapes in Pre-Industrial Society: Choices, Stability and Change.* Oxford: Oxbow Press, 271–87.

Davies, A.L. 2007. Upland agriculture and environmental risk: a new model of upland land-use based on high spatial-resolution palynological data from West Affric, NW Scotland. *Journal of Archaeological Science* 34, 2053–63.

Davies, E. 1935. Sheep Farming in Upland Wales. *Geography* 20, 97–111.

Davies, E. 1941. The patterns of transhumance in Europe. *Geography* 26, 155–68.

Davies, E. 1973. Hendre and Hafod in Merioneth. *Journal of the Merioneth Historical and Record Society* 7, 13–27.

Davies, E. 1977. Hendre and Hafod in Denbighshire. *Transactions of the Denbighshire Historical Society* 26, 49–50.

Davies, E. 1979. Hendre and hafod in Caernarvonshire. *Transactions of the Caernarvonshire Historical Society* 40, 17–46.

Davies, E. 1980. Hafod, Hafoty and Lluest: Their distribution, features and purpose. *Ceredigion* 9, 1–41.

Davies, E. 1984–85. Hafod and Lluest – the summering of cattle and upland settlement in Wales. *Folk Life* 23, 76–96.

Day, A. 1996. *Romanticism: The New Critical Idiom.* London: Routledge.

Day, A. and McWilliams, P. (eds) 1995. *Ordnance Survey Memoirs of Ireland, vol. 29, Parishes of County Antrim XI: Antrim Town and Ballyclare.* Belfast: Institute of Irish Studies.

Delaney, F. and Tierney, J. 2011. *In the Lowlands of South Galway.* Bray: Wordwell.

Delle, J.A. 1999. 'A good and easy speculation': Spatial conflict, collusion, and resistance in late-sixteenth century Munster, Ireland. *International Journal of Historical Archaeology* 3, 11–35.

Devine, T.M. 1994. *Clanship to Crofter's War: The Social Transformation of the Scottish Highlands*. Manchester: Manchester University Press.

Dickson, D. 1993. Butter comes to the market: the origins of commercial dairying in county Cork, in O'Flanagan, P. and Buttimer, C.G. (eds), *Cork: History and Society*. Dublin: Geography Publications, 367–90.

Dickson, D. 2005. *Old world colony: Cork and South Munster 1630–1830*. Cork: Cork University Press.

Dietler, M. 1994. 'Our Ancestors the Gauls': Archaeology, Ethnic Nationalism, and the Manipulation of Celtic Identity in Modern Europe. *American Anthropologist* 96, 584–605.

Dixon, P. 2009. Hunting, summer grazing and settlement: competing land use in the uplands of Scotland, in Klápště, J. and Sommer, P. (eds), *Medieval Rural Settlement in Marginal Landscapes (Ruralia 7)*. Turnhout: Brepols, 27–46.

Dixon, P. 2018. What do we really know about transhumance in medieval Scotland? in Costello, E. and Svensson, E. (eds), *Historical Archaeologies of Transhumance across Europe*. Themes in Contemporary Archaeology 6. London: Routledge, 59–73.

Dobres, M.A. and Robb, J.E. (eds) 2000. *Agency in Archaeology*. London: Routledge.

Dodgshon, R.A. 1998. *From chiefs to landlords: social and economic change in the Western Highlands and Islands, c1493–1820*. Edinburgh: Edinburgh University Press.

Doherty, C. 2000. Settlement in Early Ireland: A Review, in Barry, T.B. (ed.), *A History of Settlement in Ireland*. London: Routledge, 187–205.

Donnelly, C. 1994. The tower houses of County Limerick. Unpublished PhD thesis, School of Geography, Archaeology and Palaeoecology, Queen's University Belfast.

Donnelly, C. 2001. Tower Houses and Late Medieval Secular Settlement in County Limerick, in Duffy, P.J., Edwards, D. and FitzPatrick, E. (eds), *Gaelic Ireland, c.1250–c.1650: land, lordship, and settlement*. Dublin: Four Courts Press, 315–28.

Downey, L. 2014. The Cork Butter Exchange (1770–1924); the national and international importance and the ultimate demise of the enterprise, in Foynes, P., Rynne, C. and Synnot, C. (eds), *Butter in Ireland: From Earliest Times to the 21st Century*. Cork: Cork Butter Museum, 29–60.

Duffy, P.J. 1981. The territorial organisation of Gaelic landownership and its transformation in County Monaghan 1591–1640. *Irish Geography* 14, 1–26.

Duffy, P.J. 2007. *Exploring the History and Heritage of Irish Landscapes*. Dublin: Four Courts.

Duffy, P.J. and Nolan, W. (eds) 2012. *At the Anvil: Essays in Honour of William J. Smyth*. Dublin: Geography Publications.

Duffy, P.J., Edwards, D. and FitzPatrick, E. (eds) 2001. *Gaelic Ireland, c.1250–c.1650: Land, Lordship and Settlement*. Dublin: Four Courts Press.

Dunăre, N. 1984. Types traditionnels de vie pastorale dans les régions carpatiques de pâturages et de fenaisons (Roumanie, Ukraine, Pologne, Tchécoslovaquie, Hongrie), in *L'élevage et la vie pastorale dans les montagnes de l'Europe au moyen âge et à l'époque moderne*. Clermont-Ferrand: Institute of Studies of the Massif Central, 55–67.

Dunford, B. 2002. *Farming and the Burren*. Dublin: Teagasc.

Dunn, S.M. 2008. 'Little more than a winter home': An historical archaeology of Irish seasonal migration at Slievemore, Achill Island. Unpublished PhD thesis, Department of Anthropology, Syracuse University.

Dyer, C. 1996. Seasonal Settlement in Medieval Gloucestershire, in Fox, H.S.A. (ed.), *Seasonal Settlement* (Vaughan Paper 39). Leicester: University of Leicester, 25–33.

Dyer, C. 2004. Alternative agriculture: goats in medieval England, in Hoyle, R.W. (ed.), *People, Landscape and Alternative Agriculture: essays for Joan Thirsk*. Exeter: British Agricultural History Society, 20–38.

Emanuelsson, M., Johansson, A., Nilsson, S., Pettersson, S. and Svensson, E. 2003. *Settlement, shieling and landscape: the local history of a forest hamlet*. Stockholm: Almqvist & Wiksell International.

Empey, C.A. 1981. The settlement of the kingdom of Limerick, in Lydon, J. (ed.), *England and Ireland in the later middle ages*. Dublin, Irish Academic Press, 1–25.

Eriksson, O. 2018. What is biological cultural heritage and why should we care about it? An example from Swedish rural landscapes and forests. *Nature Conservation* 28, 1–32.

Evans, E.E. 1939. Some survivals of the Irish openfield system. *Geography* 24, 24–36.

Evans, E.E. 1940. Transhumance in Europe. *Geography* 25, 172–80.

Evans, E.E. 1945. Field Archæology in the Ballycastle District. *Ulster Journal of Archaeology* 8, 14–32.

Evans, E.E. 1951. *Mourne Country: Landscape and Life in South Down*. Dundalk: Dundalgan Press.

Evans, E.E. 1973. *The Personality of Ireland: Habitat, Heritage and History*. Cambridge: Cambridge University Press.

Evans, E.E. and Proudfoot, B. 1958. Excavations at the Deer's Meadow. *Ulster Journal of Archaeology* 21, 127–31.

Evans, J.G. 2003. *Environmental archaeology and the social order*. London: Routledge.

Everitt, A. 1977. River and wold: reflections on the historical origin of regions and pays. *Journal of Historical Geography* 3(1), 67–71.

Everson, P. and Stocker, D. 2012. Wharram before the village moment, in Wrathmell, S. (ed.), *A History of Wharram Percy and its Neighbours*. Wharram: A Study of Settlement on the Yorkshire Wolds XIII. York: York University Archaeological Publications, 164–72.

Falnes, O.J. 1933. *National romanticism in Norway*. New York: Columbia University Press.

Feehan, J. 2003. *Farming in Ireland: History, Heritage and Environment*. Dublin: UCD Faculty of Agriculture.

Feehan, J. 2012. The potato: root of the Famine, in Crowley, J., Smyth, W.J. and Murphy, M. (eds), *Atlas of the Great Irish Famine, 1845–52*. Cork: Cork University Press, 28–37.

Fenton, A. 1980. The Traditional Pastoral Economy, in Parry, M.L. and Slater, T.R. (eds), *The Making of the Scottish Countryside*. London: Taylor and Francis, 93–113.

Fenton, A. 1987. *Country Life in Scotland: Our Rural Past*. Edinburgh: John Donald.

Ferber, M. 2010. *Romanticism: A Very Short Introduction*. Oxford: Oxford University Press.

Fernández Mier, M. and Tente, C. 2018. Transhumant herding systems in Iberia, in Costello, E. and Svensson, E. (eds), *Historical Archaeologies of Transhumance across Europe*. Themes in Contemporary Archaeology 6. London: Routledge, 219–32.

FitzGerald, G. 2003. Irish-speaking in the pre-famine period: a study based on the 1911 census data for people born before 1851 and still alive in 1911. *Proceedings of the Royal Irish Academy* 103 C, 191–283.

FitzPatrick, D. 1980. Irish emigration in the later nineteenth century. *Irish Historical Studies* 22, 126–43.

FitzPatrick, E. 2013. *Formaoil na Fiann*: hunting preserves and assembly places in Gaelic Ireland. *Proceedings of Harvard Celtic Colloquium* 32, 95–118.

Fleming, A. 2012. Working with wood pasture, in Turner, S. and Silvester, R. (eds), *Life in Medieval Landscapes: People and Places in the Middle Ages*. Macclesfield: Windgather Press, 15–31.

Fleure, H.J. 1919. Human regions. *Scottish Geographical Magazine* 35, 94–105.

Ford, W.J. 1976. Some settlement patterns in the Central Region of the Warwickshire Avon, in Sawyer, P.H. (ed.), *Medieval Settlement: Continuity and Change*. London: Edward Arnold, 274–94.

Fossitt, J.A. 1994. Late-Glacial and Holocene vegetation history of Western Donegal, Ireland. *Proceedings of the Royal Irish Academy* 94 B, 1–31.

Fox, A. 1939. Early Welsh homesteads on Gelligaer Common, Glamorgan: excavations in 1938. *Archaeologia Cambrensis* 94, 163–99.

Fox, C. 1932. *The personality of Britain its influence on inhabitant and invader in prehistoric and early historic times*. Cardiff: National Museum of Wales.

Fox, H.S.A. 2012. *Dartmoor's Alluring Uplands: Transhumance and Pastoral Management in the Middle Ages*. Exeter: University of Exeter Press.

Fuhrmann, C.J. 2012. *Policing the Roman Empire: Soldiers, Administration, and Public Order*. Oxford: Oxford University Press.

Gaffney, V. 1959. Summer Shealings. *Scottish Historical Review* 38, 20–35.

Gaffney, V. 1967. Shielings of the Drumochter. *Scottish Studies* 11, 91–99.

Gailey, A. 1984. *Rural houses of the north of Ireland*. Edinburgh: John Donald.

Gailey, A. 1987. Changes in Irish rural housing, 1600–1900, in O'Flanagan, P., Ferguson, P. and Whelan, K. (eds), *Rural Ireland 1600–1900: modernisation and change*. Cork: Cork University Press, 24–40.

Galaty, J.G. and Johnson, D.L. (eds) 1990. *The World of Pastoralism: Herding Systems in Comparative Perspective*. New York: Guilford Press.

Gamble, C.S. and Boismier, W.A. (eds) 1991. *Ethnoarchaeological approaches to mobile campsites: Hunter-Gatherer & Pastoralist Case Studies*. Ethnoarchaeological Series 1. Ann Arbor, Michigan: International Monographs in Prehistory.

Gardiner, M. 2010. A preliminary list of booley huts in the Mourne Mountains, County Down. *Ulster Journal of Archaeology* 67, 145–52.

Gardiner, M. 2011a. Folklore's Timeless Past, Ireland's Present Past, and the Perception of Rural Houses in Early Historic Ireland. *International Journal of Historical Archaeology* 15, 707–24.

Gardiner, M. 2011b. Late Saxon Settlement, in Hamerow, H., Crawford, S. and Hinton, D. (eds), *A Handbook of Anglo-Saxon Archaeology*. Oxford: Oxford University Press, 198–217.

Gardiner, M. 2012a. Medieval settlement on the Garron Plateau of Northern Ireland: a preliminary report. *Medieval Settlement Research* 27, 20–28.

Gardiner, M. 2012b. Time regained: booley huts and seasonal settlement in the Mourne mountains, Co. Down, Ireland, in Turner, S. and Silvester, R. (eds), *Life in Medieval Landscapes: People and Places in Medieval Britain*. Macclesfield: Windgather Press, 106–24.

Gardiner, M. 2015. The Role of Transhumance within Rundale Agriculture, in Ó Síocháin, S., Slater, E. and Downey, L. (eds), *Rundale: Settlement, Society and Farming* (*Ulster Folklife* 58). Cultra: Ulster Folk and Transport Museum, 53–63.

Gardiner, M. 2018. The changing character of transhumance in early and later medieval England, in Costello, E. and Svensson, E. (eds), *Historical Archaeologies of Transhumance across Europe*. Themes in Contemporary Archaeology 6. London: Routledge, 110–19.

Gardiner, M.J. and Radford, T. 1980. *Ireland: General Soil Map*, 2nd edn. Dublin: Teagasc.

Geddes, D.S. 1983. Neolithic transhumance in the Mediterranean Pyrenees. *World Archaeology* 15, 51–66.

Gefu, J.O. and Gilles, J.L. 1990. Pastoralists, ranchers and the state in Nigeria and North America: a comparative analysis. *Nomadic Peoples* 25–27, 34–50.

Gelling, P.S. 1962–63. Medieval shielings in the Isle of Man. *Medieval Archaeology* 6–7, 156–72.

Gibbons, E. (ed.) 1991. *Conamara Faoi Cheilt/Hidden Conamara*. Galway: Connemara West Press.

Giddens, A. 1979. *Central problems in Social Theory: Action, Structure and Contradiction in Social Analysis*. London: Macmillan.

Giddens, A. 1981. *A Contemporary Critique of Historical Materialism: Volume 1. Power, Property and the State*. London: Macmillan.

Giddens, A. 1984. *The constitution of society: outline of the theory of structuration*. Cambridge: Polity Press.

Gilchrist, R. 2005. Introduction: scales and voices in World Historical Archaeology. *World Archaeology* 37, 329–36.

Gillespie, R. 1991. *The transformation of the Irish economy, 1550–1700*. Dublin: Economic and Social History Society of Ireland.

Gillespie, R. 2015. The changing structure of Irish agriculture in the seventeenth century, in Murphy, M. and Stout, M. (eds), *Agriculture and Settlement in Ireland*. Dublin: Four Courts Press, 119–38.

Gísladóttir, G.A., Woollett, J.M., Ævarsson, U., Dupont-Hébert, C., Newton, A. and Vésteinsson, O. 2012. The Svalbarð Project. *Archaeologica Islandica* 10, 65–76.

González-Álvarez, D., Fernández Mier, M. and López Gómez, P. 2016. An archaeological approach to the *brañas*: summer farms in the pastures of the Cantabrian Mountains (northern Spain), in Collis, J., Pearce, M. and Nicolis, F. (eds), *Summer Farms: Seasonal Exploitation of the Uplands from Prehistory to the Present*. Sheffield: J.R. Collis Publications, 203–20.

Graham, B. 1985. Anglo-Norman manorial settlement in Ireland: an assessment. *Irish Geography* 18, 4–15.

Graham, J.M. 1953. Transhumance in Ireland. *Advancement of Science* 10, 74–79.

Graham, J.M. 1954. Transhumance in Ireland, with special reference to its bearing on the evolution of rural communities in the west. Unpublished PhD thesis, Department of Geography, Queen's University Belfast.

Graham, J.M. 1970a. Rural Society in Connacht 1600–1640, in Stephens, N. and Glasscock, R.E. (eds), *Irish Geographical Studies in Honour of E. Estyn-Evans*. Belfast: Queen's University Belfast, 192–208.

Graham, J.M. 1970b. South-west Donegal in the seventeenth century. *Irish Geography* 6, 136–52.

Gray, M. 1957. *The Highland economy, 1750–1850*. Edinburgh: Oliver and Boyd.

Haldane, A.R.B. 1952. *The Drove Roads of Scotland*. Edinburgh: Nelson.

Hall, M. 2000. *Archaeology and the Modern World: Colonial Transcripts in South Africa and the Chesapeake*. London: Routledge.

Hall, M. and Silliman, S.W. 2006. *Historical Archaeology*. Oxford: Blackwell.

Hansen, J.D. 2015. *Mapping the Germans: Statistical Science, Cartography, and the Visualization of the German Nation, 1848–1914*. Oxford: Oxford University Press.

Hardin, G. 1968. The Tragedy of the Commons. *Science* 162, 1243–48.

Harris, S. and Yalden, D.W. (eds) 2008. *Mammals of the British Isles: handbook*. Southampton: Mammal Society.

Hart, K. and Sperling, L. 1987. Cattle as Capital. *Ethnos* 52, 324–38.

Hatton, T.J. and Williamson, J.G. 1993. After the Famine: Emigration from Ireland, 1850–1913. *The Journal of Economic History* 53, 575–600.

Hawthorne, D. 2015. Quantifying Fire Regimes and their Impact on the Irish Landscape. Unpublished PhD thesis, Department of Botany, Trinity College Dublin.

Hennessy, M. 1985. Parochial organisation in Medieval Tipperary, in Nolan, W. (ed.), *Tipperary: History and Society*. Dublin: Geography Publications, 60–70.

Hennessy, M. 1996. Manorial organisation in early thirteenth-century Tipperary. *Irish Geography* 29, 116–25.

Henry, F. 1956/1957. Early monasteries, beehive huts, and dry-stone houses in the neighbourhood of Caherciveen and Waterville (Co. Kerry). *Proceedings of the Royal Irish Academy* 58 C, 45–166.

Herring, P. 2012. Shadows of ghosts: early medieval transhumants in Cornwall, in Turner, S. and Silvester, R. (eds), *Life in Medieval Landscapes: People and Places in the Middle Ages*. Macclesfield: Windgather Press, 89–105.

Hickey, K. 2011. *Wolves in Ireland: a natural and cultural history*. Dublin: Four Courts Press.

Hicks, D. and Beaudry, M.C. (eds) 2006. *The Cambridge Companion to Historical Archaeology*. Cambridge: Cambridge University Press.

Hodd, A.N.L. 1974. Runrig on the eve of the agricultural revolution in Scotland. *Scottish Geographical Magazine* 90, 130–33.

Hodder, I. (ed.) 1982. *Symbolic and Structural Archaeology*. Cambridge: Cambridge University Press.

Hodder, I. and Hudson, S. (eds) 2003. *Reading the Past: Current Approaches to Interpretation in Archaeology*, 3rd edn. Cambridge: Cambridge University Press.

Hogan, E. 1910. *Onomasticon goedelicum locorum et tribuum Hiberniae et Scottiae: an index, with indentification, to the Gaelic names of places and tribes*. Dublin: Royal Irish Academy.

Hole, F. 1996. The context of caprine domestication in the Zagros region, in Harris, D. (ed.), *The Origins and Spread of Agriculture and Pastoralism in Eurasia*. London: UCL Press, 263–81.

Hooke, D. 2012. 'Weald-bære & swina mæst': wood-pasture in early medieval England, in Turner, S. and Silvester, R. (eds), *Life in Medieval Landscapes: People and Places in the Middle Ages*. Macclesfield: Windgather Press, 32–49.

Horning, A.J. 2004. Archaeological explorations of cultural identity and rural economy in the north of Ireland: Goodland, County Antrim. *International Journal of Historical Archaeology* 8, 199–215.

Horning, A.J. 2007. Materiality and mutable landscapes: Rethinking seasonality and marginality in rural Ireland. *International Journal of Historical Archaeology* 11, 358–78.

Horning, A.J. 2013. *Ireland in the Virginian Sea: Colonialism in the British Atlantic*. Chapel Hill: University of North Carolina Press.

Horning, A.J. and Palmer, M. (eds) 2009. *Crossing Paths or Sharing Tracks? Future Directions in the Archaeological Study of Post-1550 Britain and Ireland*. Woodbridge: The Boydell Press.

Horning, A.J., Ó Baoill, R., Donnelly, C. and Logue, P. (eds) 2007. *The Post-Medieval Archaeology of Ireland, 1550–1850*. Bray: Wordwell.

Hougen, B. 1947. *Fra seter til gård: studier i norsk bosetningshistorie*. Oslo: Norsk Arkeologisk Selskap.

Huang, C.C. 2002. Holocene landscape development and human impact in the Connemara Uplands, Western Ireland. *Journal of Biogeography* 29, 153–65.

Hume, N. 1964. Handmaiden to history. *North Carolina Historical Review* 41, 215–25.

Ingold, T. 1980. *Hunters, pastoralists and ranchers: reindeer economies and their transformations*. Cambridge: Cambridge University Press.

James, S. 1999. *The Atlantic Celts: ancient people or modern invention?* London: British Museum Press.

Johnson, D.L. 1969. *The Nature of Nomadism: A Comparative Study of Pastoral Migrations in Southwestern Asia and Northern Africa*. Chicago: University of Chicago.

Johnson, M. 1996. *An Archaeology of Capitalism*. Oxford: Blackwell.

Jones, D.S. 1995. *Graziers, Land Reform, and Political Conflict in Ireland*. Washington: The Catholic University of America Press.

Jones-Hughes, T. 1965. Society and settlement in nineteenth-century Ireland. *Irish Geography* 5, 79–96.

Jones-Hughes, T. 1984. Historical geography of Ireland from circa 1700, in Davies, G. (ed.), *Irish Geography 1934–1984*. Dublin: Geographical Society of Ireland, 149–66.

Joyce, M. 1949. Making the Rick. *Limerick Leader*, 20 August 1949. Available at <http://www.askaboutireland.ie/reading-room/history-heritage/pages-in-history/an-mangaire-sugach-the-li/rural-life-and-the-natura/making-the-rick/>.

Juler, C. 2014. După coada oilor: long-distance transhumance and its survival in Romania. *Pastoralism* 4(4). Available at <https://pastoralismjournal.springeropen.com/articles/10.1186/2041-7136-4-4>

Kelly, F. 1997. *Early Irish Farming: A Study Based Mainly on the Law-Texts of the 7th and 8th Centuries AD*. Dublin: Dublin Institute of Advanced Studies.

Kelly, J. (ed.) 1990. *The Letters of Lord Chief Baron Edward Willes to the Earl of Warwick, 1757–62*. Kilkenny: Boethius.

Kennedy, L. and Solar, P.M. 2007. *Irish Agriculture: A Price History from the mid-eighteenth century to the eve of the First World War*. Dublin: Royal Irish Academy.

Kennedy, L. and Clarkson, L.A. 1993. Birth, Death and Exile: Irish Population History, 1700–1921, in Graham, B.J. and Proudfoot, L.J. (eds), *An Historical Geography of Ireland*. London: Academic Press, 338–65.

Kerr, T.R., Swindles, G.T. and Plunkett, G. 2009. Making hay while the sun shines? Socio-economic change, cereal production and climatic deterioration in Early Medieval Ireland. *Journal of Archaeological Science* 36(12), 2868–74.

Khazanov, A. 1984. *Nomads and the Outside World*. Cambridge: Cambridge University Press.

Khazanov, A. 1994. *Nomads and the Outside World*, 2nd edn. Madison: University of Wisconsin Press.

Kienlin, T.L. and Valde-Nowak, P. 2004. Neolithic Transhumance in the Black Forest Mountains, SW Germany. *Journal of Field Archaeology* 29, 29–44.

Klápště, J. and Sommer, P. (eds) 2009. *Medieval Rural Settlement in Marginal Landscapes (Ruralia 7)*. Turnhout: Brepols.

Klein, J. 1920. *The Mesta: A Study in Spanish Economic History, 1273–1836*. Boston: Harvard University Press.

Konvitz, J. 1987. *Cartography in France, 1660–1848: Science, Engineering, and Statecraft*. Chicago: University of Chicago Press.

Koster, H.A. and Chang, C. 1994. Introduction, in Chang, C. and Koster, H.A. (eds), *Pastoralists at the Periphery: Herders in a Capitalist World*. Tuscon: Arizona University Press, 1–22.

Krzywinski, K., O'Connell, M. and Küster, H. (eds) 2009. *Cultural landscapes of Europe. Fields of Demeter, haunts of Pan*. Bremen: Aschenbeck Media.

Kupiec, P. 2016. Transhumance in the North Atlantic: An Interdisciplinary Approach to the Identification and Interpretation of Viking-age and Medieval Shieling Sites. Unpublished PhD thesis, Department of Archaeology, University of Aberdeen.

Kupiec, P. and Milek, K. 2018. Ethno-geoarchaeological study of seasonal occupation: Bhiliscleitir, the Isle of Lewis, in Costello, E. and Svensson, E. (eds), *Historical Archaeologies of Transhumance across Europe*. Themes in Contemporary Archaeology 6. London: Routledge, 75–92.

Kupiec, P., Milek, K., Gísladóttir, G.A. and Woollett, J. 2016. Elusive *sel* sites: the geoarchaeological quest for Icelandic shielings and the case of Þorvaldsstaðasel, in northeast Iceland, in Collis, J., Pearce, M. and Nicolis, F. (eds), *Summer Farms: Seasonal Exploitation of the Uplands from Prehistory to the Present*. Sheffield: J.R. Collis Publications, 221–36.

Lane, P. 1996. The Encumbered Estates Court and Galway land ownership, 1849-58, in: Moran, G. (ed.), *Galway: History & Society*. Dublin: Geography Publications, 395–419.

Lanters, J. 2003. Reading the Irish future in the Celtic past: texts, contexts and memory in modern Ireland, in McBride, L. (ed.), *Reading Irish histories*, Dublin: Four Courts Press, 178–95.

Larkin, E. 1972. The Devotional Revolution in Ireland, 1850–75. *The American Historical Review* 77(3), 625–52.

Larsson, J. 2012. The Expansion and Decline of a Transhumance System in Sweden, 1550–1920. *Historia Agraria* 56, 11–39.

Latour, B. 2005. *Reassembling the social: an introduction to actor-network-theory*. Oxford: Oxford University Press.

Lebaudy, G. 2006. Des « gens de moutons ». Sur les traces des bergers piémontais dans l'espace de la grande transhumance provençale-alpine, in Laffont, P.Y. (ed.) *Transhumance et estivage en Occident, des origines aux enjeux actuels, Actes des XXVI e Journées Internationales d'Histoire de l'Abbaye de Flaran (9–11 septembre 2004)*. Toulouse: Presses universitaires du Mirail, 341–53.

Leighton, D.K. 2012. *The Western Brecon Beacons*. Cardiff: Royal Commission on the Ancient & Historical Monuments of Wales.

Leone, M.P. 1995. A historical archaeology of capitalism. *American Anthropologist* 97, 251–68.

Leone, M.P. and Potter, P.B. 1988. *The Recovery of Meaning: Historical Archaeology in the Eastern United States*. Washington: Smithsonian Institute.

Leone, M.P. and Potter, P.B. (eds) 1999. *Historical Archaeologies of Capitalism*. New York: Kluwer Academic.

Leslie, S. (ed.) 1932. *Saint Patrick's Purgatory: A Record from History and Literature*. London: Burns Oates & Washbourne.

Lévêque, S. 2013. Mountain Summer Shelters in the Haut Adour Region of the Central French Pyrenees: Examples from the Campan and Lesponne Valleys (Hautes-Pyrénées), in Lozny, L.R. (ed.), *Continuity and Change in Cultural Adaptation to Mountain Environments: From Prehistory to Contemporary Threats*. New York: Springer, 97–122.

Lewis, M. 1985. The Flats of Moonacuan. *Anglesboro-Kilbehenny Parish Journal* 36.

Lewthwaite, J. 1984. The Art of Corse Herding: Archaeological Insights from Recent Pastoral Products on West Mediterranean Islands, in Clutten-Brock, J. and Grigson, C. (eds), *Early Herders and Their Flocks*, BAR International Series 202. Oxford, 25–38.

Lindholm, K.J., Sandström, E. and Ekman, A.K. 2013. The Archaeology of the Commons. *The Journal of Archaeology and Ancient History* 10, 1–49.

Locock, M. 2006. Deserted rural settlements in south-east Wales, in Roberts, K. (ed.), *Lost Farmsteads: Deserted Rural Settlements in Wales*. York: Council for British Archaeology, 41–60.

Longley, D. 2006. Deserted rural settlements in north-west Wales, in Roberts, K. (ed.), *Lost Farmsteads: Deserted Rural Settlements in Wales*. York: Council for British Archaeology, 61–82.

López-Sáez, J.A., Blanco-González, A., Abel-Schaad, D., Robles-López, S., Luelmo-Lautenschlaeger, R., Pérez-Díaz, S. and Alba-Sánchez, F. 2018. Transhumance dynamics in the Gredos range (central Spain) during the last two millennia. Environmental and socio-political vectors of change, in Costello, E. and Svensson, E. (eds), *Historical Archaeologies of Transhumance across Europe*. Themes in Contemporary Archaeology 6. London: Routledge, 233–44.

Love, J.A. 1981. Shielings of the Isle of Rum. *Scottish Studies* 25, 39–63.

Lozny, L.R. (ed.) 2013a. *Continuity and Change in Cultural Adaptation to Mountain Environments: From Prehistory to Contemporary Threats*. New York: Springer.

Lozny, L.R. 2013b. Landscape Archaeology of the Commons of the Bouleste/Labas Valley, Hautes-Pyrenees, in Lozny, L.R. (ed.), *Continuity and Change in Cultural Adaptation to Mountain Environments: From Prehistory to Contemporary Threats*. New York: Springer, 123–205.

Lucas, A.T. 1954. Bog Wood: A Study in Rural Economy. *Béaloideas* 23, 71–134.

Lucas, A.T. 1982. Contributions to the Study of the Irish House: Smokehole and Chimney, in Gailey, A. and Ó hÓgáin, D. (eds), *Gold under the Furze: Studies in Folk Tradition presented to Caoimhín Ó Danachair*. Dublin: The Glendale Press, 50–66.

Lucas, A.T. 1989. *Cattle in Ancient Ireland*. Kilkenny: Boethius Press.

Lucas, G. 2006. Historical archaeology and time, in Hicks, D. and Beaudry, M.C. (eds), *The Cambridge Companion to Historical Archaeology*. Cambridge: Cambridge University Press, 34–47.

Lucas, G. 2008. Pálstóftir: A Viking age shieling in Iceland. *Norwegian Archaeological Review* 41(1), 85–100.

Luick, R. 2004. Transhumance in Germany, in Bunce, R.G.H., Pérez Soba, M., Jongman, R.H.G., Gómez Sal, A., Herzog, F. and Austad, I. (eds), *Transhumance and Biodiversity in European Mountains*, Report of the EU-FP5 project TRANSHUMOUNT (EVK2-CT-2002–80017), IALE publication series (1). Wagingen: Alterra.

Lynch, T.F. 1971. Preceramic Transhumance in the Callejon de Huaylas, Peru. *American Antiquity* 36, 139–48.

Lynn, C.J. 1994. Houses in Rural Ireland, A.D. 500–1000. *Ulster Journal of Archaeology* 57, 81–94.

MacBain, A. 1911. *Etymological dictionary of Scottish-Gaelic*. Stirling: Enneas MacKay.

McCarthy, M. 2003. The Faunal Remains, in Cleary, R.M. and Hurley, M.F. (eds), *Excavations in Cork City, 1984–2000*. Cork: Cork City Council, 375–90.

McClatchie, M., McCormick, F., Kerr, T.R. and O'Sullivan, A. 2015. Early medieval farming and food production: a review of the archaeobotanical evidence from archaeological excavations in Ireland. *Vegetation History and Archaeobotany* 24(1), 179–86.

McCormack, A.M. 2005. *The Earldom of Desmond, 1463–1583: the decline and crisis of a feudal lordship*. Dublin: Four Courts Press.

McCormick, F. 2008. The decline of the cow: agricultural and settlement change in early medieval Ireland. *Peritia* 20, 209–24.

MacCotter, P. 2000. The Cantreds of Desmond. *Journal of the Cork Historical and Archaeological Society* 105, 49–68.

MacCotter, P. 2008. *Medieval Ireland: territorial, political and economic divisions*. Dublin: Four Courts Press.

McCourt, D. 1955. Infield and outfield in Ireland. *The Economic History Review* 7, 369–76.

McCourt, D. 1958. Surviving openfield in County Londonderry. *Ulster Folklife* 4, 19–28.

McCourt, D. 1971. The Dynamic Quality of Irish Rural Settlement, in Buchanan, R., Jones, E. and McCourt, D. (eds), *Man and his Habitat: essays presented to Emyr Estyn Evans*. London: Routledge and K. Paul, 126–64.

Mac Cuinneagáin, C. 2002. *Glencolmcille: a parish history*. Dublin: Four Masters Press.

McDonald, B.T. 1998. The Deserted Village, Slievemore, Achill Island, County Mayo, Ireland. *International Journal of Historical Archaeology* 2, 73–112.

McDonald, B.T. 2014. Booleying in Achill, Achillbeg and Corraun: survey, excavation and analysis of booley settlements in the Civil Parish of Achill. Unpublished PhD thesis, School of Geography and Archaeology, NUI Galway.

McErlean, T. 1983. The Irish Townland System of Landscape Organisation, in Reeves-Smyth, T. and Hammond, F. (eds), *Landscape Archaeology in Ireland*, British Archaeological Reports 116. Oxford, 315–39.

McGill, P.J. 1970. *History of the Parish of Ardara*. Donegal: Donegal Democrat.

McGinley, T.C. 1867. *The Cliff Scenery of South-Western Donegal*. Londonderry: The Journal Office.

Mac Giollarnáth, S. (ed.) 1934. *Peadar Chois Fhairrge: scéalta nua agus seanscéalta d'innis Peadar Mac Thuathaláin*. Baile Átha Cliath: Oifig Díolta Foilsicheáin Rialtais.

McGlynn, G. 2007. Using δ13C, δ15N, δ18O stable isotope analysis of human bone tissue to identify transhumance, high altitude habitation and reconstruct palaeodiet for the early medieval Alpine population at Volders, Austria. Unpublished PhD thesis, Faculty of Biology, LMU München.

McGrath, B. (ed.) 2006. *The Minute Book of the Corporation of Clonmel, 1608–1649*. Dublin: Irish Manuscripts Commission.

MacKay, A. and Ditchburn, D. 1997. *Atlas of Medieval Europe*. London: Routledge.

MacLysaght, E. 1939. *Irish life in the seventeenth century: after Cromwell*. Dublin: The Talbot Press.

Mac Néill, M. 2008. *The Festival of Lughnasa: A Study of the Survival of the Celtic festival of the Beginning of Harvest* (reprint). Dublin: Folklore Society of Ireland.

McNeill, T.E. 2007. Where should we place the boundary between the medieval and post-medieval periods in Ireland? in Horning, A.J., Ó Baoill, R., Donnelly, C. and Logue, P. (eds), *The Post-Medieval Archaeology of Ireland, 1550–1850*. Bray: Wordwell, 7–13.

McQuade, M., Molloy, B. and Moriarty, C. 2009. *In the Shadow of the Galtees: Archaeological Excavations along the N8 Cashel to Mitchelstown Road Scheme*. Bray: Wordwell.

McSparron, C. 2002. A note on the discovery of two probable booley houses at Ballyutoag, County Antrim. *Ulster Journal of Archaeology* 61, 154–55.

Mac Suibhne, B. 1995. Agrarian Improvement and Social Unrest: Lord George Hill and the Gaoth Dobhair Sheep War 1856–1860, in Nolan, W., Ronayne, L. and Dunlevy, M. (eds), *Donegal: History and Society*, Dublin: Geography Publications, 547–82.

MacSween, M.D. 1959. Transhumance in North Skye. *Scottish Geographical Magazine* 75, 75–88.

MacSween, M.D. and Gailey, R.A. 1961. Some shielings in North Skye. *Scottish Studies* 5, 77–84.

Maguire, W.A. 1972. *The Downshire Estates in Ireland, 1801–1845: The Management of Irish Landed Estates in the Early Nineteenth Century.* Oxford: Clarendon Press.

Matley, I.M. 1968. Transhumance in Bosnia and Herzegovina. *Geographical Review* 58, 231–61.

Miller, D.W. 2005. Landscape and religious practice: a study of Mass attendance in Pre-Famine Ireland. *Éire-Ireland* 40, 90–106.

Miller, R. 1967a. Land use by summer shielings. *Scottish Studies* 11, 193–221.

Miller, R. 1967b. Shiels in the Brecon Beacons. *Folk Life* 5, 107–10.

Mitchell, G.F. and Ryan, M. 2001. *Reading the Irish Landscape.* Dublin: TownHouse.

Moisley, H.A. 1962. *Uig: A Hebridean Parish.* Nottingham: Geography Field Group.

Mokyr, J. and Ó Gráda, C. 1984. New developments in Irish population history, 1700–1850. *The Economic History Review* 37, 473–88.

Moore, M.J. 1995. A Bronze Age settlement and ritual centre in the Monavullagh Mountains, county Waterford, Ireland. *Proceedings of the Prehistoric Society* 61, 191–243.

Moran, G.P. 1996. *Galway: History and Society.* Dublin: Geography Publications.

Moreland, J. 2011. The Mountains Survey: Loch Aoineart, in Parker Pearson, M. (ed.), *Machair to Mountains: Archaeological Survey and Excavation in South Uist.* Oxford: Oxbow, 83–117.

Moreno-Garcia, M. 2001. Sheep transhumance in Medieval Spain an ethnoarchaeological approach, in Buitenhuis, H. and Prummel, W. (eds), *Animals and Man in the Past. Essays in honour of Dr. A.T. Clason. Emeritus Professor of Archaeozoology,* ARC-Publicatie 41. Groningen, 251–62.

Morgan, H. 1999. *Tyrone's Rebellion: The Outbreak of the Nine Years War in Tudor Ireland.* Woodbridge: The Boydell Press.

Morris, H. 1939. Varia. Booleying. *Béaloideas* 9(2), 288–89.

Murphy, M. and O'Conor, K. 2006. Castles and deer parks in Anglo-Norman Ireland. *Eolas: Journal of the American Society of Irish Medieval Studies* 1, 51–70.

Murphy, M. and Potterton, M. 2010. *The Dublin Region in the Middle Ages: Settlement, Land-use and Economy.* Dublin: Four Courts Press.

Murphy, M. and Stout, M. (eds) 2015. *Agriculture and Settlement in Ireland.* Dublin: Four Courts Press.

Murray, E. 2004. Animal bone, in FitzPatrick, E., O'Brien, M. and Walsh, P. (eds), *Archaeological investigations in Galway City, 1987–1998.* Bray: Wordwell, 562–601.

Murray, E. and McCormick, F. 2012. Doonloughan: a seasonal settlement site on the Connemara coast. *Proceedings of the Royal Irish Academy* 112 C, 95–146.

Naessens, P. 2007. Gaelic lords of the sea – the coastal tower houses of south Connemara, in Doran, L. and Lyttleton, J. (eds), *Lordship in Medieval Ireland: Image and Reality.* Dublin: Four Courts Press, 217–35.

Naessens, P. 2009. The Uí Fhlaithbheartaigh Gaelic Lordship of Iarchonnacht: Medieval Lordly Settlement on the Atlantic Seaboard. Unpublished PhD thesis, Department of Archaeology, NUI, Galway.

Nash, C. 1993. Embodying the nation: the west of Ireland landscape and Irish identity, in: O'Connor, B. and Cronin, M. (eds.), *Tourism in Ireland: A Critical Analysis*. Cork: Cork University Press, 86–112.

Nash, R.C. 1985. Irish Atlantic Trade in the Seventeenth and Eighteenth Centuries. *The William and Mary Quarterly* 42, 329–56.

Nicholls, K. 1987. Gaelic society and economy in the High Middle Ages, in Cosgrove, A. (ed.), *A New History of Ireland, Volume II: Medieval Ireland 1169–1534*. Oxford: Oxford University of Ireland, 397–438.

Ní Ghabhláin, S. 1996. The origin of medieval parishes in Gaelic Ireland: the evidence from Kilfenora, in FitzPatrick, E. and Gillespie, R. (eds), *Medieval and Early Modern Ireland: Community, Territory and Building*. Dublin: Four Courts Press, 37–61.

Ní Ghabhláin, S. 2006. Late twelfth-century church construction: evidence of parish formation? in FitzPatrick, E. and Gillespie, R. (eds), *Medieval and Early Modern Ireland: Community, Territory and Building*. Dublin: Four Courts Press, 147–67.

Nolan, W. 2012. Land reform in post-Famine Ireland, in Crowley, J., Smyth, W.J. and Murphy, M. (eds), *Atlas of the Great Irish Famine, 1845–52*. Cork: Cork University Press, 570–79.

Nugent, P. 2006. The Dynamics of Parish Formation in High Medieval and Late Medieval Clare, in FitzPatrick, E. and Gillespie, R. (eds), *Medieval and Early Modern Ireland: Community, Territory and Building*. Dublin: Four Courts Press, 186–208.

Ó Bric, B. 1974. Galway Townsmen as the Owners of Land in Connacht, 1585–1641. Unpublished MA thesis, Department of History, University College Galway.

O'Brien, W. 2009. *Local Worlds: Early Settlement Landscapes and Upland Farming in South-West Ireland*. Cork: Collins Press.

Ó Cíobháin, B. 1985. *Toponomia Hiberniae IV*. Baile Átha Cliath: An Foras Duibhneach.

Ó Conaola, T.S. 1995. The great famine in Conamara: impact and assessment. Unpublished MA thesis, Department of History, University College, Galway.

Ó Conghaile, M. 1988. *Conamara agus Árainn, 1880–1980: gnéithe den stair shóisialta*. Béal an Daingin Cló Iar-Chonnachta.

O'Connell, M. and McDonnell, K. 2019. Holocene vegetation history of SW Connemara, Co. Galway with particular reference to Carna and Roundstone, in Coxon, P. (ed.), *The Quaternary of Western Ireland Field Guide*. Dublin: Irish Quaternary Association, 83–102.

O'Conor, K.D. 1998. *The archaeology of medieval rural settlement in Ireland*. Dublin: Royal Irish Academy.

O'Conor, K.D. 2002. Housing in later medieval Gaelic Ireland. *Ruralia* 4, 201–10.

O'Conor, K.D. 2007. English settlement and change in Roscommon during the late sixteenth and seventeenth centuries, in Horning, A., Ó Baoill, R., Donnelly, C. and Logue, P. (eds), *The Post-Medieval Archaeology of Ireland, 1550–1850*. Dublin: Wordwell, 189–204.

Ó Danachair, C. 1964. The combined byre-and-dwelling in Ireland. *Folk Life* 2, 58–75.

Ó Danachair, C. 1972. Traditional forms of the dwelling house in Ireland. *The Journal of the Royal Society of Antiquaries of Ireland* 102(1), 77–96.

Ó Danachair, C. 1981. An Rí (The King): an example of traditional social organisation. *Journal of the Royal Society of Antiquaries of Ireland* 111, 14–28.

Ó Danachair, C. 2004. *Irish Customs and Beliefs*. Cork: Mercier Press.

Ó Dónaill, N. 1977. *Foclóir Gaeilge-Béarla*. Baile Átha Cliath: Oifig an tSoláthair.

Ó Donnabháin, B. 2000. An appalling vista? The Celts and the archaeology of later prehistoric Ireland, in Desmond, A., Johnson, G., McCarthy, M., Sheehan, J. and Shee-Twohig, E. (eds), *New agendas in Irish prehistory: papers in commemoration of Liz Anderson*. Bray: Wordwell, 189–96.

O'Dowd, A. 1981. *Meitheal: A Study of Co-Operative Labour in Rural Ireland*. Dublin: Folklore Society of Ireland.

O'Dowd, A. 1990. *Spalpeens and Tattie Hokers: History & Folklore of Irish Migratory Agricultural*. Dublin: Irish Academic Press.

Ó Duilearga, S. 1939. Varia. Mountain shielings in Donegal. *Béaloideas* 9, 295–97.

Ó Duilearga, S. 1947. Oidhche Sheanchais i mBaile Chruaich. *Béaloideas* 17, 251–61.

Ó Duilearga, S. and Ó Gallchobhair, M. 1940. Amhráin ó Iorrus. *Béaloideas* 10, 210–84.

Oeggl, K., Schmidl, A. and Kofler, W. 2009. Origin and seasonality of subfossil caprine dung from the discovery site of the Iceman (Eastern Alps). *Vegetation History and Archaeobotany* 18, 37–46.

O'Flanagan, P. 1985. Markets and fairs in Ireland, 1600–1800: index of economic development and regional growth. *Journal of Historical Geography* 11, 364–78.

O'Flanagan, P. and Buttimer, C.G. (eds) 1993. *Cork: History & Society*. Dublin: Geography Publications.

Ó Gaora, C. 1937. *Obair is Luadhainn, nó saoghal sa nGaedhaltacht*. Baile Átha Cliath: Oifig an tSoláthair.

Ó Gráda, C. and O'Rourke, K.H. 1997. Migration as disaster relief: lessons from the Great Irish Famine. *European Review of Economic History* 1, 3–25.

Ó Héalaí, P. and Ó Tuairisg, L. (ed.) 2007. *Tobar an Dúchais: Béaloideas as Conamara agus Corca Dhuibhne*. An Daingean: An Sagart.

Ó hEochaidh, S. 1943. Buailteachas i dTír Chonaill. *Béaloideas* 13, 130–58.

Ó hÓgáin, D. 2006. *The Lore of Ireland: An Encyclopaedia of Myth, Legend and Romance*. Cork: Collins Press.

O'Keeffe, T. 2009. Irish 'Post-medieval' Archaeology: Time to Lose our Innocence? in Horning, A. and Palmer, M. (eds), *Crossing Paths or Sharing Tracks?: Future directions in the archaeological study of post-1550 Britain and Ireland*. Woodbridge: The Boydell Press, 65–80.

Ó Lochlainn, C. 1949. Miscellanea. An Bhuaile in n-Acaill. *Béaloideas* 19, 175–76.

Ó Moghráin, P. 1944. More Notes on the 'Buaile'. *Béaloideas* 14, 45–52.

Ó Moghráin, P. 1949. Miscellanea. An Tuagh Chuisle. *Béaloideas* 19, 176–77.

O'Neill, J.A. 1973. The Placenames of Glencolumbkille Parish, Co. Donegal. Unpublished PhD thesis, Queen's University Belfast.

O'Rahilly, T.F. 1946. *Early Irish history and mythology*. Dublin: Dublin Institute for Advanced Studies.

Ó Ríordáin, S.P. and Hunt, J. 1942. Mediæval Dwellings at Caherguillamore, Co. Limerick. *Journal of the Royal Society of Antiquaries of Ireland* 12, 37–63.

O'Rourke, E. 2005. Socio-natural interaction and landscape dynamics in the Burren, Ireland. *Landscape and Urban Planning* 70(1–2), 69–83.

O'Rourke, K. 1995. Emigration and living standards in Ireland since the Famine, *Journal of Population Economics* 8, 407–21.

Orr, W. 1982. *Deer Forests, Landlords and Crofters: the Western Highlands in Victorian and Edwardian times*. Edinburgh: John Donald.

Orser, C.E. Jr. 1996. *A Historical Archaeology of the Modern World*. New York: Plenum Press.

Orser, C.E. Jr. 2006a. Discovering our recent pasts: historical archaeology and early nineteenth-century rural Ireland in Orser Jr, C.E. (ed.), *Unearthing Hidden Ireland: Historical Archaeology at Ballykilcline, County Roscommon*. Bray: Wordwell, 1–18.

Orser, C.E. Jr. (ed.) 2006b. *Unearthing Hidden Ireland: Historical Archaeology at Ballykilcline, County Roscommon*. Bray: Worldwell.

Orser, C.E. Jr. 2010. Three 19th-century house sites in rural Ireland. *Post-Medieval Archaeology* 44, 81–104.

Ó Síocháín, S., Slater, E. and Downey, L. (eds) 2015. *Rundale: Settlement, Society and Farming (Ulster Folklife* 58). Cultra: Ulster Folk and Transport Museum.

O'Sullivan, A. and Sheehan, J. 1992. Fionnán enclosures: aspects of traditional land use in South Kerry. *Journal of the Kerry Archaeological and Historical Society* 25, 5–19.

O'Sullivan, A., McCormick, F., Kerr, T. and Harney, L. 2014. *Early Medieval Ireland, AD 400–1100: The Evidence from Archaeological Excavations*. Dublin: Royal Irish Academy.

Ott, S. 1981. *The Circle of Mountains: A Basque Shepherding Community*. Oxford: Clarendon Press.

Otway-Ruthven, A.J. 1964. Parochial development in the rural deanery of Skreen. *Journal of the Royal Society of Antiquaries of Ireland* 94, 111–22.

Oxford English Dictionary. Oxford: Oxford University Press. Available at <http://www.oed.com/>.

Paine, R. 1971. Animals as capital: comparisons among northern nomadic herders and hunters. *Anthropological Quarterly* 44, 157–72.

Patterson, N.T. 1994. *Cattle-lords and clansmen: the social structure of early Ireland*, 2nd edn. Notre Dame: University of Notre Dame Press.

Peate, I.C. 1944. *The Welsh House: A Study in Folk Culture*. Liverpool: Brython Press.

Pedersen, R. 1974. *Seterbruket på Hedmarken. Fra system til oppløsning*. Oslo: Hedmarksmuseet og Domkirkeodden.

Pettersson, S. 2018. From written sources to archaeological remains – medieval shielings in central Scandinavia, in Costello, E. and Svensson, E. (eds), *Historical Archaeologies of Transhumance across Europe*. Themes in Contemporary Archaeology 6. London: Routledge, 29–42.

Pillatt, T. 2012. Experiencing climate: finding weather in eighteenth century Cumbria. *Journal of Archaeological Method and Theory* 19, 564–81.

Pittock, M. 2008. *Scottish and Irish Romanticism*. Oxford: Oxford University Press.

Power, B. 2000. *White Knights, Dark Earls: The Rise and Fall of an Anglo-Irish Dynasty*. Cork: Collins Press.

Quinn, C.P., Kuijt, I., Goodale, N. and Néill, J. Ó. 2018. Along the Margins? The Later Bronze Age Seascapes of Western Ireland. *European Journal of Archaeology* 22(1), 44–66.

Ramm, H.G., McDowall, R.W. and Mercer, E. 1970. *Shielings and bastles*. London: Her Majesty's Stationery Office.

Rathbone, S. 2009. Booley houses, hafods and sheilings: a comparative study of transhumant settlements from around the Northern Basin of the Irish Sea, in Horning, A. and Brannon, N.F. (eds), *Ireland and Britain in the Atlantic World*. Dublin: Wordwell, 111–29.

Raven, J.A. 2005. Medieval landscapes and lordship in South Uist. Unpublished PhD thesis, Department of Archaeology, University of Glasgow.

Raven, J.A. 2011. The shielings survey: central South Uist, in Parker Pearson, M. (ed.), *Machair to Mountains: Archaeological Survey and Excavation in South Uist*. Oxford: Oxbow Books, 160–79.

RCAHMS 2007. *In the Shadow of Bennachie: a field archaeology of Donside, Aberdeenshire*. Edinburgh: Society of Antiquaries of Scotland.

Reckwitz, A. 2002. Toward a theory of social practices: a development in culturalist theorizing. *European Journal of Social Theory* 5, 243–63.

Rendu, C. 2006. Transhumance: prélude à l'histoire d'un mot voyageur, in P.-Y. Laffont (ed.) *Transhumance et estivage en Occident des origines aux enjeux actuels*. Toulouse: Presses universitaires du Mirail, 7–29.

Rendu, C., Calastrenc, C., Le Couédic, M. and Berdoy, A. 2016. *Estives d'Ossau: 7000 ans de pastoralsime dans les Pyrénées*. Les Lilas: Éditions le Pas d'oiseau.

Richards, E. 2000. *The Highland Clearances: people, landlords and rural turmoil*. Edinburgh: Birlinn.

Riley, P.W.J. 1978. *The Union of England and Scotland: a study in Anglo-Scottish politics of the eighteenth century*. Manchester: Manchester University Press.

Rippon, S. 2012. *Making Sense of an Historic Landscape*. Oxford: Oxford University Press.

Ritchie, A. 1977. Excavation of Pictish and Viking-age farmsteads at Buckquoy, Orkney. *Proceedings of the Society of Antiquaries of Scotland* 108, 174–227.

Roberts, K. 2006. The Deserted Rural Settlement Project: a summing up, in Roberts, K. (ed.), *Lost Farmsteads: Deserted Rural Settlements in Wales*. York: Council for British Archaeology, 171–86.

Roberts, R.A. 1968. *Yr Elfen Fugeiliol ym Mywyd Cymru*. Llundain Y Gorfforaeth Ddarlledu Brydeinig.

Robinson, T. 1990a. *Connemara. Part 1 – Introduction and Gazeteer*. Roundstone: Folding Landscapes.

Robinson, T. 1990b. *Connemara. Part 2 – Map*. Roundstone: Folding Landscapes.

Robinson, T. (ed.) 1995. *Connemara after the Famine: Journal of a Survey of the Martin Estate by Thomas Colville Scott, 1853*. Dublin: The Lilliput Press.

Robinson, T. 1997. Connemara, County Galway, in Aalen, F.H.A., Whelan, K. and Stout, M. (eds), *Atlas of the Irish Rural Landscape*. Cork: Cork University Press, 329–45.

Robinson, T. 2011. *Connemara: A Little Gaelic Kingdom*. London: Penguin.

Rockman, M. and Steele, J. (eds) 2003. *Colonization of Unfamiliar Landscapes: The Archaeology of Adaptation*. London: Routledge.

Roe, A. 2008. Naming the Waters: New Insights into the Nomadic Use of Oases in the Libyan Desert of Egypt, in Barnard, H. and Wendrich, W. (eds), *The Archaeology of Mobility: Old and New World Nomadism*. Los Angeles: UCLA Cotsen Institute, 487–508.

Rynne, C. 1998. *At the Sign of the Cow: The Cork Butter Market, 1770–1924*. Cork: Collins Press.

Rynne, C. 2014. Dairying and buttermaking in Ireland, from the earliest times to c. AD 1700, in Foynes, P., Rynne, C. and Synnot, C. (eds), *Butter in Ireland: From Earliest Times to the 21st Century*. Cork: Cork Butter Museum, 13–28.

Salzmann, P.C. 2004. *Pastoralists: Equality, Hierarchy, and the State*. Boulder: Westview Press.

Sambrook, P. 2006. Deserted rural settlements in south-west Wales, in Roberts, K. (ed.), *Lost Farmsteads: Deserted Rural Settlements in Wales*. York: Council for British Archaeology, 83–109.

Schlee, D., Comeau, R., Parker Pearson, M. and Welham, K. 2018. Carn Goedog medieval house and settlement, Pembrokeshire. *Archaeologia Cambrensis* 167, 245–55.

Shanklin, E. 1994. 'Life Underneath the Market': Herders and Gombeenmen in Nineteenth-century Donegal, in Chang, C. and Koster, H.A. (eds), *Pastoralists at the Periphery: Herders in a Capitalist World*. Tuscon: University of Arizona Press, 103–21.

Sidebotham, J.M. 1950. A settlement in Goodland townland, Co. Antrim. *Ulster Journal of Archaeology* 13, 44–53.

Silvester, R.J. 2006. Deserted rural settlements in central and north-east Wales, in Roberts, K. (ed.), *Lost Farmsteads: Deserted Rural Settlements in Wales*. York: Council for British Archaeology, 13–39.

Simakov, G.N. 1978. Opyt tipologizatsii skotovodcheskogo khoziaistva u kirgizov. (Konets XIX–nachalo XX v.). *Sovetskaya Etnografiya* 6, 14–27.

Simms, A. 2000. Perspectives on Irish settlement studies, in Barry, T.B. (ed.), *A History of Settlement in Ireland*. London: Routledge, 228–47.

Simms, K. 1986. Nomadry in medieval Ireland: the origins of the creaght or caoraigheacht. *Peritia* 5, 379–91.

Simms, K. 2015. The origins of the creaght: farming system or social unit? in Murphy, M. and Stout, M. (eds), *Agriculture and Settlement in Ireland*. Dublin: Four Courts Press, 101–18.

Sims-Williams, P. 1998. Celtomania and celtoscepticism. *Cambrian Medieval Celtic Studies* 36, 1–36.

Skene, W.F. 1880. *Celtic Scotland: a history of Ancient Alban. Volume III: Land and People*. Edinburgh: David Douglas.

Skrede, M. 2005. Shielings and landscape in western Norway. Research traditions and recent trends, in Holm, I., Innselset, S. & Øye, I. (eds), *'Utmark'. The outfield as industry and ideology in the iron age and the middle ages*, University of Bergen Archaeological Series, International 1. Bergen: University of Bergen, 31–41.

Slater, E. 2015. The 'collops' of the rundale: their evolving ecological and communal forms, in Ó Síocháin, S., Slater, E. and Downey, L. (eds), *Rundale: Settlement, Society and Farming (Ulster Folklife* 58). Cultra: Ulster Folk and Transport Museum, 65–74.

Smith, G. and Thompson, D. 2006. Results of the project excavations, in Roberts, K. (ed.), *Lost Farmsteads: Deserted Rural Settlements in Wales.* York: Council for British Archaeology, 113–32.

Smith, J.S. 1986. Deserted farms and shealings in the Braemar Area of Deeside, Grampian Region. *Proceedings of the Society of Antiquaries of Scotland* 116, 447–53.

Smyth, W.J. 1969. Clogheen-Burncourt: A Social Geography of a Rural Parish in South Tipperary, Unpublished PhD thesis, Department of Geography, University College Dublin.

Smyth, W.J. 1976. Estate records and the making of the Irish landscape: an example from County Tipperary. *Irish Geography* 9, 29–49.

Smyth, W.J. 1985. Property, patronage and population: reconstructing the human geography of mid-seventeenth century County Tipperary, in Nolan, W. (ed.), *Tipperary: history and society.* Dublin: Geography Publications, 104–38.

Smyth, W.J. 1988. Society and Settlement in Seventeenth Century Ireland: the Evidence of the '1659 Census', in Smyth, W.J. and Whelan, K. (eds), in *Common Ground: Essays on the Historical Geography of Ireland.* Cork: Cork University Press, 55–83.

Smyth, W.J. 2002. Introduction, in Pender, S. (ed.), *A Census of Ireland, circa 1659, with a New Introduction by William J Smyth.* Dublin: Irish Manuscripts Commission.

Smyth, W.J. 2006. *Map-making, Landscapes and Memory.* Cork: Cork University Press.

Smyth, W.J. 2009. The 'Conquest' of the Iveragh peninsula, in Crowley, J. and Sheehan, J. (eds), *The Iveragh Peninsula: A Cultural Atlas of the Ring of Kerry.* Cork: Cork University Press, 160–73.

Smyth, W.J. 2012a. The Famine in the County Tipperary parish of Shanrahan, in Crowley, J., Smyth, W.J. and Murphy, M. (eds), *Atlas of the Great Irish Famine, 1845–52.* Cork: Cork University Press, 385–97.

Smyth, W.J. 2012b. 'Mapping the people': the growth and distribution of the population, in Crowley, J., Smyth, W.J. and Murphy, M. (eds), *Atlas of the Great Irish Famine, 1845–52.* Cork: Cork University Press, 13–22.

Stagno, A.M. 2018. Short- and long-distance transhumant systems and common lands in post-classical archaeology. Case studies from southern Europe, in Costello, E. and Svensson, E. (eds), *Historical Archaeologies of Transhumance across Europe.* Themes in Contemporary Archaeology 6. London: Routledge, 171–86.

Star, S.L. and Griesemer, J.R. 1989. Institutional Ecology, 'Translations' and Boundary Objects: Amateurs and Professionals in Berkeley's Museum of Vertebrate Zoology, 1907–39. *Social Studies of Science* 19(3), 387–420.

Sveinbjarnardóttir, G. 1991. Shielings in Iceland: an archaeological and historical survey. *Acta Archaeologica* 61, 73–96.

Sveinbjarnardóttir, G. 1992. *Farm Abandonment in Medieval and Post-Medieval Iceland: An Interdisciplinary Study.* Oxford: Oxbow Books.

Svensson, E. 1998. *Människor i utmark.* Stockholm: Almqvist & Wiksell International.

Svensson, E. 2018. The Scandinavian shieling – between innovation and tradition, in Costello, E. and Svensson, E. (eds), *Historical Archaeologies of Transhumance across Europe*. Themes in Contemporary Archaeology 6. London: Routledge, 15–28.

Symonds, J. 2000. The dark isle revisited: an approach to the historical archaeology of Milton, South Uist, in Atkinson, J.A., Banks, I. and MacGregor, G. (eds), *Townships to Farmsteads: Rural Settlement Studies in Scotland, England and Wales*, British Archaeological Reports British Series 293. Oxford: Archaeopress, 197–210.

Teunissen, D. and Teunissen-van Oorschot, H.G.C.M. 1980. The history of vegetation in S.W. Connemara (Ireland). *Acta Botanica Neerlandica* 29, 285–306.

Thomas, F.W.L. 1857. Notice of beehive houses in Harris and Lewis; with traditions of the 'each-uisge', or water-horse, connected therewith. *Proceedings of the Society of Antiquaries of Scotland* 3, 127–44.

Vaughan, W.E. (ed.) 1996. *A New History of Ireland: Volume VI: Ireland under the Union, II: 1870–1921*. Oxford: Oxford University Press.

Waddell, J. 1998. *The Prehistoric Archaeology of Ireland*. Dublin: Wordwell.

Wallerstein, I. 1974. *The Modern World System I: Capitalist Agriculture and the Origins of the European World Economy*. New York: Academic Press.

Ward, A. 1997. Transhumance and Settlement on the Welsh Uplands: a view from the Black Mountain, in Edwards, N. (ed.), *Landscape and Settlement in Medieval Wales*. Oxford: Oxbow Books, 97–111.

Wendrich, W. 2008. From Objects to Agents: The Ababda Nomads and the Interpretation of the Past, in Barnard, H. and Wendrich, W. (eds), *The Archaeology of Mobility: Old and New World Nomadism*. Los Angeles: UCLA Cotsen Institute, 509–42.

Wendrich, W. and Barnard, H. 2008. The Archaeology of Mobility: Definitions and Research Approaches, in Barnard, H. and Wendrich, W. (eds), *The Archaeology of Mobility: Old and New World Nomadism*. Los Angeles: UCLA Cotsen Institute, 1–24.

Whelan, K. 1992. Beyond a paper landscape: J.H. Andrews and Irish historical geography, in Aalen, F.H.A. and Whelan, K. (eds), *Dublin City and County: from prehistory to present*. Dublin: Geography Publications, 379–424.

Whelan, K. 1993. Ireland in the World-System 1600–1800, in Nitz, H.-J. (ed.), *The Early Modern World-System in Geographical Perspective*. Stuttgart: Steiner, 204–18.

Whelan, K. 1995a. An Underground Gentry? Catholic Middlemen in Eighteenth-Century Ireland. *Eighteenth-century Ireland/Iris an Dá Chultúr* 10, 7–68.

Whelan, K. 1995b. Introduction, in Blake Family of Renvyle, *Letters from the Irish Highlands of Connemara, 1823/4* (reprint). Clifden: Gibbons Publications, vii–xix.

Whelan, K. 1997. The modern landscape: from plantation to present, in Aalen, F.H.A., Whelan, K. and Stout, M. (eds), *Atlas of the Irish Rural Landscape*. Cork: Cork University Press, 67–103.

Whelan, K. 2000. Settlement and Society in Eighteenth-Century Ireland, in Barry, T.B. (ed.), *A History of Settlement in Ireland*. London: Routledge, 187–205.

Whelan, K. 2003. Settlement patterns in the west of Ireland in the pre-Famine period, in Collins, T. (ed.), *Decoding the Landscape: contributions towards a synthesis of thinking in Irish studies on the landscape*, 3rd edn. NUI Galway: Centre for Landscape Studies, Galway, 60–78.

Whelan, K. 2012. Clachans: landscape and life in Ireland before and after the Famine, in Duffy, P.J. and Nolan, W. (eds), *At the Anvil: Essays in Honour of William J. Smyth*. Dublin: Geography Publications, 453–75.

Whitaker, I. 1959. Some traditional techniques in modern Scottish farming. *Scottish Studies* 3, 167–88.

Whittington, G. 1970. The problem of runrig. *Scottish Geographical Magazine* 86, 69–73.

Whyte, I. and Whyte, K.A. 1991. *The Changing Scottish Landscape: 1500–1800*. London: Routledge.

Whyte, I.D. 1985. Shielings and the Upland Pastoral Economy of the Lake District in Medieval and Early Modern Times, in Baldwin, J.R. and Whyte, I.D. (eds), *The Scandinavians in Cumbria*. Edinburgh: The Scottish Society for Northern Studies, 103–17.

Wilkie, L. 2006. Documentary archaeology, in Hicks, D. and Beaudry, M.C. (eds), *The Cambridge Companion to Historical Archaeology*. Cambridge: Cambridge University Press, 13–33.

Williams, B. and Robinson, P. 1983. The excavation of Bronze Age cists and a medieval booley house at Glenmakeeran, County Antrim, and a discussion of booleying in north Antrim. *Ulster Journal of Archaeology* 46, 29–40.

Williams, B.B. 1983. Early Christian landscapes in County Antrim, in Hamond, F. and Reeves Smyth, T. (eds), *Landscape Archaeology in Ireland*, British Archaeological Reports 116. Oxford: Archaeopress, 233–46.

Williams, B.B. 1984. Excavations at Ballyutoag, County Antrim. *Ulster Journal of Archaeology* 47, 37–49.

Wilson, W.A. 1973. Herder, folklore and romantic nationalism. *The Journal of Popular Culture* 6, 819–35.

Winchester, A.J.L. 2000. *The Harvest of the Hills: Rural Life in Northern England and the Scottish Borders, 1400–1700*. Edinburgh: Edinburgh University Press.

Winchester, A.J.L. 2012. Seasonal settlement in northern England: shieling place-names revisited, in Turner, S. and Silvester, R. (eds), *Life in Medieval Landscapes: People and Places in the Middle Ages*. Macclesfield: Windgather Press, 125–49.

Witoszek, N. 1997. The Anti-Romantic Romantics: Nature, Knowledge and Identity in Nineteenth-Century Norway, in Teich, M., Porter, R. and Gustafsson, B. (eds), *Nature and Society in Historical Context*. Cambridge: Cambridge University Press, 209–27.

Woods, C.J. (ed.) 2009. *Travellers' accounts as source material for Irish historians*. Dublin: Four Courts Press.

Wrathmell, S. (ed.) 2012. *A History of Wharram Percy and its Neighbours*. Wharram: A Study of Settlement on the Yorkshire Wolds XIII. York: York University Archaeological Publications.

Yager, T. 2002. What was rundale and where did it come from? *Béaloideas* 70, 153–86.

ONLINE PRIMARY SOURCES

Bing Maps aerial imagery. Microsoft Inc. Available at <https://www.bing.com/maps/>.

CANMORE (Online catalogue to Scotland's archaeology, buildings, industrial and maritime heritage). Historic Environment Scotland. Available at <http://canmore.org.uk/>.

Database of Irish Excavation Reports. Department of Arts, Heritage and the Gaeltacht and the Department of the Environment, Northern Ireland. Available at <http://www.excavations.ie/>.

The Desmond Survey, 1586. Corpus of Electronic Texts, University College Cork. Available at <http://www.ucc.ie/celt/published/E580000–001/>.

The Down Survey of Ireland. Trinity College Dublin. Available at <http://downsurvey.tcd.ie/index.html>

eDIL. Electronic Dictionary of the Irish Language. Available at <http://www.dil.ie/>.

Famine Atlas and Historical Population Statistics. All-Ireland Research Observatory. Available at <http://airo.maynoothuniversity.ie/mapping-resources/airo-research-themes/historical-mapping>.

Google Earth aerial imagery. Mountain View, CA: Google Inc.

Griffith's Valuation, 1848–1864. Available at <http://www.askaboutireland.ie/griffith-valuation/>.

GSI Datasets Public Viewer. Geological Survey of Ireland. Available at <http://spatial.dcenr.gov.ie/imf/imf.jsp?site=GSI_Simple>.

Ordnance Survey first edition 6 inch and 25 inch maps. Ordnance Survey Ireland. Available at <http://map.geohive.ie/mapviewer.html>.

Placenames Database of Ireland. Fiontar (DCU) & The Placenames Branch (Department of Arts, Heritage and the Gaeltacht). Available at <http://www.logainm.ie/en/>.

Record of Monuments and Places. Archaeological Survey of Ireland. Available at <http://webgis.archaeology.ie/historicenvironment/>.

RIA Corpas = Corpas Stairiúil na Gaeilge, 1600–1926. Royal Irish Academy. Available at <corpas.ria.ie>.

Schools' Folklore Collection, 1937–38. Fiontar (DCU) & National Folklore Collection (UCD). Available at <http://www.duchas.ie/en/cbes>.

Tithe Applotment Books, 1823–37. National Archives of Ireland. Available at <http://titheapplotmentbooks.nationalarchives.ie/search/tab/home.jsp>.

Wind Mapping System. Sustainable Energy Authority of Ireland. Available at <http://maps.seai.ie/wind/>

INDEX

www.ingramcontent.com/pod-product-compliance
Lightning Source LLC
Chambersburg PA
CBHW080552270326
41929CB00019B/3275